D1560041

WRITING HISTORY FOR THE KING

WRITING HISTORY FOR THE KING

HENRY II AND
THE POLITICS OF
VERNACULAR
HISTORIOGRAPHY

CHARITY URBANSKI

CORNELL UNIVERSITY PRESS
Ithaca and London

Portions of the text are drawn from Charity Urbanski, "Apology, Protest, and Suppression: Interpreting the Surrender of Caen," *Haskins Society Journal* 19 (2007): 137–53. Reprinted by permission of the *Haskins Society Journal*.

Material from the following is reprinted by permission of Oxford University Press: Orderic Vitalis, *The Ecclesiastical History of Orderic Vitalis*, ed. and trans. Marjorie Chibnall, 6 vols. (Oxford, 1969–80); William of Jumièges, Orderic Vitalis, and Robert of Torigny, *The Gesta Normannorum ducum of William of Jumièges, Orderic Vitalis and Robert of Torigni*, ed. and trans. Elisabeth M. C. van Houts, 2 vols. (Oxford, 1992–95); and William of Poitiers, *The Gesta Guillelmi of William of Poitiers*, ed. and trans. R. H. C. Davis and Majorie Chibnall (Oxford, 1998).

Material from Wace, *The Roman de Rou*, trans. Glyn S. Burgess with the text of Anthony J. Holden and notes by Glyn S. Burgess and Elizabeth M. C. van Houts (Isle of Jersey, 2002), is reprinted by permission of Société Jersiaise, Jersey, British Channel Islands.

The author was unable to locate the heirs of Carin Fahlin to request permission to use material from Benoît de Sainte-Maure, *Chronique des ducs de Normandie, publiee d'aprés le manuscrit de Tours avec les variantes du manuscrit de Londres par Carin Fahlin*, 2 vols. (Uppsala, 1951).

The author received no response from Editions Picard to multiple requests for permission to use material from Wace, *Le Roman de Rou de Wace*, ed. Anthony J. Holden, 3 vols. (Paris, 1970–73).

First published 2013 by Cornell University Press

Printed in the United States of America

Library of Congress Cataloging-in-Publication Data

Urbanski, Charity, 1970– author.
  Writing history for the king : Henry II and the politics of vernacular historiography / Charity Urbanski.
     pages cm
  Includes bibliographical references and index.
  ISBN 978-0-8014-5131-7 (cloth : alk. paper)
1. Great Britain—History—Norman period, 1066–1154—Historiography. 2. Great Britain—History—Angevin period, 1154–1216—Historiography. 3. Henry II, King of England, 1133–1189. 4. Normandy, Dukes of. 5. Normandy (France)—Historiography. 6. Wace, approximately 1100–approximately 1175. Roman de Rou. 7. Benoît, de Sainte-More, active 12th century. Chronique des ducs de Normandie. I. Title.

  DA195.U73 2013
  942.02072—dc23   2013012541

Cornell University Press strives to use environmentally responsible suppliers and materials to the fullest extent possible in the publishing of its books. Such materials include vegetable-based, low-VOC inks and acid-free papers that are recycled, totally chlorine-free, or partly composed of nonwood fibers. For further information, visit our website at www.cornellpress.cornell.edu.

Cloth printing   10 9 8 7 6 5 4 3 2 1

In memory of my grandmother,
Inice May Johnson

Contents

ACKNOWLEDGMENTS

I have been helped by a multitude of people over the course of writing this book. I am enormously grateful to my husband, Michael Carver, for his devotion and more than occasional personal sacrifice. He has displayed enduring patience and given me unfailing support. I owe my family, and especially my mother, Laura Swick, my grandmother, Inice Johnson, and my aunt, Nancy Adkins, special thanks for always encouraging me to cultivate my talents and to persevere.

I have also been fortunate to enjoy the support of a number of friends and colleagues who have provided me with intellectual stimulation, helpful criticism, comfort, and fortification. I would especially like to thank Amanda Hingst, David Spafford, Rebecca Moyle-Lange, Tyler Lange, Purnima Dhavan, Adam Warner, Elena Campbell, Noam Pianko, and Devin Naar for their assistance in reading countless drafts, offering thoughtful feedback, and endlessly discussing material with me. I am also sincerely grateful to Deseree Lyon, Alejandro Salazar, Christa Stelzmuller, Derrick Stansfield, and Ruth Jewett for their years of support and encouragement. A special thanks is due to Nicholas Goode and Jill Henry-Goode for their friendship and for generously housing me while I conducted my research.

I am profoundly grateful to those who have shepherded my research and guided me. I would particularly like to thank Geoffrey Koziol, who has been a constant source of careful attention, excellent insight, sound advice, and optimism. His vast knowledge and steady guidance have enriched my work. I must also offer my sincere gratitude to Maureen Miller, who has provided me with thoughtful criticism, good counsel, and incomparable attentiveness, and to Jennifer Miller, who has shared her astute interpretive insights and given me perceptive guidance. Their honest appraisals and unflagging support have been invaluable. I would also like to thank Joseph Duggan, Martin Aurell, Jean Blacker, John Gillingham, Glyn Burgess, Emily Albu, Peter Damian-Grint, Patrick Geary, Téo Ruiz, Robert Jordan, Robert Stacey, the members of the University of Washington's History Reading Group, and the members of the UCLA Center for Medieval and

Renaissance Studies' California Medieval History Seminar for generously reading portions of my work and giving me their time and comments. Their advice has enriched my work, though any errors that remain are entirely my own. And a special thanks is due to John Ackerman of Cornell University Press for his patience in guiding me through the publication process.

Finally, I would like to thank the institutions that made my research possible: the History Department of the University of California at Berkeley, the British Library, the Bibliothèque nationale de France, the Bibliothèque municipale de Rouen, the Bibliothèque municipale de Tours, the Bibliothèque municipale de Alençon, and their staffs. I would also like to thank the Graduate Division of the University of California at Berkeley and the University of California's Office of the President for providing me with the fellowships that financed my research.

LIST OF ABBREVIATIONS

ANS	*Anglo-Norman Studies*
ASC	*Anglo-Saxon Chronicle*
CCM	*Cahiers de civilisation médiévale*
CDN	*Chronique des ducs de Normandie*
EHD	*English Historical Documents*
EHR	*English Historical Review*
GG	*Gesta Guillelmi*
GND	*Gesta Normannorum ducum*
GRA	*Gesta Regum Anglorum*
HA	*Historia Anglorum*
HE	*Historia Ecclesiastica*
HN	*Historia Novella*
HRA	*Historia Rerum Anglicarum*
HRB	*Historia Regum Britanniae*
HSJ	*Haskins Society Journal*
MGH	*Monumenta Germaniae Historia*
RR	*Roman de Rou*
RRAN	*Regesta Regum Anglo-Normannorum*
TRHS	*Transactions of the Royal Historical Society*

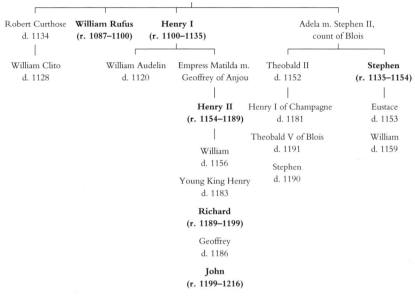

William the Conqueror
(r. 1066–1087)

Robert Curthose
d. 1134

William Rufus
(r. 1087–1100)

Henry I
(r. 1100–1135)

Adela m. Stephen II,
count of Blois

William Clito
d. 1128

William Audelin
d. 1120

Empress Matilda m.
Geoffrey of Anjou

Theobald II
d. 1152

Stephen
(r. 1135–1154)

Henry II
(r. 1154–1189)

Henry I of Champagne
d. 1181

Eustace
d. 1153

William
d. 1156

Theobald V of Blois
d. 1191

William
d. 1159

Young King Henry
d. 1183

Stephen
d. 1190

Richard
(r. 1189–1199)

Geoffrey
d. 1186

John
(r. 1199–1216)

FIGURE 1.   Norman Genealogy

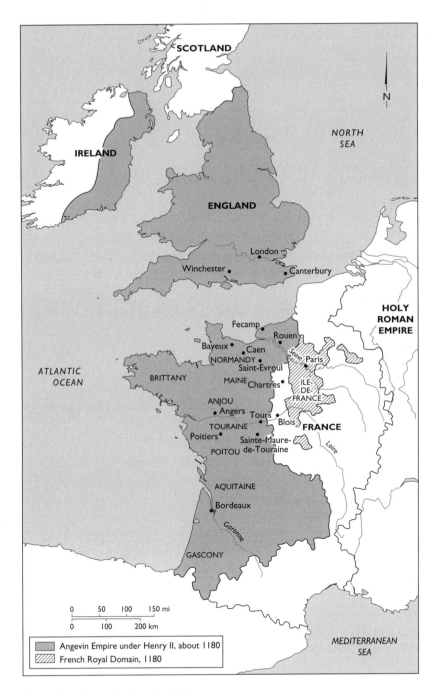

FIGURE 2. Angevin Empire, circa 1180

WRITING HISTORY FOR THE KING

Introduction

Sometime around 1160, a Norman cleric named Wace began a history of the Norman dukes and kings of England at the behest of Henry II of England (r. 1154–89). Wace had come to Henry's attention after dedicating an earlier work, the *Roman de Brut*, to Henry's queen, Eleanor of Aquitaine. Adapting material from various Latin histories, Wace had already completed a narrative that chronicled the deeds of the Norman dynasty from their Viking founder, Rollo (or Rou), to the reign of Henry I when he was abruptly fired around 1174. The reasons for his dismissal are unknown, but Wace was clearly vexed by this turn of events. He complains that he has been replaced by another author in the explicit of his history, the *Roman de Rou*.[1] "Let he whose business it is continue the story. I am referring to Master Beneeit, who has undertaken to tell of this affair, as the king [Henry II] has assigned him the task; since the king has asked him to do it,

---

1. Wace, *Le Roman de Rou de Wace*, ed. Anthony J. Holden, 3 vols. (Paris, 1970–73) and Wace, *The Roman de Rou*, ed. and trans. Glyn Burgess (Isle of Jersey, 2002). The *Roman de Rou* (c. 1160–74) is an adaptation of several Latin sources, which uses Orderic Vitalis's E redaction of William of Jumièges's *GND* as its framework. It includes anecdotes and the *De obitu Willelmi* from the anonymous B redaction of the *GND*, and draws on Orderic Vitalis's *HE*, the *Brevis Relatio*, William of Malmesbury's *Gesta regum Anglorum*, and William of Poitiers's *Gesta Guillelmi*.

I must abandon it and fall silent."[2] This Master Beneeit, more commonly known as Benoît de Sainte-Maure (author of the enormously popular *Roman de Troie* and a native of the Touraine), then undertook his own version of the history of the Normans, also at the king's request. Benoît dispensed with Wace's version of Norman history entirely, and began anew with the Latin sources, eventually producing the *Chronique des ducs de Normandie*.[3]

On the surface these facts seem unremarkable. What could be more predictable than a king turning to popular authors working in a fashionable style and commissioning a history of his ancestors, presumably in the hope of glorifying his dynasty and himself? This project, however, marked the first time that a medieval European monarch had ever commissioned a dynastic history in Old French. The project was innovative in another sense as well, as works of any kind in Old French had only just begun to appear at the beginning of the twelfth century. Aside from the novelty of the project, Henry's foray into literary patronage also presents us with a mystery: Why was Wace fired?

This book began with a simple question: Why were these histories written? Attempting to answer that question raised countless others. Why were these histories written in the vernacular rather than in Latin? What were Henry's desires for a history of his dynasty and how can we recover them? Did Wace understand his patron's expectations? What did Wace do to provoke the king's ire? Did Benoît's history satisfy Henry and how can we know? For whom were these histories intended and how did they receive them? We have no records that directly reveal what Henry wanted from a dynastic history or what he may have hoped to achieve by disseminating this history in the vernacular, nor can we fully recover the intentions of either Wace or Benoît de Sainte-Maure. Likewise, we have little that directly reveals how audiences reacted to these texts, and nothing that tells us exactly what they thought of them. These problems are agonizingly familiar to medieval historians. In spite of what appears to be a dearth of evidence, we can posit answers to the important questions of political culture raised by these

---

2. "Die en avant qui dire en deit; / j'ai dit por Maistre Beneeit, / qui cest' ovre a dire a emprise / com li reis l'a desor lui mise; / quant li reis li a rové faire / laissier la dei, si m'en dei taire." Wace, *RR*, vv. 11419–24 (all references to the *Roman de Rou* are to part III of Holden unless otherwise noted).

3. Benoît de Sainte-Maure, *Chronique des ducs de Normandie par Benoît*, ed. Carin Fahlin, 2 vols. (Uppsala, 1954), [hereafter CDN]. Benoît returned to most of the same Latin sources Wace had used to construct his history; however, the *CDN* (c.1174–before 1189) relies on Robert de Torigny's F redaction of the *GND* for its framework.

histories by examining the materials that we do have extant: the histories themselves, their Latin sources, contemporary texts, and documents from Henry II's reign. We are especially fortunate to have two versions of the same history to compare: one that failed to please the king, and one that presumably met his expectations. This experiment in vernacular historiography presents us with a rare opportunity to examine a royal attempt to control the meaning of the past.

A series of assumptions has guided my examination of these histories. First, Wace is taken at his word that he was personally commissioned to write a history for Henry II and then fired by the king after he had worked on the project for about fifteen years.[4] We cannot know, however, whether the king initiated the project and then fired Wace entirely of his own volition, or on the advice of unknown counselors. A group of counselors around the king may well have been involved in the production of these histories, even though neither Wace nor Benoît mentions any intermediaries in their texts. Neither author so much as implies that they received their commission or instructions from anyone but the king, nor do they address anyone but him. We must, therefore, surmise that Henry II sponsored this historiographical enterprise, either on his own or in consultation with others.[5]

Henry would not have fired Wace and transferred the commission to Benoît de Sainte-Maure had he been pleased with Wace's work. It is also

---

4. Wace includes an autobiographical sketch that refers to the prebend in Bayeux that he says Henry awarded him in return for his efforts. "Jo di e dirai que jo sui / Wace de l'isle de Gersui, / al fieu de Normendie apent. / En l'isle de Gersui fui nez, / a Chaem fui petiz portez, / illoques fui a letres mis, / pois fui longues en France apris; / quant jo de France repairai / a Chaem longues conversai, / de romanz faire m'entremis, / mult en escris e mult en fis. / Par Deu aïe e par le rei / – altre fors Deu servir ne dei – / m'en fu donee, Deus li rende, / a Baieues une provende. / Del rei Henri segont vos di, / nevo Henri, pere Henri." Wace, RR, vv. 5301–18. He also records his firing and the transfer of the commission to Benoît at the end of the Roman de Rou. "Die en avant qui dire en deit; / j'ai dit por Maistre Beneeit, / qui cest' ovre a dire a emprise / com li reis l'a desor lui mise; / quant li reis li a rové faire / laissier la dei, si m'en dei taire. / Li reis jadis maint bien me fist, / mult me dona, plus me pramist, / e se il tot donee m'eüst / ço qu'il me pramist, mielz me fust; / nel poi aveir, ne plout al rei, / mais n'est mie remés en mei. / Treis reis Henris ai coneüz, / en Normendie toz veüz; / d'Engletere e de Normendie / orent tuit trei la seignorie. / Li segont Henri que jo di / fu niés al premerain Henri, / né de Mahelt, l'empereiz, / e li tierz fu al segont fils. / Ci faut le livre Maistre Wace; / quin velt avant faire sin face." Wace, RR, vv. 11419–40.

5. Karen Broadhurst has identified the Roman de Rou and the Chronique des ducs de Normandie as the only vernacular works that can be linked to Henry II with any confidence. Karen M. Broadhurst, "Henry II of England and Eleanor of Aquitaine: Patrons of Literature in French?" Viator 27 (1996): 53–84. Cf. Diana B. Tyson, "Patronage of French Vernacular History Writers in the Twelfth and Thirteenth Centuries," Romania 100 (1979): 180–222, and John Gillingham, "The Cultivation of History, Legend, and Courtesy at the Court of Henry II," in Writers of the Reign of Henry II, ed. Ruth Kennedy and Simon Meecham-Jones (New York, 2006), 25–52.

very unlikely that the king would have bothered to transfer the commission and begin the project all over again if it were only of passing interest to him. Although it was not unheard of for a medieval monarch or aristocrat to patronize literary labors in which they had only the most marginal interest, I contend that this project in particular was close to Henry. It is, after all, *his* history, the deeds of his most important ancestors, and not those of some distant dynasty, that Wace and Benoît were charged with writing.[6] And the purpose of writing dynastic or genealogical history was "above all to exalt a line and legitimize its power."[7] This writing took the form of translating and adapting a variety of existing Latin texts, which indicates that this vernacular history was meant to reach a much wider and more varied audience than its Latin predecessors—almost certainly the same aristocratic and clerical audience that had already been commissioning and consuming Old French histories of the Britons and Anglo-Saxons since at least 1135. Wasting time, money, and effort on adapting existing Latin histories of the Normans into the vernacular would have been foolish otherwise.

Although these Old French texts are histories, they are not completely reliable repositories of historical facts. None of the texts that historians use to reconstruct the past are without blemish, and historical narratives are particularly susceptible to manipulation.[8] Constructing narrative history demands that information be shaped to conform to the constraints of the narrative structure, but this deficiency has hardly led us to avoid enlisting historical narratives to build our own narrative reconstructions of the past. We would have precious little left to work with if we did so. These histories indisputably contain some fictional elements, and the same can be said of the entire corpus of ancient and medieval historiography. Miraculous events,

---

6. Henry II's maternal, Norman ancestors were the source of his claim to the English throne. Henry's Anglo-Saxon ancestry through his maternal grandmother, Edith-Matilda, was important as well, and was used to bolster Henry's legitimacy (especially by writers such as Aelred of Rievaulx), but the Normans had conquered the Anglo-Saxons and taken the throne from them. His Norman ancestors were therefore more important to him in real terms than either his Anglo-Saxon ancestors or his paternal ancestors, the counts of Anjou. Henry also patronized histories of his father's family, but they were produced in Latin and were thus almost certainly intended for a more limited audience. Cf. John of Marmoutier, "*Historia abbreviata consulum Andegavorum*," in *Chroniques d'Anjou*, ed. Paul Marchegay and André Salmon (Picard, 1856); and John of Marmoutier, "*Historia Gaufredi ducis Normannorum et comitis Andegavorum*," in *Chroniques des comtes d'Anjou et des seigneurs d'Amboise*, ed. Louis Halphen and C. Poupardin (Paris, 1913).

7. Gabrielle Spiegel, "Genealogy: Form and Function in Medieval Historical Narrative." *History and Theory* 22 (1983): 43–53, at 47.

8. Cf. Hayden White, *The Content of the Form: Narrative Discourse and Historical Representation* (Baltimore, 1987).

omens, and rhetorical set pieces were part of the Latin historiographical tradition, and such flaws have led legions of modern historians to regard medieval historiography as "inauthentic, unscientific, unreliable, ahistorical, irrational, borderline illiterate, and worse yet, unprofessional."[9] These elements, however, were not only commonplace, they were expected, and a twelfth-century audience with any previous knowledge of Latin histories would have been quite familiar with them.

In spite of their deficiencies, verifiable facts are present in most narrative histories, and this is certainly the case for these vernacular histories as well. As recent scholarship has shown, the *Rou* in particular contains information that is not only substantially accurate but otherwise unavailable.[10] My purpose, however, is not to contend that these histories are completely trustworthy. On the contrary, they are riddled with deliberate untruths and distortions. Every individual involved in the production of the *Rou* and the *Chronique* had an agenda to advance or an axe to grind. Bias and prejudice constantly rear their heads in these texts; politics and ideology permeate and distort their representations of the past. Indeed, these "flaws" are precisely the qualities that make these histories so interesting.

These histories and their distortions are valuable for what they reveal about contemporary political culture. Far from being neutral and objective records, historical narratives are by their very nature partial and constructed representations of the past.[11] Authors must choose to elide or reveal

---

9. Spiegel, "Genealogy," 44.

10. Although the verifiable facts that appear in the *Chronique* are undoubtedly due to the accuracy of Benoît's sources, recent scholarship has demonstrated that Wace included unique and substantially accurate information in the *Rou* that is simply unavailable elsewhere. This information includes his list of the companions of William the Conqueror, his account of the number of ships prepared for the Conquest, and his account of the surrender of Caen. Cf. Elisabeth van Houts, "The Adaptation of the *Gesta Normannorum ducum* by Wace and Benoît." In *Non nova, sed nove: Mélanges de civilisation médiévale dédiés à Willem Noomen*, ed. M. Gosman and J. van Os. Groningen, 115–24. 1984 (reprinted in Elisabeth M. C. van Houts. *History and Family Traditions in England and the Continent, 1000–1200*, 115–12 [Aldershot, 1999]); van Houts, "The Ship List of William the Conqueror." *ANS* 10 (1988): 159–83; van Houts, "Wace as Historian," in *Family Trees and the Roots of Politics: The Prosopography of Britain and France from the Tenth to the Twelfth Century*, ed. Katherine S. B. Keats-Rohan, 104–32 (Cambridge, 1997) (reprinted in Elisabeth M. C. van Houts. *History and Family Traditions in England and the Continent, 1000–1200*, 103–132 [Aldershot, 1999]); Matthew Bennett. "Poetry as History? The *Roman de Rou* of Wace as a Source for the Norman Conquest." *ANS* 5 (1983): 21–39; Bennett, "Wace and Warfare." *ANS* 11 (1989): 37–57 (reprinted in *Anglo-Norman Warfare: Studies in Late Anglo-Saxon and Anglo-Norman Military*).

11. White, *Content of the Form*; Yitsak Hen and Matthew Innes, eds., *The Uses of the Past in the Early Middle Ages* (Cambridge, 2000); Rosamond McKitterick, *The Carolingians and the Written Word* (Cambridge, 1989); Rosamond McKitterick, *History and Memory in the Carolingian World* (Cambridge, 2004); Rosamond McKitterick, "Constructing the Past in the Early Middle Ages," *TRHS*,

information; they must forge causal connections and simplify complex series of events in order to fashion a satisfying and coherent narrative. Historical narratives thus reveal as much about the cultures and societies that produced them as they do about the cultures and societies they purport to represent. These histories offer representations of the past that are informed by, shaped by, and suited to their present, and they must be read within their political, social, and cultural contexts.[12]

The *Rou* and the *Chronique* are as valuable for what they can tell us about their authors and the reign of Henry II as for anything they might reveal about the historical deeds of his predecessors or the origins of the Normans. My examination of these histories mines their narratives of the past in order to illuminate their present. In particular, the following chapters analyze how Wace and Benoît used their sources, how they consciously manipulated, contradicted, inserted, eliminated, or obscured information to reshape the *meaning* of the past. Wace and Benoît were responding to current realities in attempting to control the meaning of the past, and they used their representations of Norman history as forums for debating the nature of royal power and the legitimacy of Henry II's policies. Their histories must therefore be understood as reflecting, responding to, and participating in the politics of Henry II's reign.

Writing about the past—especially in the exemplary or didactic modes so prevalent in the Middle Ages—must be understood as "an act of power, in that it seeks to influence action in the present" and to shape the future.[13] All historians are agents with agendas of their own that may or may not correspond to the needs and desires of their patrons. There are, however, important limitations to the reshaping of the past, especially the more recent past, by the needs of the present. Human memory and rival narratives both conspire to circumscribe this refashioning. In this study, Wace presents a rival (and subversive) narrative that, in conjunction with human memory,

---

6/7 (1997): 101–30; Mary Carruthers, *The Book of Memory: A Study of Memory in Medieval Culture* (Cambridge, 1990); Janet Coleman, *Ancient and Medieval Memories: Studies in the Reconstruction of the Past* (Cambridge, 1992); Walter Goffart, *The Narrators of Barbarian History (A.D. 550–800): Jordanes, Gregory of Tours, Bede, and Paul the Deacon* (Notre Dame, 2005); Patrick Geary, *Phantoms of Remembrance: Memory and Oblivion at the End of the First Millennium* (Princeton, 1994); Michael Clanchy, "Remembering the Past and the Good Old Law," *History* 55 (1970): 165–75; and Clanchy, *From Memory to Written Record: England 1066–1307* (Oxford, 1993).

12. Matthew Innes, "Introduction: Using the Past, Interpreting the Present, Influencing the Future," in Hen and Innes, *Uses of the Past in the Early Middle Ages*, 1–8, at 4.

13. Innes, "Introduction," 4.

constrains other efforts to manipulate the representation and meaning of Norman history.

Commissioning a history, especially a history of one's own lineage, is also an act of power, and Henry must be assigned a certain amount of agency as the patron of these histories. As J. M. Wallace-Hadrill pointed out, a sudden interest in the past was often cultivated by dynasties under threat, at times when the very survival of the dynasty was at stake, and this certainly seems to have been the case when the king commissioned these histories.[14] Modifying earlier scholars' assessments of the extent and nature of Henry II's power, I contend that his authority in England and Normandy was remarkably tenuous in some ways, and that the future of his dynasty was far from certain. Faced with the historical unpredictability of the Anglo-Norman succession, and the decades of civil war and fragmentation of power under his predecessor, Henry had to work assiduously to consolidate his power and ensure that his heirs would succeed him. By examining some of his contemporaneous actions, it becomes clear that he commissioned these dynastic histories as part of a much larger political program intended to shape public opinion.[15] The term "public," however, has a very restricted meaning in this context. The Anglo-Norman nobility and clergy comprised the only public that would have mattered to the king. They exercised influence, they used Old French as the language of their daily lives, and they already displayed an avid interest in vernacular histories. Henry's most likely agenda was to counter the traditional power of his barons and clergy by disseminating a genealogical history that would illustrate the hereditary right of his family to rule England and Normandy, justify his efforts to monopolize power by giving them a basis in historical precedent, and help to guarantee the succession of his children.[16]

---

14. J. M. Wallace-Hadrill, "The Franks and the English in the Ninth Century: Some Common Historical Interests," in J. M. Wallace-Hadrill, *Early Medieval History* (Oxford, 1975), 201–16, at 201.

15. Cf. Renate Blumenfeld-Kosinski, "Introduction: The Middle Ages," in *The Politics of Translation in the Middle Ages and the Renaissance*, ed. Renate Blumenfeld-Kosinski, Luise von Flotow, and Daniel Russell (Ottawa, 2001), 17–27, at 19–20; and Blumenfeld-Kosinski, "The Earliest Developments of the French Novel: The *Roman de Thèbes* in Verse and Prose," in *The French Novel: Theory and Practice*, French Literature Series 10 (1984), 1–10.

16. For a discussion of the political utility of portraying innovations as customary or traditional, see Gabrielle Spiegel, "Political Utility in Medieval Historiography: A Sketch," *History and Theory* 14 (1975): 314–25, esp. 315; and Marc Bloch, *Feudal Society* (Chicago, 1965), I:114.

CHAPTER 1

Situating the *Roman de Rou* and *Chronique des ducs de Normandie*

For much of the Middle Ages there was a division between spoken and written language in Western Europe. Latin, which had been adopted by the early Christian church, continued to be used as the written language of much of Europe and the lingua franca of the Catholic Church long after it had ceased to be spoken as a native tongue. Literacy, however, was defined as the ability to both read and write in Latin, and Latin literacy was generally confined to the upper echelons of society. During the disorders of the tenth and eleventh centuries, Latin literacy declined among the laity and became the almost exclusive preserve of the Christian clergy.[1] With a few notable exceptions, such as of the emergence of Old English as a written administrative and literary language in eighth-century England, vernacular writing began to reappear in Western Europe only around 1100.[2] Old French was one of the first vernaculars to emerge as a literary language

---

1. This definition of literacy as the ability to both read and write in Latin does not take into account the functional ability of many laypeople to read Latin to some degree.

2. Although written scraps of other vernaculars do exist, such as the Old High German and Old French texts of the 842 Oaths of Strasbourg preserved in a tenth- or eleventh-century manuscript (BnF Cod. Lat. 9768), there is no indication that either language was commonly written until the twelfth century. The earliest poem in Occitan dates from the tenth century, but there is little evidence that Occitan was widely used as a written language until the late eleventh century.

during this period, and the earliest literary works in Old French were produced in England.

The emergence of vernacular literature marked the beginning of the reunification of spoken and written language. Vernacular literacy rates began to climb rapidly in twelfth-century Europe, just as the patronage and production of vernacular literature began to flourish. Although Wace's *Roman de Rou* and Benoît de Sainte-Maure's *Chronique des ducs de Normandie* were products of this momentous shift from Latin to the vernacular, and they were commissioned by no less a patron than Henry II, they have suffered a peculiar fate at the hands of modern historians who have variously ignored, celebrated, derided, and rehabilitated them.

In this chapter I examine the place of the *Roman de Rou* and the *Chronique des ducs de Normandie* in modern scholarship, and the fraught relationship that historians have had with these texts for much of the nineteenth and twentieth centuries. Although the *Roman de Rou* is a special case, in that it was directly attacked and discredited as a historical source, historians have largely ignored these histories (or used them furtively) because they are written in a vernacular, in verse, and because they do not conform to modern generic expectations or distinctions. These works, however, were constructed and received as histories. Vernacular genres were still in the process of forming when they were written, and verse was a perfectly acceptable vehicle for the transmission of historical truth in the twelfth century—in fact, it was the form in which almost all twelfth-century vernacular histories appeared. The rise of prose as the language of historical truth in the thirteenth century was not the result of a crisis of confidence in verse histories. On the contrary, it was driven by a desire on the part of educated vernacular historians to distance themselves and their learned work from the *jongleurs* and the *chansons de geste*.

In this chapter I also examine the political and cultural contexts of the birth of Old French historiography in England, and the reasons that Old French vernacular historiography emerged in England almost a century before it appeared elsewhere in Europe. Post-Conquest England was unique in that it had both a newly established aristocracy with a pressing need to project its own legitimacy and integrate itself into insular culture and a native tradition of vernacular history writing in Old English that the new Norman elite could draw upon. By the turn of the twelfth century, when the first histories written in Old French began to appear, the foreign Norman and native Anglo-Saxon nobilities had largely merged into a single Anglo-Norman aristocracy through intermarriage. It was these Anglo-Norman nobles who patronized the earliest Old French histories, histories that almost invariably focused on the various inhabitants (and conquests) of Britain. For the first few generations of nobles born of unions between the Anglo-Saxons and their Norman conquerors, insular history was at once an object of fascination, a way to make sense of their own more recent history, and a means of forging a new Anglo-Norman identity. Finally, I argue that Henry II was following a well-established Norman tradition of using history to legitimize his power when he did something truly innovative—he appropriated the new genre of Old French verse historiography in an attempt to shape opinion among the Anglo-Norman aristocracy and clergy.

Poetry and History

The texts at the center of this study, Wace's *Roman de Rou* and Benoît de Sainte-Maure's *Chronique des ducs de Normandie*, will be unfamiliar to many medieval historians. Although they are dynastic histories commissioned by Henry II to commemorate the deeds of his Norman ancestors (and their authors are well known for their other works), these texts have been largely neglected by historians until quite recently. They present several problems for the historian: written in Old French, and in verse, neither has traditionally been regarded as a reliable, or even as an explicitly historical, text. Both have suffered the ignominy of being excluded from the historical canon and dismissed by many historians for much of the twentieth century.

The *Roman de Rou* in particular experienced a fall from favor in the late nineteenth century. In 1873, Edward A. Freeman promoted Wace as an "honest" authority and used the *Rou* as a source for his history of the Norman Conquest.[3] In his vigorous objection to Freeman's use of the *Rou*, J. H. Round noted that Wace had included contradictory material in his account of the Conquest, and argued that such conflicts rendered the *Rou* virtually useless as a historical source.[4] Considering that the historians of Freeman and Round's day were occupied with the difficult work of reconstructing a basic historical framework of ascertainable facts, and were already confronted with a morass of information requiring painstaking verification and chronological ordering, it is understandable that some of them should have

---

3. Edward A. Freeman, *The History of the Norman Conquest of England, Its Causes and Its Results* (New York, 1873).

4. J. H. Round, "Wace and His Authorities," *EHR* 8 (1893): 677–83, and J. H. Round, "Mr. Freeman and the Battle of Hastings," *EHR* 9 (1894): 209–60. Reprinted in *Feudal England: Historical Studies on the Eleventh and Twelfth Centuries* (London, 1964), 258–321.

deemed Wace's penchant for including conflicting accounts drawn from a variety of Latin sources as a hindrance to their efforts. Round's assessment that the *Rou* was unhelpful in establishing such historical facts proved compelling and was subsequently adopted by many prominent scholars of Norman history, most notably by David C. Douglas.[5] As a result of this doubt about the *Rou's* utility as a reliable source for the Conquest, both Wace and his history were shunned by historians for several generations. It has only been in the last few decades that historians such as René Stuip, Elisabeth van Houts, and Matthew Bennett have begun to rehabilitate the *Roman de Rou* and exonerate Wace by reexamining his list of the Conqueror's companions, his description of warfare, and his representation of the battle of Hastings.[6]

The lack of interest that historians have displayed toward Benoît de Sainte-Maure's *Chronique des ducs de Normandie*, on the other hand, has no root in a similar debate over its utility. Indeed, the distinction between the two texts is that the *Rou* was once regarded as an original and trustworthy source, but was rejected by later historians who found Wace's tendency to include contradictory material an impediment to their work. Perhaps because Benoît stuck rather closely to his Latin sources and offered little material that was new or exceptional, no comparable attempt was ever made to promote the *Chronique* as an original source. It was regarded as thoroughly derivative and thus ignored.[7]

These histories suffer from the additional handicap of being written in a vernacular. Historians of the Middle Ages have had an uneasy relationship with vernacular sources for a rather obvious reason: the vast majority of our surviving primary sources are written in Latin. As the language of the medieval, educated elite, Latin was the language almost invariably used for the administration of the ecclesiastical and secular institutions on which historians lavished their attention for much of the nineteenth and twentieth centuries. The preponderance of surviving medieval vernacular texts, on the other hand, are literary works and have long been regarded as falling within the purview of literary scholars. It should come as no great surprise that

---

5. David C. Douglas, "Companions of the Conqueror," *History* 27 (1943): 129–47. See also, Antonia Gransden, *Historical Writing in England* (London, 1982), I:187.

6. René Stuip, "La Conquête de l'Angleterre dans la littérature française du XIIe siècle," *Rapports–Het Franse Boek* 58 (1988): 123–31; Elisabeth van Houts, "Adaptation of the *Gesta Normannorum ducum* by Wace and Benoît," 115–24. Reprinted in Elisabeth M. C. van Houts, *History and Family Traditions in England and the Continent, 1000–1200* (Aldershot, 1999), 115–24; van Houts, "Ship List of William the Conqueror," 159–83; van Houts, "Wace as Historian," 104–32; Bennett, "Poetry as History?" 21–39; and Bennett, "Wace and Warfare," *ANS* 11 (1989): 37–57.

7. Gransden, *Historical Writing*, I:212.

historians developed a preference for Latin sources over time as they were quite simply what were most frequently encountered and utilized.

Medieval vernacular texts, especially those produced during the burgeoning of romance literature in the twelfth century, are still generally viewed with a degree of suspicion by historians—they are instinctively regarded as at least quasi fictional and therefore inherently inferior to their Latin cousins. This is partly due to the influence of the medieval hierarchy of language that we have absorbed from our sources. Latin was the language of the educated elite and Latinity was explicitly equated with literacy in the Middle Ages. Vernacular languages were held in such low esteem that a medieval person was considered *illiteratus* or *idiota* if he could not read and write Latin, even if he possessed the ability to read and write in a vernacular.[8] Both the *Rou* and the *Chronique* were destined for an audience of *illiterati* as defined by these standards, a fact that contributed to their marginalization as it implies that they are inferior literary products intended for an unlearned audience. This audience of *illiterati*, however, was primarily royal and aristocratic, and the twelfth-century authors who adapted Latin texts into the vernacular for them, men such as Wace and Benoît, were educated clerics whose Latin literacy enabled them to work as translators. To put it another way, these histories were produced by men of learning for the upper echelons of medieval society in spite of their low form.

Although several generations of cultural historians have advanced the study of medieval vernacular texts in general, twelfth-century vernacular

---

8. Walter Ong, "Orality, Literacy, and Medieval Textualization," *New Literary History* 16/1 (1984): 1–12, at 6–7; Peter Damian-Grint, *The New Historians of the Twelfth-Century Renaissance: Inventing Vernacular Authority* (Woodbridge, 1999), chap. 5; Brian Stock, "Literacy and Society in the Twelfth Century," in *The Spirit of the Court: Selected Proceedings of the Fourth Congress of the International Courtly Literature Society*, ed. Glynn S. Burgess and Robert A. Taylor (Woodbridge, 1985), 1–4; Brian Stock, "Medieval Literacy, Linguistic Theory, and Social Organization," *New Literary History* 16/1 (1984): 13–29; Michael Clanchy, "The Written Word: From Domesday Book to Caxton," in *The Making of Britain: The Dark Ages*, ed. Lesley M. Smith (London, 1984), 163–77; Vivian H. Galbraith, "The Literacy of the English Medieval Kings," *Proceedings of the British Academy* 21 (1935): 201–37 (reprinted in *Kings and Chroniclers: Essays in English Medieval History*, by V. H. Galbraith [London, 1982], 78–111); Ralph V. Turner, "The Miles Literatus in Twelfth- and Thirteenth-Century England: How Rare a Phenomenon?" *American Historical Review* 83 (1978): 928–65 (reprinted in *Judges, Administrators and the Common Law in Angevin England*, by Ralph V. Turner [London, 1994], 119–36; Nicholas Orme, "Lay Literacy in England, 1100–1300," in *England and Germany in the High Middle Ages: Essays in Honour of Karl J. Leyser*, ed. Alfred Haverkamp and Hanna Vollrath (Oxford, 1996), 35–56; Rosamond McKitterick and Paul Binski, "History and Literature: Sacred and Secular," in *The Cambridge Illuminations: Ten Centuries of Book Production in the Medieval West*, ed. Paul Binski and Stella Panayotova (London, 2005), 235–40; Bloch, *Feudal Society*; James Thompson, *The Literacy of the Laity in the Middle Ages* (Berkeley, 1939); and Lynn Thorndike, "Elementary and Secondary Education in the Middle Ages," *Speculum* 15 (1940): 400–408.

histories still find themselves at a disadvantage when Latin sources covering the same material are available.[9] This has certainly been the case for both the *Rou* and the *Chronique*. Both have suffered from the fact that we have a wealth of alternative sources in Latin that recount the history of the Normans and that have been regarded as more worthy of serious historical study. Since these more reputable Latin histories of the Norman dukes and kings of England are the very sources that Wace and Benoît translated and adapted to construct the *Rou* and the *Chronique*, this fact has tended to legitimate our neglect of these vernacular histories rather than encourage their study.

Neglect of these histories has also been abetted by the fact that they do not conform to the expectations that modern readers attach to generic distinctions. The problem of genre is most apparent in the case of the *Roman de Rou*. Saddled as it is with both a suspect vernacular text and the label *roman* (romance), it seems destined to be condemned to the realm of literature. The term *roman*, however, has both generic and linguistic applications. It can refer to the genre of a text, or simply to the language in which a text appears, as was most often the case in the twelfth century. When the word *romanz* first appeared at the beginning of the twelfth century, "its only meaning was 'the vernacular French language.'"[10] During the twelfth century the term *romanz* was most often used to refer to vernacular texts that were translated/adapted from Latin. Although the *Roman de Rou* is certainly written "*en romanz*," it does not necessarily follow that it is a *roman* in the later sense of a romance.

Partly due to the fact that the *Roman de Rou* has been called a *roman* for the last four centuries, historians have tended to regard it as fiction and have accordingly steered clear of it.[11] But the problem of genre is illusory in this case. The modern title of the *Roman de Rou* is merely a confection of the seventeenth century.[12] Its earliest modern editor, François Pluquet, published the

---

9. There are important, and mostly recent, exceptions to this trend: René Stuip, Matthew Bennett, Elisabeth van Houts, and Gabrielle Spiegel.

10. *The Roman de Rou*, ed. Glyn Burgess, xxvii and n. 41. He also points out that "in Wace's time translation usually implied adaptation rather than literal translation" (p. xxxiv, n. 65).

11. The most notable exception to this was Edward A. Freeman's use of the *Roman de Rou* as a source for the Conquest in the nineteenth century in *The History of the Norman Conquest of England*. Marjorie Chibnall also found many of Wace's details compelling enough to include them in the notes to her edition of the *Historia Ecclesiastica*. Orderic Vitalis, *The Ecclesiastical History of Orderic Vitalis*, ed. and trans. Marjorie Chibnall, 6 vols. (Oxford, 1969–80).

12. Peter Damian-Grint also makes this point in an unpublished paper, "Robert Courteheuse et Henri Beauclerc, *frères ennemis* dans les *estoires* de Wace et de Benoît" (2006). I am grateful to have

work as the *Roman de Rou et ducs de Normandie* in the late 1820s, following André Duchesne's seventeenth-century designation of the work as *Le Roumanz de Rou et des Dus de Normendie*.[13] Wace, however, never refers to his work as the *Roman de Rou*, but calls it either the *geste* (deeds) or the *estoire* (history) of the Normans.[14] On the basis of the internal textual evidence, it is abundantly clear that Wace's work should be called the *Geste des Normanz*.[15] Although Wace and Benoît included some material that modern historians might find objectionable, they relied primarily on authoritative Latin sources (the *Gesta Normannorum ducum* and Orderic Vitalis's *Historia Ecclesiastica*) for the content of their histories, and employed a familiar genealogical format borrowed from Latin historiography. Both histories trace the line of agnatic descent from Rollo (or Rou), the founder of the Norman dynasty, to Henry I, recounting the deeds of each of the Norman dukes and kings of England in turn.

Although the appellation of "chronicle" has been far less problematic for historians, the title of Benoît's work is similarly a contrivance of the text's earliest modern editor, Francisque Michel.[16] In his own references to his work, Benoît invariably calls his text an *estoire*, leading Peter Damian-Grint to suggest that the work be called the *Estoire des dus Normanz*.[17] What emerges from a review of the internal textual evidence in both cases is the very clear

---

been given an advance draft of this paper, and I strongly agree with his conclusion that we should strip away these anachronistic accretions and view both the *Roman de Rou* and the *Chronique des ducs de Normandie* in contemporary generic terms as *estoires*.

13. *Roman de Rou et ducs de Normandie*, ed. François Pluquet (Rouen, 1827–29). The later editions are *Maistre Wace's Roman de Rou et des ducs de Normandie*, ed. H. Andresen (Heilbronn, 1877–79); *Le Roman de Rou*, ed. A. J. Holden (Paris, 1970–73); and *The Roman de Rou*, trans. Glyn Burgess, notes Glyn Burgess and Elisabeth van Houts (Isle of Jersey, 2002). The first reference to *Le Roumanz de Rou et des Dus de Normendie* as the title of the work appears at the head of the *Première Partie* (a section now regarded as a false start and included as an appendix in Holden's and Burgess's editions) in Duchesne's seventeenth-century copy of the text; BnF Duchesne 79, fol. 1–84.

14. Wace refers to his text as a *geste* on three separate occasions. *RR*, I, v. 43; II, v. 1360; and III, vv. 5297–98. On one occasion, he clearly refers to his work as an *estoire*. *RR*, I, v. 4.

15. This was first suggested by Gaston Paris in his review of Hugo Andresen's edition of the *Roman de Rou*. Gaston Paris, "Wace, *Roman de Rou*, hgg. von Andresen," *Romania* 9 (1880): 592–614. See also Damian-Grint, "Robert Courteheuse et Henri Beauclerc," 3.

16. The first edition published was the *Chronique des ducs de Normandie, par Benoît, trouvère anglo-normand du XIIe siècle; publiée pour la première fois d'après un manuscrit du Musée britannique, par Francisque Michel*, 2 vols. (Paris, 1836–44). The subsequent, and more authoritative, edition is the *Chronique des ducs de Normandie par Benoît*, ed. Carin Fahlin, 4 vols. (Uppsala, 1951–79). All of my references to the *Chronique* are to the Fahlin edition.

17. Peter Damian-Grint bases this suggestion upon two pieces of internal evidence. "Ai translaté des dus normanz, / d'eus l'estoire qui moct est granz." Benoît, *CDN*, vv. 42049–50. "De lui [Duke Richard I] est l'estoire fenie." Benoît, *CDN*, v. 28708. Damian-Grint notes that it is equally possi-

indication that the *Roman de Rou* and the *Chronique des ducs de Normandie* were envisioned by their authors as *estoires*.[18] Wace and Benoît thought that they were writing history, and we must take their intentions seriously if we hope to understand how these authors, their patron, and their audiences viewed these works. Any attempt to interpret these texts requires that we preface our investigation of them with the understanding that their authors conceived of, constructed, and presented them as histories.

Not only do Wace and Benoît self-consciously style their texts as *estoires* or *gestes*, they assure their audiences of the reliability of their narratives by calling on the *auctoritas* (authority) of their Latin sources.[19] In a tradition familiar to anyone who has spent time reading ancient or medieval histories, Wace and Benoît summon the *auctoritas* of their sources to vouch for the credibility and quality of their own texts.[20] Although they seldom name these authorities (Benoît's references to Pliny, Augustine, and Isidore in his proemium are exceptional), they constantly reveal that they are working with authoritative Latin texts by referring to their labor as translators.[21]

---

ble to use the title *Estoire de Normandie* suggested by Anne Berthelot in her *Histoire de la littérature française du Moyen Âge* (Rennes, 2006), 65.

18. Damian-Grint, "Robert Courteheuse et Henri Beauclerc," 4. Damian-Grint also points out that the term *chronique* was almost never used as a generic designation in a historiographical work in the twelfth century—he notes that the only known exception to this rule is Gaimar's use of the word "*chroniz*" in the *Estoire des Engleis* when referring to the proper name of *The Anglo-Saxon Chronicle*. Damian-Grint, *New Historians of the Twelfth-Century Renaissance*, 225–26. Cf. Peter Damian-Grint, "*Estoire* as Word and Genre," *Medium Aevum* 66 (1997): 189–99.

19. Peter Damian-Grint has detailed the various rhetorical strategies used by Wace, Benoît, and their contemporaries to authorize their vernacular histories in *New Historians of the Twelfth-Century Renaissance*.

20. After an extensive cosmological and geographical proemium invoking Pliny and Augustine, Benoît calls on the authority of Isidore of Seville to authenticate the account he has given. Benoît, *CDN*, vv. 353–56. Although neither Wace nor Benoît ever name their authorities for Norman history, they often refer to them. After his account of the 1105 surrender of Caen, for instance, Benoît declares that he has reported the event "si cum je truis"—implying that he has an authoritative text at hand. Benoît, *CDN*, vv. 43531–36. Wace refers to his sources in a similar manner and sometimes reveals that he is working with more than one source. In his account of Harold Godwinson's trip to Normandy, for instance, he reveals that he has found conflicting accounts of the event in two separate books, but he does not name them or their authors. Wace, *RR*, vv. 5597–604 (all references to the *Roman de Rou* are to part III unless otherwise noted). Cf. Damian-Grint, *New Historians*, chap. 4.

21. Wace often complains about the difficulty of translating his work into the vernacular. In one case, he connects such a complaint to a short autobiography in which he appears to assert himself as an authority with personal knowledge of Norman history, rather than appealing to the more traditional *auctoritas* of a Latin source. Wace, *RR*, vv. 5300–318. In another instance, Wace complains of the difficulty of translating Latin works. Wace, *RR*, II, vv. 1357–59. Cf. Jean Blacker, "'La geste est grande, longue et grieve a translater': History for Henry II," *Romance Quarterly* 37 (1990): 387–96. Benoît makes similar complaints, including one in which he declares that he wishes to

While appealing to Latin sources to authenticate their narratives, Wace and Benoît also seek to establish themselves as authorities by exhibiting their learning in rhetorical tours de force that range from cosmological and geographical expositions to etymological lessons.[22] They also deploy other rhetorical strategies to convince their readers that they are reliable and their histories trustworthy. For instance, Wace and Benoît foster the confidence of their audiences by frequently noting that they are relying on personal knowledge or eyewitness testimony in relating an event.[23] Quite often, Wace reveals that he does not know the truth of some matter or that he realizes that his information comes from a disreputable source, such as the songs of *jongleurs*.[24] Like more traditional invocations of *auctoritas*, all of these are conventional rhetorical strategies designed to persuade an audience of the author's reliability and the veracity of his text.[25] Most twelfth-century Anglo-Norman readers and auditors, who were accustomed to the conventions of ancient and medieval Latin historiography and attuned to invocations of *auctoritas*, would have recognized these prompts and accepted these vernacular texts as they were intended—that is, as histories translated from authoritative Latin sources by men of learning.[26]

---

please Henry II, but the work of translation is burdensome. Benoît, *CDN*, vv. 28708–26. Cf. Damian-Grint, *New Historians*, chap. 4.

22. Wace begins part III of the *Roman de Rou* with a reminder that everything would be forgotten if not for the work of historians like himself, who not only write histories but read them aloud at festivals. He then goes on to recall the ancient names of cities and countries, delivers a lecture on how Neustria acquired the name Normandy with the coming of the "Northmen," and declares that all that is ultimately left of great men, such as Alexander or Caesar, is what can be found in books. Wace, *RR*, vv. 1–142. Peter Damian-Grint has shown that Benoît, likewise, performs a rhetorical tour de force in the proemium of the *Chronique* (vv. 1–352) that presents his credentials as a learned scholar to his audience. Peter Damian-Grint, "Learning and Authority in Benoît de Sainte-Maure's Cosmography," *Reading Medieval Studies* 24 (1998): 42. Cf. Damian-Grint, *New Historians*, chap. 4.

23. Damian-Grint, *New Historians*, chaps. 1–4.

24. Wace frequently calls on the authority of his own personal knowledge or the authority of eyewitnesses, as when he relates the translation of the bodies of Dukes Richard I and II, to which he says he was an eyewitness. Wace, *RR*, vv. 2241–46. Wace often resorts to claiming ignorance or being unable to find a reliable account of an event. In one instance, he recounts songs he has heard the *jongleurs* sing about William Longsword's misdeeds, but then says he can find out nothing more about these events. Since he can find no authoritative written evidence, he declares that he will not say any more about it. Of course, in this case Wace uses a plea of ignorance to spread fairly vicious rumors about Longsword without appearing to intend to do so, but it is the fact that he claims to have sought corroboration that is significant in this context. Wace, *RR*, II, vv. 1361–67. Cf. Damian-Grint, *New Historians*, chap. 4.

25. Cf. Damian-Grint, *New Historians, passim*.

26. For discussions of twelfth-century lay literacy, see Michael Clanchy, *From Memory to Written Record: England 1066–1307* (Oxford, 1993), esp. 185–96; Brian Stock, *The Implications of Literacy:*

Yet another problem confronts any historian who wishes to use these texts: they are not only vernacular texts of suspect genre, but they are written in verse. This fact alone seems designed to ward off historians as we associate verse with fiction and regard prose as the only medium capable of conveying historical truth. This unfavorable view of verse is partly a modern prejudice, but it has been reinforced by the works of later medieval prose historians who fervently denounced verse in an attempt to elevate their own work.

In *Romancing the Past*, Gabrielle Spiegel examined the adoption of prose as the language of historical truth by vernacular authors in the early thirteenth century.[27] Spiegel connected the birth of vernacular prose historiography to the trials of early thirteenth-century Flemish aristocrats, their loss of political power, and their desire to assert their relevance by inventing a glorious past that would enhance their ebbing prestige. The vernacular authors entrusted with constructing this magnificent past thus had to make unusually emphatic claims to veracity, and they did so by equating their use of prose with historical accuracy. As Spiegel has also pointed out, the new prose historians promoted their works through diatribes that extolled the virtues of prose and decried the mendacity of verse.

The inclination to dismiss verse historiography has been so pervasive that one might well question why historians should bother with verse histories at all. If verse was reputed to be the language of lies, and the vernacular was the lowest stratum of medieval language, what can the study of vernacular verse historiography possibly yield? This question assumes, however, that the assessment of the relative merits of verse and prose made by these early thirteenth-century authors remains static for all time and in all places.

Although the opposition of verse and prose is an ancient one, the assumption that a greater truth value inherently resides in one form or the other demonstrably shifts over time. It revolves in large cycles that we can trace from the preference for epic poetry exhibited by ancient cultures to the intentionally dispassionate prose historiography that we value today (this

Written Language and Models of Interpretation in the Eleventh and Twelfth Centuries (Princeton, 1983); Damian-Grint, *New Historians*, chap. 5; Ong, "Orality, Literacy, and Medieval Textualization"; Stock, "Literacy and Society in the Twelfth Century"; Stock, "Medieval Literacy"; Clanchy, "Written Word"; Galbraith, "Literacy of the English Medieval Kings"; Turner, "Miles Literatus"; Orme, "Lay Literacy in England, 1100–1300"; McKitterick and Binski, "History and Literature: Sacred and Secular"; Bloch, *Feudal Society*; Thompson, *Literacy of the Laity in the Middle Ages*; and Thorndike, "Elementary and Secondary Education in the Middle Ages."

27. Gabrielle Spiegel, *Romancing the Past: The Rise of Vernacular Prose Historiography in Thirteenth-Century France* (Berkeley, 1993).

is not meant to imply that modern historiography is actually dispassionate or unbiased, only to stress that, in order to be taken seriously, modern historians must adhere to a set of rhetorical conventions that convey the intent and appearance of objectivity). Whereas later historians, and some contemporaries, may have accused epic poets and verse historians of sacrificing truth to meet the demands of meter, all audiences at all times did not apply the same criteria.[28] Verse was not always considered inherently inferior to prose or intrinsically fictitious, a point that Spiegel has also emphasized.[29] Although Spiegel correctly pointed out that poetry and history were, in fact, intimately related in the ancient and early medieval rhetorical tradition, this important point bears repeating. It was not until the end of the twelfth century that "counter to the received wisdom of the ancients, poetry was found lacking and prose acknowledged as the only proper (at least preferred) language of historical truth in the Middle Ages."[30] Verse was a perfectly acceptable and unproblematic vehicle for the transmission of historical truth during the twelfth century, and it was the form in which almost all twelfth-century vernacular historiography appeared.[31]

Verse was not reserved for fiction in the twelfth century; it was associated with a number of vernacular genres, but especially with history and hagiography. As Peter Damian-Grint has argued, the tendency of modern scholars to associate verse with fiction in the twelfth century ignores all known facts regarding the development of vernacular literature.[32] The earliest verse history appeared well before the earliest extant romance, twelfth-century vernacular histories were almost always written in verse, they were dynastic, and they had very little in common with the romances that appeared later. If anything, these facts suggest that romances emulated the popular verse

---

28. The reception of the Homeric epic provides an instructive example. Although many Roman and medieval intellectuals regarded Homer with skepticism, Homer's influence on the Greek historian Herodotus has been well documented. It should be noted, however, that the prose form of *The Histories* was ultimately of little use in insulating Herodotus himself from judgment. Cicero may have called him "*pater historiae*" (*De Legibus*, i.5), but he was criticized nonetheless by Thucydides (*History of the Peloponnesian War*, i.22) and Plutarch (*De Herodoti malignitate*).

29. Gabrielle Spiegel, "Forging the Past: The Language of Historical Truth in the Middle Ages," *History Teacher* 17/2 (1984): 267–83, at 267–69. Cf. Damian-Grint, *New Historians*, chap. 1.

30. Spiegel, "Forging the Past," 267–68.

31. Spiegel's equation of prose with truth and the genre of history is perfectly acceptable for the thirteenth century when the vernacular was entering maturity and genres were hardening, but it cannot be successfully projected back into the twelfth century when vernacular literature and its generic categories were still forming. See also Damian-Grint, "*Estoire* as Word and Genre," 189–99; Damian-Grint, *New Historians*, chap. 6; and *Roman de Rou*, ed. Glyn Burgess, xxvii–xxxiv.

32. Damian-Grint, *New Historians*, chap. 6, esp. 181–98.

form of the earliest vernacular histories. The fact that the *Rou* and the *Chronique* were composed in verse should be taken as evidence that they were designed to suit the tastes of the twelfth-century aristocrats who commissioned and consumed them, not as an indication that they were intended or received as fiction.

The rise of vernacular prose historiography in the thirteenth century should be understood as both a reaction to, and an extension of, the proliferation of vernacular verse historiography during the twelfth century.[33] As Spiegel has clearly pointed out, it was only at the end of the twelfth century, when vernacular historians emphatically sought to claim equality with Latin historians and distance themselves from the *jongleurs*, that any debate emerged over the merits of verse.[34] Unfortunately, historians have had a tendency to lump twelfth-century "rhymed chronicles" together with the *chansons de geste*.[35] Verse histories and *chansons de geste* both purported to represent history, but they differed in at least one critical way. Although the *chansons de geste* employed a variety of rhetorical tropes attesting to their veracity, *jongleurs* did not claim to be producing accurate translations of authoritative Latin texts.[36] Twelfth-century verse historians such as Wace and Benoît, on the other hand, took special care to present themselves as men of learning and their works as reliable translations of authoritative Latin sources. Wace, who called himself "Maistre Wace" and invariably described himself as either a *clerc lisant* (reading clerk) or a *maistre lisant* (reading master), would undoubtedly have been horrified to find himself thrown into the company of lowly *jongleurs*, as would Benoît, who was also careful to project his learning and authority.[37]

Although the precise meanings of the terms *clerc lisant* and *maistre lisant* are a matter of some debate, the term *clerc lisant* can be generally understood to designate an author who specialized in adapting Latin texts for a vernacular audience and who read those texts aloud. The distinction between a *clerc*

---

33. Ibid., chap. 6.

34. Spiegel, "Forging the Past," 268–73.

35. Ibid., 269.

36. *Chansons de geste* usually claimed to reproduce an eyewitness's account. Damian-Grint, *New Historians*, 38, 72, 116, 152–68.

37. At various points in the *Roman de Rou* Wace refers to himself as "un clerc de Caen," "clerc lisant," "maistre lisant," and "Maistre Wace," and he regularly refers to the *chansons de geste* sung by the *jongleurs* as unreliable sources. Wace also refers to his successor as "Maistre Beneeit" in his epilogue. Gaimar likewise describes himself as a *clerc lisant* in the *Estoire des Engleis*. Geffrei Gaimar, *Estoire des Engleis: History of the English*, ed. and trans. Ian Short (Oxford, 2009) v. 2380. See also Damian-Grint, *New Historians*, chap. 4.

lisant and a *maistre lisant* appears to have been that the *maistres lisant* were authorized to teach. The appearance of these terms notably coincided with the emergence of authors translating Latin works into the vernacular in the early twelfth century.[38] These titles emphasized the verse historian's reliance on authoritative written sources, as well as his Latinity, erudition, morality, and clerical training, and they were used to differentiate his learned work from that of the *jongleurs*. These terms also indicate that verse histories, like the *chansons de geste*, had a performative aspect: they were destined to be read before an audience.

Wace and Benoît were not just authors and translators; their professional duties included reading their works aloud for the entertainment and instruction of an aristocratic audience. Wace asserts as much in the *Roman de Rou* when he muses on the purpose of history writing: "To remember the deeds, words and ways of our ancestors, the wicked deeds of wicked men and the brave deeds of brave men, books, chronicles and histories should be read out at festivals." He goes on to say that "if documents were not composed, and then read and recounted by clerics, many things which transpired in times gone by would be forgotten."[39] Wace envisions his history being read to a large crowd during a festival, such as Christmas or Easter, at a time when the king normally held court with his most important nobles and clerics, as well as foreign dignitaries, in attendance. Benoît similarly draws our attention to the fact that his work is destined to be read aloud by continually asking his reader to *hear* (*oir*) his words and by anticipating a time when he will personally read his work to Henry II.

Since *clercs lisant* and *jongleurs* both composed and recited rhymed works treating historical events and the lives of saints, their works could be easily conflated.[40] In fact, the polemic of early prose historians suggests that audiences were increasingly prone to confuse the work of vernacular historians and *jongleurs* at the end of the twelfth century.[41] Even though twelfth-century clerical authors such as Wace and Benoît used various rhetorical strategies

---

38. See also Jean-Guy Gouttebroze, "Entre les historiographes d'expression latine et les jongleurs: Le clerc lisant," in *Le Clerc au moyen âge* (Aix-en-Provence, 1995), 215–30; M. Dominica Legge, "Clerc Lisant," *Modern Language Review* 47 (1952): 554–56; and Faith Lyons, "*Clerc lisant* and *maître lisant*," *Modern Language Review* 56 (1961): 224–25.

39. "Pur remembrer des ancesurs / les fiez e les diz e les murs, / les felunies des feluns / e les barnages des baruns, / deit l'um les livres e les gestes / e les estoires lire a festes. / Si escripture ne fust feite / e puis par clers litte e retraite, / mult fussent choses ublïees / ki de viez tens sunt trespasses." Wace, *RR*, vv. 1–10.

40. Cf. Damian-Grint, *New Historians*, 204

41. Peter Damian-Grint has also argued that this was the case. Damian-Grint, *New Historians*, chap. 5.

and the designation of *clerc lisant* to project their learning and authority, and they did so in part to distance their work from that of traveling entertainers, these strategies ultimately proved inadequate. The vernacular prose historians of the late twelfth and early thirteenth centuries attempted to make the distinction between themselves and the *jongleurs* even more apparent by insisting that prose was the only language capable of conveying truth and by banishing verse from their histories altogether.[42]

Spiegel singled out the early thirteenth-century translators of the *Pseudo-Turpin Chronicle* as especially vehement in their invective, and their rhetoric reveals their ulterior motives—the translators claimed that prose distinguished their works from the mendacious songs of the *jongleurs*, and that adopting prose allowed them to faithfully translate the Latin prose of their exemplars in a way that their predecessors had not.[43] These self-promoting declarations announced that all previous verse histories should be discarded and the newly fashioned prose narratives preferred because they were inherently more reliable by virtue of their very form. Prose historians thus rhetorically claimed even greater authority than their verse predecessors had by asserting that only their prose could accurately reproduce the Latin of their exemplars.

Based on this invective, we would expect to find that verse histories such as the *Rou* and the *Chronique* fell into disregard sometime around 1200 and ceased to circulate shortly thereafter, but that is not the case. Not only did these verse histories continue to circulate (in fact, all but one of the surviving copies of the *Rou* and the *Chronique* date from the thirteenth century or later), both of them were adapted into prose sometime after 1200.[44] Both works were still considered accurate and important enough to have their lives prolonged by merely adjusting their language to conform to the new conventions. As harsh as prose historians were in their criticism of verse histories,

---

42. Ibid., chap. 6.

43. For instance, Nicholas of Senlis declares in his translation of the *Pseudo-Turpin Chronicle* that "never have so many lies been told as by those singers and jongleurs who spoke and chanted [songs about Charlemagne's expedition to Spain]." Spiegel also notes that Johannes "asserted the authority of his version against those which had preceded it on the basis of his faithful reproduction, in French, of the Latin prose of his exemplar." He thus reveals a desire to elevate his work by emulating the prose of his Latin source. Spiegel, "Forging the Past," 271–72. See also Damian-Grint, *New Historians*, chap. 6.

44. A prose version of the *Chronique des ducs de Normandie* is held by the J. Paul Getty Museum (Getty, Ms. Ludwig XIII 4); prose versions of the *Roman de Rou* are at the British Library (BL Royal Fr. 15.E.VI) and the Bibliothèque nationale de France (BN fr. 16939). There may well be more manuscripts containing prose versions of the *Rou* and *Chronique* that I have yet to find.

their efforts to enshrine prose as the language of historical truth did not result in a dramatic change in the actual content of vernacular histories.

Spiegel has also noted that the earliest prose historians were far less interested in genuine veracity than in its appearance, and that they freely adopted elements from romance and epic to enliven their narratives and suit the tastes of their audiences.[45] I would add that prose authors did so because the tastes of their audiences had already helped to shape, and had been shaped by, verse histories. The Anglo-Norman aristocracy in particular seems to have played an active role as patrons in forging the aesthetic of the earliest Old French verse histories, and their tastes do not appear to have undergone a revolution at the turn of the thirteenth century.

The shift to prose vernacular historiography was thus not due to a greater concern for veracity on the part of prose historians, nor was it a response to the changing tastes of their audience. It was largely motivated by a growing desire on the part of educated and literate clerics, the successors of authors like Wace and Benoît, to further elevate their work, to clearly distinguish themselves from *jongleurs* and align themselves with Latin historians.[46] The venom with which prose historians denounced both verse and its purveyors suggests that their efforts to reinvent vernacular historiography were constrained by the older aesthetic and by their audience's lingering preference for rhymes and songs.[47]

The transition from verse to prose was, in fact, a protracted process that spanned at least three decades from roughly 1180 to 1210. It accompanied a gradual hardening of vernacular genres (as history was increasingly constructed and recognized as a genre distinct from romance or poetry) and was driven by a desire on the part of translators to differentiate their learned work from that of the *jongleurs* they maligned.[48] This transition was not instigated by a widespread crisis of confidence in verse histories or by a general public that was demanding prose; it was implemented by the very authors who translated Latin texts as a means of reinforcing their claims to learning and authority. Prose would eventually triumph as the language of historical truth during the thirteenth century as vernacular modes of representing history continued to evolve, but this would only occur decades after

---

45. Spiegel, "Forging the Past," 273–74.

46. See Damian-Grint, *New Historians*, chap. 6.

47. As Peter Damian-Grint has noted, *chansons de geste* and epics continued to be popular long after prose was adopted as the preferred form for vernacular historiography. Damian-Grint, *New Historians*, 189–90.

48. See Damian-Grint, *New Historians*, chaps. 5 and 6.

the appearance of the *Roman de Rou* and *Chronique des ducs de Normandie*. And the evolution of vernacular historiography did not end with the triumph of prose; verse historiography was eventually granted a reprieve and enjoyed a marked resurgence in the fourteenth century.[49]

The Origins of Old French Historiography

One of the idiosyncrasies of Old French historiography is that it was not born in France at all. The first extant Old French histories appeared in Norman England around 1135, almost a full century before they appeared elsewhere in Europe.[50] The spread of vernacular literacy across Europe, the indigenous tradition of Old English historiography in England, and the concerns over legitimacy unleashed by the Norman Conquest converged at the beginning of the twelfth century to produce what appears to have been a veritable clamoring in England for histories of the Anglo-Saxons, Welsh, and Normans written in Old French.[51] The earliest Old French histories, those written by Geffrei Gaimar, Wace, and Benoît de Sainte-Maure, were designed to appeal to a mixed audience that lacked sufficient Latin, Welsh, or Old English literacy to access this history at first-hand.[52]

---

49. Damian-Grint, *New Historians*, chap. 6.

50. M. Dominica Legge, "La précocité de la littérature anglo-normande," *CCM* 8 (1965): 327–49; M. Dominica Legge, *Anglo-Norman Literature and Its Background* (Westport, 1978); M. Dominica Legge, "L'influence littéraire de la cour d'Henri Beauclerc," in *Melanges offerts à Rita Lejeune* (Gembloux, 1969), 679–87; Reto R. Bezzola, *Les origines et la formation de la littérature courtoise en occident (550–1200)*, 3 vols. (Paris, 1958–63), II:418–22, 451–55, and III:149; and Ruth Dean, *Anglo-Norman Literature: A Guide to Texts and Manuscripts* (London, 1999). Peter Damian-Grint has pointed out that "the European tradition of vernacular historiography is otherwise represented during the twelfth century by a single work, the Middle High German *Kaiserchronik*; composed around 1150, it had no imitators and no noticeable influence on historiographical writing in the lands of the Holy Roman Empire, where chronicles continued to be written in Latin only." Damian-Grint, *New Historians*, 11–12.

51. See also Damian-Grint, *New Historians*, chap. 1; Nancy Partner, *Serious Entertainments: The Writing of History in Twelfth-Century England* (Chicago, 1977), 5; Bernard Guenée, *Histoire et culture historique dans l'Occident médiéval* (Paris, 1980), 320; Ian Short, "Patrons and Polyglots: French Literature in Twelfth-Century England," *ANS* 14 (1991): 229–49; and Ian Short, "Gaimar et les débuts de l'historiographie en langue française," in *Chroniques nationales et chroniques universelles*, ed. Danielle Buschinger (Göppingen, 1990), 155–63.

52. Gaimar's *Estoire des Engleis* and his now lost *Estoire des Bretuns* (c. 1135), as well as Wace's *Roman de Brut* (c. 1155), preceded the *Roman de Rou* (c. 1160–74) and *Chronique des ducs de Normandie* (c. 1174–89). Cf. Damian-Grint, *New Historians*, chaps. 1–3. Although Damian-Grint distinguishes between the classical material presented in the *romans antiques* and twelfth-century verse historiography proper, I would argue that the *romans antiques* were virtually indistinguishable from the earliest

The *Roman de Rou* and the *Chronique des ducs de Normandie* were designed for the tastes of the Anglo-Norman nobility, and they must be understood as part of a larger tradition of vernacular historiography in England.[53] Unlike their contemporaries on the Continent, the Anglo-Saxons had been making regular note of history in their vernacular since at least the ninth century. The very existence of *The Anglo-Saxon Chronicle* probably suggested the utility and practicality of vernacular history writing to the Normans.[54] After all, histories were useful only to the extent that one could access them. Latin histories were directly accessible only to the tiny minority of the medieval population who were literate in Latin, and anyone else wishing to hear them had to rely on translators to convey information to them. Writing history in the vernacular thus removed a significant barrier between historical narratives and the nobles who generally commissioned and consumed them. Vernacular historians often emphasized precisely the point that their work allowed non-Latinate audiences to access historical material.[55] As the Normans had no known experience in producing vernacular history themselves, but gained exposure to an insular tradition of vernacular history writing after the Conquest, we must assume that their early experimentation with the form was the result of this contact.[56] Such a chain of events would certainly explain the precocious appearance of Old French histories in England about sixty years after the Conquest.

Not only was *The Anglo-Saxon Chronicle* the most likely precursor of Old French historiography, it was also the first history known to have appeared in Old French.[57] Geffrei Gaimar produced his verse translation/adaptation

---

vernacular histories. Both translated authoritative sources into verse for vernacular audiences, and were clearly intended to be didactic. The *romans antique* may have incorporated popular motifs, introduced anachronisms, and fictionalized their narratives to an extent that we might find objectionable in a work of history, but they clearly purported to represent ancient "history" for an aristocratic audience. See Renate Blumenfeld-Kosinski, "Old French Narrative Genres: Towards a Definition of the *Roman Antique*," *Romance Philology* 34 (1980): 143–59, and Renate Blumenfeld-Kosinski, "The Gods as Metaphor in the *Roman de Thèbes*," *Modern Philology* 83 (1985): 1–11.

53. See Damian-Grint, *New Historians*, 14–16.

54. *The Anglo-Saxon Chronicle: A Revised Translation*, trans. Dorothy Whitelock, with David C. Douglas and Susie I. Tucker (London, 1961). See also Damian-Grint, *New Historians*, 14–16; Ian Short, "Gaimar's Epilogue and Geoffrey of Monmouth's *Liber vetustissimus*," *Speculum* 69 (1994): 323–43, at 323; and Reginald R. Darlington, *Anglo-Norman Historians* (London, 1947), 19.

55. See Damian-Grint, *New Historians*, chap. 1–3.

56. Ibid., 14–16; and David Howlett, *The English Origins of Old French Literature* (Portland, 1996), 51.

57. Gaimar describes in his epilogue a rhymed vernacular chronicle of the life of Henry I written by a certain David that would have been the first known history in Old French had it survived. "Ore dit Gaimar, s'il ad guarant, / del rei Henri dirrat avant, / ke s'il en volt un poi parler / e de sa

of *The Anglo-Saxon Chronicle* in 1135 at the behest of Lady Constance, wife of Ralph fitzGilbert.[58] That work, the *Estoire des Engleis*, is the earliest extant history in Old French. Gaimar's translation of *The Anglo-Saxon Chronicle* was initially accompanied by a second work described by the author as the *Estoire des Bretuns* that has long since been lost. The *Estoire des Bretuns* appears to have been an adaptation of Geoffrey of Monmouth's *Historia regum Britanniae*, which in turn claimed to be a Latin translation of an ancient Welsh book.[59] In fact, Gaimar links his work to Geoffrey of Monmouth's in the epilogue of the *Estoire des Engleis*; while he does not mention Geoffrey or his book by name, he does refer to Geoffrey's patron, Robert of Gloucester, and to the book that he commissioned.[60] Referring to his source for the lost *Estoire des Bretuns*, Gaimar says that Robert of Gloucester "had this historical narrative adapted/translated in accordance with the books belonging to the Welsh" and loaned it to Walter Espec, who then loaned it to Ralph fitzGilbert. Lady Constance borrowed the book from her husband and charged Gaimar with translating it into Old French.

Although Gaimar may be exaggerating Lady Constance's involvement in order to flatter her, his account of this commission gives us some sense of how patronage worked for these vernacular verse histories and suggests that patrons played an active role in their production. In his epilogue, Gaimar also claims to have had access to copies of a variety of other books written in Old English, Old French, and Latin, which he used to construct his work.[61] Gaimar appears to have relied on two copies of *The Anglo-Saxon*

---

vie translater, / tels mil choses en purrad dire / ke unkes Davit ne fist escrivere, / ne la räine de Luvain." Gaimar, *Estoire des Engleis*, vv. 6477–84. See also Short, "Gaimar's Epilogue," 326.

58. The references to Lady Constance appear in the epilogue (vv. 6429–75) reproduced below. Gaimar's epilogue also functions as a *captatio benevolentiae*, in that it seeks to elicit the goodwill of his patron, and should therefore not be taken as conclusive evidence that either Lady Constance or contemporary Anglo-Norman nobles lacked Latin literacy. See also Jean Blacker, "'Dame Custance la gentil': Gaimar's Portrait of a Lady and Her Books," in *The Court and Cultural Diversity: Selected Papers from the Eighth Triennial Congress of the International Courtly Literature Society, The Queen's University of Belfast, 26 July–1 August 1995*, ed. Evelyn Mullally and John Thompson (Woodbridge, 1997), 109–19.

59. The missing *Estoire des Bretuns* and the provenance of his source materials are described by Gaimar in his epilogue. Gaimar, *Estoire des Engleis*, vv. 6429–76, and *The Historia regum Britannie of Geoffrey of Monmouth*, ed. N. Wright and J. C. Crick, 4 vols. (Woodbridge, 1984–91).

60. Ian Short suggests that the source Gaimar describes as "le bon livre de Oxford" may have been part of "a pre-Geoffrey of Monmouth historical corpus to which Gaimar had access independently of Geoffrey." This corpus may have comprised materials in Latin, Old English, or possibly even Welsh. Short, "Gaimar's Epilogue," 340–41.

61. "Ici voil [jo] del rei finer. / Ceste estorie fist translater / Dame Custance la gentil. / Gaimar i mist marz e averil / e tuz les dusze mais / ainz k'il oust translaté des reis. / Il purchaça maint esam-

Chronicle, as well as a wealth of unidentified sources in Old English and Latin, and a copy of Geoffrey of Monmouth's *Historia regum Britanniae*.[62] Although Gaimar's account of his source materials in his epilogue must be taken with a certain measure of skepticism, as it serves to authenticate his narrative, it does suggest that Old French texts had already begun to appear in England by 1135, and that texts in Old English, Old French, and Latin enjoyed a fairly brisk circulation among the Anglo-Norman aristocracy and clergy at the time.[63]

In each of the four surviving manuscripts containing Gaimar's *Estoire des Engleis* we find another early Old French verse history, Wace's *Roman de Brut*.[64] A rival vernacular adaptation of Geoffrey of Monmouth's *Historia*

---

plaire, / liveres engleis e par gramaire / e en romanz e en latin, / ainz k'en pust traire a la fin. / Si sa dame ne li aidast, / ja a nul jor ne l'achevast. / Ele enveiad a Helmeslac / pur le livere Walter Espac. / Robert li quens de Glöucestre / fist translater icele geste / solum les liveres as Waleis / k'il aveient des bretons reis. / Walter Espec la demandat, / li quens Robert li enveiat, / puis la prestat Walter Espec / a Räul le fiz Gilebert. / Dame Custance l'enpruntat / de son seignur k'ele mult amat. / Geffrai Gaimar cel livere escrit / [e] les transsadances i mist / ke li Waleis ourent leissé, / k'il aveit ainz purchacé — / u fust a dreit u fust a tort — / le bon livere de Oxeford / ki fust Walter l'arcediaen, / si en amendat son livere bien; / e de l'estorie de Wincestre / fust amendé ceste geste, / de Wassingburc un livere engleis / u il trovad escrit des reis / e de tuz les emperurs / ke de Rome furent seignurs / e de Engleterre ourent trëu, / des reis ki d'els ourent tenu, / de lur vies e de lur plaiz, / des aventures e des faiz, / coment chescons maintint la terre, / quel amat pes e liquel guere. / De tut le plus pout ci trover / ki en cest livere volt esgarder; / e ki ne creit ço ke jo di, / demand a Nicole de Trailli." Gaimar, *Estoire des Engleis*, vv. 6429–76.

62. Gaimar claims to have had four major sources, two for the history of the Britons and two for the history of the Anglo-Saxons. According to Alexander Bell, "le livere Walter Espac" appears to have been a copy of the *Historia regum Brittaniae* most likely given to Walter Espec by Robert of Gloucester soon after the *Historia* was completed, while "le bon livre de Oxford" appears to have been a Welsh or English book that Gaimar initially acquired before he had access to the *Historia* and afterward used to supplement the *Historia*. Neither has been identified. Bell suggests that "l'estorie de Wincestre" and "de Wassingburc un livere engleis" were copies of *The Anglo-Saxon Chronicle* held at Winchester and Washingborough in the twelfth century. Bell also notes that Gaimar made use of a variety of unknown sources, including a *Life of Saint Guthlac*, a collection of writings concerned with Saint Edmund, a list of the resting places of saints, and a Danish account of Haveloc. Gaimar's French sources are unknown. Geffrei Gaimar, *Estoire des Engleis*, ed. Alexander Bell (Oxford 1960), liii–lxxvii.

63. See also Short, "Gaimar's Epilogue," 232, 327, and 340; C. Warren Hollister, "Anglo-Norman Political Culture and the Twelfth-Century Renaissance," in *Anglo-Norman Political Culture and the Twelfth-Century Renaissance*, ed. C. Warren Hollister (Woodbridge, 1997), 1–16, at 6; and John Gillingham, "Gaimar, the Prose *Brut*, and the Making of English History," in John Gillingham, *The English in the Twelfth-Century: Imperialism, National Identity, and Political Values* (Woodbridge, 2000), 113–22.

64. Gaimar, *Estoire de Engleis*, xii. Wace, *Le Roman de Brut*, ed. Le Roux Lincy, 2 vols. (Rouen, 1836–38) and *Le Roman de Brut*, ed. Ivor Arnold, 2 vols. (Paris, 1938 and 1940). The complete or nearly complete text of the *Roman de Brut* survives in nineteen manuscripts and an additional twelve manuscripts contain fragments of the text. For the most recent list of surviving manuscripts,

regum Britanniae, the *Roman de Brut* supplanted Gaimar's *Estoire des Bretuns* soon after its completion in 1155. Leaving aside questions of Geoffrey of Monmouth's reliability or the existence of his putative Welsh source, these early verse adaptations of *The Anglo-Saxon Chronicle* and the *Historia regum Britanniae* were histories commissioned by and designed for the Anglo-Norman aristocracy.[65] The sole exception to this rule of aristocratic patronage for the earliest surviving Old French histories was Wace's *Roman de Brut*, which was dedicated to Eleanor of Aquitaine but not commissioned by her. Wace's choice to dedicate his work to England's new queen in 1155 was most likely motivated by a desire to generate future royal commissions; it should not be taken as an indication that he was already working for either Eleanor or Henry II. It seems that Wace had begun the *Roman de Brut* without a patron, but assumed that his history of the Britons would find a receptive audience among the Anglo-Norman nobility.[66] He was right. The *Roman de Brut* proved to be so popular that it was adapted into Middle English verse by Layamon at the beginning of the thirteenth century, and adapted yet again into Middle English prose in the fifteenth century.[67]

The birth of Old French historiography in England thus owes a large debt to the indigenous Anglo-Saxon (and possibly Welsh) tradition of vernacular historiography, but it was equally predicated on the peculiar circumstances of the twelfth-century Anglo-Norman nobility. Scholars have long observed that the precocious eruption of historiography in the Anglo-Norman world was one of England's central contributions to the twelfth-century renaissance, that it developed out of an intellectual tradition fostered in Benedictine monasteries, and that it was "remorselessly political."[68] The

---

see Judith Weiss, *Wace's Roman de Brut, A History of the British People: Text and Translation* (Exeter, 1999), xxvii–xxix.

65. Despite the controversy his work generated, Geoffrey claimed to faithfully represent Welsh history and many, if not all, of his contemporaries took his work seriously. Those who believed that Geoffrey had utterly invented his source and his "facts" were compelled to rebut his work *because* it was enjoying a large degree of acceptance. See Short, "Gaimar's Epilogue," 340–41.

66. Wace seems to have begun the work in 1150, and it is likely that he originally envisioned dedicating the *Roman de Brut* to King Stephen or to a member of the Anglo-Norman nobility.

67. Layamon, *Brut*, ed. G. L. Brook and R. F. Leslie, 2 vols. (London, 1963 and 1978); Thomas J. Harford, *A Comprehensive Study of Layamon's Brut* (Lewiston, NY, 2002); *The Oldest Anglo-Norman Prose Brut Chronicle: An Edition and Translation*, ed. Julia Marvin (Woodbridge, 2006); and Lister M. Matheson, *The Prose Brut: The Development of a Middle English Chronicle* (Tempe, 1998).

68. R. W. Southern, *Medieval Humanism and Other Studies* (Oxford, 1970), 160–62; R. W. Southern, "England in the Twelfth-Century Renaissance," *History* 45 (1960): 201–16; R. W. Southern, "Aspects of the European Tradition of Historical Writing," *TRHS* 5/20 (1970): 174–96; 5/21 (1971): 159–79; 5/22 (1972): 159–80; and 5/23 (1973): 243–63; Partner, *Serious Entertainments: The*

years immediately following the Norman Conquest produced a flurry of politicized history writing in Latin as the Normans found themselves in a truly extraordinary situation: a bastard Norman duke had forcibly supplanted a noble Anglo-Saxon family on the throne of England.[69] And we must remember that the conquest of one Christian people by another Christian people was quite unsettling at the time, even if it was not altogether novel.[70] Violence among Christians was clearly a source of increasing concern, as the practice of attempting to restrict it through mechanisms such as the Peace and Truce of God in the centuries leading up to the Norman Conquest demonstrates.[71] Unsurprisingly, many of the histories produced after the Conquest took the form of Norman apologies that catalogued William the Conqueror's hereditary and legal rights to England, his appeals for clerical and papal blessing to press his claim to England, and the benefits that his rule bestowed on the English. They also attempted to shift the blame for the Conquest onto Harold Godwinson, by detailing the great wrongs Harold had allegedly perpetrated against William.

Writing of History in Twelfth-Century England; Damian-Grint, *New Historians*, chap. 1; and Hollister, "Anglo-Norman Political Culture," 5.

69. Among these are Wace's and Benoît's main sources. William of Poitiers's *Gesta Guillelmi*, the *Gesta Normannorum ducum*, Orderic Vitalis's *Historia Ecclesiastica*, the *De obitu Willelmi*, the *Brevis relatio de Guillelmo nobilissimo comite Normannorum*, and Guy of Amiens's *Carmen de Hastingae Proelio.* "De obitu Willelmi," in *Guillaume de Jumièges, Gesta Normannorum ducum*, ed. Jean Marx (Caen, 1914) 145–49, and translated into English in R. Allen Brown, *The Norman Conquest of England* (Woodbridge, 1995), 47–50; Anonymous monk of Battle Abbey, "*The Brevis relatio de Guillelmo nobilissimo comite Normannorum*, written by a Monk of Battle Abbey: Edited with an Historical Commentary by Elisabeth M. C. van Houts," in *Chronolgy, Conquest and Conflict in Medieval England: Camden Miscellany XXXIV* (London, 1997), 1–48, reprinted with an English translation in Elisabeth M. C. van Houts, *History and Family Traditions in England and the Continent, 1000–1200* (Aldershot, 1999); and *The Carmen de Hastingae Proelio of Guy of Amiens*, ed. and trans. Frank Barlow (Oxford, 1999). See also Hollister, "Anglo-Norman Political Culture," 5. Of course, England had also been conquered by the Danes earlier in the eleventh century, but they seem to have been much less interested in using history writing to justify their conquest.

70. Elisabeth van Houts, "The Trauma of 1066," *History Today* 46/10 (1996): 9–15; Elisabeth van Houts, "The Memory of 1066 in Written and Oral Traditions," *ANS* 19 (1997): 167–79; and Elisabeth van Houts, "The Norman Conquest through European Eyes," *EHR* 110/438 (1995): 832–53.

71. It is ironic that William the Conqueror, who did so much to promote clerical reform and enforce the Peace and Truce of God within his duchy, found himself invading another Christian kingdom. This discomfort with violence among Christians could be defused by enlisting clerical and papal support for one's cause, and this is precisely what William did. William's appeal to Rome actually reveals the tension and uncertainty surrounding his proposed enterprise. The fact that he thought it necessary to win papal approval for his invasion of England exposes a degree of anxiety that would not have existed if such violence were considered perfectly acceptable. Elisabeth van Houts has demonstrated that the Conquest was not only a source of trauma for the Anglo-Saxons, it was a source of profound unease for contemporaries on the Continent. See Ibid.

Although the passage of dominion from one dynasty to another was not unknown on the Continent, the Norman acquisition of power in England presented special problems. In France, for instance, the Capetians had clearly orchestrated a coup to seize the reins of power from the Carolingians, just as the Carolingians had done centuries earlier when they banished the last Merovingian and took power for themselves.[72] These transfers of power, while certainly sources of concern and the impetus for a great deal of justificatory history writing, were easier to smooth over in some ways. To begin with, they were not conquests but political coups mounted by high-ranking nobles with either the tacit assent or active cooperation of members of the clergy and nobility. The Carolingians, and the Capetians after them, could and did argue that dominion had come to them as a result of God's will, that the older dynasty had degenerated and its latest rulers had been kings in name only, while they had been the only real power in the kingdom for quite some time. They also enlisted the aid of powerful clerics, or appealed to the pope, in order to legitimize their actions. They were thus able to frame their coups as legal formalities that merely acknowledged an existing reality. Continuity was always stressed as the new dynasty claimed to be restoring an old order, and stifled any suggestion that they might have actually destroyed the established order. The fact that both the Carolingians and Capetians had actually occupied positions of power under the dynasties they had just overthrown, as either mayors of the palace or powerful barons, and had sympathizers among the nobles and clerics made it easier for them to emphasize this continuity with the past in a convincing manner. That they were familiar, were already powerful, and spoke the same language as the people they ruled

---

72. The Capetians had struggled for power with the last Carolingians for decades before Hugh Capet, with the assistance of Archbishop Adalberon of Reims, managed to seize the throne after the death of Louis V in 987. Louis V had died without a legitimate heir, and although Louis V's uncle laid claim to the throne by hereditary right, Hugh and Adalberon refused to accept him. Instead, Adalberon crowned Hugh Capet. Pippin le Bref had similarly deposed Childeric III, the last Merovingian, in 751 and exiled him to a monastery after receiving papal approval for his plans. McKitterick, *Frankish Kingdom*, chaps. 1–3, 7, and 12; McKitterick, *History and Memory in the Carolingian World*, chaps. 1–6; Werner Goez, *Translatio Imperii* (Tübingen, 1958); Karl Ferdinand Werner, "Die Legitimität der Kapetinger und die Entstehung des 'Reditus regni Francorum ad stirpem Karoli,'" *Die Welt als Geschichte* 12 (1952): 203–25; Karl Ferdinand Werner, "Les sources de la légitimité royale à l'avènement des Capétiens (Xe–XIe siècle)," in *Le Sacre des Rois* (Paris, 1985), 49–60; Joachim Ehlers, "Die 'Historia Francorum Senonensis' und der Aufstieg des Hauses Capet," *Journal of Medieval History* 4/1 (1978): 1–24, 107; and Bernard Guenée, "Les Généalogies entre l'histoire et la politique: La fierté d'être Capétien, en France, au Moyen Âge," in Bernard Guenée, *Politique et histoire au Moyen Âge: Recueil d'articles sur l'histoire politique et l'historiographie médiévale (1956–1981)* (Paris, 1981).

and the regimes they had just deposed also helped to ameliorate the perception of a severe rupture with the past.

The Norman Conquest could not be justified so easily. Although Edward the Confessor had a Norman mother (Queen Emma) and was fostered in the Norman ducal household, the Normans were not members of the Anglo-Saxon nobility, nor did they intermarry with Anglo-Saxons with great frequency prior to the Conquest.[73] The Normans might have been familiar to the Anglo-Saxons (Queen Emma had brought Norman clerics with her to England and many Normans had populated Edward the Confessor's court), but they had been a noticeably foreign presence among the Anglo-Saxons. In the case of the Normans who Edward had attracted to his court, they had been invited to England to serve as a counterweight to the power of the Godwin family and were unceremoniously run off of the island when Godwin returned to favor.[74] The Anglo-Saxons had apparently been quite happy to be rid of these interlopers at the time, and they certainly did not welcome the Normans back with open arms.

The most serious impediment to Norman attempts to emphasize continuity with the Anglo-Saxon past was quite simply the fact that the Normans were foreign conquerors. Aside from the obvious trauma that the Conquest had inflicted on the Anglo-Saxons, the Normans were noticeably different from the people they had conquered. They were distinctly alien in their dress, their manners, and their language. Nor did it help in the least that Norman relations with the Anglo-Saxons had been tainted by fear and mistrust for at least a generation prior to the Conquest.[75] The rupture with

---

73. Edward's mother, Emma, was the daughter of Duke Richard I. Æthelred, Emma, and their sons fled to Normandy after Cnut's invasion; Edward and his brother Alfred remained there and were raised in the ducal household after Æthelred's death and Emma's remarriage to Cnut. See Elisabeth van Houts, "The Political Relations between Normandy and England before 1066 according to the *Gesta Normannorum ducum*," in *Les Mutations sociales au tournant des XIe–XIIe siècles. Etudes anselmiennes (IVe section). Colloque organisé par le CNRS sous la présidence de Monsieur Jean Pouilloux, membre de l'Institut. Abbaye Notre Dame du Bec, Le Bec-Hellouin 11–16 juillet 1982* (Paris, 1984), 85–97 and 191–92; van Houts, "Trauma of 1066," 9–15; van Houts, "Memory of 1066," 167–79; and van Houts, "Norman Conquest," 832–53.

74. See van Houts, "Political Relations," 85–97.

75. Æthelred and his father-in-law, Richard I, had not always been on good terms. They had argued over Normandy's tendency to shelter, and buy stolen goods from, Vikings who were looting the English coast. Edward had an even more unpredictable relationship with his Norman cousins. He had once contemplated invading Normandy, then decided against it and brought Normans to his court to counter the power of the Godwin family, only to kick the Normans out when Godwin returned to favor. During Edward's reign the Anglo-Saxons generally feared the power and influence of their king's Norman cousins as they were so often pitted against each other. van Houts, "Political Relations," 85–97.

the past caused by the advent of Norman dominion in England was thus of a far greater magnitude than recent transfers of power on the Continent had been, and the need to construct and project the legitimacy of the new regime was accordingly exacerbated.

Speaking a foreign language and representing an alien culture, the Normans could not even think of passing themselves off as Anglo-Saxons. They did, however, attempt the next best thing. They intermarried with the conquered Anglo-Saxon nobility and cultivated their kinship ties with what was left of the Anglo-Saxon royal dynasty. Henry I's marriage to Edith-Matilda in 1100 was a shrewd attempt to integrate the two dynasties. By marrying Edith, a member of the Anglo-Saxon royal house who assumed the Norman name Matilda upon her marriage to Henry I, the king attempted to ensure that future occupants of the English throne could claim both royal Anglo-Saxon and Norman blood. It would take two generations, however, before this strategy paid off (Henry II was the first king to carry the blood of both royal houses).

It just so happened, however, that the Normans already had a bit of experience in producing justificatory history. The early history of the Normans is murky at best, but it appears that the Viking Rollo and his followers had invaded and settled parts of Neustria (modern Normandy) well before Charles the Simple ceded them land along the lower Seine by the Treaty of Saint-Clair-sur-Epte in 911.[76] Rollo and his son, William Longsword, were generally left in peace by their Carolingian lords, but this changed after William Longsword's murder at the hands of the count of Flanders in 942.[77]

---

76. C. Warren Hollister, "Normandy, France and the Anglo-Norman Regnum," *Speculum* 51 (1976): 202–42; Pierre Bauduin, "Chefs normands et élites franques, fin IXe–début Xe siècle," in *Les Fondations scandinaves en Occident et les débuts du duché de Normandie. Colloque de Cerisy-la-Salle (25–29 septembre 2002)*, ed. Pierre Bauduin (Caen, 2005), 181–94; Jacques Le Maho, "Les Normands de la Seine à la fin du IX siècle," in Baudin, *Les Fondations scandinaves en Occident et les débuts du duché de Normandie*, 161–79; Lucien Musset, "Ce que l'on peut savoir du traité de Saint-Clair-sur-Epte," *Annuaire des cinq départements de Normandie* 147 (1981): 49–82 (reprinted in Lucien Musset, *Nordica et Normannica: Recueil d'études sur la Scandinavie ancienne et médiévale, les expéditions des Vikings et la fondation de la Normandie* [Paris, 1997], 377–81); Lucien Musset, "Considérations sur la genèse et le tracé des frontières de la Normandie," in *Media in Francia: Recueil de mélanges offerts à Karl Ferdinand Werner*, ed. Georges Duby (Paris, 1989), 309–18 (reprinted in Lucien Musset, *Nordica et Normannica: Recueil d'études sur la Scandinavie ancienne et médiévale, les expéditions des Vikings et la fondation de la Normandie* [Paris, 1997], 403–13); Michel Roblin, "Petromantalum, Saint-Clair et le Vexin," *Journal des savants* 1 (1976): 3–31; and David C. Douglas, "Rollo of Normandy," *EHR* 57 (1942): 417–36.

77. William Longsword had been at war with Arnulf I of Flanders. Arnulf had invited William to a meeting to settle their differences; when William arrived at the meeting he was killed by Arnulf's men. McKitterick, *Frankish Kingdom*, 236–38.

Instead of protecting William's son, Richard I, the Carolingian king, Louis IV, kidnapped him and attempted to take Normandy from him. Richard soon escaped from captivity, returned to Rouen, and reestablished Norman rule.[78] Several decades later, Richard took his revenge on the Carolingians by supporting the Capetian coup and helping to elect Hugh Capet as king in 987.[79] It was toward the end of Duke Richard I's reign that Dudo of Saint-Quentin, a foreigner who had made a favorable impression at the Norman court, was urged to write a history of the Normans. Although Dudo did not undertake the task until well after Richard's death in 996, his history was still colored by a pressing need to justify the autonomy of the Norman dukes and Norman control of what had formerly been Carolingian Neustria.

Dudo's *De moribus et actis primorum Normanniae ducum* (c. 1015–26) defended Norman autonomy from Carolingians and Capetians alike.[80] Dudo accomplished this feat by asserting that Norman control over Neustria had been formally granted to Rollo by the Carolingian king Charles the Simple at Saint-Clair-sur-Epte in 911. In fact, Dudo's history contains our only account of the treaty.[81] Dudo also presented the progenitor of the Norman dynasty, the Viking Rollo, as a noble pagan called by God to convert to

---

78. Ibid., 238.

79. Odo and Robert I had also been kings of the West Franks, however briefly, but Hugh Capet's elevation to the throne cemented Capetian hegemony. Cf. McKitterick, *Frankish Kingdom*, 326–28.

80. Dudo of Saint-Quentin, *De moribus et actis primorum Normanniae ducum auctore Dudone sancti Quintini decano*, ed. Jules Lair (Caen, 1865), and *Dudo of St Quentin: History of the Normans*, trans. Eric Christiansen (Woodbridge, 1998). Cf. Olivier Guillot, "La conversion des Normands à partir de 911," in *Histoire religieuse de la Normandie* (Chambray, 1981), 23–53; Olivier Guillot, "La conversion des Normands peu après 911: Des reflets contemporains à l'historiographie ultérieure (Xe–XIes.)," *CCM* 24 (1981): 101–16 and 181–219; Douglas, "Rollo of Normandy," 417–36; Eleanor Searle, "Fact and Pattern in Heroic History: Dudo of Saint-Quentin," *Viator* 15 (1984): 119–37; Victoria B. Jordan, "The Role of Kingship in Tenth-Century Normandy: Hagiography of Dudo of Saint-Quentin," *HSJ* 3 (1991): 53–62; Felice Lifshitz, "Dudo's Historical Narrative and the Norman Succession of 996," *Journal of Medieval History* 20 (1994): 101–20; Leah Shopkow, "The Carolingian World of Dudo of Saint-Quentin," *Journal of Medieval History* 15 (1989): 19–37; Leah Shopkow, *History and Community: Norman Historical Writing in the Eleventh and Twelfth Centuries* (Washington, DC, 1997); Emily Albu, "Dudo of Saint-Quentin: The Heroic Past Imagined," *HSJ* 6 (1994): 111–18; and Emily Albu, *The Normans in Their Histories: Propaganda, Myth, and Subversion* (Woodbridge, 2001).

81. Cf. Hollister, "Normandy, France and the Anglo-Norman Regnum," 202–42; Bauduin, "Chefs normands et élites franques, fin IXe–début Xe siècle," 181–94; Le Maho, "Les Normands de la Seine à la fin du IX siècle," 161–79; Musset, "Ce que l'on peut savoir du traité de Saint-Clair-sur-Epte," 377–81; Musset, "Considérations sur la genèse et le tracé des frontières de la Normandie"; Roblin, "Petromantalum, Saint-Clair et le Vexin," 3–31; and Douglas, "Rollo of Normandy," 427–29.

Christianity and rule over a confederation of diverse peoples that would settle Normandy.[82] Dudo's presentation of Rollo's divine mission augmented the legitimacy of Norman rule by portraying Norman dominion and autonomy as providentially ordained.

Although the political circumstances were quite different, the Conquest ignited another wave of Norman concern over legitimacy.[83] That the Normans turned once more to politicized history writing to justify their actions was not novel by any means; what was new was the tradition of vernacular historiography that the Normans encountered among the inhabitants of England.[84] And vernacular historiography had much to recommend it to the Normans. It made histories that had been directly accessible only to those literate in Latin available to a mixed audience of lay and cleric, male and female. It thus promised to be a much more effective vehicle for memorializing the Norman dynasty and asserting their claims to legitimacy than histories written in Latin.

What is most remarkable about the earliest Old French histories is the fact that they do not attempt to justify Norman rule directly, nor do they treat the Norman dynasty in any substantive manner. Whereas the Latin histories produced in the wake of the Conquest relentlessly focused on legitimizing Norman claims to England, the earliest extant Old French histories tended to avoid the issue altogether. Instead, Gaimar's *Estoire des Engleis* and Wace's *Roman de Brut* offered histories of the Anglo-Saxons and the Britons to an Anglo-Norman audience, many of whom were by now descended from both Norman and Anglo-Saxon nobles. Rather than directly addressing their own recent history, and their concerns over Norman legitimacy, it seems that the Anglo-Norman nobles who were commissioning vernacular histories around 1135 were interested in viewing their recent ascent to power in England in terms of continuity with the Anglo-Saxon and

---

82. Dudo of Saint-Quentin, *History of the Normans*, 29–30. Cf. Guillot, "La conversion des Normands à partir de 911," 23–53; Guillot, "La conversion des Normands peu après 911," 101–16 and 181–219; Douglas, "Rollo of Normandy," 417–36; Searle, "Fact and Pattern," 119–37; Jordan, "Role of Kingship," 53–62; Lifshitz, "Dudo's Historical Narrative," 101–20; Shopkow, "Carolingian World of Dudo of Saint-Quentin," 19–37; Shopkow, *History and Community*, 68–70; Albu, "Dudo of Saint-Quentin," 111–18; and Albu, *Normans in Their Histories*, 16–19, 22–23, and 26.

83. Albu, *Normans in Their Histories*; G.A. Loud, "The 'Gens Normannorum'—Myth or Reality?" *ANS* 4 (1982): 104–16; R. H. C. Davis, *The Normans and Their Myth* (London, 1976); and Eleanor Searle, *Predatory Kinship and the Creation of Norman Power, 840–1066* (Berkeley, 1988).

84. Peter Damian-Grint has also argued that the early appearance of Old French historiography in England was largely due to the existence of an indigenous Anglo-Saxon historiographical tradition. Damian-Grint, *New Historians*, 10–16.

Welsh history of the island. As Ian Short has noted, the second-generation descendants of the Norman conquerors were seeking to integrate themselves historically and socially into Anglo-Saxon culture during Henry I's reign.[85]

Insular history could be understood as a continuous cycle of degeneration and rebirth, in which dynasties regularly arose, declined, and were providentially supplanted (most often by foreign invaders).[86] The fall of the Britons in particular had long been attributed to their degeneracy, most notably by Bede, who had interpreted their subjugation to the Anglo-Saxons as God's vengeance for their sins and the corruption of their rulers.[87] Geoffrey of Monmouth appropriated this interpretation in his *Historia regum Britanniae* (c. 1135), which forcefully espoused the idea that God had punished the reprobate Britons with Anglo-Saxon dominion.[88] Geoffrey thereby implicitly advanced the notion that the Anglo-Saxons had degenerated in their turn and that God had thus sent the Normans to punish them. Placed within this larger historical context, the Anglo-Saxons could be viewed, somewhat sympathetically, as the victims of providence, while the Normans could be seen as merely the most recent in a long series of agents charged with executing God's plan.[89] There is no evidence, however, that either Gaimar or Wace appropriated this interpretation of insular history in their vernacular adaptations of Geoffrey's work. Of course, Geoffrey's history also had another important lesson for contemporary audiences. It made clear that factionalism invariably played to the advantage of one's enemies and invited destruction, thus pointing out the dangers of discord to an aristoc-

85. Short, "Gaimar's Epilogue," 323.

86. Henry of Huntingdon organized his *Historia Anglorum* around the conceit that the successive invasions of Romans, Picts and Scots, Angles and Saxons, Danes, and Normans were punishments sent by God to chastise the sinful inhabitants of England. See *Henry, Archdeacon of Huntingdon: Historia Anglorum, The History of the English People*, ed. and trans. Diana Greenway (Oxford, 1996).

87. Bede, *The Ecclesiastical History of the English People; The Greater Chronicle; Bede's Letter to Egbert*, ed. Judith McClure and Roger Collins (Oxford, 1994), I:14–16. Cf. R. William Leckie Jr., *The Passage of Dominion* (Toronto, 1981), chap. 2; Walter Goffart, *The Narrators of Barbarian History (A.D. 550–800): Jordanes, Gregory of Tours, Bede, and Paul the Deacon* (Princeton, 1988), chap. 4 and esp. page 250; and Robert Hanning, *The Vision of History in Early Britain: From Gildas to Geoffrey of Monmouth* (New York, 1966), 67–90.

88. Leckie, *Passage of Dominion*, chap. 2; John Gillingham, "The Context and Purposes of Geoffrey of Monmouth's *History of the Kings of Britain*," *ANS* 13 (1991): 99–118; Fiona Tolhurst, "The Britons as Hebrews, Romans, and Normans: Geoffrey of Monmouth's British Epic and Reflections of Empress Matilda," *Arthuriana* 8/4 (1998): 69–87; and Susan M. Shwartz, "The Founding and Self-Betrayal of Britain: An Augustinian Approach to Geoffrey of Monmouth's *Historia Regum Britanniae*," *Medievalia et humanistica* 10 (1981): 33–53.

89. Leckie, *Passage of Dominion*, 55–72.

racy that found itself enmeshed in civil war after the death of Henry I.[90] It was this theme that resonated with Wace.

Although Gaimar also began writing his history of the Anglo-Saxons around 1135, the *Estoire des Engleis* suggests that Gaimar's concerns were quite different from Geoffrey's. Gaimar attempted to seamlessly integrate the Anglo-Norman kings into insular history by following the format of *The Anglo-Saxon Chronicle* and completely neglecting the dynastic rupture caused by the Conquest. In fact, Gaimar evinces a remarkable gingerness in his treatment of the Conquest. He largely avoids the battle of Hastings and ignores the political situation leading up to it.[91] William the Conqueror "is not a major dramatic figure in the *Estoire*" and Gaimar "does not mention William by name until after the battle of Hastings."[92] Notably, Gaimar neither praises nor condemns William and offers no judgment regarding the Conquest; he simply records it, gives the briefest account of William's reign, and moves on to describe Robert Curthose's military prowess and the elegance of William Rufus's court before closing with Rufus's death. Gaimar's account thus attempts to depoliticize the Conquest by ignoring the dynastic rupture it caused and treating William's accession to the throne as an almost neutral event. Despite Gaimar's meticulous efforts to avoid these areas of contention, their suppression only serves to underscore the profound trauma caused by the Conquest and the difficulty of addressing it.

Gaimar must have begun his adaptation of Geoffrey of Monmouth's *Historia regum Britanniae* soon after he completed the *Estoire des Engleis*. Since Gaimar's *Estoire des Bretuns* is no longer extant, we have no way of knowing whether it reproduced Geoffrey's condemnation of the Britons and implicit criticism of the Anglo-Saxons. We do, however, have Wace's adaptation of Geoffrey's work, the *Roman de Brut*.

Writing almost twenty years after Geoffrey of Monmouth and Gaimar, Wace was not inclined to relentlessly chastise the Britons for their own demise in the *Roman de Brut* or imply that the Anglo-Saxons had somehow followed the degenerate example of their predecessors. Perhaps this was due

---

90. Ibid., chap. 2; Gillingham, "Context and Purposes of Geoffrey of Monmouth's *History of the Kings of Britain*," 99–118; Tolhurst, "Britons as Hebrews, Romans, and Normans," 69–87; Blacker-Knight, "Transformations of a Theme: The Depoliticization of the Arthurian World in the *Roman de Brut*," 54–57; and David Rollo, *Historical Fabrication, Ethnic Fable, and French Romance in Twelfth-Century England* (Lexington, 1998), chap. 3.

91. See also Gaimar, *L'Estoire des Engleis*, ed. Alexander Bell, lxxii; and Jean Blacker, *The Faces of Time: Portrayal of the Past in Old French and Latin Historical Narrative of the Anglo-Norman Regnum* (Austin, 1994), 92.

92. Blacker, *Faces of Time*, 92.

to the fact that he began the *Roman de Brut* around 1150, at a time when both of the men vying to succeed Stephen on the English throne were descended from both Anglo-Saxon and Norman royalty.[93] Since Henry II and Stephen's son Eustace both carried Anglo-Saxon and Norman blood, Wace probably felt it was no longer necessary to belabor the point that Norman dominion was part of a divine plan that was first manifested when God punished the reprobate Britons with Anglo-Saxon conquerors. In any case, Wace omitted Geoffrey's screeds blaming the Britons for provoking God's wrath. The *Roman de Brut* was not completely depoliticized, however.[94] To explain Anglo-Saxon hegemony, Wace focused on the cunning of the early Anglo-Saxons and their exploitation of British discord. His history thus promoted the virtues of political unity at a time when England was emerging from two decades of civil war.

Although neither the *Estoire des Engleis* nor the *Roman de Brut* treated Norman history in any substantive way, they proved to be extremely popular among the Anglo-Norman aristocracy. It was thus almost certainly in the hope of appealing to this ready audience for vernacular history that Henry II, and/or a group of his counselors, eventually took up the idea of producing a dynastic history of the Normans in Old French. The political landscape had, of course, changed dramatically by the time Wace began working on the *Roman de Rou* in 1160, and Henry II was reacting to forces distinct from those that had motivated the Anglo-Norman nobles responsible for commissioning vernacular histories during the early years of Stephen's reign. The important point remains that by 1160 there was a well-established Anglo-Norman tradition of vernacular verse historiography that Henry II could co-opt to commemorate his own dynasty and project its legitimacy.[95] And Henry II had many reasons to do just that, as his accession to the throne in 1154 had been preceded by a disputed succession in 1135

---

93. Henry II's grandmother, Edith-Matilda, and Stephen's wife, Matilda of Boulogne (Edith-Matilda's niece), were both direct descendants of Edmund Ironside. Henry II and Stephen's son Eustace were thus descended from both Anglo-Saxon and Norman kings. Cf. Jim Bradbury, *Stephen and Matilda: The Civil War of 1139–1153* (Far Thrupp, 1996), 6; and Frank Barlow, *The Feudal Kingdom of England, 1042–1216* (London, 1988), 139 and 146.

94. See also Jane Zatta, "Translating the *Historia*: The Ideological Transformation of the *Historia regum Britannie* in Twelfth-Century Vernacular Chronicles," *Arthuriana* 8/4 (1998): 148–61; Jean Blacker-Knight, "Transformations of a Theme: The Depoliticization of the Arthurian World in the *Roman de Brut*," 54–57; Dolores Buttrey, "Authority Refracted: Personal Principle and Translation in Wace's *Roman de Brut*," in *The Politics of Translation in the Middle Ages and the Renaissance*, ed. Renate Blumenfeld-Kosinski, Luise von Flotow, and Daniel Russell (Ottawa, 2001), 85–106.

95. See also Renate Blumenfeld-Kosinski, "Introduction: The Middle Ages," 17–27, at 19–20; and Renate Blumenfeld-Kosinski, "The Earliest Developments of the French Novel: The *Roman de*

and a civil war that had lasted for almost twenty years. If history writing responds to the crises and necessities of the present, then Henry II's irregular accession to the English throne, his drive to consolidate power, and his campaign to ensure the succession of his children were certainly potent stimuli for such an enterprise.

Thèbes in Verse and Prose," in *The French Novel: Theory and Practice*, French Literature Series 10 (Columbia, SC, 1984), 1–10.

CHAPTER 2

Henry II

Henry fitzEmpress arrived in England in December of 1154 to claim the throne of a kingdom that had been ruled by his mother's family for almost a century.[1] At the age of twenty-one, Henry was already duke of Normandy, duke of Aquitaine, and count of Anjou. His father, Geoffrey the Fair of Anjou, had turned the duchy of Normandy over to him by 1150 and had left him the family patrimony, the counties of Anjou and Maine, upon his untimely death on September 7, 1151.[2] Henry had subsequently acquired the duchy of Aquitaine in 1152 through his marriage

---

1. Henry of Huntingdon reports that it was "a few days before Christmas." Henry of Huntingdon, *Historia Anglorum*, x.40, 775. Ralph of Diceto and Robert de Torigny give December 7, while Gervase of Canterbury notes the date as December 8. Ralph of Diceto, *Radulfi de Diceto Decani Lundoniensis Opera Historica*, ed. William Stubbs, 2 vols. (London, 1876), I:299; Robert de Torigny, *Chronique de Robert de Torigni*, ed. L. Delisle, 2 vols. (Rouen, 1872), I:289; and Gervase of Canterbury, *The Historical Works of Gervase of Canterbury*, ed. William Stubbs, 2 vols. (London, 1879–80), I:159.

2. Henry of Huntingdon says that Henry received both Normandy and Anjou upon his father's death. Huntingdon, *HA*, x.31, 757. Cf. *Gesta Stephani: The Deeds of Stephen*, ed. K. R. Potter (London, 1955), 149; John of Hexham's continuation of Symeon of Durham's "*Historia regum*," in *Symeonis Monachi Opera Omnia*, ed. T. Arnold, 2 vols. (London, 1882–85), II:326; and Torigny, *Chronique*, I:255–56. Geoffrey died on September 7, 1151, and was succeeded as count of Anjou by Henry, but he had given Henry the duchy of Normandy between November 1149 and March 1150; see Z. N. Brooke and C. N. L. Brooke, "Henry II, Duke of Normandy and Aquitaine," *EHR* 61 (1946): 81–89, at 84.

to Eleanor, heiress to Aquitaine and ex-wife of the French king, Louis VII.[3] Henry made his way from the Hampshire coast to London in the winter of 1154 secure in the knowledge that the final territory to which he could lay claim by hereditary right would now be his.[4]

England had been kingless for six weeks since Stephen's death on October 25, and yet the kingdom was at peace and waited for Henry.[5] There had been little reason for him to hurry across the Channel in order to take control of the treasury and claim his crown before a more nimble and aggressive competitor beat him to it; instead, he was able to settle his affairs in Normandy and wait for a favorable wind before he crossed to England, a luxury that none of his Norman predecessors had ever possessed. Henry and Eleanor were jointly crowned in London on December 19, 1154, by Archbishop Theobald of Canterbury.[6] Contemporaries noted that the occasion was memorable for its opulence, but otherwise uneventful. It was certainly unmarred by the riot that accompanied the coronation of Henry's great-grandfather, William the Conqueror, or by the unseemly haste and the undertones of treachery that surrounded those of his grandfather, Henry I, and his immediate predecessor, Stephen. After six weeks of peaceful, if tense, expectation, England received her new king and queen.[7]

Henry II's accession was remarkable for its orderliness, but it had by no means been inevitable. As contemporaries were painfully aware, it had been preceded by a disaster and a disputed succession that had given way to a period of bitter civil war (later known as the Anarchy). Only years of fighting, intrigue, and diplomacy, aided by the unusually accommodating hand of death, had finally assured Henry's control over the duchy of Normandy and his rise to the throne of England.

---

3. Huntingdon, *HA*, x.31, 755–58; Torigny, *Chronique*, I:259–60; *Gesta Stephani*, 149; and John of Hexham, *Historia regum*, II:327.

4. Henry had been recognized as Stephen's heir under the Treaty of Winchester in 1153. Huntingdon, *HA*, x.37, 771; Torigny, *Chronique*, I:280–81; and Gervase of Canterbury, *Historical Works*, I:156.

5. Huntingdon, *HA*, x.40, 775.

6. Henry of Huntingdon gives no date, but Robert de Torigny and the *Chronicle of Battle Abbey* note that the coronation occurred on Sunday, December 19. Huntingdon, *HA*, x.40, 775; Torigny, *Chronique*, I:289–90; and *The Chronicle of Battle Abbey*, ed. and trans. Eleanor Searle (Oxford, 1980), 152. Gervase of Canterbury contends that Henry arrived in London on December 19, but was crowned two days later. Gervase of Canterbury, *Historical Works*, I:159.

7. Henry of Huntingdon remarked that "although England was therefore without a king for six weeks, by God's protecting grace she did not lack peace, either through love or fear of the king who was about to come." Huntingdon, *HA*, x.40, 775.

The calm that characterized the interregnal period between Stephen's death and Henry's coronation was unprecedented in recent English history, and it was a clear indication of the extent to which Henry was recognized as the legitimate heir to the Anglo-Norman realm. Although historians have long recognized that Henry faced a multitude of challenges in restoring royal power in England, many appear to have interpreted the widespread recognition of Henry's right to the throne as evidence that the problem of the English succession had finally been solved with Henry's coronation.[8] The reality was far more complex. Even though Henry enjoyed the advantage of being the almost universally acknowledged heir to England in 1154, he continued to face numerous threats to his authority and the survival of his dynasty after he succeeded to the throne.

As I (and many other historians) have suggested elsewhere, monarchs most often resorted to sponsoring history writing at times when the very survival of their dynasty was under threat. Henry's early years as king certainly qualified as such a time, following as they did a succession crisis that had taken the throne from his mother and resulted in twenty years of civil war. In this chapter I offer a critical reassessment of the nature of Henry's power and demonstrate that his decision to commission a vernacular history of his Norman ancestors was motivated by a pressing need to project royal authority and establish dynastic stability. I focus on the four most important threats to Henry's power: the Norman disdain for his father, Geoffrey of Anjou; the very means by which Henry had come to the throne; the need to continuously legitimize the restoration of royal government by appealing to justice, tradition, and precedent; and the threat that the lack of clear rules governing the Anglo-Norman succession posed for the survival of his dynasty. After restoring a sense of the precariousness of Henry's power and the urgent necessity of his efforts to delineate clear rules governing the succession, I place his patronage of Wace's *Roman de Rou* and Benoît de Sainte-Maure's *Chronique des ducs de Normandie* within the larger context of his sustained efforts to enhance the prestige of his dynasty and promote its survival through the cultivation of the public memory of his ancestors.

---

8. Even George Garnett implies that this was the case. He points out that Henry had already received liege homage from the Anglo-Norman barons and that this solved "the problem of interregnal uncertainty"; however, it did not solve the greater problem of a lack of clear rules for the succession. George Garnett, *Conquered England: Kingship, Succession, and Tenure 1066–1166* (Oxford, 2007), 296.

Lineage and Regional Rivalries

When Henry took the throne in 1154 he was still practically a stranger in his new kingdom. Even his lineage was a double-edged sword, being both the foundation of his claim to the Anglo-Norman realm and his greatest impediment to legitimacy and acceptance. The son of an Angevin count and a Norman mother who was practically an alien among her own people (she had been raised in the German imperial court), Henry was the product of an unpopular marriage that had been forced on the Anglo-Norman baronage by his grandfather Henry I.[9] In fact, Henry I's barons had used this marriage as a pretext for denying the throne to his designated heir, his daughter Matilda—an action that effectively dispossessed Henry II as well. Even after he was crowned, Henry II still had to contend with the stigma of being the son of Geoffrey of Anjou, and with the fact that the Normans generally regarded him as an Angevin heir.

The Norman disdain for Henry II's father was rooted in a long-standing regional rivalry that was intensified by the political landscape of medieval France. In the early twelfth century, the power of the Capetians (the French royal house) was limited to the region immediately surrounding Paris, and they were struggling to establish their dominance over most of the country that they claimed to rule. In the absence of effective royal power, territories that shared a border spent much of their time vying with each other for regional power and resisting royal efforts to bring them to heel. Such was the fractious relationship between Normandy and Anjou. The Angevins had alternately allied with and fought against their Norman neighbors throughout the tenth and eleventh centuries, and it was precisely this unpredictable shifting that Henry I had hoped to stabilize by negotiating a marriage alliance with them.

Aside from his desire to stabilize relations with Anjou, Henry's efforts to forge an alliance were also motivated by internecine rivalry as he was seeking to exclude his nephew, William Clito, from the Norman succession. Henry had taken the English throne during his older brother Robert's absence on crusade in 1100, then defeated Robert at the battle of Tinchebray in 1106 and forcibly took Normandy from him. Henry imprisoned Robert for the remainder of his life and ruled Normandy in his place, dispossessing Robert's son, William Clito, in the process. When it became clear that Henry

---

9. William of Malmesbury, *Historia Novella*, ed. K. R. Potter (London, 1955), 2–5; and *Gesta Stephani*, 7.

had no intention of relinquishing Normandy after this victory, many of the Anglo-Norman barons felt that Henry had unjustly imprisoned his own brother and dispossessed his nephew, and a series of rebellions broke out in support of Clito's claims to Normandy. The Angevins seized this opportunity to undermine Henry and supported the rebels against the king. Henry's initial attempt to negotiate a marriage alliance between Normandy and Anjou occurred in 1113, in the wake of one of these rebellions. The timing of the negotiations reveals that Henry was motivated, at least in part, by his desire to ensure that the Angevins permanently abandoned Clito's cause.[10]

It took another six years before a marriage was finally celebrated and an alliance cemented. In the meantime Anjou had continued to pursue its own interests, quite often to the detriment of Henry I and the Normans. The first Norman-Angevin alliance was finally created in 1119 through the marriage of Henry I's heir, William Audelin, and Matilda of Anjou, daughter of Count Fulk V of Anjou.[11] The marriage fulfilled three important goals for Henry: it promised to produce a legitimate heir of his line who would succeed to both Normandy and England; it neutralized the threat that Anjou posed to Normandy by encouraging the Angevins to abandon their support for Clito; and it brought the disputed county of Maine back into Norman hands as Matilda's dowry. The marriage also had the advantage of ensuring that no Anglo-Norman lands would be alienated as part of the agreement. Unfortunately, Henry's success in orchestrating this coup was extremely short-lived. The drowning death of William Audelin, Henry I's only legitimate son, in the wreck of the White Ship in November 1120 destroyed the king's carefully laid plans for an alliance with Anjou and threw the succession of Normandy and England into chaos.[12]

Henry I was infamous for his production of bastards, and it is thus a cruel irony that the premature death of his only legitimate son left the future of

---

10. For more on these maneuvers, see Judith Green, *Henry I: King of England and Duke of Normandy* (Cambridge, 2006); Judith Green, *The Government of England under Henry I* (Cambridge, 1986); and William Aird, *Robert Curthose* (Woodbridge, 2008).

11. Orderic Vitalis, *Ecclesiastical History*, xii, VI:224; *Anglo-Saxon Chronicle*, an. 1119; and "*Gesta consulum Andegavorum*," in *Chroniques des Comtes d'Anjou et des Seigneurs d'Amboise*, ed. Louis Halphen and René Poupardin (Paris, 1913), 161.

12. Accounts of the wreck of the White Ship are found in Orderic Vitalis, *HE*, xii, VI:294–301; *ASC*, an. 1120; William of Malmesbury, *De gestis regum Anglorum*, ed. W. Stubbs, 2 vols. (London, 1887–89), II:496–98; Symeon of Durham, II:259; Eadmér of Canterbury, *Eadmeri historia novorum in Anglia*, ed. Martin Rule (London, 1884), 288–89; Huntingdon, *HA*, vii.31, 467; and Hugh the Chantor, *History of the Church of York*, ed. C. Johnson (London, 1961), 99.

England and Normandy dangling in suspense and threatened to reverse Henry's hard-fought battle to establish his own dynasty at the expense of his eldest brother, Robert Curthose, and his nephew, William Clito. From the moment he had seized control of England, Henry I had worked to establish a dynasty of his own and to ensure its legitimacy. His first move had been to marry Edith-Matilda, a scion of the Scottish and Anglo-Saxon royal houses.[13] The two children born to Henry I and Edith-Matilda, William Audelin and the empress Matilda, embodied the peaceful unification of the Anglo-Saxon royal bloodline with that of their Norman conquerors. With William Audelin's death in 1120, the pressure for Henry I to assure the continuity of his line was mounting and the possibilities for doing so were more and more limited. Queen Edith-Matilda had died in 1118, and their only other surviving child, their daughter Matilda, had been married to the German emperor, Henry V, since 1114.[14] Henry I hastily remarried two months after the wreck of the White Ship in an attempt to produce legitimate offspring who could inherit the patrimony he had painstakingly built, but he and his second wife, Adeliza of Louvain, were never able to conceive.[15]

After William Audelin's death, relations between the Normans and the Angevins quickly began to deteriorate. To make matters worse for Henry, many of the Anglo-Norman barons now assumed that William Clito was Henry's logical successor. Henry used every means at his disposal to exclude his nephew from the succession, and, once more, his unjust treatment of Clito caused widespread indignation among the Anglo-Norman barons. Many of them rose against Henry in support of Clito and were joined, again, by the Angevins. When Count Fulk V of Anjou demanded that Henry return the county of Maine along with Matilda of Anjou in 1123, open war broke out between the Normans and Angevins.[16] Fulk further incensed Henry by openly favoring Clito, and giving Clito his daughter Sibyl in marriage, along with the disputed county of Maine.[17] It looked as though Henry

---

13. Huntingdon, *HA*, vii.22, 449; Orderic, *HE*, x, V:298–300; *ASC*, an. 1100; Florence of Worcester, *Florentii Wigorniensis Monachi, Chronicon ex chronicis*, ed. B. Thorpe (London, 1848–49), 47–48; and Eadmer of Canterbury, *Historia novorum*, 121–25. See Barlow, *Feudal Kingdom of England*, 139.

14. Orderic, *HE*, xii, VI:189; William of Malmesbury, *De gestis regum Anglorum*, 494–95; Eadmer of Canterbury, *Historia novorum*, 248; Florence of Worcester, *Chronicon ex chronicis*, 271; and *ASC*, an. 1118.

15. Barlow, *Feudal Kingdom of England*, 159.

16. Symeon of Durham, *Historia Regum*, II:263; *ASC*, an. 1121; and Orderic, *HE*, xii, VI:330.

17. Orderic, *HE*, xi, VI:164–66.

had been outmaneuvered, but the king was able to stave off this disaster by persuading Pope Calixtus II to block Clito's marriage to Sibyl on the grounds of consanguinity. Henry, however, still had to contend with his own lack of a viable heir.[18]

Clito's very existence menaced Henry with the threat that Normandy, and even England, might revert to him upon Henry's death. In order to prevent Clito from gaining a foothold, Henry strengthened the positions of his oldest illegitimate son, Robert of Gloucester, and his nephew, Stephen of Blois.[19] Both men were given extensive English and Norman lands and married to heiresses. Robert was already married to Mabel, heiress of Gloucester, when Henry elevated the honor of Gloucester to an earldom in 1122, and Stephen married Matilda of Boulogne, Queen Edith-Matilda's niece, in 1125.[20] Although Henry favored both men, neither was specifically groomed for the succession. Robert of Gloucester in particular seems to have been excluded from serious consideration on the grounds of his illegitimacy alone. For five very long years the future of England and Normandy was uncertain, and then fate seemed at last prepared to smile on Henry. Emperor Henry V of Germany died in 1125, leaving the empress Matilda widowed, childless, and available for a new marriage.[21]

Henry I recalled his daughter to England where he presented her to the Anglo-Norman barons at the 1126 Christmas court at Windsor.[22] Within weeks Henry had convinced the English barons of Matilda's right to succeed him by arguing that she was his legitimate issue and carried the blood of both Anglo-Saxon and Norman kings. The situation, however, was far from ideal as the Normans had no experience with female rulers. Equally disconcerting was the fact that Norman law assumed that the property and rights of females were at the disposal of their husbands. In the twelfth century in particular, lands and titles passed through the hands of heiresses with such regularity that aristocratic men sometimes hunted these women like

---

18. Ibid.; and William of Jumièges, Orderic Vitalis, and Robert de Torigny's continuation of the *Gesta Normannorum ducum*, ed. and trans. Elisabeth M. C. van Houts, 2 vols. (Oxford, 1992–95), viii, II:262. Cf. Barlow, *Feudal Kingdom of England*, 158.

19. W. L. Warren, *Henry II* (Berkeley, 1973), 14; and R. W. Southern, "The Place of Henry I in English History," *Proceedings of the British Academy* 48 (1962): 127–69.

20. Bradbury, *Stephen and Matilda*, 6, and Barlow, *Feudal Kingdom of England*, 146.

21. Orderic, *HE*, xii, VI:360, and Torigny, *GND*, viii, II:240.

22. *ASC*, an. 1126 and 1127; Torigny, *GND*, viii, II:240; and Huntingdon, *HA*, vii, 37, 477.

game.[23] The prospect of a female ruler who would almost certainly remarry, giving her husband grounds to claim lands and rights *iure uxoris* (by his wife's right) must have caused the barons considerable hesitation in accepting Matilda as Henry's heir. Yet Henry lacked any real alternatives if he was as determined as he seems to have been to have an heir of his flesh installed on the English throne and in the Norman duchy, so he pressed for Matilda's recognition in spite of these obstacles. On January 1, 1127, Henry assembled the barons and clergy present in London to formally recognize Matilda as heir to England and Normandy by the swearing of oaths.[24] For good measure, all of the magnates and bishops assembled at Henry I's Easter court took a second oath to the same effect on April 29, 1128.[25] Since the barons and clergy were instrumental in making a king, having them swear solemn oaths to recognize Matilda as the rightful heir was a vital step in securing her succession.

Soon after Matilda was formally recognized as his heir, Henry turned his attention to finding a suitable marriage for her. Henry still had to contend with Clito, whose claims to the Anglo-Norman realm many of the barons secretly supported despite their oaths to Matilda. Once again, Henry thought of forging an alliance with Anjou. As with the earlier Norman–Angevin alliance, this renewed effort was driven by Henry's need to persuade the Angevins to abandon their support for his nephew. Within the year Henry had negotiated the marriage of his daughter Matilda to Fulk V's son Geoffrey through Robert of Gloucester, Brian fitzCount, and John, bishop of Lisieux.[26] Henry does not appear to have consulted any of his other magnates about the marriage. Indeed, Bishop Roger of Salisbury, one of Henry's most trusted ministers, later used the secrecy of the negotiations as a pretext for abjuring the oaths he had taken to uphold Matilda's claim to the throne and

23. John Gillingham, *The Angevin Empire* (London, 1984), 6, and Warren, *Henry II*, 12. Eleanor of Aquitaine, heiress to the largest duchy in France, had to evade the snares of several would-be "suitors," including the count of Blois and Henry II's own younger brother Geoffrey, on her way to Poitou to marry Henry II in 1152. Warren, *Henry II*, 45.

24. John of Worcester, *The Chronicle of John of Worcester*, ed. R. R. Darlington and P. McGurk, trans. Jennifer Bray and P. McGurk, 3 vols. (Oxford, 1995), 22–23; *ASC*, an. 1127; Symeon of Durham, *Historia Regum*, II:281; Eadmer of Canterbury, *Historia Novorum*, 292; and William of Malmesbury, *HN*, 3–5. See also Barlow, *Feudal Kingdom of England*, 159, and Marjorie Chibnall, *The Empress Matilda: Queen Consort, Queen Mother, and Lady of the English* (Oxford, 1991), 51–52.

25. John of Worcester, *Chronicle*, 26–27. Neither the *ASC* nor William of Malmesbury mentions the Easter oath. Chibnall, *Empress Matilda*, 52

26. William of Malmesbury, *HN*, 5.

encouraging others to do so.[27] Matilda and Geoffrey were married at Le Mans cathedral on June 17, 1128, and this time the alliance provoked outright hostility from some of the barons.[28]

Although the Normans and Angevins were rivals in the early twelfth century, they were not implacable enemies.[29] The problem with the new version of the Norman-Angevin alliance was not that the Normans held some deep and abiding hatred for the Angevins by 1128, or even that the Angevins had so often acted against Norman interests. After all, the barons had readily accepted the earlier marriage of William Audelin to Matilda of Anjou. The new alliance was unacceptable to many of them because it was of an entirely different nature from the earlier arrangement and had been executed in a manner that excluded them. It appears that Henry had made little effort to persuade his barons of the usefulness of an alliance with Geoffrey of Anjou or to seek their counsel on the matter. Instead, he had pursued the negotiations in secret and then forced the marriage on the barons as a fait accompli. To complicate matters further, many of the Anglo-Norman barons still harbored sympathy for William Clito. Ironically, William Clito died in July of 1128 and ceased to be a threat to Henry almost as soon as this unpopular marriage had been solemnized.

The new alliance with Anjou offered other slights to Anglo-Norman sensibilities as well. Whereas the earlier marriage had secured the friendship of Anjou and brought the county of Maine firmly back under Norman control, while preventing the alienation of Anglo-Norman lands, the new alliance threatened to place the whole of the Anglo-Norman realm under the rule of an Angevin count; some of Henry's magnates predictably began to recoil at this prospect. We do not know what the exact arrangements for the succession were and, it seems, neither did the barons. We do know what precedents the Anglo-Normans and the Angevins had before them, however, and they were not at all promising from the Anglo-Norman point of view.[30] Geoffrey was the son of Fulk V of Anjou, who had gained Maine

---

27. Bishop Roger of Salisbury claimed that "he was released from the oath he had taken to the empress because he had sworn only on condition that the king should not give his daughter in marriage to anyone outside the kingdom without consulting himself and the other chief men." William of Malmesbury, *HN*, 5.

28. Orderic gives the year as 1129, but Chibnall corrects this to 1128. Orderic, *HE*, xii, VI:391 and n. 2.

29. Chibnall, *Empress Matilda*, 54.

30. Chibnall includes the fullest discussion of the conflicting sources on the succession. John of Marmoutier and the Le Mans and Durham chroniclers assume or state that there was an agreement that Geoffrey would succeed as king and duke, while Orderic Vitalis asserts that Geoffrey's role was

through marriage to an heiress and was about to set off to the Holy Land to marry another heiress, Melisende of Jerusalem, with the intention of governing the Kingdom of Jerusalem *iure uxoris*.[31] Under the circumstances the Anglo-Norman magnates could only assume, as we must, that Geoffrey would follow his father's example and attempt to assert his rights in his wife's name upon Henry I's death.

The Normans may not have been relentlessly hostile to the Angevins at this point, but they were certainly too proud to be ruled by one. The Normans were more powerful and important than their Angevin neighbors, Normandy was far larger than Anjou, and England was far richer. The Anglo-Norman barons had no interest in taking orders from a mere count when they were accustomed to serving kings, they had no desire to see a foreigner installed as duke of Normandy, nor had they conquered England and secured it with such effort only to see it fall into the hands of their rivals.

Matilda herself was less than thrilled by the alliance and appears to have thought it beneath her.[32] At the time of her marriage to Geoffrey she was twenty-six, the widow of an emperor, and the descendant of kings, while her husband was the fifteen-year-old son of a count whom her father had knighted a week before the wedding. After their first year of marriage, Matilda left Geoffrey and returned home to her father.[33] Henry took his daughter back to England in 1131, where he secured another round of oaths acknowledging Matilda as his heir in order to suppress the dissension simmering among his barons.[34] Some of them were already arguing that they were no longer bound by the oaths they had taken to recognize Matilda as Henry's heir because her marriage to Geoffrey had been forced on them without their consent.[35] In spite of baronial grumbling, Henry's will prevailed, as it so often did. The assembled court at Northampton renewed

---

merely to assist his wife. Chibnall is also of the opinion that Henry tried to keep the question open in order to wait for a grandson who would moot the issue. Chibnall, *Empress Matilda*, 57.

31. Gillingham, *Angevin Empire*, 9.

32. Robert de Torigny, who knew Matilda, wrote that she was unhappy with the match. Chibnall, *Empress Matilda*, 55; and Torigny, *GND*, viii, II:230.

33. Symeon of Durham records Matilda's quarrel with Geoffrey. Symeon of Durham, *Historia Regum*, 283.

34. Huntingdon, *HA*, vii.41, 487–89. Hollister notes that a group of nobles who were resisting Matilda's claims had formed shortly after 1126. It notably included Bishop Roger of Salisbury, who later abjured his oath to Matilda. He also suggests that they may have been inclined to accept William Clito as the legitimate heir to England and Normandy at this time. C. Warren Hollister, *Henry I* (New Haven, 2001), 315.

35. Barlow, *Feudal Kingdom of England*, 161.

their oaths to recognize Matilda as Henry I's heir on September 8, 1131, and decided to send her back to Geoffrey.[36] Whatever her misgivings, Matilda dutifully returned to her husband and began producing heirs. The first, a son named Henry in honor of his grandfather, was born on March 5, 1133. Shortly afterward, during the summer of 1133, Henry I had his barons swear to recognize both Matilda and the infant Henry as his heirs.[37]

Henry's decision to force an unpopular marriage on his magnates, his failure to clearly define their respective roles or associate them in his rule, and Matilda and Geoffrey's own actions eventually undermined Henry's carefully engineered plans for the succession. Henry I died on December 1, 1135. Just before the king's death, Matilda and Geoffrey had briefly rebelled against him. The rift had arisen over certain castles on the Norman-Angevin border, which Henry had promised to his son-in-law as Matilda's dowry, but which he then refused to cede to Geoffrey.[38] The dispute was intensified by Geoffrey's demand to receive homage from the Norman barons as a means of solidifying his and Matilda's support.[39]

Henry had acted unilaterally in marrying Matilda to Geoffrey, but, if we accept the testimony of the chroniclers, he had also tried to address the concerns of his barons and leave his own options open by having his magnates swear fealty to his daughter Matilda and his grandson Henry, but never to Geoffrey. Geoffrey and Matilda's poorly timed demand for castles and homage brought the real problem with the succession to the forefront: no one knew exactly what Geoffrey and Matilda's respective roles were going to be. The Norman magnates might have been able to accept Geoffrey as Matilda's consort, if this had been made explicit, but his ambiguous presence at Matilda's side made the barons nervous. If anything, Geoffrey's insistence on receiving homage must have confirmed the barons' worst fears—he was already attempting to assert his rights in his wife's name before Henry was even dead. His actions appear to have decisively tipped the scales against the couple.

36. Ibid.; Chibnall, *Empress Matilda*, 59; Huntingdon, *HA*, vii.41, 486–88; Ralph of Diceto, *Opera Historica*, I:246; and William of Malmesbury, *HN*, 10.

37. Barlow, *Feudal Kingdom of England*, 161; and Roger of Howden, *Chronica Rogeri de Hoeudene*, ed. William Stubbs, 4 vols. (London, 1868–71), I:186–87. Chibnall points out that if fealty was sworn again during this period, as Roger of Howden claims it was, it can only have been at Rouen as Matilda did not return to England after 1131 and was actively witnessing charters from Rouen at this time. It does seem clear, however, from precisely this charter evidence that Matilda was being groomed for succession at the Norman administrative center of Rouen. Chibnall, *Empress Matilda*, 61–63.

38. Huntingdon, *HA*, vii.43, 490; and Vitalis, *HE*, xiii, VI:444–46.

39. Barlow, *Feudal Kingdom of England*, 161.

Henry I had probably hoped to avoid the issue of the role his son-in-law was to play altogether by living long enough for his grandson to reach maturity. Normandy and England could then pass directly to a male heir of Henry's own line. He may have also desired to raise the boy in his own court, just as he had done with Stephen of Blois, or in the household of one of his magnates, thus making him recognizably Norman rather than Angevin, and therefore more palatable to the Anglo-Norman barons. Whatever he might have wanted, Henry I died apparently still at odds with Matilda and Geoffrey, his grandson was still an infant, and it was left to the barons and clergy to determine whom they would accept as the next ruler of England and Normandy.

Stephen's Reign and the Civil War

Stephen of Blois's success in gaining control of England and Normandy upon Henry I's death was thus partly due to the Anglo-Norman magnates' profound unease over Geoffrey's role in the succession, and partly due to the fact that Matilda and Geoffrey had so recently alienated many of them by demanding homage and openly rebelling against the king. Stephen's coup, however, was ultimately the result of his own speed and decisiveness in racing to claim the throne.[40] It certainly helped Stephen that his cousin Matilda was unable to reach England fast enough to assert her rights. Matilda's absence from England also made it easier for the Anglo-Norman barons to rationalize their acceptance of Stephen's usurpation by arguing that the oaths they had sworn to Matilda were coerced, and therefore invalid, or by accepting the assertion of Hugh Bigod, a powerful Norman baron, that Henry I had undergone a change of heart on his deathbed and had absolved them from their obligation to keep their oaths to uphold Matilda as his heir.[41] That Hugh Bigod was almost certainly absent from Henry's deathbed, and thus could have had no special knowledge of the king's last wishes, did little to dampen the fervor of some of the magnates to use this as an excuse to abjure their oaths to Matilda.[42]

40. Cf. Garnett, *Conquered England,* 138.

41. John of Salisbury, *Historia Pontificalis: Ioannis Saresberiensis Historia Pontificalis: John of Salisbury's Memoirs of the Papal Court,* ed. Marjorie Chibnall (Oxford, 1956), 85; Ralph of Diceto, *Opera Historica,* 248; and Gervase of Canterbury, *Historical Works,* I:94.

42. Warren, *Henry II,* 18.

Whatever their rationale, the Anglo-Norman clergy and magnates found themselves faced with a clear choice between Matilda and her foreign husband, and Stephen, Henry's adult nephew. They could accept Henry's known wishes for the succession and muddle through the vagaries of female rulership, which would almost certainly entail accepting Geoffrey of Anjou as their lord. Or, they could choose someone who could immediately deliver the kind of rule with which they were familiar and comfortable. Faced with such a choice, many decided to discard the oaths they had sworn to Matilda at Henry's demand, and to throw their support behind Stephen.

It should be readily apparent that Stephen's claim to the throne was tenuous. He was not the heir designate, none of the barons had pledged to recognize him as Henry's heir, he had personally sworn the oath to uphold Matilda on at least one occasion, and he was not descended in the male line from the Norman royal house, as was Matilda.[43] His hereditary claim was made through his mother, Henry I's sister Adele, daughter of William the Conqueror. The greatest advantage Stephen possessed was that he was an adult male of the Conqueror's line, who was known to, related to, and acceptable to the Anglo-Norman barons. In other words, he was neither an Angevin nor a stranger, and he certainly was not a woman or, more damning still, Geoffrey of Anjou. In many ways, Stephen had the advantages that mattered most to the barons. He had been raised in Henry I's court, he had extensive holdings in England and Normandy, his wife Matilda was of Anglo-Saxon royal blood (she was Queen Edith-Matilda's niece), and his brother Henry was bishop of Winchester. Stephen was well placed, he knew the land, he had influential relatives and supporters, and his children carried the blood of both the Norman and Anglo-Saxon royal houses, just as Henry I and Edith-Matilda's children had. Most important, Stephen had the backing of several of the most powerful Anglo-Norman magnates, including Hugh Bigod, Robert of Leicester, and Waleran of Meulan.

Stephen also had the dubious advantage of irregular succession being the rule rather than the exception in England. England still lacked clear rules governing the royal succession for most of the twelfth century—neither hereditary right nor primogeniture yet applied.[44] Royal blood was an important consideration, but designation, oaths, and election by the nobles and clergy were more important than hereditary claims. In fact, there was no

43. William of Malmesbury reports that Stephen and Robert of Gloucester had engaged in a friendly dispute over who should be the first to swear at the January 1, 1127, oath-taking ceremony for Matilda. Stephen had won. William of Malmesbury, *HN*, 4.

44. Cf. Garnett, *Conquered England*.

basis whatever in English law or custom for claiming that the crown should pass to the nearest blood relative (as W. L. Warren has pointed out, Matilda and Henry II resorted to claiming the throne by hereditary right only because designation and oath swearing had failed them so completely).[45] It was partly as a result of this ambiguity that all three of Stephen's Norman predecessors had taken possession of the throne in bitterly disputed circumstances. Given the historical precedents, Stephen's actions in asserting himself over a clearly designated, female heir, whose rights he had personally taken an oath to uphold, were audacious, but they were not entirely unusual.

The Anglo-Norman barons were also declaring their preference for one alliance over another in taking sides. Although other factors, such as Geoffrey and Matilda's recent rebellion, certainly influenced their decisions, it is clear that the Anglo-Norman magnates favored their Blésois relations over their new Angevin in-laws. This was almost certainly due to the fact that Stephen was the product of a marriage alliance, rather than a participating party in one. After all, it is one thing to marry into a family, as Geoffrey had done, but it is quite another thing to be born into that family. Stephen was viewed as an insider whose loyalties were not in question, while Geoffrey was still an interloper and his motives would always be suspect.

Of course, the Anglo-Norman baronage was not single-minded. Not all of them supported Stephen, and a few appear to have been reluctant to perjure themselves. King David of Scotland, Matilda's uncle, stands out for his refusal to do homage to Stephen—he sent his son Henry to perform homage in his stead.[46] Whatever their personal reservations, most of the Anglo-Norman barons were sensible of the delicacy of the situation, and they chose to accept their new lord rather than risk having their estates confiscated. Those who defied Stephen found themselves exiled.[47] Even Matilda's half-brother, Robert of Gloucester, initially reconciled himself to the reality of Stephen's usurpation before rallying to Matilda's cause and becoming her staunchest supporter.[48] Stephen's reign was thus made possible by the consent and through the assistance of the majority of the Anglo-Norman barons and clergy, but from the start there was dissent within their ranks. Civil war began almost immediately in Normandy, and moved to England

---

45. Warren, *Henry II*, 19.

46. Huntingdon, *HA*, x.4, 707; and William of Malmesbury, *HN*, 4.

47. Huntingdon, *HA*, x.4, 709; and *Gesta Stephani*, 28–46.

48. Chibnall, *Empress Matilda*, 73–74.

in earnest after Robert of Gloucester openly renounced his homage to Stephen in May of 1138.[49]

The civil war sparked by Stephen's usurpation had a host of negative consequences that Henry II ultimately inherited. In England it depleted the treasure amassed by Henry I, produced a fractured baronage that was divided in its allegiances, and resulted in an increase in baronial power, as Stephen multiplied the number of earldoms and delegated royal prerogatives to his barons in attempts to maintain order in the kingdom.[50] Although England's government was far from being in shambles under Stephen, it was split into two different spheres during the civil war: one administered by Stephen and another, smaller sphere in western England that was administered by Matilda.

The Angevins, on the other hand, definitively won Normandy fairly early on as an indirect result of Stephen's capture at the battle of Lincoln in February 1141.[51] Geoffrey of Anjou was able to push into central and eastern Normandy while Stephen was imprisoned and his partisans were busy in England.[52] By 1144 Geoffrey had established his dominance in Normandy and was recognized as its duke by Louis VII.[53] This early victory in Normandy was a mixed blessing for the Angevins though. It had taken nine years of campaigning before the Angevins finally wrested control of Normandy from Stephen's partisans. The protracted fighting had tarnished their reputation in the meantime and left memories of Angevin brutality deeply imprinted on Norman minds.[54]

Apparently aware that he was personally a focus of baronial resentment, Geoffrey transferred Normandy to the future Henry II as soon as he was reasonably able. Henry received the duchy from his father by 1150 and almost immediately faced attacks by the combined forces of Louis VII and Stephen's eldest son, Eustace. Like Henry I before him, Stephen was determined to leave the Anglo-Norman realm to an heir of his flesh and was grooming Eustace for the succession. Eustace's bid to regain Normandy

---

49. William of Malmesbury, *HN*, 21–24; and Huntingdon, *HA*, x.7, 713.

50. See R. H. C. Davis, *King Stephen, 1135–1154* (Berkeley, 1967); and David Crouch, *The Reign of King Stephen, 1135–1154* (London, 2000).

51. Henry of Huntingdon gives a lengthy description of the battle. Huntingdon, *HA*, x.13–19, 725–41.

52. Gillingham, *Angevin Empire*, 12–15.

53. Emilie Amt, *The Accession of Henry II in England: Royal Government Restored, 1149–1159* (New York, 1993), 8; and Torigny, *Chronicle*, 147–48.

54. Orderic, *HE*, xiii, VI:467–75

from the Angevins and subject the whole of the Anglo-Norman realm once
more to Stephen's rule would have been a major coup for the Blésois had
it succeeded. It would almost certainly have tipped the scales in Stephen's
favor and ensured Eustace's succession, but it failed spectacularly and cemented the Angevin hold on the duchy. In August of 1151, Louis VII formally recognized Henry as duke of Normandy and received Henry's homage
for the duchy.[55]

The Angevin cause was further aided in 1152 when Pope Eugenius III
and Archbishop Theobald of Canterbury blocked Stephen's attempt to
crown his son Eustace and associate him in the rule of the kingdom.[56] Stephen had alienated much of the English clergy in 1139 when he summarily
arrested and imprisoned the Bishops Roger of Salisbury, Nigel of Ely, and
Alexander of Lincoln on suspicion of conspiracy, and he had never fully
regained the clergy's trust and support. His relations with the papacy had
also been strained at best. The irregularities that had marked Stephen's accession, and the taint of perjury that still clung to him, had caused a series
of popes to keep their distance from him. Although they did not advocate
deposing Stephen, the English clergy and Eugenius III refused to crown his
son.[57] In an attempt to defer the problem of the English succession, Pope
Celestine II had decreed a ban against any innovations concerning the English crown in the early 1140s—at the height of the civil war. The English
did not traditionally crown their heirs while the king still lived, so the ban
effectively prevented both Stephen and the empress Matilda from crowning
an heir during their own lifetimes. Pope Eugenius III and Archbishop Theobald justified their refusal to crown Eustace on the grounds that they were
simply observing Pope Celestine II's ban, but it seems clear that their actions
were designed to exclude Eustace from the succession. The Norman clergy
had supported Henry fitzEmpress's claims to England for almost a decade by
this time, and now Eugenius III and the English church appeared to be join-
ing them.

Geoffrey of Anjou had died shortly after his son's formal recognition as
duke of Normandy, on September 7, 1151.[58] Although Matilda was still living, she had withdrawn from actively pursuing her claim to the English

---

55. Torigny, *Chronicle*, 160–63.

56. John of Salisbury, *Historia Pontificalis*, 85–86; and Huntingdon, *HA*, x.32, 759.

57. Henry of Huntingdon notes that "the pope in a letter had forbidden the archbishop to elevate
the king's son as king. It was understood that this was because Stephen had seized the kingdom
contrary to the oath [he had taken to support Matilda]." Huntingdon, *HA*, x.32, 759.

58. Torigny, *Chronicle*, 161–63.

throne in 1148 and returned to Rouen. The Angevin quest to regain England was now entirely in Henry's hands. Henry was actively campaigning in England in 1153, in the hopes of winning a decisive victory over Stephen that would secure him the unquestioned right to the English throne.[59] Stephen and Eustace for their part were just as doggedly fighting back, hoping to permanently eliminate the threat that Henry posed to them. Neither Stephen nor Henry appears to have wanted a negotiated peace. Both men hoped to triumph in a decisive battle; it was only the pressure exerted by the barons and the clergy that forced them to come to terms with each other.[60] The clergy's refusal to recognize Eustace as Stephen's successor had sent a powerful signal to the baronage, and even Stephen's staunchest supporters, that arranging a settlement with Henry was in their best interest. The barons, for the most part, had thus become more interested in preventing battles than taking part in them.

Although it appears incongruous that the notoriously warlike Normans had suddenly become reluctant to fight, there were practical advantages to preventing either side from attaining a decisive victory. One of the most important advantages was that the barons on both sides could hedge their bets and preserve an exploitable ambiguity in the outcome. If neither side fought, neither could be decisively defeated, and thus be left open to retaliation. Just as important, preventing a pitched battle and a decisive victory meant that neither Stephen nor Henry would be able to govern from a position of strength.[61] It is unlikely that all of the barons were so cynical in their motives. There must have been many who simply wanted to avoid destroying the kingdom and see the contest decided peacefully, as did most of England's clergy.[62] Archbishop Theobald of Canterbury and Bishop Henry of Winchester, the king's brother, took the lead in negotiating a truce, and were joined in their efforts by barons from both sides.[63]

While the barons and clergy attempted to negotiate a permanent settlement, Henry was making considerable gains in the midlands and winning important supporters away from Stephen. He was also coming to be regarded by more and more of the clergy and baronage, including many of

---

59. Huntingdon, *HA*, x.33–34, 761–67; *Gesta Stephani*, 146–148; Torigny, *Chronique*, I:271; and Gervase of Canterbury, *Historical Works*, I:151–52.

60. Amt, *Accession of Henry II in England*, 11–13.

61. Huntingdon, *HA*, x.34, 767.

62. *Gesta Stephani*, 157.

63. Huntingdon, *HA*, x.37, 771; and *Gesta Stephani*, 157–59.

Stephen's adherents, as the rightful heir to England.[64] The future of the Blésois cause was already looking grim when the most serious blow came. Eustace died suddenly of unknown causes on August 17, 1153.[65] With him went Stephen's best hope for establishing his own dynasty and Henry's only real competition.[66] Eustace died after throwing a monumental temper tantrum provoked by a five-day truce arranged by the barons. Eustace had interpreted the truce as an indication that baronial support had shifted toward Henry. Perhaps sensing that his cause was inexorably slipping into irrelevance, Eustace vented his anger on Cambridgeshire and the Abbey of Saint Edmund. His death shortly afterward was seen by many as divine retribution for the destruction he had wrought on the abbey.[67]

Eustace's untimely death removed the greatest obstacle to peace. A treaty was finally arranged between Stephen and Henry before the assembled barons and clergy at Winchester on November 6, 1153. The Treaty of Winchester recognized Henry as heir to England by hereditary right and granted England to him and his heirs. In return for this recognition, Henry had done homage to Stephen and each had promised to protect the other.[68] Despite being forced to perform homage to Stephen as part of the terms of the treaty, Henry was otherwise meticulous in refusing to recognize Stephen's legitimacy either during Stephen's life or after his death. All of Henry's actions and stated intentions underscore his belief that Stephen's rule had been an unlawful suspension of legitimate government. Indeed, Henry's lifelong obsession with asserting every hereditary right to which he could conceivably lay claim appears to have been matched only by his zeal for denying Stephen's legitimacy and effacing any evidence he could of his predecessor's reign. Henry could at least console himself for having performed homage to

---

64. Gervase of Canterbury, *Historical Works*, I:154; and *Gesta Stephani*, 142, 148.

65. The author of the *Gesta Stephani* says that "Eustace for his part, greatly vexed and angry because the war, in his opinion, had reached no proper conclusion, left his father and went out of sight of the court, and met his end from grief within a few days." *Gesta Stephani*, 158.

66. Although Eustace's younger brother William was still alive, he does not appear to have been considered a serious contender for the English throne. The clergy and baronage were already gravitating toward Henry as the rightful heir to the throne, and it is unlikely that they would have supported William when they had denied support to Eustace. This consideration was probably the decisive factor in William's refusal to challenge Henry's claim to the throne, and in his loyal support for Henry as king. William was allowed to retain most of his lands under Henry II and remained earl of Warenne and count of Boulogne and Mortain until his death in 1159 while accompanying Henry on the expedition to Toulouse.

67. Gervase of Canterbury, *Historical Works*, I:155; Torigny, *Chronicle*, 176; *Gesta Stephani*, 158.

68. Torigny, *Chronicle*, 177; Huntingdon, *HA*, x.37–38, pp. 771–73; and *RRAN*, III, n. 272.

Stephen with the fact that he had won a very important point: Stephen was forced to concede and record in writing Henry's legitimate hereditary claim to the English throne. It was a claim that Henry had spent the whole of his young life asserting.

The Restoration of Royal Authority

Henry fitzEmpress at last gained the final piece of his maternal inheritance after Stephen's death the following year and was crowned Henry II, king of England. Although Henry had gained the English throne with the support of many of the barons and clergy, he still faced numerous challenges to his authority.[69] Henry was now master of a kingdom that had long been almost entirely unencumbered by the yoke of royal authority, and he had been forced to make promises and concessions that often bordered on the extravagant in order to win supporters in England and Normandy. In the intervening year between the Treaty of Winchester and Stephen's death, Henry had returned to Normandy and begun slowly to reassert ducal authority there. He also set about regaining the rights and lands that he and his father had been forced to cede to the Norman barons and Louis VII.[70] He continued this painstaking process after his accession to the English throne.

Henry had very ambitious plans for someone who had won the kingdom through treaty rather than military victory; his unambiguous and often-stated goal was to return the Anglo-Norman realm to the status quo established by his grandfather Henry I.[71] This entailed not only the restoration of Henry I's government and laws but also the return of lands and rights to those who had possessed them on the day when Henry I "was alive and dead," something much easier said than done. Many of the chroniclers go so far as to assert that the Treaty of Winchester included terms for returning lands to their legitimate possessors "who held them in the time of the excellent King Henry" and for razing the castles that had been built since Henry I's death. The treaty itself contains no such provisions, but these accounts make clear the extent to which Henry II's wishes on these issues were known.[72]

---

69. See Amt, *Accession of Henry II in England.*

70. Torigny, *Chronicle*, 179.

71. *RRAN*, III, nos. 44, 61, 65, 86, 111, 128, 130, 140, 239, 309, 462, 574–75, 582, 653, 710, 728–29, 735, 795, 901–2, 962, 997.

72. Torigny, *Chronicle*, 177; *Gesta Stephani*, 158–59; Huntingdon, *HA*, x.38, pp. 770–72; Ralph of Diceto, *Opera Historica*, I:297; John of Hexham, *Historia regum*, II:331.

Henry's way was made easier by the convenient deaths of many to whom he had promised the most. W. L. Warren has pointed out that death appeared to be quite literally in Henry's service, as both Eustace and Stephen met untimely ends. Indeed, death continued to remove obstacles for Henry early in his reign. Stephen's youngest legitimate son, William, to whom Henry had made excessive concessions in the Treaty of Winchester, died in 1159. Henry's own younger brothers, Geoffrey and William, whom he had excluded from their paternal inheritance, died in 1158 and 1164.[73] Their deaths removed potential contenders for the throne and helped strengthen Henry's own position and ensure the succession of his children.

Many of the earls King Stephen had created, and those to whom Henry had made lavish concessions, also died early in Henry's reign.[74] Upon each of their deaths, Henry either allowed their earldom to lapse, or denied their heirs the concessions he had made to their fathers. King David of Scotland died in 1153, leaving Henry free to take back the counties of Cumberland, Westmorland, and Northumberland that David had forced Stephen to concede to him, and that Henry had then confirmed to him in 1149. King David had long been a supporter of the Angevin cause—he had even knighted the young Henry fitzEmpress in 1149—but his partisan standing earned no special treatment for his heir. David's death allowed Henry to regain much of the north of England without a fight.[75]

In spite of death's assiduous work on Henry's behalf, the lapse of earldoms and the reappropriation of royal castles and lands did not proceed without difficulty. It was not uncommon in the first years of Henry's reign for his magnates to refuse his demands and prepare to use violence to protect the properties, and especially the fortresses they had gained from the Crown under Stephen. The castles that dotted the English countryside were often outposts of resistance and strongholds from which the barons not only exercised regional power but defied the king. Henry repaid any defiance by his barons, both Stephen's supporters and his own, with military action. The threat of Henry's approaching army was often all that was required to persuade a recalcitrant baron to surrender the source of the contention, as Earl

---

73. Torigny, *Chronicle*, 163; and William of Newburgh, *Historia rerum Anglicarum*, in *Chronicles of the Reigns of Stephen, Henry II, and Richard I*, ed. R. Howlett, 4 vols. (London, 1884–90), I:1–408 and II:409–53, in I:112–13. See also John Gillingham, *Angevin Empire*, 16–19.

74. *Gesta Stephani*, 158; Gerald of Wales, *Giraldus Cambrensis Opera*, ed. J. S. Brewer, J. F. Dimmock, and G. F. Warner, 8 vols. (London, 1861–91), VIII:155–56.

75. Torigny, *Chronicle*, 192; William of Newburgh, *HRA*, I:105–6.

Roger of Hereford learned when Henry marched against him.[76] Others, seasoned by the years of civil war and not so easily cowed by the threat of violence, came to blows with Henry over his demands that they relinquish royal lands. Hugh Mortimer, a supporter of Henry's who was indignant at the king's demand that he surrender three of his strongholds, suffered the further indignity of having them taken from him by force and having to formally submit to Henry before an assembly of magnates and clergy after his surrender.[77] Henry extended an olive branch by restoring two of the castles to Hugh, after making clear that they were Crown properties.

The defeats of Hugh Mortimer and others like him stood as examples to the rest of the magnates, who might now think twice before defying Henry, especially since they would likely be allowed to continue in their possession of castles as long as they acknowledged that they properly belonged to the Crown. Henry's success in suppressing baronial dissent, reclaiming royal lands, and asserting his rights and authority was, however, clearly accompanied by a simmering resentment on the part of the barons. Discontent was obviously nursed by men such as Hugh Mortimer and Roger of Hereford, who had previously provided Henry with unwavering support. Henry's impartiality in imposing his will on everyone, regardless of whether they had fought for or against him, may have earned him a certain degree of grudging respect, but it did not necessarily endear him to his magnates. It must have been an especially bitter pill for faithful Angevin partisans, who quite reasonably felt that they deserved better treatment, if not a special dispensation, for their loyalty.

By 1157 Henry was in a position to deal with two of the most powerful and problematic men in his kingdom, King Stephen's surviving son William of Blois and Hugh Bigod, who were apparently embroiled in a struggle for control of Norfolk.[78] The conflict over Norfolk seems to have escalated to a level that required Henry's attention, and he demanded that both men hand over all of their castles, both royal and private, at a council convened at Bury Saint Edmunds in May of 1157.[79] Henry was clearly having second

---

76. William of Newburgh, *HRA*, I:103–4.

77. Ibid., I:105; Gervase of Canterbury, *Historical Works*, I:161–62; *Chronicon Monasterii de Bello*, ed. J. S. Brewer (London, 1846), 75.

78. Warren offers a convincingly reconstructed outline of the dispute based on charter evidence and the scant reference to it made by chroniclers. Warren, *Henry II*, 66–68; *RRAN*, III:272; and Thomas Rhymer, *Foedera, Conventiones, Litterae, et Acta Publica*, ed. A. Clarke and F. Holbrooke, 7 vols. (London, 1816–69), I:42.

79. Torigny, *Chronicle*, 192–93; *Chronicon Monasterii de Bello*, 85.

thoughts about the extensive concessions he had been forced to make to William under the terms of the Treaty of Winchester.[80] The quarrel between William and Hugh Bigod thus afforded Henry the opportunity to simultaneously arrange for new terms with William that were more advantageous for himself and to neutralize the potential threat that both men posed to royal authority. Henry now recognized William's right only to those lands that Stephen had held at the time of Henry I's death in 1135 and required both men to surrender all of the castles they held in Normandy and England.[81] Both men protested the loss of their castles, but William appears to have been more easily reconciled to the new situation, a reconciliation that Henry made easier by granting William an allowance from the royal revenues.[82] William was apparently satisfied with this arrangement, and he remained loyal to Henry until his death in 1159.

Hugh Bigod, on the other hand, appears to have deeply resented Henry's interference in his bid for hegemony over East Anglia. In fact, he held a grudge against the king until his death in 1177, becoming one of the leaders of the rebellion against Henry in 1173/74 known as the Great War. Henry restored two of Hugh's castles to him in 1165 in return for the payment of a large fine, but after the Great War Henry again obliged Hugh to surrender all of his castles. In a forceful demonstration of royal authority, Henry personally saw to it that Hugh's castle of Framlingham, the foundation of the Bigod family fortune, was razed to the ground by one of the royal engineers.[83] Hugh Bigod's bitter displeasure with Henry over the confiscation of his castles in 1157 was likely conditioned by the support he had given to the Angevins when Henry was still vying for the throne. Much like Hugh Mortimer and Earl Roger of Hereford, he probably felt he deserved better from the king, especially since his quarrel was with William of Blois, who might naturally be considered their mutual enemy.

Henry's program for the development of English government has been understood—and was defined by Henry himself—as merely the restoration

---

80. The exchequer was under orders to defer William's danegeld and county *donum* as earl of Warenne, and his assessments were recorded separately from those for the rest of the Norfolk on the county pipe rolls: *The Great Rolls of the Pipe of the Reign of Henry the Second, 5th to 34th years,* 30 vols. (London, 1884–1925), *Pipe Rolls 2–3–4 HII,* 7, 9, 31, 61.

81. Torigny, *Chronicle,* 192–93; Warren, *Henry II,* 67; and Amt, *Accession of Henry II in England,* 27.

82. *Pipe Rolls 2–3–4 HII,* 73, 79, 86, 94–98, 132.

83. R. A. Brown, "Framlingham Castle and Bigod," *Proceedings of the Suffolk Institute of Natural History and Archaeology* 25 (1950): 127–48; R. A. Brown, "Royal Castle Building in England, 1154–1216," *EHR* 70 (1955): 353–98; R. A. Brown, *English Medieval Castles* (London, 1954); and Warren, *Henry II,* 66 and 235.

of Henry I's government. This characterization, however, is disingenuous to some degree and obscures the fact that Henry II's government actually surpassed his grandfather's in terms of its centralization and effectiveness.[84] Henry may have viewed, and he certainly sold, his efforts to assert royal power and restore the possession of lands to their "lawful" possessors primarily as restoration, but this made the transition to greater royal authority no less painful for the barons who had grown used to having a fairly free hand under Stephen. The confiscation of castles they regarded as theirs, the curtailment of their rights, and even their ability to wage private war, surely must have rankled them. Henry's attempts to monopolize power and forbid violence among his barons were positively unbearable to some of them, as the example of Hugh Bigod attests. However ready the barons may have been for an end to interminable warfare and for the imposition of order, they were certainly unprepared to cede all of the power they had gained under Stephen. As W. L. Warren has pointed out, the barons had probably accepted Henry as Stephen's successor because they had assumed that Henry would be busy administering his vast continental possessions, and that they would be actively governing England. In this assumption "they were to be rudely disillusioned."[85] Henry's desire to rule as his grandfather had came as a shock to the barons, and it must be remembered that they did not necessarily regard his grandfather as a paragon of justice and virtue. In fact, Henry I's efforts to hold the reins of government firmly in his own hands had not been universally welcomed in his own time by the barons, who invariably lost in the perennial struggle for power whenever the king gained.

In spite of his ambitious plans, Henry II was sensible of the need to assuage and persuade his magnates in order to rule effectively. Warren and many scholars after him have argued convincingly that Henry II either lacked his mother's imperiousness and arrogance or that he had learned from her example to avoid exhibiting these features. Nor did Henry II have his grandfather's overbearing and authoritarian presence. Unlike his mother, Henry pursued his policies in a manner that was calculated to offer room for reconciliation and to avoid the appearance of unilateralism. He was careful to consult his barons frequently and attempted to persuade them so that his decisions at least appeared to be the result of their counsel. He also

---

84. Cf. Thomas Bisson, *The Crisis of the Twelfth Century: Power, Lordship, and the Origins of European Government* (Princeton, 2009), chap. 5.

85. Warren, *Henry II*, 59.

appointed men who had been loyal to Stephen (such as Henry of Essex, Richard de Lucy, and Robert de Beaumont) to important administrative positions to further reconciliation.[86]

Henry also surrounded himself with people who knew his new kingdom better than he did, such as Archbishop Theobald of Canterbury and Thomas Becket, and acted on their advice in carrying out his plans. Henry's impartiality in reclaiming Crown properties from both his own and Stephen's partisans, his efforts to reconcile with rather than punish Stephen's adherents, and his insistence that he was only restoring royal government to its former pristine condition all point to a deep concern on Henry's part that his rule be seen as legitimate and just, and, above all, in line with accepted custom and tradition. It seems to have mattered less to Henry that his policies actually alienated a majority of the barons, including those who had supported him in his struggle for the throne.

Henry followed his initial successes in reclaiming Crown properties and asserting royal authority with further efforts to regain lost rights and to formally compile and codify lists of royal properties and vassals who owed military service to the Crown.[87] The king also attempted to adjust customary rights, rents, and dues to reflect contemporary realities. These measures to enumerate royal prerogatives inevitably fueled baronial and clerical resentment. The 1164 Constitutions of Clarendon were perhaps the most famous of Henry's attempts to codify what had always been a matter of custom, and they backfired spectacularly.[88] The Constitutions of Clarendon attempted to limit papal influence within England by requiring royal approval for appeals to Rome, and sought to subject clerical lawbreakers to the full rigors of royal justice. The clergy, led by Archbishop Thomas Becket, fought back by vehemently rejecting any royal claims to jurisdiction over them and disputing the king's right to interfere in their relations with Rome. Henry presented the Constitutions of Clarendon as an innocuous

---

86. Torigny, *Chronicle*, 174; *RRAN*, III:543, 546–50, 552, and 559; and *Recueil des Actes de Henri II*, 434.

87. On Henry's legal innovations, see Thomas Keefe, *Feudal Assessments and the Political Community under Henry II and His Sons* (Berkeley, 1983); John Beeler, *Warfare in England, 1066–1189* (Ithaca, 1966); Doris Stenton, *English Justice between the Norman Conquest and the Great Charter, 1066–1215* (Philadelphia, 1964); R. C. van Caenegem, *The Birth of the English Common Law* (Cambridge, 1973); Patrick Wormald, *The Making of English Law: King Alfred to the Twelfth Century; Legislation and Its Limits* (Oxford, 1999); and Paul Brand, "'Multis vigiliis excogitatam et inventam': Henry II and the Creation of the English Common Law," *HSJ* 2 (1990): 197–222.

88. William Stubbs, ed., *Select Charters and Other Illustrations of English Constitutional History from the Earliest Times to the Reign of Edward the First* (Oxford, 1900), 135; and Warren, *Henry II*, 97. See also Frank Barlow, *Thomas Becket* (Berkeley, 1986); and Anne Duggan, *Thomas Becket* (Oxford, 2004).

attempt to compile English custom, but his insistence on retaining the two most provocative provisions (clauses three and four on royal jurisdiction over criminous clerks and royal approval for clergy leaving the kingdom) outraged the clergy. Rather than defining the relationship between king and clergy in a mutually acceptable manner, the Constitutions of Clarendon were the opening salvo in a battle between Henry and the clerical aristocracy who, under the influence of several generations of Gregorian, Cluniac, and Cistercian reformers, were moving away from working comfortably with secular rulers and toward increasing cooperation with the papacy. Henry's attempt to formally enunciate an outdated view of the relationship between clerical and royal authority actually stiffened clerical resistance to royal authority and opened the breach in his relations with Archbishop Thomas Becket that resulted in Becket's exile and eventual martyrdom.

Henry made several other moves to improve the functioning of royal government that gave his secular magnates equal or greater cause for alarm. The 1166 Assize of Clarendon threatened baronial control of the courts by giving sheriffs the authority to override baronial franchises in their pursuit of felons, and it threatened lords with the loss of their customary revenues from the profits of justice if they were found to be deficient in executing their duties or slow in bringing criminals to trial.[89]

In 1166 Henry also ordered a comprehensive inquest into all of the vassals of his barons who held their fiefs by knight-service (meaning that they owed military service in return for their land).[90] It was particularly important for Henry to have up-to-date, accurate numbers of these knights as the last such inquest had been conducted almost a hundred years earlier, and the barons had since developed a habit of enfeoffing additional knights without informing the king, and thus depriving the king of their service. More important, this chicanery deprived the king of an important source of revenue since military service was most often commuted to a cash payment known as scutage. The 1166 inquest was intended to update an antiquated system and enable Henry to demand that his barons increase their scutage payments to reflect the actual number of knights they possessed. It predictably met with resistance from the barons. In 1168 they forced Henry to settle for

---

89. Stubbs, *Select Charters*, 143; and Warren, *Henry II*, 124.

90. The returns from this inquiry were compiled in the *Cartae Baronum*. See also *Red Book of the Exchequer*, ed. Hubert Hall, 3 vols. (London, 1896), I; *Liber niger Scaccarii*, ed. Thomas Hearne, 2 vols. (London, 1774); and *Domesday People: A Prosopography of Persons Occurring in English Documents, 1066–1166*, ed. K. S. B. Keats-Rohan, 2 vols. (Woodbridge, 1999–2002), II: pipe rolls to *Cartae Baronum*.

scutage payments based only solely on the number of knights they had traditionally owed the king.[91] In spite of the furor this had caused in England, Henry held a similar inquest into the holdings of his barons in Normandy in 1172. Robert de Torigny reported that the measure enabled Henry to double his revenue from the duchy that year.[92] Henry also held inquests to determine precisely which lands had belonged to his grandfather on the day of his death and how much of these lands had since been encroached on by the barons and their tenants. The king's purpose, of course, was to levy rents and fines for the use of any lands that his grandfather had possessed.

The Great War, 1173/74

Henry's determined efforts to lay claim to any and all rights, rents, dues, services, and lands that he possibly could, as well as his attempts to improve the collection of revenues and the administration of justice, had the cumulative effect of eroding traditional centers of baronial power and subjecting their affairs to unwelcome royal scrutiny. In 1173 the resentment that had been building for nearly twenty years found a convenient outlet and the barons finally rebelled against Henry. The ostensible cause of the rebellion was the dissatisfaction of Henry II's son, the Young King Henry. In an effort to assure the succession, and in emulation of the successful Capetian practice of associating the heir in the kingship during the old king's lifetime, Henry II had crowned his eldest son in 1170, and again in 1172. The only problem with this plan was that, whereas the Capetian heirs were generally satisfied with this practice and waited patiently for the deaths of their fathers, Norman heirs had a tendency to rebel.[93] In the Young King Henry's case, he resented his lack of any real power, his constant shortage of money, and the counselors his father imposed on him. His mother, Queen Eleanor, along with his brothers, Richard and Geoffrey, who were also frustrated by

---

91. Warren, *Henry II*, 124; and J. H. Round, *Feudal England: Historical Studies on the Eleventh and Twelfth Centuries* (London, 1964), 189. See also C. Warren Hollister, *The Military Organization of Norman England* (Oxford, 1965), 203 and 266–67.

92. Torigny, *Chronique*, 349–53; J. Boussard, "L'enquête de 1172 sur les fiefs de chevalier en Normandie," in *Recueil de travaux offert à M. Clovis Brunel*, 2 vols. (Paris, 1955), I:193–208; and Warren, *Henry II*, 124.

93. Robert Curthose had only recently rebelled against William the Conqueror and the two were still estranged when the Conqueror died in 1087; their strained relationship almost perfectly mirrors that of the Empress Matilda and Henry I in 1135.

Henry II's continuing refusal to cede any real authority to them after the 1169 dynastic settlement, combined forces with Young King Henry. They were joined by Eleanor's ex-husband, Louis VII, who rarely passed up a promising opportunity to take the wind out of Henry II's sails.

The ensuing revolt encompassed all of Henry II's lands and reveals a widespread discontent with his authority. Ralph of Diceto writes of the rebels in Normandy that "those men . . . joined the party of the son, not because they regarded his as the juster cause, but because the father . . . was trampling upon the necks of the proud and the haughty, [and] was dismantling or appropriating the castles of the country. . . ."[94] Their motivation was almost universally shared by the rest of the participants in the rebellion. The rebels, for the most part, were marcher lords whose power and independence had been severely checked by Henry. They were joined by a formidable list of nobles who each nursed their own personal grievances against the king and jumped at the chance to regain the power they had previously enjoyed and rekindle the territorial ambitions Henry had quashed.[95] Hugh Bigod, who had never forgiven Henry for thwarting his designs in East Anglia and confiscating his castles in 1157, was among them, as were King William of Scotland and many of King Stephen's relatives.

The number of vassals in open rebellion against the king, combined with those who refused to clearly proclaim their loyalty to Henry, was large enough to cause Roger of Howden to comment that "nearly all the earls and barons of England, Normandy, Aquitaine, Anjou, and Brittany arose against the king of England the father."[96] The situation was dire enough for Henry and contemporary observers to assume that those who were not actively aiding the king were already among the rebels or "wavering in their allegiance to the king and ready to defect."[97] Henry, of course, had good reason to fear defections as his policies had offended so much of the aristocracy and clergy. No matter what authority or precedent Henry claimed for his expansion of royal power, or how reasonable his efforts to codify tradition and custom might have seemed to him, the aristocracy rightly perceived that Henry's actions directly threatened their own power, and they were determined not to relinquish it without a fight.

---

94. Ralph of Diceto, *Opera Historica*, I:371.

95. Boussard, Norgate, and Warren have all compiled lists of the rebels: J. Boussard, *Le gouvernment d'Henri II Plantagenêt* (Paris, 1956), 477; Kate Norgate, *England under the Angevin Kings*, 2 vols. (London, 1887), II:136; Warren, *Henry II*, 121.

96. Roger of Howden, *Chronica*, II:47.

97. William of Newburgh, *HRA*, I:181.

Faced with rebellion in all of his dominions, Henry focused his energy on maintaining order in Normandy and England, and set about securing his castles and rallying his supporters. The war reached a turning point in July 1174 after Henry publically performed penance at the tomb of Thomas Becket and thus neutralized one of the most powerful rationales his barons had offered for opposing him.[98] Within a month royalists had captured King William of Scotland and Henry had put Louis VII and the French army to rout. Deprived of their most important supporters, the rebels had little choice but to come to terms with the king. Peace was negotiated between Henry II and his sons at Montlouis in September 1174. As usual, Henry was conciliatory and offered favorable terms to the rebels, who were allowed to go back to their estates and return to the status quo ante bellum.[99] The only exception to this general amnesty was Henry's queen, Eleanor of Aquitaine, who had incurred Henry's wrath by encouraging their children to rebel against him and enlisting the aid of her ex-husband, Louis VII. Henry imprisoned Eleanor at the beginning of the war for her role in fomenting the rebellion, and she remained incarcerated for almost fifteen years, until Henry's death in 1189. The leniency Henry displayed toward the rebels was calculated to end the war quickly and to encourage reconciliation. It was not, however, an indication that he was in any way humbled or that he intended to abandon the policies that had so inflamed the barons in the first place.

In fact, the following years were punctuated by vigorous reassertions of royal power and continued efforts to extend the reach of royal authority, some of them more outrageous from a baronial point of view than any before them. Just after the Great War, in 1176, the king took all baronial castles into his possession. In 1177 he rotated the custodianship of these castles to ensure that everyone explicitly understood the principle that these were royal possessions. He also sought to prevent the custodians from becoming too closely associated with their castles and attempting to claim custody of them by hereditary right.[100] As Warren neatly observed, these actions "put the principle beyond doubt—though not beyond resentment."[101] The Assize of Northampton, issued in 1176, expanded upon the Assize of Claren-

---

98. Jordan Fantosme points out that things went very well for Henry after he accepted blame for his part in Becket's murder and performed penance. Jordan Fantosme, *Jordan Fantosme's Chronicle*, ed. and trans. R. C. Johnston (Oxford, 1981), 141–43.

99. Roger of Howden, *Gesta Regis Henrici Secundi*, ed. William Stubbs, 2 vols. (London, 1867), I:75–79; Roger of Howden, *Chronica*, II:66–69; and Ralph of Diceto, *Opera Historica*, I: 394–95.

100. Roger of Howden, *Gesta*, I:160–61; Warren, *Henry II*, 141–42.

101. Warren, *Henry II*, 142.

don and increased the severity of punishments for those convicted, or even suspected, of serious crimes.[102] And, notably, Henry angered his magnates even further in 1176 by retroactively punishing offenses against the forest laws committed by barons and clergy, including his own loyalists, during the Great War.[103]

Although Henry's determination to restore royal authority was based as much on his loathing for anything associated with Stephen's reign as it was on his admiration for the government and authority of his grandfather, Henry was careful to appease Stephen's adherents and to appeal to precedent, custom, and tradition in reviving his grandfather's government and restoring order. Unfortunately for the barons, whether they had supported Stephen or Henry, Henry's restoration came at a price: the loss of baronial autonomy, authority, and power. Henry's method of governing before the Great War was apparently designed to make this bitter reality as palatable as possible, as he combined efforts to reconcile his barons with actions that were designed to limit their power and sure to insult their sensibilities. Henry's reassertion of royal authority after the Great War predictably followed the same pattern of conciliatory and even magnanimous gestures accompanied by inflammatory actions. It was impossible for Henry to rule as he wanted without trampling on the ambitions of his magnates, but neither could he rule without their assistance. In the absence of a completely professionalized bureaucracy, judicial system, or army, the barons still actively participated in the administration of government, in the prosecution of justice, and in defending the country from internal rebellions and external attacks, and they had to be accommodated to some extent. Henry's efforts to mitigate the negative consequences of his reassertion of royal power indicate that he was aware of the limitations of his power and knew that he was performing a delicate balancing act.

The Succession Question

Perhaps the most serious threat that Henry faced was the very nature of the royal succession in England. Neither hereditary right nor primogeniture yet applied to the English succession, as Henry was well aware from his own

---

102. Stubbs, *Select Charters*, 179; Warren, *Henry II*, 139 and 355.

103. Torigny, *Chronicle*, 267; Ralph of Diceto, *Opera Historica*, I:402; Roger of Howden, *Gesta*, I:92–94; and Roger of Howden, *Chronica*, II:79.

experience. Primogeniture was gaining ground among noble households in England by the time Henry came to the throne, and it was the standard practice for noble and royal successions in neighboring France, but it did not necessarily apply to the English royal succession as the Norman kings of England had never previously used it. The Normans had applied primogeniture to their patrimony, the duchy of Normandy, for several generations, but since the Norman conquest of England in 1066 the English royal succession had been consistently decided on the basis of a combination of hereditary claim, designation, and consent.[104] William the Conqueror had famously passed over his oldest son Robert (who received Normandy, William's patrimony), and designated his second son, William Rufus, as his successor in England (land he had acquired by conquest and could thus dispose of separately). When William Rufus died, his younger brother Henry I raced to claim the English throne while Robert was away on crusade. Henry was confronted by several of Robert's supporters who opposed this power grab, but Henry soon convinced a majority of the barons and clergy to accept him as king. Henry had planned to leave both England and Normandy to his only legitimate son, William Audelin, and this would have provided some precedent for applying primogeniture to the English succession if the plan had worked, but William Audelin died in 1120, leaving Henry with little choice but to designate his daughter Matilda as his heir. The fact that the barons and clergy were able to exclude Matilda and give the throne to her cousin Stephen when Henry I died in 1135, and were able once again to exclude Stephen's son Eustace in favor of Henry II, demonstrates that the element of consent was still quite strong. Royal blood gave one a claim to the throne, and designation certainly helped, but the consent of the barons and clergy still determined whether a claimant was actually elevated to the throne. Given such dismaying precedents and his own experience, Henry II could have had no confidence that the barons and clergy would respect his own wishes for the succession once he was dead.

Remarkably, many scholars have viewed Henry as completely unconcerned with the succession of his children. They appear to assume that, once Henry had gained the throne, there was no need for him to worry about the possibility of another succession dispute. Henry's consecration as king may have secured his possession of England, but it in no way guaranteed that his children would succeed him. Henry had only just succeeded in firmly establishing himself on the throne in 1159, and his children with

---

104. See Garnett, *Conquered England*, chaps. 1–3.

Eleanor were still very young when Henry first commissioned Wace to write a history of his Norman ancestors in 1160.[105] The couple's first son, William, had passed away from a seizure at the age of two in 1156 (as if to underscore the realities of medieval mortality rates and the contingent nature of any plans for the succession). Their surviving sons, Henry, Richard, and Geoffrey, ranged in age from five to two years old in 1160, and their last son, John, was not was not born until 1167. When this project first began, none of Henry's sons were old enough to fight for the succession if their father died prematurely, and it was entirely conceivable that they might be passed over for the throne if disaster struck.

The capriciousness of fate and the vagaries of human mortality must have been very much on Henry's mind in 1160 given his own history. He had only been two years old when his grandfather died, and both he and his mother were passed over for the throne. He had been too young at the time to object to the machinations of the nobles and clergy, and both his mother and his father had been powerless to stop them from giving the throne to Stephen. It was also entirely possible that none of Henry's sons would survive their father, and in fact three of his five sons with Eleanor did precede him to the grave. Had all of the boys died before their father, as sometimes happened in noble families, Henry would have found himself in precisely the same difficult situation as his grandfather Henry I had been in—his only surviving legitimate children would have been female and he would have been forced to attempt to convince the nobles and clergy to accept one of his daughters as their queen. In 1160 there was still the distinct possibility that either of these unpleasant scenarios might come to pass: Henry might die early and leave behind sons too young to fight for their claim to the throne, or he might live to a ripe old age as his grandfather had done, but see all of his sons predecease him.

Like all of his predecessors, Henry wanted to ensure that his children succeeded him, and many of his actions suggest that the succession was on his mind from his earliest months as king. His greatest challenge was therefore to establish firm rules governing the succession that would supersede the influence traditionally wielded by the barons and clergy. Shortly after taking the throne, on April 10, 1154, Henry required his barons to swear to uphold the rights of his infant sons William and Henry as his heirs (William died shortly afterward).[106] The oath swearing was an important first

---

105. See Amt, *Accession of Henry II in England*.

106. Torigny, *Chronicle*, 184.

step in securing the succession, but Henry was aware that it was insufficient to ensure that another succession dispute would not break out upon his death—after all, the oaths sworn to support Matilda on multiple occasions had failed to prevent a crisis in 1135. What Henry desperately needed was to establish hard and fast principles governing the succession that the barons and clergy could not override. To achieve this end, Henry began to innovate.

In January 1169, at Montmirail, Henry announced a dynastic settlement that further detailed his wishes for the succession.[107] Henry, as the eldest surviving son, was to inherit England, Normandy, and Anjou (a reconstituted patrimony consisting of the lands Henry II had inherited from both his mother and father). Richard was to have his mother's duchy of Aquitaine (a separately alienable acquisition), while Geoffrey, who was betrothed to the heiress of Brittany, was to hold Brittany as the Young King Henry's vassal. John, the youngest son, received no lands. The settlement was announced as part of peace negotiations between Henry II and Louis VII (the Young King Henry and Richard performed homage to Louis VII for their lands, while Geoffrey performed homage to his brother Henry), but it was equally motivated by Henry's desire to ensure that his lands would pass to his children. Henry made a will confirming the grants made at Montmirail in August 1170 while suffering from a serious illness.[108] Although these preparations may also have been part of a longer-term effort to prevent internecine rivalry among Henry's sons by clearly delineating which of his lands they would inherit, there is no evidence that the boys were already fighting each other in 1169.

Shortly after the dynastic settlement, Henry took the unprecedented step of having his eldest son crowned by the archbishop of York at Westminster on May 24, 1170.[109] Henry borrowed this tactic from the Capetian kings of France, who had avoided succession disputes through their long habit of crowning their new king while the old king still lived. Henry seems to have had little confidence that his wishes would be respected and decided to take matters into his own hands. By emulating the established French practice,

---

107. Herbert of Bosham, *Materials for the History of Thomas Becket*, ed. J. C. Robertson, 7 vols. (London, 1875–85), III:419.

108. Howden, *Gesta*, I:6–7.

109. The coronation was exceptionally performed by the archbishop of York due to Henry's ongoing quarrel with Thomas Becket. Henry's wife, Margaret, the daughter of Louis VII, was delayed in Caen and missed the coronation. Torigny, *Chronicle*, 245; Howden, *Gesta*, I:5–6; Howden, *Chronica*, II:4–5; and Gervase of Canterbury, *Historical Works*, I:219–20.

Henry must have hoped to remove any possibility of interference on the part of the barons and the clergy. A second coronation was performed at Westminster by the bishop of Rouen in 1172, and this time the young king's wife, Margaret, was crowned by his side.[110] All of these measures were designed to avert a succession dispute like the one that had occurred in 1135. More important, they sought to enshrine hereditary right as the basis for the succession. The fact that the Young King Henry predeceased his father in 1183, and that Henry II never crowned another son while he lived, since these coronations had directly contributed to the outbreak of the Great War in 1173, is immaterial. Henry was indisputably innovating when it came to ensuring the succession of his children.

As it turned out, Henry lived long enough for his sons to mature and was survived by two of them. There was no succession crisis when Henry died in 1189, but Henry had no way of knowing in 1160 (or even 1169, 1170, or 1172) that this would be the case. Furthermore, the problem of the lack of clear rules for the succession was not entirely resolved even with Richard's accession to the throne in 1189; yet another crisis broke out upon Richard's death in 1199 over whether his younger brother, John, or nephew Arthur (Geoffrey's son), should be king. There was still room for debate when it came to the royal succession, and once again the nobles and clergy had to choose whom they would accept as king.

It may be argued that Henry had no need to worry about the succession as there was no one to challenge his children for the English throne. There were certainly no legitimate, direct male descendants of William the Conqueror left (Henry I had been the last). Henry II's own brothers were dead by 1164 and Stephen's only remaining son died in 1159. There were, however, other descendants of the Conqueror on the Continent. Stephen's older brother, Theobald of Blois, had sons that were still living, and the barons and clergy could easily have chosen to support one of them upon Henry's death (especially if Henry had died prematurely or all his sons had predeceased him). Theobald himself had been offered the crown by the Anglo-Norman barons and clergy before they had turned to Stephen, and Theobald's sons, Henry the Liberal of Champagne (d. 1181), Theobald V of Blois (d. 1191), Stephen of Sancerre (d. 1191), and William, archbishop of Reims (d. 1202), had a hereditary claim to the English throne that was almost as good as that possessed by Stephen's sons (though Stephen's sons had two further advantages: their father had been king and their mother was descended from the

---

110. Howden, *Gesta*, I:31.

Anglo-Saxon royal house).[111] Even though none of Theobald's sons were actively vying for the throne, the fact remains that they had strong hereditary claims. Had the Anglo-Norman nobles and clergy decided to defy Henry's wishes for the succession, they had suitable replacements for his children close at hand.

History and Dynastic Memory

Henry's reassertion of royal authority was accompanied by concerted efforts to shape the realm of public opinion. Just as Henry took care to appeal to justice, precedent, and tradition in his political actions, he was careful to foster an image of himself as a legitimate king. In Henry's case, projecting such an image was more necessary than usual as his path to the throne had been beset with so many difficulties and his policies alienated so many of his most powerful subjects. To assert his legitimacy and assure the succession of his children, Henry turned to the time-honored practice of cultivating the memory of his dynasty.

By 1160, the year in which Henry commissioned Wace to write the first vernacular history of his Norman ancestors, the king had made substantial gains in the restoration of royal authority and appears to have been thinking about his own legacy and that of his dynasty. Many of his actions during the first years of his reign indicate that he took a particular interest in cultivating the memory of his ancestors and controlling the public's perception of his place within that lineage. Indeed, Henry's decision to commission a vernacular history of his Norman ancestors must be understood as part of a larger political program designed to strengthen his own legitimacy by enhancing the prestige of his dynasty. These efforts included petitioning for the canonization of Edward the Confessor, translating the bodies of Dukes Richard I and II, and tending the public memory of Henry I.

Henry began agitating for the canonization of Edward the Confessor almost as soon as he obtained the English throne.[112] As the crucial pivot

---

111. Cf. Garnett, *Conquered England*, 141. Orderic reports that Theobald was indignant at being passed over for the throne, but Robert de Torigny says that Theobald was offered the throne and that the offer was only rescinded after news arrived that Stephen had already been crowned. Orderic, *HE*, vi, III:454; and Torigny, *Chronicle*, 129

112. Henry II's petition is one of thirteen extant petitions that were sent to Pope Alexander III requesting the canonization of Edward the Confessor (Henry's petition makes particular mention of his own kinship with Edward). Bernard Scholz, "The Canonization of Edward the Confessor,"

between Anglo-Saxon and Anglo-Norman control of England, Edward the Confessor occupied a privileged place in Anglo-Norman history. Edward was the son of King Æthelred and Queen Emma, the daughter of the Norman duke Richard I. After Æthelred's death and their mother's remarriage to Cnut, both Edward and his brother Alfred had been raised in the household of Emma's brother and William the Conqueror's grandfather, Duke Richard II. Edward had maintained close, if not always friendly, ties with his Norman relatives after his accession to the English throne. From the Anglo-Norman point of view, the celibate and childless Edward had lawfully designated his cousin William as his heir with the consent of the Anglo-Saxon barons. The legitimacy of the Norman kings was predicated on Edward's lack of children and his designation of William as his heir, and Anglo-Norman kings regularly used it to justify their claims to England.[113] It was therefore essential that Edward's legacy, his holy celibacy, and his formal designation of William as his heir be memorialized. Having Edward formally canonized precisely for his celibacy would ensure that his cult would be dominated by the memory of his childlessness and transform the demise of the Anglo-Saxon dynasty into an act of holiness. Edward's cult would thus continuously reiterate the legitimate and sacred origin of Norman rule in England.

The possession of a saint in one's genealogy also increased a family's prestige, and the Normans were sorely in need of assistance on that front as the founder of their dynasty was a pagan Viking who had invaded Normandy, and their crowning glory had been William the Bastard's conquest of England. Unlike his Anglo-Norman predecessors, who were related to the Anglo-Saxon dynasty only through marriage, Henry II carried the blood of both royal lines and could therefore enjoy the reflected glory of Edward's sanctity in a way that his predecessors could not.[114] "The holy 'King and Confessor' was expected to add to the charismatic character of his royal kins-

---

Speculum 36/1 (1961): 38–60. See also Frank Barlow, *Edward the Confessor* (Berkeley, 1970); and Richard Mortimer, *Edward the Confessor: The Man and the Legend* (Woodbridge, 2009).

113. Since Edward's designation of William as his heir was disputed by the Anglo-Saxon sources, pro-Norman historians such as William of Poitiers also portrayed William's victory over Harold at Hastings as proof that William had the more legitimate claim to the throne.

114. Aelred of Rievaulx's *Life of Edward the Confessor*, written just after the canonization, is dedicated to Henry II and memorializes him as the fulfillment of Edward's prophecy that the Norman and Anglo-Saxon dynasties would finally be united in a single king. Aelred also credits Henry II's support and royal authority as the source of Edward's canonization in his prologue to the Vita. *Patrologia Latina: Patrologiae Cursus Completus*, ed. J. P. Migne, 221 vols. (1844–55), 195.

man and to the sacred nature of [Henry's] kingship."[115] Edward was one of the first saints anywhere to be officially canonized by the papacy, as the practice was still in its infancy in the 1160s. Although a popular cult had already formed around Edward, Henry II was determined to pursue the new avenue of securing official, papal recognition for his saintly ancestor.[116] With so much depending on the recognition of Edward's sanctity, Henry appears to have been unwilling to trust his fate to the hazards of popular opinion. Henry's petition was successful. Pope Alexander III canonized Edward the Confessor in February 1161, and the saint's translation was publicly celebrated at Westminster on October 13, 1163, in the presence of Henry and his barons.[117]

Bernard Scholz has argued that Edward's canonization was a matter of enormous ideological importance for Henry. According to Scholz, the formal recognition of Edward's sanctity was intended "to shed new glory on the ancestors and the family of the king, and thus to provide the Plantagenets with the halo of inherent sanctity."[118] It was propaganda for a cult of the ruler's dynasty that was intended to reinforce Henry's hereditary right to the throne. Imbuing the kingship with an aura of sanctity served to "increase [the king's] independence from the ecclesiastical mediators of the anointing and to distinguish his lordship from that of his barons."[119] Although Henry's kingship was founded on his hereditary claim to the crown, the elevation of an English king also depended on the consent of the barons and consecration by the Church. Henry, however, had good reason to promote hereditary right as the sole basis of any legitimate claim to the throne. As we have seen, hereditary right was only one factor germane to the royal succession; royal designation and oath swearing were far more important. Matilda's

115. Scholz, "Canonization of Edward the Confessor," 57.

116. Cf. Eric Kemp, *Canonization and Authority in the Western Church* (London, 1948); Stephan Kuttner, "La réserve papale du droit de canonisation," *Revue historique de droit français et étranger* 4/18 (1938): 172–228; André Vauchez, *La sainteté en occident aux derniers siècles du moyen âge d'après les procès de canonisation et les documents hagiographiques* (Rome, 1981), 13–69; and Bernhard Schimmelpfennig, "Heilige Päpste-päpstliche Kanonisationspolitik," in *Politik und Heiligenverehrung im Hochmittelalter, Vorträge und Forschungen, 42,* ed. Jürgen Petersohn (Sigmaringen, 1994), 73–100. For a review of the earlier tradition of episcopal canonization, see Agostino Amore, "Culto e Canonizzazione dei Santi nell'antichitá Cristiana," *Antonianum* 52 (1977): 38–80; and Agostino Amore, "La canonizazzione vescovile," *Antonianum* 52 (1977): 231–66.

117. *Gesta Abbatum Monasterii Sancti Albani: Chronica Monasterii S. Albani: Gesta Abbatum Monasterii Sancti Albani, a Thoma Walsingham,* ed. H. T. Riley (London, 1867), I:159; Warren, *Henry II,* 223.

118. Scholz, "Canonization," 59.

119. Ibid., 59–60.

claim to the throne (and the oaths sworn to her) had been discounted by both the barons and the clergy in 1135, and their actions in assisting Stephen's usurpation had very nearly deprived Henry himself of the kingdom. The barons and clergy had, of course, been instrumental in bringing about Henry's own succession, but the king must have been painfully aware that they retained the power to affect the succession upon his death. From the moment he found himself safely ensconced on the throne, Henry had worked to ensure that his children would succeed him by limiting the ability of the magnates and clergy to meddle in the succession and promoting the principle of hereditary right as the sole basis of royal succession. "Such a policy was mandatory after the question of succession had brought disaster upon the country on the death of Henry I."[120] Edward the Confessor's canonization under Henry II's auspices was "thus able—and perhaps intended—to support the belief in an entirely independent and indispensable hereditary right of succession of the individual monarch based on his legitimacy."[121]

A year after the translation of Edward the Confessor, on April 19, 1164, Henry II and Archbishop Becket, along with ten other English bishops, consecrated the recently completed conventual church at Reading Abbey.[122] Like the canonization of Edward the Confessor, the consecration of Reading Abbey had a special dynastic significance. Henry I had begun construction of the abbey in 1121, after the deaths of Edith-Matilda and William Audelin, and dedicated it to all of his predecessors and successors as kings of England.[123] Henry I's generous endowment and rebuilding of Reading also had another important motivation. Reading was one of three Anglo-Saxon abbeys destroyed by the Danes that Henry undertook to restore as part of his project of establishing firm connections with his Anglo-Saxon predecessors. In fact, Pauline Stafford links "the lands used to endow Reading with those of late Saxon queens and of female communities themselves linked to queens."[124]

What was arguably more important to Henry II than Reading's connection to Anglo-Saxon queens was the fact that the abbey had maintained a cult dedicated to the memory of Henry I since his death in 1135. Reading

---

120. Ibid., 60.

121. Ibid.

122. R. W. Eyton, *Court, Household, and Itinerary of Henry II* (London, 1878), 71.

123. Edith-Matilda was buried at Westminster Abbey; William Audelin's body was never recovered from the sea. Hollister, *Henry I*, 437.

124. Pauline Stafford, "Cherchez la femme: Queens, Queen's Lands and Nunneries: Missing Links in the Foundation of Reading Abbey," *History* 85 (2000): 4–27, at 4.

was actually something of a royal mausoleum by 1164. Henry I's body rested in a place of honor before the high altar of the monastery's church, not far from the bodies of his second wife, Adeliza of Louvain, and an illegitimate son, Reginald (the Young King Henry would later be interred near his great-grandfather at Reading). At the consecration in 1164, Henry II renewed the liberties granted by his grandfather and made a point of putting the abbey under his own special protection.[125] Henry II's attention to the completion of Reading Abbey demonstrates his desire to ensure that his royal ancestors continued to be visibly memorialized. It is worth adding that publicly celebrating the memory of Henry I, through the completion and consecration of the abbey, viscerally recalled the source of Henry II's authority in a way that little else could. And, by linking himself so firmly to his grandfather, Henry was attempting to smooth over the issue of his Angevin paternity and present himself as a Norman heir.

In a clearly related attempt to control the memory of his dynasty, Henry was also attending to the commemoration of two of his most important Norman ancestors. In 1162, Henry and his Norman bishops supervised the translation of the bodies of Dukes Richard I and Richard II to places of honor behind the altar at Sainte-Trinité, Fécamp.[126] Just as Henry sought to control Edward's memory and enhance his family's prestige through seeing to his canonization, he also sought to cultivate the memories of Richard I and Richard II through placing their bodies in prominent positions in a monastery his family had refounded. Like the assumption of Edward the Confessor into the ranks of the saints, the very public celebration of the translation of the bodies of Richard I and Richard II was intended to promote the principle of hereditary right and to strengthen Henry's position in relation to the Church.

Richard I and Richard II had been notably pious secular rulers. Richard I had rebuilt the modest church dedicated to Sainte-Trinité on the site facing the ducal palace after personally finding its most precious relics, drops of the Holy Blood of Christ, hidden away in the old church.[127] The recovery of the Holy Blood and the construction of the new church rapidly transformed Fécamp into Normandy's most famous pilgrimage site. Richard II

125. *Reading Abbey Cartularies: British Library Manuscripts Egerton 3031, Harley 1708 and Cotton Vespasian E XXV*, ed. B. R. Kemp, 2 vols. (London, 1986–87), n. 32. Henry II's successors followed his example. *Reading Abbey Cartularies*, nos. 35, 39 (Richard I) and 71 (Henry III).

126. Torigny, *Chronicle*, 212–13.

127. For the evolution of the myth of the Holy Blood and its discovery, see Jean-Guy Gouttebroze, *Le Précieux Sang de Fécamp* (Paris, 2004).

had continued to transform Fécamp, replacing the canons established there by Richard I with a Benedictine community and installing William of Volpiano as its first abbot. Even the tomb from which the bodies of the dukes were removed held great significance. During his lifetime, Richard I had set up a humble tomb for himself just outside the church door and had ordered that it be filled with food to be distributed to the poor every Friday. This same unadorned tomb under the eaves of Sainte-Trinité was meant to be Richard's unassuming final resting place, but his corpse gave off such an odor of sanctity at the time of his burial that a chapel dedicated to Saint Thomas was erected over Richard's tomb.[128]

Richard II chose to be interred in the same tomb as his father when he died in 1027. For almost 150 years, monks and pilgrims had passed this chapel containing the tomb of Richard I and Richard II as they entered the church to venerate the Holy Blood. Their bodies were now moved to an even more splendid structure behind the high altar. The translation of the ducal bodies in Henry II's presence thus recalled the great piety of his Norman ancestors and their reputed sanctity, while the placement of the bodies behind the altar conferred on them an aura of quasi sanctity.[129] More important for Henry II, the translation celebrated the Norman dynasty. It reinforced the importance of lineage and the principle of hereditary succession as Richard I and Richard II were not just successive dukes of Normandy but were also father and son. Their joint translation thus emphasized the continuity of the ducal line and underscored Henry's own place within that distinctly Norman lineage.

Henry's decision to commission a vernacular history of his maternal ancestors in 1160 was thus part of a larger effort to publically memorialize his

128. According to Dudo of Saint-Quentin, Richard I had died an especially pious death at Fécamp. When he fell ill at Bayeux, Richard had himself transported to Fécamp dressed in a hairshirt. There he made an offering to the church, received communion and the viaticum, and died among the community of canons he had established. Dudo also recounts that Count Raoul d'Ivry and the bishops found Richard I's body to be pliable and sweet smelling when they visited his tomb several days after his death. Dudo of Saint-Quentin, *History of the Normans*, 170–73. Cf. Joseph Bédier, "Richard de Normandie dans les chansons de geste," *Romanic Review* 1 (1910): 113–24, at 118.

129. The translation of relics by a bishop functioned as ecclesiastical recognition of the deceased's sanctity at this time. Jean-Guy Gouttebroze, "Pourquoi congédier un historiographe, Henri II Plantagenêt et Wace (1155–1174)," *Romania* 112 (1991): 289–311, at 304. See also Amore, "Culto e Canonizzazione dei Santi nell'antichitá Cristiana," 38–80, and Amore, "La canonizazzione vescovile," 231–66. The translation of the bodies was probably also related to a movement in the eleventh and twelfth centuries to attribute saintly powers to Duke Richard I. See Joseph Bédier, "Richard de Normandie dans les chansons de geste," 113–24, and Nicole Cazauran, "Richard sans puer: Un personnage en quête d'auteur," *Travaux de Littérature* 4 (1991): 21–43.

ancestors and to establish a cult of his dynasty that would help to guarantee its survival. Considering the magnitude of the disruption caused by the succession dispute in 1135 and the decades of civil war that preceded Henry's accession to the throne, it is unsurprising that the king turned to history writing as part of his project of restoring order in the Anglo-Norman realm. The dominant theme of Anglo-Norman history, as Marjorie Chibnall and other historians have noted, was legitimacy, both dynastic and individual.[130] "To the legitimacy of William I's conquest of England, which had been hammered home by Norman historians from William of Poitiers onwards, was now added the legitimacy of Henry II's claim by hereditary right."[131]

Henry II was politically astute enough to recognize that patronizing history writing offered him the opportunity to disseminate a particular version of the past that would reinforce his dynasty's legitimacy, his own authority, and help to ensure the succession of his children. Henry apparently also felt it was necessary to advertise the legitimacy of his controversial reassertion of royal power by insisting that he was simply reclaiming the authority enjoyed by his predecessors. As W. L. Warren has pointed out, Henry II was hardly alone in attempting to limit the power of his nobles. William the Conqueror and his sons had also prohibited private warfare, allowed castles to be built only with their permission, and tried to limit the power of the English earls. As Warren notes, "These were salutary policies, but they seemed at the time the self-interested prejudices of authoritarian rulers."[132] Henry II's vigorous resumption of these practices must have seemed just as self-interested and authoritarian to his barons, but he could nonetheless claim that they were based on the precedents established by his Norman ancestors. A history commemorating the deeds of his grandfather and great-grandfather could be fashioned to emphasize that Henry II was not introducing new and burdensome regulations, and enable him to claim that he was merely restoring good government. Of course, the barons could still object to these policies, but Henry II would be in a much better position to argue that he had tradition and precedent on his side if a history demonstrating precisely that point was circulating among the aristocracy.

As useful as a new history of the Norman dynasty could be for Henry II, its production presented him with one major problem: Stephen had ruled England for almost twenty years and commemorating his reign was potential

---

130. Chibnall, *Empress Matilda*, 195.

131. Ibid.

132. Warren, *Henry II*, 363.

minefield. Fortunately, Henry II had a useful model at hand for dealing with such a troublesome predecessor. His own great-grandfather, William the Conqueror, had had a similar problem with Harold Godwinson. William's solution was to characterize Harold's reign as a usurpation that defied Edward the Confessor's wishes, and a usurpation that was carried out by William's own perjured vassal at that. In order to quash any potential defense of Harold's reign, pro-Norman histories of the Conquest, such as that of William of Poitiers, emphasized Edward's designation of William as his heir in 1051 and a series of events that historians believe probably occurred in 1064: Harold's shipwreck on the coast of France, William's rescue of Harold from the count of Ponthieu, and the oath of fealty that Harold had allegedly sworn over relics at Bonneville to uphold William's right to the throne and to assist him in gaining it should he be opposed.[133] These elements all served to vilify Harold and to exacerbate his crime by adding perjury and treason to the usurpation, just as Stephen's usurpation after taking at least one well-known oath to uphold Matilda's rights had arguably added perjury and treason to his crime.

In addition to representing Harold as a treasonous and perjured usurper who stole the throne on the very day of Edward's funeral, William also nullified Harold's legacy by using Edward's reign as the foundation for his rule. To give only two prominent examples, William's laws proclaimed that "all shall have and hold the law of King Edward in respect of their lands and all their possessions."[134] and the Domesday inquest used land holdings during King Edward's reign as the baseline for assessing contemporary holdings and deciding disputes over possession.[135] While William was appealing to Edward to legitimate his acts, he also intended to negate any laws or grants made during Harold's short reign by appealing only to the precedents established by Edward the Confessor, the king from whom his own legitimacy derived.[136] Viewed from this perspective, Henry II's approach to dealing with Stephen's reign in his charters as king follows a familiar and established pattern. Henry II appeals only to the precedents established by the last lawful king of England, Henry I, and utterly rejects Stephen's acts. Commemorat-

---

133. William of Poitiers, *Gesta Guillelmi*.

134. The Laws of William the Conqueror in *English Historical Documents, vol. 2 (1142–1189)*, ed. David C. Douglas and G. W. Greenaway (London, 1953) [hereafter *EHD*], n. 18; Stubbs, *Select Charters*, 98–99. Henry I also appealed to legal precedents set by Edward the Confessor in his Coronation Charter: Douglas, *EHD*, n. 19.

135. Douglas, *EHD*, 849 and n. 215.

136. Cf. Garnett, *Conquered England*, chap. 1.

ing Stephen in a history, even as a usurper, was a trickier business, and it is probably indicative of the dangers inherent in attempting to memorialize Stephen's reign that he does not appear prominently in either Wace's *Roman de Rou* or Benoît de Sainte-Maure's *Chronique des ducs de Normandie*.

Finally, by controlling the representation of his family in a dynastic history, Henry could construct his own identity and ensure that he would be viewed by posterity (if not by his contemporaries) as a legitimate English king. As should be abundantly clear, Henry's Angevin father was a potential stumbling block for him. Although Henry could not, and probably did not wish to, escape the fact that he was Geoffrey's son, the barons and clergy had used Geoffrey of Anjou as a pretext for denying the throne to Matilda, and his father was of very limited use to Henry in promoting his legitimacy as king of England and duke of Normandy. Although modern scholars often refer to Henry II as Henry of Anjou, his contemporaries knew him as Henry fitzEmpress (a cognomen that emphasized his mother's royal lineage and his claim to the English throne). It seems highly unlikely that he ever would have called himself Henry of Anjou, or that anyone around him would have done so unless they were spoiling for a fight. As W. L. Warren has pointed out, "That he was the son of a count no one chose to remind him."[137] Except, of course, for Herbert of Bosham, who famously reminded Henry of precisely that, and he meant it as an insult.[138] Although no one who wished to remain in Henry's good graces ever dared to raise the subject, Herbert of Bosham's example is instructive. Anyone who wanted to undermine Henry's power or legitimacy had only to conjure the specter of his father and remind him that he was the son of an Angevin count. It was therefore beneficial (perhaps even necessary) for Henry to emphasize his Norman ancestry and clearly illustrate his rightful place within that lineage. The genealogical format of a dynastic history could do just that.

To demonstrate how Henry could selectively fashion his own identity, we need only look to his charters. Stephen's usurpation of the English throne had dominated Henry's life from his earliest years, and it seems that it also affected Henry's expressions of his own identity. His early charter formulae almost always asserted his legitimacy as a Norman heir through references to his maternal, Norman ancestors. From his earliest charters until the end of his reign, Henry identified himself at important moments

137. Warren, *Henry II*, 222.

138. My thanks to Martin Aurell for pointing out that Herbert of Bosham insulted Henry II precisely by reminding him that he was not the son of a king. Martin Aurell, *L'Empire des Plantagenêt* (Paris, 2003), 248.

as *filius Matildis* (son of Matilda).[139] Before Geoffrey of Anjou was recognized as duke of Normandy in 1144, Henry was most often styled either *filius Matildis* or *Henricus filius filie Regis Henrici rectus heres Angliae et Normanni(ae)* (Henry, son of the daughter of King Henry, rightful heir to England and Normandy) as he appears in a charter confirming grants made by Matilda in 1141.[140]

Matilda herself was always styled as *Matildis imperatrix Henrici regis filia* (Empress Matilda, daughter of King Henry) in her charters, with *Anglorum domina* (Lady of the English) being added for a short time after 1141. As W. L. Warren has pointed out, the use of the formula *Matildis imperatrix Henrici regis filia* made hereditary claims to the lands and titles held by Henry I.[141] Warren has also correctly observed that Matilda and Henry II were forced to rely on hereditary claims, which had little force in English custom or law, because oath swearing had so utterly failed them.[142] Henry was thus following Matilda's lead in indirectly asserting his right to titles that he could not actually use in order to advance his claims to the Anglo-Norman realm. No one could doubt that, by emphasizing their lineage in their charters, both Matilda and Henry were hammering home their hereditary rights to the lands of Henry I during the period when Stephen was legally *rex Anglorum et dux Normannorum*. It is more telling, however, that Henry continuously used the cognomen fitzEmpress, and that he occasionally identified himself as Matilda's son and Henry I's grandson even after he was king of England and duke of Normandy in his own right. It appears that Henry never quite escaped the need to remind everyone exactly whence his authority derived.

Of course, Henry was also the son of Geoffrey of Anjou, but Henry's hereditary rights to Normandy and England were quite obviously more contested than his right to the county of Anjou. It thus stands to reason that there would be a greater need to forcefully assert the contested claim. Henry does sometimes appear in charters as *Henricus ducis Normannorum et comitis Andegavorum filius* (Henry, son of the duke of Normandy and count

---

139. Henry appears as *filius Matildis imperatrix* in the 1174 Treaty of Falaise, in the 1184 Assize of the Forest, and in an 1183 memorandum from Caen. Douglas, *EHD*, nos. 26 and 27; *Recueil des Actes de Henri II*, II:250; Warren, *Henry II*, 222–23; R. L. G. Ritchie, *The Normans in Scotland* (Edinburgh, 1953), 354–55.

140. *RRAN*, III, n. 635.

141. Warren, *Henry II*, 19.

142. "The oaths were crucial for Matilda. She later claimed hereditary right, but this was because the oaths failed her. . . . In reality there was no ground for claiming that the English crown should descend by right to the nearest blood relative. Kinship with the royal family was undoubtedly a factor in influencing the choice of successor, but an element of choice remained." Warren, *Henry II*, 18.

of Anjou), but this usually occurs in charters relating to Anjou before Geoffrey's death in 1151, and in charters relating to Normandy during the period
from 1144 to 1150 when Geoffrey was the acknowledged *dux Normannorum*.[143] Before being acknowledged as duke of Normandy in 1150, Henry
had no title of his own, and during this period he occasionally appears as
the son of the duke of Normandy and count of Anjou.[144] Just as the designation *filius Matildis* made an indirect claim before 1144 to Henry's rights in
England and Normandy, his identification with his father, who was duke of
Normandy after 1144, asserted his right to succeed Geoffrey as *dux Normannorum*. Moreover, in the English charters in which Henry appears as *ducis
Normannorum et comitis Andegavorum filius*, he is generally granting something
pro animabus regis Henrici avi mei et Matildis regine avie mee (for the souls of
King Henry, my grandfather, and Queen Matilda, my grandmother).[145]
This formulation links Henry as much to his maternal grandparents as to his
father, and it acts as a reminder that Henry II's hereditary right to England
was derived not only from his Norman grandfather, King Henry I, but also
from his Anglo-Saxon grandmother, Queen Edith-Matilda.

It should come as no surprise that Henry II wished to be identified as the
son of Matilda and the grandson of Henry I and Edith-Matilda: all of his
rights in England and Normandy depended on it, and Henry had spent the
first twenty years of his life immersed in a battle over his place as the *rectus
heres* (rightful heir) in the Anglo-Norman succession. Henry could never
have forgotten that the barons and the clergy had interfered in the succession in 1135, and his actions indicate that he felt the need to put the supremacy of hereditary succession beyond doubt for the rest of his life. His
decisions to have the barons swear oaths to his sons in 1154, to provide a
clear dynastic succession in 1169, and to associate the Young King Henry in
the rule of England by having him crowned in 1170 and 1172, all indicate
that Henry was still convinced that the principle had to be fostered to ensure
that another dispute would not break out upon his own death. A dynastic
history of Henry's maternal ancestors could provide a clear genealogical map
of his lineage, as well as cautionary examples of the dangers of baronial and

---

143. *RRAN*, III, nos. 18, 304, 320, and 735.

144. *RRAN*, III, nos. 111, 420, 666, 704, and 795.

145. This is the case in *RRAN*, III, nos. 420, 666, 704, and 795. In *RRAN*, III, n. 111, Henry appears with his mother confirming the lands of Humphrey de Bohun as he held them on the day on
which Henry I was alive and dead. The formula used is *Matildis imperatrix Henrici regis filia et Anglorum domina et Henricus filius comitis Andegavorum*. Although Henry appears in this charter as the son
of the count of Anjou, he is expressly linked to both his mother and Henry I in it.

clerical meddling in the succession. It could once again reiterate the legitimate and hereditary source of his authority, should anyone have any lingering reservations. Most important, a history of the Anglo-Norman dynasty could offer Henry the chance to control the representation of his ancestors, mythologize the reign of his grandfather, and cast himself as Henry I's heir in both blood and deed.

CHAPTER 3

The *Roman de Rou*

Around 1160, Henry II commissioned Wace, a *clerc lisant* born on the Norman island of Jersey and living in the Bessin, to produce the first vernacular history of his maternal ancestors, the Norman dukes and kings of England.[1] Wace had recently finished another vernacular history, the *Roman de Brut*. Based on Geoffrey of Monmouth's *Historia regum Brittaniae*, the *Brut* recounted the history of the Britons from their Trojan founder, Brutus, to the death of King Cadwallader.[2] To judge by the number of extant manuscripts, the *Brut* had enjoyed a success akin to that of a contemporary best seller and had made Wace's reputation as a historian.[3]

---

1. Wace began writing the *Roman de Rou* in 1160. "Mil chent et soisante anz out de temps et d'espace / puiz que Dex en la Virge descendi par sa grace, / quant un clerc de Caen, qui ont non Mestre Vace, / s'entremist de l'estoire de Rou et de s'estrasce." Wace, *RR*, I, vv. 1–4. Wace, *The Roman de Rou*, trans. Glyn S. Burgess with the text of Anthony J. Holden and notes by Glyn S. Burgess and Elizabeth M. C. van Houts (Isle of Jersey, 2002); and Wace, *Le Roman de Rou de Wace*, ed. Anthony J. Holden, 3 vols. (Paris, 1970–73).

2. Wace, *Le Roman de Brut*, ed. Le Roux Lincy, 2 vols. (Rouen, 1836–38); Wace, *Le Roman de Brut*, ed. Ivor Arnold, 2 vols. (Paris, 1938 and 1940); and *Wace's Roman de Brut, A History of the British People: Text and Translation*, ed. and trans. Judith Weiss (Exeter, 1999).

3. The complete or nearly complete text of the *Roman de Brut* survives in nineteen manuscripts. An additional twelve manuscripts contain fragments of the text. For the most recent list of surviving manuscripts, see Weiss, *Wace's Roman de Brut*, xxvii–xxix.

According to the English poet Layamon, who translated the *Brut* into Middle English in the thirteenth century, Wace dedicated this work to Queen Eleanor after its completion in 1155.[4] Wace's dedication of the *Brut* to Eleanor was likely intended to make a favorable impression on the new king and queen and to elicit future royal patronage. It appears that Wace's gesture was well aimed, as he was repaid a few years later with a royal commission for the *Roman de Rou*.[5]

In modern editions, the *Roman de Rou* is divided into three main parts and an appendix that contains what was apparently a false start. Part I, also known as the *Chronique Ascendante*, is a 315-line poem composed in twelve-syllable *laisses*, which briefly sets out the history of the Norman dukes and kings of England in ascending order, beginning with Henry II and ending with the dynasty's founder, Rollo (rendered in Old French as Rou).[6] It functions both as a summary of the history that follows and as a plea for largesse directed to Henry II.[7] Wace appears to have written the *Chronique Ascendante* after 1174; it contains references to the Great War of 1173/74 and the 1174 siege of Rouen, and is rife with denunciations of the French who had supported Henry II's sons in their recent rebellion against their father.[8]

---

4. Layamon, *Brut*, ed. G. L. Brook and R. F. Leslie, 2 vols. (London, 1963 and 1978), I:20–23. Wace tells us that he completed the *Brut* in 1155. Wace, *Roman de Brut*, II, vv.14864–65.

5. Wace's *Roman de Rou* and Benoît de Sainte-Maure's *Chronique des ducs de Normandie* were the only vernacular works directly commissioned by Henry II. See Broadhurst, "Henry II of England and Eleanor of Aquitaine," 53–84.

6. A *laisse* is a stanza of variable length in which lines are grouped together on the basis of a single assonance. *The Roman de Rou*, trans. Burgess, xxiv, n. 29. There is some debate over whether Wace was the author of the *Chronique Ascendante*. Reto Bezzola has suggested that it is the work of a second author who was working from a lost dedication copy of the *Roman de Rou*. Bezzola, *Les Origines et la formation de la littérature courtoise*, 3:178. Anthony Holden counters these arguments in "L'Authenticité des premières parties du *Roman de Rou*," *Romania* 75 (1954): 22–53. See also Philippe Auguste Becker, "Die Normannenchroniken: Wace und seine Bearbeiter," *Zeitschrift für romanische Philologie* 63 (1943): 481–519, and "Der gepaarter Achtsilber in der französischen Dichtung," in *Abhandlungen der philologisch-historischen Klasse der Sächsischen Akademie der Wissenschafte*, 43, 1 (Leipzig, 1934).

7. Wace complains that "largesse has now succumbed to avarice; it cannot open its hands, they are more frozen than ice" [mez avarice a frait a largesce sa grace, / ne peut lez mainz ouvrir, plus sont gelez que glace]. Wace, *RR*, I, vv. 9–10. He goes on to say that although Henry and Eleanor have rewarded him with gifts and promises, need "often presents itself and often forces me to make pledges in order to obtain money" [Ne me font mie rendre a la court le musage, / de dons et de pramesses chascun d'euls m'asouage; / mez besoing vient sovent qui tost sigle et tost nage, / et souvent me fait meitre le denier et le gage]. Wace, *RR*, I, vv. 20–23.

8. In fact, Wace asserts that the French and their treachery had been the real cause of the Great War, effectively excusing both Henry's sons and his barons for their roles in the rebellion: "Se lez Franceiz pooient lor pensez achever, / ja li roiz d'Engleterre n'avrait rienz decha mer, / a honte l'en feroient, s'il pooient, passer. / Au siege de Roem le cuiderent gaber; / s'il le peüssent prendre ou par

Parts II and III contain the history proper and were composed between 1160 and 1174. Part II traces the history of the Normans from Rollo to the beginning of Duke Richard I's reign in 4,425 twelve-syllable lines known as Alexandrines. Part III continues the history from Richard I's marriage to Gunnor to the 1106 battle of Tinchebray, but it abandons the rhyme scheme of parts I and II in favor of octosyllabic rhyming couplets. My attention will be focused on part III, which is by far the longest portion of the poem (consisting of 11,440 lines) and which circulated independently of parts I and II.[9] The earliest extant manuscripts of the *Roman de Rou* contain part III only, and it is in this section that Wace displays the most originality.[10]

Like Wace's earlier history, the *Roman de Rou* is an adaptation of a Latin source, or, in this case, sources. Wace relied on Orderic Vitalis's redaction of William of Jumièges's *Gesta Normannorum ducum*, along with Orderic's own original work, the *Historia Ecclesiastica*.[11] He also drew on Dudo of Saint-Quentin's *De moribus et actis primorum normanniae ducum*, William of Poitiers's *Gesta Guillelmi Ducis Normannorum et Regis Anglorum*, and William of Malmesbury's *Gesta regum Anglorum*, among others.[12] But Wace was no mere translator

---

force enz entrer / tout temps mez li feïssent par eschar reprover, / mez quant Henri y vint n'i ouserent ester / ne il n'i peüssent mie asseür sejorner. / Par nostre novel roi, qui roi ne peut regner, / cuiderent Normendie toute prendre ou gaster; / lez fiz mesconseillierent por le pere encombrer." Wace, *RR*, I, vv. 59–69.

9. Of the five surviving manuscripts containing the *Roman de Rou*, three contain only part III (BL, Royal 4.C.XI; BnF, fr. 375; and BnF, nouv. aq. 718) and one contains only the first forty-four lines of part III (BL, Royal 13.A.XVIII). The only manuscript containing the complete text of the poem is a seventeenth-century copy of a lost exemplar made by André Duchesne (BnF, Duchesne 79) from which three further copies were made. Duchesne's copy also contains a 750-line poem that appears to have been a false start to part II; it appears as the appendix in both Holden's edition of the *Roman de Rou* and in Glyn Burgess's English translation of the text. Finally, the rhyme scheme of the first two-thirds of the poem was already old fashioned by the time Wace stopped writing around 1174, and this may partially account for the fact that part III circulated independently of parts I and II.

10. All references to the *Roman de Rou* are to part III unless otherwise noted.

11. *The Gesta Normannorum ducum of William of Jumièges, Orderic Vitalis and Robert of Torigni*, ed. and trans. Elisabeth M. C. van Houts, 2 vols. (Oxford, 1992–95); and Orderic Vitalis, *The Ecclesiastical History of Orderic Vitalis*, ed. and trans. Marjorie Chibnall, 6 vols. (Oxford, 1969–80). Wace relied primarily on Orderic's E redaction of the *Gesta Normannorum ducum* and also used four anecdotes from the anonymous B redaction. See van Houts, "Adaptation of the *Gesta Normannorum ducum* by Wace and Benoît," 115–24; and van Houts, "Wace as Historian," in Elisabeth M. C. van Houts, *History and Family Traditions in England and the Continent,* 103–32, at 106, n. 20.

12. Dudo of Saint-Quentin, *De moribus et actis primorum Normanniae ducum auctore Dudone sancti Quintini decano; Dudo of St Quentin: History of the Normans*; William of Poitiers, *Gesta Guillelmi*; William of Malmesbury, *De Gestis Regum Anglorum Willelmi Malmesbiriensis Monachi*, ed. William Stubbs, 2 vols. (London, 1889); and *William of Malmesbury, Gesta regum Anglorum: The History of the English Kings*, ed. and trans. R. A. B. Mynors, completed by R. M. Thomson and M. Winterbot-

of Latin histories for a vernacular audience. On the contrary, he navigated a myriad of sources, using or discarding material as he went, judging the veracity and quality of his sources, and augmenting his written sources with oral testimony and his own memories as his narrative approached his own time.[13] Wace's penchant for departing from his authorities and carrying out his own historical inquiries did not necessarily endear him to his patron though; it almost certainly cost him Henry's support. Wace worked for nearly fifteen years on the *Roman de Rou*, but in its final lines he tersely informs his reader that the project has been transferred to another author associated with Henry's court, Benoît de Sainte-Maure.[14]

Wace's abrupt termination of the *Roman de Rou* and his obvious bitterness over the rescission of his commission beg his reader to investigate the cause(s) of Henry's displeasure. Of course, in order to determine why Henry rejected the *Rou*, we must also speculate on his desires for the project. Although Henry left no document detailing his wishes, we are fortunate to have Benoît de Sainte-Maure's version of Norman history with which to compare the *Rou*. Both Wace's *Roman de Rou* and Benoît de Sainte-Maure's *Chronique des ducs de Normandie* were commissioned by Henry II, and both recount Norman history.[15] The most important difference between the two texts is that Henry II apparently disapproved of the *Rou* and hired Benoît to replace it. By reading the *Roman de Rou* and the *Chronique des ducs de Normandie* together, and attending carefully to Benoît's rewriting of Norman history, we can reach some conclusions as to what Henry expected from a history of his dynasty.

Benoît's work will be addressed in the next chapter. This chapter will examine some of the more peculiar aspects of Wace's representation of Norman history and attempt to determine why Wace lost the king's sup-

---

tom, 2 vols. (Oxford, 1998–99). For a comprehensive description of Wace's sources see Burgess, *Roman de Rou*, xxx–xxxiv.

13. van Houts, "Wace as Historian," 115.

14. "Die en avant qui dire en deit; / j'ai dit por Maistre Beneeit, / qui cest' ovre a dire a emprise / com li reis l'a desor lui mise; / quant li reis li a rové faire / laissier la dei, si m'en dei taire. / Li reis jadis maint bien me fist, / mult me dona, plus me pramist, / e se il tot donee m'eüst / ço qu'il me pramist, mielz me fust; / nel poi aveir, ne plout al rei, / mais n'est mie remés en mei. / Treis reis Henris ai coneüz, / en Normendie toz veüz; / d'Engletere e de Normendie / orent tuit trei la seignorie. / Li segont Henri que jo di / fu niés al premerain Henri, / né de Mahelt, l'empereiz, / e li tierz fu al segont fils. / Ci faut le livre Maistre Wace; / quin velt avant faire sin face." Wace, *RR*, vv. 11419–40.

15. Benoît de Sainte-Maure, *Chronique des ducs de Normandie, publiee d'après le manuscrit de Tours*, and Benoît de Sainte-Maure, *Chronique des ducs de Normandie, par Benoit, trouvére anglo-normand du XIIe siècle*.

port. In order to approach even these most basic questions, it is necessary to have some assumptions derived from a comparison of the two works already in place. I propose that Henry's most fundamental desire in patronizing a vernacular history of his ancestors was to aggrandize his dynasty and to commemorate his legitimate descent from the Norman and Anglo-Saxon royal houses, thereby reiterating his hereditary right to rule England and Normandy. Henry must have also hoped that this history would assist him in his efforts to enshrine the principle of hereditary right as the sole basis of kingship by vividly illustrating the traditional passage of power from one generation of his lineage to the next. He also may have hoped that a dynastic history would aid him in his efforts to curb baronial power by furnishing him with precedents, either culled or concocted from the examples of his predecessors, for his expansion of royal authority.[16] Admittedly, precedents alone were unlikely to persuade Henry's barons to acquiesce to the erosion of their own power—they were quite capable of formulating their own interpretations of the past and they had far too much at stake in the present to simply bow before precedent. Such material, however, might well prove effective in helping Henry's heirs maintain the centralized authority that he had worked so assiduously to build. At the very least, this history might contribute one more weapon to the arsenal of arguments in favor of vigorous royal government. The next chapter will examine how Benoît de Sainte-Maure's version of Norman history advanced those goals, while this chapter will explore Wace's failures as a royal propagandist.

Although much of the *Rou* presents Norman history in a manner unlikely to have generated controversy, Wace's tendency to depart from his sources as his narrative approached his own time, and to include material that weakened traditional Norman claims to legitimate rule in England, resulted in several episodes found in part III that Henry II would have found objectionable. Indeed, Wace's termination appears to have stemmed from his willingness to question rather than cleave to the Norman historiographical orthodoxy; an inclination that Wace justifies by articulating a desire to construct an accurate account of the past (as I will argue later, Wace's statements attesting to his desire for accuracy often mask other motivations).[17] Although the truth claims of medieval authors are notoriously unreliable

---

16. For a discussion of the political utility of appealing to tradition and historical precedent, see Spiegel, "Political Utility in Medieval Historiography," 314–25.

17. For discussions of Wace's impartiality and desire for accuracy, see Stuip, "La Conquête de l'Angleterre," 123–31; Blacker, *Faces of Time*, 42; Jean Blacker-Knight, "Wace's Craft and His Audience: Historical Truth, Bias, and Patronage in the *Roman de Rou*," *Kentucky Romance Quarterly* 31

indicators of the actual veracity of their narratives, and the *Rou* contains many fictions, Wace's reconstruction of the more recent Norman past is, in fact, remarkably accurate in many respects.[18] The historical accuracy of Wace's work, however, is largely irrelevant, as Henry II appears to have wanted a vernacular history that reproduced the conventional view of the past found in Latin histories of the Normans, not one that sought to "correct" it.

The most notable instances of Wace's deviation from the Norman historiographical orthodoxy are found in his representations of the Norman conquest of England, William the Conqueror's death, Henry I's accession to the English throne, and Henry I's forcible acquisition of Normandy at the expense of his elder brother, Robert Curthose.[19] In each case, Wace presents a contentious event in a manner that questions rather than reinforces Norman claims to legitimacy, thus indirectly undermining Henry II's own legitimacy. Whereas Wace's portrayals of these events are likely to have provoked Henry II's displeasure, his assessment of the characters and relative merits of Robert Curthose and Henry I must have irritated his patron as well, contributing to his dismissal.

The Conquest of England

Wace begins his description of the Norman conquest of England predictably enough with Harold Godwinson's ill-fated trip to Normandy in 1064. But, in reconstructing the events preceding the Conquest, Wace commits a potentially damnable sin: he includes both the Norman and the Anglo-

---

(1984): 355–63, at 356; Burgess, *Roman de Rou*, xxxv–xxxvii; Bennett, "Poetry as History?" 21–39, at 23 and 38; and van Houts, "Wace as Historian," 104–32.

18. On the limitations of medieval authorial claims to veracity, see Ruth Morse, *Truth and Convention in the Middle Ages: Rhetoric, Representation, and Reality* (Cambridge, 1991), chap. 2. For Wace's reliability as a historian and his use of archival sources, oral traditions, and eyewitness testimony, see van Houts, "Wace as Historian," and Françoise Le Saux, *A Companion to Wace* (Cambridge, 2005), part III, esp. 210–12.

19. Jean Blacker-Knight's examination of some of these aspects confirms my own findings: Blacker-Knight, "Wace's Craft and His Audience," 355–63. She has also suggested that Henry II was unhappy with the slow progress Wace was making. Blacker, "'La geste est grande," 387–96. Matthew Bennett has advanced the argument that Wace's list of the ship companions of William the Conqueror, which included ancestors of many of the 1173/74 rebels, must have been an irritant to Henry II in the aftermath of the Great War. Bennett, "Poetry as History," 21–39. Finally, Jean-Guy Gouttebroze has argued that Wace may have angered Henry by sympathizing with Thomas Becket's stance against the king. Gouttebroze, "Pourquoi congédier un historiographe," 289–311.

Saxon versions of events and, in doing so, undermines Norman legitimacy. According to Wace's initial depiction of the event, Harold's purpose in traveling to Normandy was not to confirm William as Edward the Confessor's heir, as the Norman accounts unanimously insist. Rather, Harold's intention was to gain the release of hostages that his father Godwin had been forced to hand over to Edward, and that Edward had then transferred to his cousin Duke William.[20] Wace notes that Edward had long feared Godwin, his own father-in-law and the most powerful of the Anglo-Saxon earls, and with good reason as Godwin had delivered Edward's brother Alfred to a gruesome death in 1036 and often quarreled with Edward himself.[21] Edward had exiled Godwin and his family in 1051 in the wake of a particularly nasty rift, but Godwin returned to England the following year accompanied by armed supporters.[22] An alarmed Edward had then demanded hostages in order to secure peace and Godwin had turned over his son Wulfnoth and his nephew Hakon to appease the king.[23] When Harold asked Edward's permission to retrieve his brother and cousin, Wace says that Edward refused to give it and warned Harold against the trip, cautioning him that he might easily fall prey to William's cunning.[24] Wace follows this rather striking bit of information, given everything he has previously had to say about the great love and trust between Edward and William, with another surprise.[25] Wace declares that he has found this account in writing, but that another

---

20. "Heraut fu bien de son seignor. / qui a feme aveit sa seror. / Quant sis peres fu devïez, / qui del morsel fu estranglez, / en Normendie volt passer / por les hostages delivrer, / donc il aveit mult grant pitié." Wace *RR*, III, vv. 5580–87.

21. "Goïgne fu en Engleterre, / manant d'aveir, riche de terre, / mult se tint orgueillos e fier, / Ewart out sa fille a moillier; / mais Goïgne fu fel e faus, / en la terre fist plusors maus; / Ewart le dota e haï / por son fere que il traï, / e por les Normanz que il diesma / e por maint mal qu'il engigna. / Par paroles que entrels crurent / e par ovres que aparurent, / crut entrels une grant meslee, / ki a peine fu acordee; / Ewart Goïgne mult dota, / de sa terre le congea, / ço jura qu'il n'I remaindreit / ne en son regne ne l'avreit, / se feelté ne li jurout / e s'ostages ne l'en livrout, / que il eüst a remanant / de tenir pais a son vivant. / Goïgne ne l'osa neer; / tant por le rei asseürer, / tant por ses parenz maintenir, / tant por ses homes garantir, / un soen nevo e un soen filz, / qu'il aveit ensenble norriz, / a en hostage al rei bailliez; / e li reis les a enveiez / al duc Guilliame en Normendie / com a celui ou mult se fie." Wace, *RR*, vv. 5413–44.

22. See *The Anglo-Saxon Chronicle: A Revised Translation*, an. 1051 and 1052.

23. Wace does not name the hostages but Eadmer gives both their names and their precise relationship to Godwin. Eadmer of Canterbury, *Historia Novorum,* 6.

24. "Al rei Ewart a pris congié, / e Ewart bien li deveia / e defendi e conjura / qu'en Normendie ne passast / n'al duc Guilliame ne parlast; / tost i porreit estre engigniez / ker li dus ert mult vezïez; / s'il voleit aveir ses hostages / si enveiast altres messages." Wace, *RR*, vv. 5588–96.

25. Wace says that Edward loved William just as much as he would his own brother and child. "Le duc Guillaume ama tant / comme son frere e son enfant." Wace, *RR*, vv. 4751–52.

book says that Edward sent Harold to William to ensure that the kingdom would pass to William after his death.[26] He then claims that he does not know which explanation is correct, but that both can be found in writing.[27]

Wace was clearly aware of the Norman version of events, as his main sources included William of Poitiers's *Gesta Guillelmi*, William of Jumièges's *Gesta Normannorum ducum*, and Orderic Vitalis's *Historia Ecclesiastica*, all of which promote the Norman orthodoxy that Edward expressly sent Harold to confirm William as his heir.[28] Wace, however, chose quite consciously to question the veracity of these sources and to include the Anglo-Saxon interpretation presented by Eadmer of Canterbury.[29] By presenting the Anglo-Saxon account first and then declining to pronounce judgment on the accuracy of either version, Wace undermined the traditional insistence on William's legitimate claim to England as Edward's designated heir.

With Wace unwilling to assert the veracity of one account over another, Harold sets off for Normandy on unknown business.[30] Rather than arriving in Normandy, however, Harold went astray—again Wace pleads ignorance of exactly how this happened—and landed in Ponthieu, where he fell into the hands of the local count. Imprisoned by Count Guy and desperate for assistance, Harold sent a messenger to William asking for his help. According to Wace, William thought that "he could gain some advantage from keeping Harold himself" so he secured his release from the count's prison with threats and promises. William then held Harold in "great honor," giv-

---

26. "Issi l'ai jo trové escrit; / e uns altres livres me dit / que li rei le rova aler, / por le realme asseürer / al duc Guilliame, son cosin, / que il eüst emprés sa fin; / ne sai mie certe achaison, / mais l'un e l'autre escrit trovon." Wace, *RR*, vv. 5597–604.

27. Françoise Le Saux points out that many of Wace's declarations of ignorance are, in fact, crafty refusals to openly take a side on politically charged matters. Le Saux, *Companion to Wace*, 171–72, 208–10, and 220–21. Although they do afford Wace a certain amount of cover, I would emphasize that they also draw our attention to these areas of conflict, and that this may have been precisely what Wace intended. As Le Saux amply demonstrates, Wace often pleads ignorance when omitting, including, or otherwise manipulating material that his audience would recognize as controversial. These claims of ignorance thus serve as markers indicating that Wace is fully aware of the problems surrounding a certain issue, and of the controversy that his representation of an event is likely to provoke. In this case, Wace's declaration that he does not know which written source is correct is likely intended to shield him from recrimination, while at the same time revealing his awareness that this depiction of Harold's trip to Normandy is subversive by Norman standards and potentially incendiary.

28. Poitiers, *GG*, 70–71; Jumièges, *GND*, vii, II:158–61; and Orderic, *HE*, iii, II:134–37.

29. Eadmer, *Historia Novorum*, 6–8. See also Blacker-Knight, "Wace's Craft and His Audience," 357; and Rollo, *Historical Fabrication, Ethnic Fable, and French Romance*, 161.

30. "Que que besoigne qu'il quesist / e que que rien faire volsist, / Heraut a la veie se mist / coment que pois li avenist." Wace, *RR*, vv. 5605–8.

ing him horses and weapons, taking him to tournaments and to fight against the Bretons.[31] During Harold's stay, Wace reports that William convinced him to deliver England to him upon Edward's death and to take his daughter Adele as his wife. William also persuaded Harold to swear an oath to this effect. Wace's account stresses William's duplicity in staging Harold's oath, as well as Harold's fear in pronouncing it. According to Wace, William took Harold to Bayeux where he ordered that any relics that could be found be collected and placed into a tub where they were concealed by a cloth and yet another reliquary was placed on top of them. After Harold had recited the oath "as it was dictated to him" and kissed the reliquary, William drew back the covering on the tub to display the cache of relics hidden below. Wace says that the revelation of the mass of relics on which he had unwittingly sworn caused Harold to be overcome with fear. As Wace gives no explanation for Harold's reaction, we can only infer that his fear was caused either by the knowledge that he had no intention of abiding by his oath (the additional relics made the oath more binding and thus made breaking it more perilous), or by the realization that he should have heeded Edward's prescient warning that William's cunning would be his ruin. After securing Harold's oath, William finally allowed him to depart for England, although apparently still without the hostages whose freedom he had come to secure in the first place.[32]

Wace next moves to Edward's deathbed where Harold has gathered his family and allies around the ailing king. At Harold's command one of the

---

31. "Guilliame tint Heraut maint jor, / si com il dut, a grant enor, / a maint riche torneiement / le fist aler mult noblement, / chevals e armes li dona / e en Bretaigne le mena, / ne sai de veir treis faiz ou quatre, / quant as Bretons se dut combatre. / Entretant a li dus parlé / tant que Heraut li a graé / qu'Engleterre li livrera, / tres que li reis Ewart morra, / e a moillier, s'il velt, prendra / Ele une fille que il a; / ço, se lui plaist, li jurera, / e Guillame le graanta. / Por receivre cest serement / fist assenbler un parlement, / a Baieues, ço solent dire, / fist assenbler un grant concire; / tos les corsainz fist demander / e en un leu toz assenbler, / tote un cove fist emplir, / pois les fist d'un paile covrir, / que Heraut ne sout ne ne vit, / n'il ne li fu mostré ne dit; / desus out mist un filatiere, / tot le meillor qu'il pou eslire / e le plus chier qu'il pout trover, / oil de boef l'ai oï nomer. / Quant Heraut sus sa main tendi / la main trembla, la char fremi; / pois a juré e arami, / si com uns hoem li eschari: / Ele, la fille al duc, prendra / e Engleterre al duc rendra, / de ço li fera son poeir / solonc sa force e son saveir, / emprés la mort Ewart, s'il vit, / si veirement Deus li aït / e li corsaint qui iloc sunt; / plusors dient: 'Que Deus li dont!' / Quant Heraut out les sainz baisiez / e il fu sus levez en piez, / vers la cuve li dus l'atrait / e lez la cuve ester le fait; / de la cuve a le paile osté, / qui tot aveit acoveté, / a Heraut a dedanz mostré / sor quels corsainz il a juré; / Heraut forment s'espoënta / des religues qu'il li mostra. / Quant son eire out apareillié / al duc Guilliame l'a conveié / e de bien faire asez preié, / pois l'a al departir baisié / par nom e fei e d'amisté. / Heraut passa delivrement / en Engleterre salvement." Wace, *RR*, vv. 5665–725.

32. Eadmer notes that Harold took his nephew back to England with him, but Wace drops the subject of the hostages altogether. Eadmer of Canterbury, *Historia Novorum*, 8.

Anglo-Saxon lords begs the dying Edward to ensure the future peace of the kingdom by naming Harold as his successor. Edward replies that they all know he has left the kingdom to his cousin William and that some of the barons gathered around him have already sworn oaths to him.[33] Harold, however, again asks Edward for his assent, which Edward grudgingly gives, along with a prophecy. "Harold, you will have this, but I know that you will die. If I ever truly knew the duke and his barons who are with him and the great forces he can summon, nothing can protect you other than God."[34] Although Wace says that he does not know whether Edward granted the English their way with a willing heart, he glosses the episode by saying "thus he made Harold his heir since he could not have William."[35] Caught between the Anglo-Saxon and Norman versions of events, Wace asserts that Edward revised his wishes for the succession on his deathbed, but advances the Norman contention that Edward had previously named William as his heir and still preferred him. In the end, Wace achieves a compromise by implying that Harold and his supporters bullied the dying Edward into leaving the kingdom to Harold.[36] This compromise, however, hinders Norman claims to legitimacy more than it helps them as the Anglo-Saxons held that deathbed bequests, coerced or not, superseded all other bequests.[37] In the *Roman de Rou* then, Harold is arguably Edward's legitimate heir.

---

33. "'Seignors,' dist il, 'assez savez / e mainte feiz oï avez / que mon regne ai emprés ma vie / doné al duc de Normendie, / e ço que jo li ai doné / li ont alquanz de vos juré.'" Wace, *RR*, vv. 5797–802.

34. "'Heraut,' dist li reis, 'tu l'avras, / mais jo sais bien que tu morras; / se jo onques e duc conui, / e ses barons qui sunt od lui / e la grant gent qu'il poet mander, / rien ne t'en poet, fors Deus, garder.'" Wace, *RR*, vv. 5809–14.

35. "Donc dist Heraut que bien fereit, / deïst li reis ço que il voldreit, / il fereit ço qu'a faire aveit, / Normant ne altre ne cremeit. / Donc se torna li reis, si dist / − ne sai se par bon coer le fist − / 'Ore facent Engleis duc ou rei, / Heraut ou altre, jo l'otrei.' / Issi a fait Heraut son eir / quant Guilliam ne pout aveir; / rei a regne aveir estoveit, / regne sainz rei estre ne deit; / a ses barons a graanté / qu'il en facent lor volenté. / Li reis morut, ne pout remaindre, / mult en orent Engleis a plaindre; / li cors, qui mult fu enorez, / a Westmostier fu enterrez, / mult fu riche sa sepolture / que fait fu e encore dure. / Des que li reis Ewart fu morz, / Heraut, qui ert mananz e forz, / se fist enoindre e coroner, / onques al duc n'en volt parler; / homages prist e feeltez / des plus riches e des ainznez." Wace, *RR*, vv. 5815–40.

36. Wace is using Orderic Vitalis's *Historia Ecclesiastica* as one of his sources here, but the two accounts differ in one important respect. Wace implies that Harold and his supporters bullied Edward, whereas Orderic states that Harold deceived Edward on his deathbed, telling him that William had given him his daughter as his wife and granted England to him as his future son-in-law. Orderic says that although Edward was amazed, he believed Harold's story and gave his approval. Orderic, *HE*, iii, II:137. The scene of Edward's deathbed is not described by Eadmer of Canterbury, William of Poitiers, or William of Jumièges.

37. Even William of Poitiers acknowledges Anglo-Saxon custom on this matter and records Harold's argument that Edward's deathbed bequest superseded his earlier promise to William. It should

Wace presents the reason for Harold's trip to Normandy as a subject that is open to interpretation, but Harold's oath is a slightly different matter. In accordance with the Norman version of the events leading to the Conquest, Wace maintains the validity of Harold's oath, asserting that Harold perjured himself in taking the throne from the man he had sworn to assist in attaining it.[38] Although Wace portrays Harold's oath in a manner that strongly suggests it was coerced, nowhere does he claim that Harold protested that the oath was invalid. Nor does Wace indicate that Harold ever sought to be absolved of the oath until the eve of the battle of Hastings when Harold defiantly asserts that, *if* he took such an oath, it was only to save himself and he will take it upon himself to seek absolution if he has wronged William.[39] Initially, however, Harold almost gleefully repudiates the oath and invites William's vengeance.[40]

It is extremely unlikely that Wace, although a Norman, was unaware that Anglo-Saxon tradition privileged deathbed bequests. After all, even William of Poitiers had rehearsed the Anglo-Saxon contention that Edward's bequest to Harold superseded his promise to William. Wace, however, appears to assert that Harold's oath to William outweighed Edward's deathbed designation of Harold as his heir.[41] Wace's portrayal of Harold's oath indicates

---

be noted, however, that William of Poitiers discounts Harold's argument and immediately follows this information with a vindication of William's rights. Poitiers, *GG*, 118–19. Beckerman points out that while Norman testamentary custom in the mid-eleventh century held that the designation of a successor *inter vivos* was binding and could not be revoked, Anglo-Saxon custom privileged deathbed bequests. John Beckerman, "Succession in Normandy, 1087, and in England, 1066: The Role of Testamentary Custom," *Speculum* 47/2 (1972): 258–60, at 260. See also Michael Sheehan, *The Will in Medieval England: From the Conversion of the Anglo-Saxons to the End of the Thirteenth Century* (Toronto, 1963), 109; *Vita Aedwardi Regis: The Life of King Edward Who Rests at Westminster*, Attributed to a Monk of St. Bertin, ed. and trans. Frank Barlow (London, 1962), 79–80; and Barlow, *Edward the Confessor*, 249.

38. Cf. Poitiers, *GG*, 120–21; Jumièges, *GND*, vii, II:160–61; and Orderic, *HE*, iii, II:134–37.

39. "'Dites al duc que jo li mant / qu'il ne m'apelt de covenant, / ne ne m'apelt de serement / se jo li ai fait folement; / se jo onques rien li pramis / por ma deliverance lifis, / por mei delivrer li jurai, / quantqu'il me quist li otrerai; / ne me deit estre reprové / ker nel fis nïent de mon gré. / La force ert soe, si cremeie, / se sa volenté ne faiseie, / que jo ja mais ne revertisse; / e que toz tens la remainsisse; / e se de rien mesfait li ai / jo maïsmes m'en assoldrai.'" Wace, *RR*, vv. 6815–30.

40. "Guilliame li manda sovent / k'il li tenist son serement, / e Heraut li mandout vilment / qu'il ne fereit por lui nïent, / ne il sa fille ne prendreit / ne il terre ne li rendreit; / e Guilliame le desfia / e desfiance lui manda, / e Heraut toz tens responeit / que nule rien mais nel cremeit." Wace, *RR*, vv. 5925–34.

41. Although Wace never explicitly makes this argument in the *Roman de Rou*, William of Poitiers includes a less ambiguous rebuttal of Harold's claim. In the *Gesta Guillelmi*, William the Conqueror sends a messenger to Harold who reminds him that Edward had named the duke as his heir, that the designation had been approved and oaths had been accordingly sworn by the English magnates and

that it was wildly improper and that Harold could easily have been absolved of it if only he had been sensible about it. We must therefore surmise that it was Harold's arrogant repudiation of the coerced oath that brought about his fall. In Wace's account it is certainly Harold's perjury that causes him to lose the kingdom, just as it is William's complaint of Harold's perjury that wins him papal approval for his invasion of England.[42] Notably, Earl Gyrth's fear of the consequences of Harold's perjury leads him to suggest that his brother avoid the battle and allow him to lead the English in his place.[43]

In spite of Wace's emphasis on Harold's perjury, his depiction of the events preceding the battle of Hastings results in a subtle erosion of Norman claims to legitimate rule in England, which were founded above all on William's lawful and recognized designation as Edward's heir (and were reinforced by William's victory at Hastings).[44] Wace undermines Norman legitimacy first by privileging the Anglo-Saxon contention that Harold went to Normandy to secure the release of hostages, rather than hewing to

---

clergy, and that Edward had provided hostages to William to ensure his succession. He goes on to remind Harold that he is, in fact, the duke's vassal and that he has personally sworn to uphold William's claim to the English throne. William then offers to put his case to the judgment of either the Normans or the English, as Harold prefers. Poitiers, *GG*, 120–22.

42. "Li dus volt mult raisnablement / faire son apareillement. / A l'apostoile fist mander / par clers qui sorent bien parler / comme Heraut l'aveit servi, / serement falsé e menti; / e quant il sa fille ne prent, / ne il le regne ne li rent / que Ewart li aveit doné / e Heraut li aveit juré, / del parjure feïst justise / solonc l'esgart de Sainte Iglise. / E se ço ert que Deus volsist / que il Engletere conquesist, / de saint Pierre la recevreit, / altres fors Deu n'en servireit. / L'apostoile le otreia, / un gonfanon li enveia, / un gonfanon e un anel / mult precios e riche e bel; / si com il dist, desoz la pierre / aveit un des denz saint Pierre. / A cez enseignes li manda / e de par Deu li otreai / que Engletere conquesist / e de saint Pierre la tenist." Wace, *RR*, vv. 6293–318.

43. "'Bel frere,' dist il, 'remanez, / mais voz amisnies me livrez, / en aventure me metrai, / a Guillame me combatrai; / n'ai od lui nule covenance / par serement ne par fiance, / ne jo ne sui od lui par fei / ne jo serement ne li dei. / Tel chose porreit avenir, / n'i estovreit plus colp ferir. / Jo criem, se vos vos combatez, / ad ço que vos vos parjurez, / que del parjure piés vos seit / e que cil venque qui a dreit.'" Wace, *RR*, vv. 6905–18.

44. William of Poitiers offers the most succinct statement of Norman claims to legitimate rule in England in his account of William the Conqueror's consecration. "And his children and grandchildren will rule by lawful succession over the English land, which he possesses both by hereditary designation confirmed by the oath of the English, and by right of conquest. He was crowned by the consent, or rather by the wish, of the leaders of the same people. And if anyone asks the reason for this blood claim, it is well known that he was related to King Edward by close ties of blood, being the son of Duke Robert, whose aunt, Emma, the sister of Richard II and daughter of Richard I, was Edward's mother." ["Cuius liberi atque nepotes iusta successione praesidebunt Anglicae terrae, quam et hereditaria delegatione sacramentis Anglorum firmata, et iure belli ipse possedit: coronatus tali eorundem consensu, uel potius appetitu eiusdem gentis primatum. Et si ratio sanguinis poscitur, pernotum est quam proxima consanguinitate regem Edwardum attigerit filius ducis Rodberti, cuius amita Ricardi secundi soro, filia primi, Emma, genitrix fuit Edwardi."] Poitiers, *GG*, 150–51.

the Norman contention that Edward sent Harold to confirm William as his heir. He follows this by asserting that Edward warned Harold not to go to William because the duke would almost certainly trick him, implying that Edward found his cousin to be less than trustworthy. Having presented the two conflicting accounts, Wace demurs and claims he does not know which is true. Wace then contends that William hoped to gain some advantage from Harold's presence in Normandy and he stresses the manner in which William entertained Harold, outfitting him with weapons and horses and taking him into battle with him as one would one's vassal. The implication is clearly that William wished to bind Harold to him through the ties of lordship, but Wace fails to assert that Harold made a formal submission of fealty to William during his oath swearing. Finally, Wace suggests that William did, in fact, deceive Harold, that he coerced him into swearing a dictated oath over a mass of concealed relics, while his sources aver that Harold's oath had been sworn freely.[45]

The complete absence of any oath of fealty binding Harold to William in the *Roman de Rou* is deeply problematic. Wace's account of Harold's trip to Normandy merely suggests that William was trying to bind Harold to him as his vassal, but Wace's sources unanimously insist that Harold incontrovertibly became William's vassal before usurping England.[46] The oath of fealty made Harold doubly guilty of being the duke's own perjured vassal, paving the way for his richly deserved fall. According to these sources, Harold's crime was not so much that he took the English throne from William, but that in doing so he abjured his oath and rebelled against his lord. The latter was far more reprehensible and was the lynchpin of Norman arguments against Harold's legitimacy. In the *Roman de Rou*, however, Harold is not William's vassal and therefore owes him no special allegiance. As a result, Harold's crime is wholly transformed. Rather than abjuring an oath freely sworn to his lord, Harold renounces a coerced and very inconvenient oath sworn to a person with whom he shares no particular bond and to whom he owes no extraordinary loyalty—such an oath was a relatively

---

45. William of Poitiers specifically insists that Harold's oath was not coerced. "Harold swore fealty to him according to the holy rite of Christians. And, as the most truthful and distinguished men who were there as witnesses have told, at the crucial point in the oath he clearly and of his own free will pronounced these words." ["illic Heraldus ei fidelitatem sancto ritu christianorum iurauit. Et sicut ueracissimi multaque honestate praeclarissimi homines recitauere, qui tunc affuere testes, in serie summa sacramenti libens ipse haec distinxit."] Poitiers, *GG*, 70–71.

46. Ibid. Jumièges, *GND*, vii, II:161; and Orderic, *HE*, iii, II:135.

minor matter and Harold could easily have been absolved of it through ecclesiastical channels. In Wace's account, however, Harold never attempts to
be released from his coerced oath to assist William, and thus leaves himself
open to the charge of perjury.

In Wace's contradictory retelling, the Norman Conquest can be interpreted as the product of William's cunning, rather than the vindication of
William's rights, and the difference is important. (To be sure, neither Harold nor William is portrayed in a particularly flattering light in the *Roman de
Rou*—William's cunning merely triumphs over Harold's arrogance.) Wace
indicates that Harold was Edward's legitimate heir, that William deceived
and coerced Harold in order to gain the English throne, and that Harold
was never William's vassal. Wace's account thus significantly weakens the
traditional Norman insistence on the legitimacy of the Conquest, and
thereby calls into question the legitimacy of Norman rule and Henry II's
own rights in England.

The Death of William the Conqueror

The damage to Norman legitimacy inflicted by Wace's representation of the
Conquest is compounded by Wace's account of William the Conqueror's
death. Ironically, Wace causes further injury to Norman legitimacy in this case
by adhering to Orderic Vitalis's account of William's death and burial.[47] Orderic generally offers a sympathetic portrayal of the Norman dukes, but he
stands out among his peers for condemning William's treatment of the conquered English, for reporting the less savory details of his death, and for vocif-
erously criticizing the Norman character. In Orderic's eyes, the Normans were
warlike and fearless, but prone to interminable civil war, devastating their own
country and persecuting the innocent if left unrestrained.[48] Although Orderic
admired William for his harsh rule and his ability to curb Norman aggression
by forcefully subduing anyone who threatened disorder, he deplored certain
effects of the Conquest and held William accountable for what he considered
to be unconscionable actions, such as the murder of the Anglo-Saxon earl
Waltheof and the brutal suppression of rebellions in the north of England.
Ultimately, Orderic viewed William as a necessary evil, a hard man raised in

---

47. For Wace's reliance on Orderic in this passage see Holden, *Le Roman de Rou de Wace*, III:111. The
passage in Orderic's *Historia Ecclesiastica* that Wace is following occurs in book VII, chaps. 14–16.

48. See Albu, *Normans in Their Histories*.

the midst of violence and therefore capable of restraining the notoriously violent Normans. Above all, Orderic's William is a scourge sent by God to punish the Anglo-Saxons. It is therefore startling that Wace chose to use the *Historia Ecclesiastica* as his primary source for William's death.[49]

Before recounting William's demise, Wace first encapsulates the whole of William's twenty-one year English reign in as many lines, reducing his long rule to a perfunctory account of his gifts to his followers and his decision, in consultation with his English and Norman barons, to uphold the customs and laws of King Edward.[50] With William's English reign neatly dispatched, Wace proceeds to the Conqueror's final illness in 1087. According to Wace, William sensed that his end was approaching and decided to parcel his lands out to his sons to prevent internecine war after his death.[51] After summoning his barons, William confirmed his gift of Normandy (his patrimony) to Robert Curthose, his eldest son.[52] He had granted Normandy to Robert before he conquered England, and now he gave him Le Mans as well. William also gave Robert a warning about the infamous Norman temperament, telling him that the Normans were brave, valiant, and fierce, but naturally undisciplined and prone to giving bad service when left to their own inclinations. Wace repeats Orderic's caveat that the Normans must be constantly restrained by a strong ruler in order to harness their better qualities and keep their vices at bay. He declares that Robert will have his hands full watching over such men.

---

49. William of Malmesbury, Henry of Huntingdon, and the *Anglo-Saxon Chronicle* were also critical of William the Conqueror.

50. Wace, *RR*, vv. 8989–9010. See chapter 2 for a discussion of the importance of constructing a fiction of continuity between Edward the Confessor and William the Conqueror as a means of projecting Norman legitimacy in post-Conquest England.

51. "Sa terre a ses filz a donee, / qu'emprés sa mort ne seit meslee; / toz ses barons a apelez. / 'Oez,' dist il, 'si m'entendez! / Normendie, mon eritage, / ou le plus est de mon lignage, / doins a Robert, mon filz l'ainzné, / e jo li ai posa graé / des anceis que jo fusse reis, / e ore li doins le Mans en creis; / le Mans e Normendie avra, / le rei de France en servira. / En Normendie a gent mult fiere, / jo ne sai gent de tel maniere, / chevaliers sunt proz e vaillant, / par totes terres conquerant. / Se Normant one boen chevetaigne / mult fait a criendre lor compaigne; / se il nen one de seignor crieme, / qui les destreigné e aprieme, / tost en avra malvais servise, / Normant ne sunt proz sainz justise, / foler e plaisier les covient; / se reis soz piez toz tens les tient, / e qui bien les defolt e poigne, / d'els porra faire sa besoigne. / Orgueillos sunt Normant e fier / e vanteor e boubancier, / toz tens les devreit l'en plaisier, / ker mult sunt fort a justisier; / mult a a faire e a penser / Robert, qui deit tel gent garder.'" Wace, *RR*, vv. 9101–32.

52. The duchy was normally transmitted to the duke's eldest son, and oaths of fealty were generally sworn to the heir designate during his father's lifetime. The Norman barons had already sworn fealty to Robert on several occasions by the time the Conqueror died. Cf. Garnett, *Conquered England*, 154–78.

Unlike Orderic or the anonymous author of the *De obitu Willelmi*, who explicitly noted Robert's ineptitude, his estrangement from his father, and his absence from William's deathbed as the underlying reasons for William's decision to leave England to his second son, Wace says nothing about the family tensions.[53] Wace never even alludes to Robert's recent rebellion

---

53. Orderic's account of William's death begins at the end of book VII, chapter 14 of the *Historia Ecclesiastica* and continues through chapter 16. Orderic notes that William the Conqueror called his sons William Rufus and Henry to his deathbed, but his son Robert was conspicuously absent. "His son Robert, who was the eldest, had often quarreled with his father and again quite recently taking offense for some trivial cause, had gone off to the king of France." [Rodbertus enim filius eius qui maior natu erat, multotiens olim contra patrem suum litigauerat, et tunc nouiter pro quibusdam ineptiis similiter stomachatus ad regem Francorum discesserat.] Orderic, *HE*, vii, IV:80–81. Orderic also implies that William would have disinherited Robert if it were possible. "'I invested my son Robert with the duchy of Normandy before I fought against Harold on the heath of Senlac; because he is my first-born son and has received the homage of almost all the barons of the country the honor then granted cannot be taken from him. Yet I know for certain that any province subjected to his rule will be most wretched. He is a proud and foolish fellow, doomed to suffer prolonged and grim misfortune.'" ["Ducatum Normanniae antequam in epitimio Senlac contra Heraldum certassem Rodberto filio meo concessi cui quia primogenitus est et hominum pene omnium huius patriae baronum iam recepit concessus honor nequit abstrahi. Sed indubitantur scio quod uere misera erit regio quae subiecta fuerit eius domino. Superbus enim est et insipiens nebulo trucique diu plectendus infortunio."] Orderic, *HE*, vii, IV:92–93. The *De obitu Willelmi* is appended to book VII in the B redaction of the *GND*. It also suggests that William wanted to dispossess Robert entirely, but could not legally do so. "He allowed his son William to have the crown, the sword, and the golden sceptre with inlaid jewels. Whereupon the venerable Bishop William and the others who were present feared that he would remain implacable towards his eldest son Robert, knowing that a wound frequently cut or cauterized causes sharper pain to the wounded. They relied therefore on the invincible patience, which he always displayed, and sought gently to make him change his mind by way of Archbishop William, whose words he never spurned. At first the king showed some bitterness, but after pondering for a little while, pulling together what strength was left in him, he seemed to consider how many serious injuries Robert had inflicted upon him, and he said: 'Because he does not want to come or he spurns to come in order to apologize, I shall do what I think is correct. With you and God as my witnesses I forgive him all the sins he has committed against me, and I grant him all the duchy of Normandy,' (which by the testimony of God and all the magnates of the palace he had previously entrusted to him). 'You, however, will have to warn him, that, even though I have forgiven him his sins many times, he should not forget that he led his father's grey hairs in sorrow to the grave, and in doing so disregarded the commands and the warnings of our God the Father.'" ["Et Willelmo quidem suo filio coronam, ensem, sceptrum auro gemmique redimitum hadendum permisit. Inter hec tam uenerabilis antistes Willelmus quam ceteri qui aderant, uerebantur ne forte suo filio primogenito Roberto implacabilis esse uellet, scientes quod uulnus frequenter inscisum aut cautherio adustum acerbiorem sustinenti propagaret dolorem; fisi tamen de eius inuicta paciencia, qua semper usus est, per archiepiscopum Willelmum, cuius uerba spernere nolebat, animum illius leniter pulsant. Qui primum quidem amaritudinem sui monstrauit animi. At uero parumper deliberans et uiribus quantuliscumque collectis, enumerare uidebatur quot et quantis ab eo afflictus sit incomodis, dicens: 'Quia ipse,' inquit, 'uenire satisfacturus non uult aut dedignatur, ego quod meum est, ago: uobis testibus et Deo, omnia que in me peccauit, illi remitto, et omnen ducatum Nomannie sibi concedo,' (quem Deo teste et proceribus palacii illi iamdudum ante largitus fuerat). 'Vestrum autem erit illum monere, ut, si ego illi tociens prepere gesta indulsi, ille tamen sui non obliuiscatur, qui canos paternos deducit cum dolore ad mortem, et in talibus communis patris Dei precepta minasque contempsit.'"] *GND*, vii, II:186–89.

against his father, or to the possibility that William wanted to disinherit Robert. Instead, Wace transforms Orderic's biting critique of innate Norman ferocity into an explanation for William the Conqueror leaving England (territory which he had acquired through conquest and could therefore dispose of separately) to his second son, William Rufus. Wace implies that, since Robert will be completely occupied with curbing the famously volatile Normans, he would be unable to effectively rule England as well. By consciously obscuring the fact that Robert was in open rebellion against his father at the time of his death and that William would have disinherited Robert entirely if he could have, Wace relieves Robert from any responsibility for having lost his father's confidence, and thus for having lost England to his younger brother. Although Wace appears to be largely impartial in his account of Norman history, when he does reveal a prejudice it is generally in Robert Curthose's favor. Wace generally neglects to include any material from Orderic that impugns Robert (of which there is a great deal), or that supports Henry too enthusiastically. This favoritism becomes more pronounced as Wace's narrative reaches its conclusion and surely would have rankled Henry II.

Wace next moves to William the Conqueror's desire to leave England to William Rufus.[54] William declares that he would like to advance the cause of his second son, who desires England for himself and would like to be its king, but William refrains from leaving him the kingdom. Loosely following Orderic, Wace has William observe that he cannot name his heir to England because "I conquered England wrongfully and many men were killed there wrongfully; I killed their heirs wrongfully and took over the kingdom wrongfully. What I stole wrongfully and had no right to I ought not give to my son, neither should I endow him with it wrongfully."[55] Instead of naming Rufus as his heir, William decides to send him to Archbishop Lanfranc. If it is within the archbishop's power to grant Rufus the crown, then William begs that he should do so.[56]

---

54. "Guilleme, qui ci est, mis filz, / qui mult est nobles e gentilz, / voldreie jo mult avancier / se Deus le voleit otreier; / Engletere a son oés coveit, / qu'il en fust reis, s'estre poeit, / mais jo nel pois faire par mei, / raisnablement savez por quei. / Engleterre conquis a tort, / a tort i out maint home mort, / les eirs en ai a tort ocis / e a tort ai le regne pris; / e ço que j'ai a tort toleit, / ou jo nen aveie nul dreit, / ne dei mie a mon filz doner / ne a tort nel dei eriter. / Mais ultre mer l'enveierai, / a l'archevesque preierai / que la corone li otreit / se il le poet faire par dreit; / s'il le poet faire par raison / jo prié qu'il l'en face de don." Wace, *RR*, vv. 9133–54.

55. Wace, *RR*, vv. 9141–48.

56. Orderic offers a slightly different version of this. "The king, fearing that rebellion might break out in a realm as far-flung as his, had a letter to secure the recognition of the new king addressed to

Wace's insistence here that William does not have the right to leave England to anyone is derived from Orderic's deathbed speech for William, but Wace pushes Orderic's criticism of William's rule to the conclusion that William's rule was illicit, rather than merely unjust and unnecessarily cruel. Although Orderic has William list a multitude of sins he committed in conquering England and state that he dare not transmit the kingdom that he won with so many sins for fear that his evil deeds should become the cause of even worse things, nowhere does he say that William wrongfully stole a kingdom to which he had no right.[57] Orderic adheres to the Norman contention that William, Edward's rightful and designated heir, took England from his perjured vassal Harold, albeit with terrible bloodshed and the loss of much innocent life. This, however, is a far cry from charging William

---

Archbishop Lanfranc and sealed with his seal. Giving it to his son William Rufus, he ordered him to cross to England without delay. Then he gave him his blessing with a kiss, and sent him post-haste overseas to receive the crown." ["Metuens rex ne in regno tam diffuso repentina orireture turbatio, epistolam de constituendo rege fecit Lanfranco archiepiscopo , suoque sigillo signatum tradidit Guillelmo Rufo filio suo iubens ut in Angliam transfretaret continuo. Deinde osculatus eum benedixit, et trans pontum ad suscipiendum diadema properantur direxit."] Orderic, *HE*, vii, IV:96–97.

57. "'I name no man as my heir to the kingdom of England; instead I entrust it to the eternal Creator to whom I belong and in whose hand are all things. For I did not come to possess such a dignity by hereditary right, but wrested the kingdom from the perjured king Harold with bitter strife and terrible bloodshed, and subjected it to my rule after killing or driving into exile all his partisans. I treated the native inhabitants of the kingdom with unreasonable severity, cruelly oppressed high and low, unjustly disinherited many, and caused the death of thousands by starvation and war, especially in Yorkshire. . . . In mad fury I descended on the English of the north like a raging lion, and ordered that their homes and crops with all their equipment and furnishings should be burnt at once and their great flocks and herds of sheep and cattle slaughtered everywhere. So I chastised a great multitude of men and women with the lash of starvation and alas was the cruel murderer of many thousands, both young and old, of this fair people. I dare not transmit the government of this kingdom, won with so many sins, to any man, but entrust it to God alone, for fear that after my death my evil deeds should become the cause of even worse things. I hope that my son William, who has always been loyal to me from his earliest years and has gladly obeyed me in every way he could, may long prosper in the Lord, enjoy good fortune, and bring lustre to the kingdom if such is the divine will.'" ["Neminem Anglici regni heredem constituo sed aeterno conditori cuius sum et in cuius manu sunt omnia illud commendo. Non enim tantum decus hereditario iure possedi sed diro conflictu et multa effusione humani cruoris periuro regi Heraldo abstuli, et interfectis uel effugatis fauctoribus eius dominatui meo subegi. Naturales regni filios plus aequo exosos habui, nobiles et uulgares crudeliter uexaui, iniuste multos exheredituai, innumeros manime in pago Eborachensi fame seu ferro mortificaui. . . . Vnde immoderato furore commotus in boreales Anglos ut uesanus leo properaui domos eorum iussi segetesque et omnem apparatum atque supellectilem confestim incendi, et copiosos armentorum pecudumque greges passim mactari. Multitudinem itaque utriusque sexes tam dirae famis mucrone multaui et sic multa milia pulcherimae gentis senum iuuenumque proh dolor funestus trucidaui. Fasces igitur huius regni quod cum tot peccatis optinui, nulli audeo tradere nisi Deo soli, ne post funus meum adhuc deteriora fiant occasione mei. Guillelmum filium meum qui michi a primis annis semper inhesit, et michi pro posse suo per omnia libenter obediuit opto in spiritu Dei diu ualere, et in regni solio si diuina uoluntas est feliciter fulgere."] Ibid., 92–95.

with stealing the kingdom. Orderic enumerates the sins for which William must atone, his destruction of the innocent and his overly harsh rule, but Orderic accepts that William's rule was legitimate. Wace, on the other hand, transforms Orderic's condemnation of William's reign into a condemnation of Norman rule in general.

Wace was on very dangerous ground here, and his assault on the very foundation of Norman claims to legitimate rule in England can only have incensed Henry II. Orderic's obvious sympathy for the conquered English may have been irritating to some Norman readers, but he at least never wavered in his belief that the conquest of England was divinely ordained and that William was well within his rights in taking England from the perjured Harold. That Orderic came to view William as a scourge sent to punish the English is another matter entirely. Orderic still believed that God had placed William over the English, for good or ill, and there was no arguing with divine providence. Orderic is able at once to accuse William of unspeakable atrocities and to defend his rule because he sees the hand of the Creator in William's conquest. Wace, on the other hand, places far less emphasis on the Conquest as a divinely sanctioned trial by battle. Although he does include elements that mark the Conquest as a trial by battle, such as William's receipt of papal approval for his actions, the pious preparations for battle made by the Normans, and Harold's blinding at Hastings, Wace only perfunctorily attributes the battle's outcome to God's favor.[58] His true interest lies in describing the prowess of the combatants and their military exploits at the battle of Hastings, not in discerning the hand of God in the battle's outcome. In fact, Wace appears to intentionally distort Orderic's assessment of William. Orderic does not assert that William stole a kingdom to which he had no legal or hereditary right, but that he proved to be an unworthy steward of the kingdom God had given him.

As for the transmission of the kingdom, Wace again appears to willfully alter Orderic's argument. By asserting that William became king through conquest rather than by hereditary right, Orderic was actually making a distinction between Normandy as William's patrimony (*propre*) and England as William's conquest (*conquêt* or *acquêt*).[59] The two had to be legally distinct

58. Wace, *RR*, vv. 6293–331, 7095–103, 7335–90, and 7777–80. Wace includes Harold's blinding, but does not explicitly interpret it as divine punishment for his perjury. Wace, *RR*, vv. 8161–74. See also Dorothy Bernstein, "The Blinding of Harold and the Meaning of the Bayeux Tapestry," *ANS* 5 (1982): 40–64, at 47.

59. Although John Le Patourel denied the existence of a legal distinction between *conquêt/acquêt* and *propre* in eleventh-century Normandy, more recent research has revised his assessment. Emily

in order for William to transmit them separately. Orderic was not contending that William had no hereditary claim to England, only that England was not part of his patrimony.[60] When Wace has William declare that "what I stole wrongfully and had no right to I ought not to give to my son" he transforms Orderic's argument for the legality of the separate transmission of England and Normandy into an outright denial of any legitimate Norman right to England. Furthermore, Orderic says only that William "dare not" transmit the kingdom to anyone, not that he "cannot" or has no right to do so, as Wace claims.[61] Orderic's William will not name anyone as his heir to England in acknowledgement of his sins, but Wace's William quite literally says that he is powerless to transmit the kingdom and that "you know the reason why."[62] As if it were not enough that Wace accuses William of stealing a kingdom

---

Tabuteau argues that by the time of the Conquest the rule was already emerging that lands or goods acquired by conquest or purchase were distinct from, and therefore more freely alienable, than those inherited as part of one's patrimony. She details numerous instances of Norman nobles who participated in the Conquest leaving their Norman lands (patrimonies) to their eldest sons and their English lands (conquests) to their second sons, alienating conquests through gifts to churches, or otherwise disposing of conquests separately from their patrimonies. She also notes that most of the charters already employ the term *adquirere* (rather than *conquirere*) in distinguishing between conquests and patrimonies. Emily Tabuteau, *Transfers of Property in Eleventh-Century Norman Law* (Chapel Hill, 1988), 34, 101–12, 177–78, and 225. Cf. John Le Patourel, "The Norman Succession, *1066–1144*," *EHR* 86 (1971): 225–50, at 227; John Le Patourel, *Norman Barons* (1066 Commemoration Series of the Hastings and Bexhill Branch of the Historical Association, 4, 1966), 25–26; John Le Patourel, *The Norman Empire* (Oxford, 1976), 183, n. 1; Robert Génestal, "La formation du droit d'aînesse dans la coutume de Normandie," in *Travaux de la Semaine d'histoire du droit normand tenue a Guernesey* (Caen, 1928), 221–40, at 168; Jean Yver, "Les caractères origineaux du groupe de coutumes de l'Ouest de la France," *Revue historique de droit français et étranger* 4/24 (1952): 18–79, at 58–62; James Holt, "Feudal Society and the Family in Early Medieval England: I. The Revolution of 1066," *TRHS* 5/32 (1982): 193–212, at 198–99 and 204–5; and James Holt, "Feudal Society and the Family in Early Medieval England: II. Notions of Patrimony," *TRHS* 5/33 (1983): 193–220, at 213.

60. Preceding his account of the Conquest, Orderic notes: "Indeed, Edward king of England, son of King Ethelred by Emma, daughter of Richard the elder, duke of Normandy, had died shortly before; and Harold, son of Earl Godwin, had usurped the kingdom of England. . . . The truth was that Edward had declared his intention of transmitting the whole kingdom of England to his kinsman William duke of Normandy, first through Robert archbishop of Canterbury and afterwards through the same Harold, and had with the consent of the English made him heir to all his rights." [Eduardus enim rex Anglorum Edelredi regis ex Emma Ricardi senioris Normannorum ducis filia filius paulo ante obierat, et Haroldus Goduini comitis filius regnum Anglorum usurpauerat. . . . Eduardus nimirum propinquo suo Willelmo duci Normannorum primo per Rodbertum Cantuariorum summum pontificem postea per eundem Heraldun interam Anglici regni mandauerat concessionem, ipsumque concedentibus Anglis fecerat totius iuris sui haeredem."] Orderic, *HE*, iii, II:135.

61. To my knowledge Wace is alone in claiming that William has no right to name his heir to England.

62. "Raisnablement savez por quei." Wace, *RR*, v. 9140.

to which he had no right, he then implies that the barons and clergy assembled around William's deathbed, as well as Wace's own audience, know this to be true.

Wace's contention that William wrongfully killed the English heirs and illicitly took their kingdom must also have provoked a certain measure of Henry II's ire as it further undermined Norman claims to legitimacy. It matters very little that both Wace and Orderic were essentially correct in their assessments of William's destruction, dispossession, and exile of the Anglo-Saxon nobility.[63] The Norman orthodoxy presented most succinctly by William of Poitiers insisted that William not only showed clemency to the conquered English and treated them with generosity but that "nothing was given to any Frenchman which had been taken unjustly from any Englishman."[64] The charge of dispossessing rightful heirs must have been particularly repugnant to Henry II on a more personal level as well, since he had spent his own youth as the dispossessed but rightful heir to England and Normandy. Henry's obsession with the overriding importance of hereditary rights is evident in his lifelong reluctance to dispossess even vassals who made war against him, as well as in two of his most important legal innovations: *novel disseisin* and *mort d'ancestor*. The former treated unjust dispossessions (those made without a legal judgment) as breaches of the king's peace and subjected the lawbreaker to a formal inquiry (the *assize of novel disseisin*), while the latter applied hereditary right

---

63. William's dispossession and exile of the Anglo-Saxon nobility was, indeed, catastrophic. The greatest of the Anglo-Saxon earls were quickly supplanted by William's relatives and supporters: Harold died at Hastings, along with his brothers Gyrth and Leofwine, Oswulf died in 1067, Cospatric transferred his allegiance to King Malcolm of Scotland in 1068, Edwin and Morcar were dispossessed in 1069, and Waltheof, the last Anglo-Saxon earl, was dispossessed and murdered in 1075. Many Anglo-Saxon thegns and their heirs died at Fulford, Stamford Bridge, and Hastings, and many of those who survived the Conquest lost their lives in rebellions between 1068 and 1071. Those remaining Anglo-Saxon nobles who had not forfeited their land through rebellion, seen their heirs slain, taken refuge in Scotland, or gone into exile elsewhere did retain possession of their lands. Their status, however, was greatly diminished and it appears that a significant number of their daughters were married to Norman noblemen who then inherited the estates of their fathers-in-law, often by excluding legitimate Anglo-Saxon male heirs. As a result, very few Anglo-Saxon names appear in Domesday Book in 1086 and it has been estimated that only 8 percent of English land was still in Anglo-Saxon hands by the time of William's death in 1087. The condition of the remaining Anglo-Saxon nobles did not substantially improve until Henry I's reign, more than thirty years after the Conquest. For the impact of the Conquest on the Anglo-Saxon nobility, see Frank Stenton, "English Families and the Norman Conquest," *TRHS* 4/26 (1944): 1–12.

64. "Nulli tamen Gallo datum est quod Anglo cuiquam iniuste fuerit ablatum." Poitiers, *GG*, 162–65.

to the transmission of fiefs.[65] Orderic stands out among the major Norman historians in charging William with the unjust dispossession and killing of the English, and Wace's decision to follow him at this crucial point
in his narrative must have been just as egregious and insulting to his patron
as his decision to include the Anglo-Saxon version of Harold's trip to
Normandy.

Finally, the dying William turns to his third son, the future Henry I.
Having already revealed his wishes for the transmission of Normandy and
England, William has no land left to bestow on Henry. Instead of land,
Wace says that William left his youngest son five thousand pounds and commanded Robert and William to "make Henry rich and wealthy, more than
any man holding land from [them]."[66] Wace says no more. Orderic (who was
a fierce supporter of Henry I) could not leave Henry so empty handed; his
account of William's deathbed speech goes on to assure both Henry and his
readers that Henry will one day surpass his brothers in dominions, wealth,
and power.[67] Robert de Torigny includes a similar assurance that Henry

---

65. The evolution of *novel disseisin* has to be largely inferred as direct evidence such as edicts and
writs are no longer extant. Henry's first step, probably taken between 1156 and 1160, was to declare that disseisin (dispossession) could only follow upon a legal judgment. Indirect evidence for
this comes from a letter of Archbishop Theobald referring to a writ ordering him to restore a
church to a clerk named Osbert who had been disseised contrary to the king's edict. John of
Salisbury, *The Letters of John of Salisbury, I, The Early Letters (1153–1161)*, ed. W. J. Miller and H.
E. Butler, revised by C. N. L. Brooke (London, 1955), 162–63. Around 1166 Henry began treating disseisins as breaches of the king's peace; fines "pro disseisina contra assisam regis" begin to
appear on the pipe rolls after 1166. *Pipe Roll 12 Henry II*, 65; *Pipe Roll 13 Henry II*, 48 and 134;
and *Pipe Roll 14 Henry II*, in *The Great Rolls of the Pipe of the Reign of Henry the Second, 5th to 34th
years*, 30 vols. (London, 1884–1925). The 1176 Assize of Northhampton, clause 5, also orders
justices to "make inquiry about disseisins contrary to the assize, committed since the lord king
returned to England after making peace with his son." *Select Charters and Other Illustrations of English Constitutional History*, 180. Finally, the *assize of novel disseisin* was introduced in which a royal
justice questioned a "jury of recognition" to establish whether someone had been unlawfully
disseised and who had committed the disseisin. Upon the justice's decision the losing party paid
a fine. The first explicit reference to the *assize of novel disseisin* occurs in the pipe rolls in 1181. For
mort d'ancestor, see the Assize of Northampton, clause 4; and Stubbs, *Select Charters*, 179–80. See
Warren, *Henry II*, 341.

66. "'A Henri, mon filz le poinsé, / ai .v. mile livres doné, / e a Guilleme ci comant / e a Robert
l'aure filz mant, / que chascun en sa poësté, / issi com il m'a en chierté, / face Henri riche e manat
/ plus que home de lui tenant.'" Wace, *RR*, vv. 9155–62.

67. "Henry, his younger son, who had heard that no share of the royal wealth was to come to him,
said sorrowfully and with tears to the king, 'And what, father, do you give me?' The king answered
him, 'I give you five thousand pounds in silver from my treasure.' To which Henry said, 'What shall
I do with treasure, if I have no place to make my home?' and his father replied, 'Be satisfied, my
son, and take comfort in the Lord. Patiently allow your elder brothers to take precedence over you.
Robert will have Normandy, and William England. But you in your own time will have all the
dominions that I have acquired and be greater than your brothers in wealth and power.'" ["Henri-

ultimately obtained all of his father's lands.[68] Wace's omission here may appear insignificant, but it is symptomatic of a larger trend that becomes clearer as his narrative approaches its end. Wace's decision to exclude any reassurance that Henry will outshine his brothers is almost certainly a result of his sympathy for Robert Curthose, and it fits into an emerging pattern that begins with Wace's decision to disguise the nature of Robert's relations with his father at the time of his death.

Wace recounts that after divesting himself of his worldly possessions and releasing all of the prisoners in his custody, William died on September 8, calling upon God and the Virgin Mary.[69] Following Orderic, Wace says that William's servants stole whatever they could from his household and shamefully left the king, "whom people were accustomed to fear when he was alive, to lie alone."[70] When the news spread that the king had died, barons and bishops came rushing to prepare the body for burial. William's body was then taken to Caen. As William's funeral procession made its way to the church of Saint-Étienne, a fire broke out in the town, causing everyone

---

cus iunior filius ut nil sibi de regalibus gazis dari audiuit, merens cum lacrimus ad regem dixit, 'Et michi pater quid tribus?' Cui rex ait, 'Quinque milia libras argenti de thesauro meo tibi do.' Ad haec Henricius dixit, 'Quid faciam de thesauro, si locum habitationis non habuero?' Cui pater respondit, 'Equanimis esto fili et confortare in domino. Pacifice patere ut maiores tui precedant te. Robertus habebit Normanniam et Guillelmus Angliam. Tu autem tempore tuo totum honorem quem ego nactus sum habebis, et fratribus tuis diuitiis et potestate prestabis.'"] Orderic, *HE*, vii, IV:95–97.

68. "Henry was the only one of his sons to be present at the funeral, and he benefitted thereby, for one day he would obtain the whole of his father's inheritance, which his brothers after his father's death possessed only in parts." ["Solus autem filiorum suorum Henricus exequias patris prosecutus est, dignus qui paternam hereditatem aliquando solus obtineret, quam fratres sui particulatim post mortem patris possederunt."] *GND*, vii, II:194–95.

69. September 9, 1087, is generally agreed on as the date of William's death. "Entrant sttenbre, al'oisme di / morut li reis, del siecle issi. / a l'ore que prime sona, / qu'il oï bien e demanda / que ço esteit que donc sonout, / Deu reclama si com il pout / e ma dame Sainte Marie; / tot en parlant fina sa vie, / que de son sens nen empeira / ne sa parole ne mua." Wace, *RR*, vv. 9223–32.

70. "Al terme que li reis fina / e que del siecle trespassa, / veïssiez mult servanz errer / e cels issir e cels entrer, / velos e covertos embler / e quantqu'il porent trestorner. / Une loee prof entiere, / ainz que le cors fust mis en biere, / laissierent sol le rei gesant / que l'en soleit criendre viviant; / donc fu la novele espandue / e la gent fu grant acorue, / e li evesque e li baron / vindrent a grant procession. / Le cors ont mult bel conreé, / overt, enoint e enbasmé; / a Chaem one le cors porté / si com il aveit commandé. / N'out nul evesque en la province, / abé ne conte ne haut prince / qui ne fust al cors enterrer, / por ço que il peüst aler; / mult i out moines revestuz / e proveires e clers menuz. / Quant le cors orent conreé / haut chanterent Libera me; / a l'iglise one porté le cors. / Mais la biere ert encore fors / quant iloc sorst une criee / donc la gent fu tote esfree, / ker la vile esteit alumee, / tote la gent i est alee; / tuit fors les moines i corurent, / cil remestrent al cors e furent. / Quant li feu chaï e quassa / la gent arriere retorna; / le cors porterent el mostier / e li clerc firent lor mestier, / tuit ont od bone volenté / Requiem eternal chanté." Wace, *RR*, vv. 9239–78.

except for a few monks to flee and abandon the king's body. After the tumult died down, the people returned and the funeral proceeded. As the sarcophagus was being prepared, however, a second interruption occurred. A vavasor named Ascelin fitzArthur stood in front of the assembly and charged William with having taken by force the very land on which the church stood, including the ground in which William was to be buried.[71] Ascelin claimed that the church, for the most part, belonged to him, that it was part of his fief and he had not given it, sold it, forfeited it, or mortgaged it. On no account would he allow the burial to proceed until he received restitution. Wace remarks that the people coming and going thought it a great marvel that "the king, who had made so many conquests and captured so many cities and castles, did not have any land free of claim in which his body could lie in death."[72] The assembled bishops quickly inquired into Ascelin's charges and found that the land had indeed been his father's and had been held by his family for generations.[73] The barons present then appealed to Ascelin to accept a payment of sixty shillings for the space of the tomb in order for the burial to proceed, promising him that things would be better for him in the future.

Wace's account, though much abbreviated, is generally faithful to Orderic's version of the events.[74] Wace, however, has much less to say than Orderic

---

71. "Endementres que l'en faiseit / le sarkeu ou gesir deveit, / e li evesque e li baron / esteient iloc environ, / eis vos un vavasor errant, / qui la presse vint derompant; / Acelin out nom, filz Artur, / par la presse vint asseür, / sor une pierre en haut monta, / devers la biere se torna, / clers e evesque apela, / en haut s'estut, en haut parla, / e tot le pople l'esgarda. / 'Seignors,' dist il, 'entendez ça! / Jo devié a toz e defent / de par Jhesu omnipotent / e par l'apostoile de Rome / – nel pois veer par plus haut home – / que vos Guilleme n'enterrez / el lieu ou metre le devez, / ne que il en mon dreit ne gise; / ker tot le plus de ceste iglise / est de mon dreit e de mon fieu, / jo n'ai dreit graignor en nul lieu. / Jo nel vendi ne n'engagai / ne nel forfis ne nel donai, / ne il de mei ne l'engaga / n'en gage rien ne m'en dona; / par sa force le me toli, / onques pois dreit ne m'en offri. / Jo l'en apel nomeement, / que dreit m'en face al jugement / ou tuit iront communement, / devant celui qui pas ne ment; / a cel jor m'en rende raison, / oiant toz l'en semon par non.'" Wace, *RR*, vv. 9279–314.

72. "E cil qui vont e cil qui vienent / tel chose a grant merveille tienent, / del rei qui tant aveit conquis, / tantes citez, tanz chastels pris, / nen a de terre quite tant / ousis cors giese al moriant." Wace, *RR*, vv. 9319–24.

73. "Li evesque ont l'ome apelé / e as veisins one demandé / se ço ert veir que il diseit, / e il distrent qu'il aveit dreit; / terre son pere aveit esté / de parenté en parenté. / A l'ome ont dit que deniers prenge, / si laist quite tot son chalenge; / seisante solz li one doné / e por tant a quite clamé / le sepulcre ou li cors fu mis, / e por ço a les deniers pris; / e li baron li ont pramis / que mielz l'en sera mais toz dis. / Acelin l'a issi graé, / lores ont le cors enterré." Wace, *RR*, vv. 9325–40.

74. Orderic's lengthy account of William's death, funeral, and burial appear at the end of book VII. The important details that he includes are William's calling upon God and the Virgin after the hour

about their meaning. Where Orderic seizes on the circumstances of William's death to meditate on the vanity of the world and the transience of earthly glory and loyalty, Wace repeats the series of events but offers little gloss on their significance. Whereas Orderic moralizes on William's sins, the majority of Wace's account is occupied with retelling the story of Ascelin's challenge to William's burial.[75] This episode is sensational enough, following as it does in both accounts the ignominious treatment of William's corpse and the interruption of the funeral procession by a freak fire, but it also conjures a host of unpleasant associations. Ascelin accuses William of stealing the very land on which he erected the abbey of Saint-Étienne, an abbey William built to expiate the sin he had committed in marrying Matilda of Flanders, a relative within the prohibited degrees of consanguinity. Although Wace does not mention this in connection with Ascelin's challenge, he does provide the relevant information elsewhere.[76] Ascelin's challenge thus recalls the memory of William the Conqueror's illicit marriage, which in turn casts doubt on the legitimacy of his descendants, including Henry II. The acknowledgment of Ascelin's rights by the bishops and the payment arranged by the barons also impugn William as they make perfectly clear that he died without having expiated all of his sins—he never compensated Ascelin's family for the land he had taken from them by force. The episode has the unfortunate effect of once again bringing up the issue of wrongful disinheritance, this time the unjust disinheritance of one of William's own men rather than that of an entire foreign aristocracy. As we have already seen, disinheritance and legitimacy—the legitimacy of the Conquest, the Norman dynasty, and of his own rule—were particularly sore subjects for

---

of prime had sounded, the abandonment of William's corpse and the looting of William's household by his servants, the transfer of the body to Caen, the burning of Caen during the funeral, Ascelin's challenge to William's burial, and William's bloated corpse bursting when forced into its sarcophagus. Orderic, *HE*, vii, IV:101–9.

75. Aside from the explicit moralizing Orderic engages in, he also implies that William's decomposing body is a distinctly unholy corpse. Unlike the bodies of the saintly that resist decay and exude a sweet fragrance, William's body displays the consequences of his sins. It is worth noting that the *GND* is completely silent on the curious events surrounding William's death and funeral, offering an extremely brief and altogether more reverent treatment of the events in that it includes absolutely nothing that might impugn William. *GND*, vii, II:195.

76. Wace mentions William's marriage to Matilda and Archbishop Malger's interdict, as well as the abbeys founded by William and Matilda to make amends. Wace, *RR*, vv. 4496–540. Wace follows this information, however, with an indictment of Malger and says that he behaved foolishly. He also notes that Malger fled his family and ended his days in the company of a concubine and a demonic familiar named Toret. Wace, *RR*, vv. 4541–618. Orderic, on the other hand, is silent on the subject and mentions neither the debate over the legality of the marriage nor Malger's interdict in his *Historia Ecclesiastica*.

Henry II, and the steady accretion of charges against his great-grandfather cannot have pleased him.

Henry I and Robert Curthose

Wace's ambivalent, and at times wholly subversive, presentation of the Conquest and William the Conqueror's death strike at the very heart of Norman claims to legitimate rule in England. This alone may have been enough to offend Henry II and warrant Wace's termination; however, Wace goes on to offer a portrayal of Henry II's grandfather that can only have incensed his patron further. Henry I was a problematic figure for contemporary Anglo-Norman historians. Although most writers praised Henry's leadership, his rise to power in both England and Normandy had been morally ambiguous at best, and treacherous at worst. Henry I seized the English throne in 1100 while his oldest brother and the late king's heir, Robert Curthose, was returning in triumph from the First Crusade.[77] Six years later Henry took the duchy of Normandy from Robert by force, defeating him at Tinchebray in 1106, imprisoning him for the remainder of his life, and ruling Normandy in his stead. Henry's apologists, such as Orderic Vitalis and Robert de Torigny, reported these troublesome facts, but they also attempted to justify Henry's actions by portraying Robert as dangerously inept and incapable of governing.[78] They also excused Henry's questionable method of seizing

---

77. C. Warren Hollister pointed out that an agreement between William Rufus and Robert Curthose designating each as the other's heir had been made in 1091, but that Robert had repudiated it in 1093 and that it is not known to have been renewed. C. Warren Hollister, *Henry I* (New Haven, 2001), 105. Although this is true, Robert Curthose was still considered the heir apparent by many of the Anglo-Norman barons. Indeed, Henry's attempt to claim the treasury at Winchester after Rufus's death was challenged by William of Breteuil, who reminded him, as well as the assembled barons, that they had all sworn homage to Robert Curthose and should remain faithful to him whether he was present or not. Henry impatiently drew his sword in response to William of Breteuil's challenge and was granted the castle and its treasure. Orderic, *HE*, x, V:290.

78. Robert de Torigny composed an entire book (originally book VII, it appears in van Houts's edition as book VIII) in praise of Henry I and his reign, appending it to his redaction of the *GND*. Its first chapter is indicative of the tone of the whole book; in it, Robert proposes to show how Henry I was far superior to his brothers as he exhibited all of their good qualities as well as excellent qualities that his brothers lacked. *GND*, viii, II:197–289. Robert de Torigny says that "common repute deservedly extolled Robert in matters of warfare, but truthfully declared that he was far from effective in giving wise advice or ruling the duchy." [Robertum in rebus bellicis fama non immerito extollebat, sed hec eadem in maturitate consilii et in regimine ducatus ipsum minus utilem non mendaciter asserebat.] *GND*, viii, II:203. About Robert's deficiencies as duke, Orderic says: "All men knew that Duke Robert was weak and indolent; therefore troublemakers despised him and stirred up loathsome factions when and where they chose. For although the duke was bold and dar-

power by emphasizing his positive achievements in reunifying the Anglo-Norman realm and exercising a harsh but effective justice that produced an era of prosperity and peace—both Orderic and Robert de Torigny defended Henry's dubious rise to power by attributing it to divine intervention.[79] Wace, however, offers a strikingly different representation of Henry I as an opportunist driven by greed who violated Robert's rights in taking

---

ing, praiseworthy for his knightly prowess and eloquent in speech, he exercised no discipline over either himself or his men. He was prodigal in distributing his bounty and lavish in his promises, but so thoughtless and inconsistent that they were utterly unreliable. Being merciful to suppliants he was too weak and pliable to pass any judgment on wrongdoers; unable to pursue any plan consistently he was far too affable and obliging in all his relationships, and so he earned the contempt of corrupt and foolish men. . . . He diminished his inheritance daily by his foolish prodigality, giving away whatever anyone asked; and as he impoverished himself he strengthened the hands of others against him." [Omnes ducem Robertum mollem esse desidemque cognoscebant, et iccirco facinorosi eum despiciebant, et pro libitu suo dolosas factiones agitabant. Erat quippe idem dux audax et ualidus, militiaeque laude dignus eloquio facundus, sed in regimine sui suorumque inconsideratus. In erogando prodigus, in promittendo diffusus, ad mentiemdum leuis et incautus. Misericors supplicibus, ac ad iusticiam super iniquos faciendam mollis et mansuetus, in definitione mutabilis, in conuersatione omnibus nimis blandus et tractabilis ideoque peruersis et insipientibus despicabilis. . . . Prodigus dominium patrem suorum cotidie imminuebat insipienter tribuens unicuique quod petebat, et ipse pauperescebat, unde alios contra se roborabat.] Orderic, *HE*, viii, IV:115. Although Wace champions Robert Curthose in much of the *Roman de Rou*, even he briefly acknowledges that people considered Robert to be negligent after he returned from the Holy Land and that they chastised him for it. "N'ert mie mult encïentos / e si esteit mult pereços; / por pereços fu mult tenuz / pois qu'il fu d'oltre mer venuz; / peresce semble malvaistié, / plusor l'en orent chastïé, / mais por nul boen chastisement / ne pout aveir amendement." Wace, *RR*, vv. 10923–30.

79. After recounting Henry's accession to the English throne, Orderic says, "He governed the realm committed to him by God prudently and well through prosperity and adversity; among all the rulers of Christendom he is considered outstanding for his preservation of peace and justice." [Hic inter prospera et aduersa regnumm sibi diuinitus commissum prudenter et commode moderatus est ac inter precipuos totius Christianitatis principes optentu pacis et iusticiae fulgens insignis habitus est.] Orderic, *HE*, x, V:295. After the battle of Tinchebray at which Henry defeated Robert, Orderic says: "All pious men were overjoyed when they heard the news of the king's victory; outlaws and evil-doers, on the other hand, were filled with grief and sorrow because they had no doubt that a yoke had been laid on their hitherto unconquered necks by God's will. When these seditious predators discovered that the monarch whose effective justice they had already experienced had conquered his enemies in battle by God's help, they acknowledged his greatness and fled at once in all directions, abandoning their habitual oppressions solely out of fear of him." [Auditus rumoribus de uictoria regis religiosi quique letati sunt exleges autem et malignitatis amatores contristati luxerunt, quia iugem indomitae ceruici suae diuinitus impositum pro certo nouerunt. Nam seditiosi predones ex quo sceptrigerum quem forem iusticiarium olim comprobauerunt, adminiculante Deo superiorum hostibus in bello comperierunt agnita uiri uirtute per diuersa statim loca diffugerunt, et solo timore illius a solitis infestationibus cessauerunt.] Orderic, *HE*, xi, VI:93. Robert de Torigny passes over Henry's accession to the throne of England with little commentary, but he describes Henry's success at Tinchebray as God's judgment: "But God's judgment came upon them and both men [Robert Curthose and William of Mortain] along with many others were taken prisoner by King Henry's men and led before the king. In this manner did God concede a bloodless victory to a king who feared him, as once he did to his servant the Emperor Theodosius." [Sed iudicio Dei super eos ueniente, capti sunt ambo et multi alii cum eis ab hominibus Henrici regis atque ante eum

the English throne, brought civil war to Normandy, and shamelessly bribed men to betray Robert. Wace's characterization of Henry I rejects the positive assessments of Henry's apologists and focuses on the monarch's negative qualities to such an extent that it ultimately questions his very legitimacy. Contemporary audiences were very likely to have been familiar with the defenses offered by Henry I's apologists, and they could not have failed to comprehend the import of Wace's revisions and insinuations.

Wace's representation of Henry I is unusual enough when compared to that of his sources, but it seems even stranger when we remember that Wace was writing for Henry I's grandson, Henry II. The *Roman de Rou*, at least from Henry II's perspective, was intended to glorify his dynasty, celebrate his own legitimacy as Henry I's heir, and help guarantee the succession of his children. And Henry II had another important motive for patronizing the *Roman de Rou*. The first years of Henry's reign were spent vigorously reasserting royal authority and limiting baronial power, a program that Henry II characterized as the restoration of his grandfather's government but that still bred resentment among the barons. Henry II must have hoped that Wace, like Orderic Vitalis and Robert de Torigny, would portray his grandfather sympathetically and concentrate on the benefits of his severe rule, rather than dwelling on the attendant loss of baronial autonomy or delving too deeply into how he came to power.

Wace's account of Henry I's reign begins with the English magnates and clergy pressuring Henry to take the throne after William Rufus's death in a hunting accident.[80] They argue that Henry should take the throne because Robert is far away and no one knows whether he will ever return. At first Henry resists, wanting to wait for Robert, but he soon agrees to become king. Although the account blames Henry's usurpation partly on the advice of the English barons and clergy, Henry is also implicated. Wace makes it clear that Henry knew that his accession to the throne violated his elder brother's rights, and he makes the charge that Henry injured Robert twice—once just after Robert returns from Jerusalem, and again before

---

adducti. Concessit hoc modo Deus regi se timenti uictoriam incruentam, sicut quondam Theodosio imperatoris seruo suo fecerat.] *GND*, viii, II:222–23.

80. "Li evesque s'entrasenblerent / e li baron s'entremanderent, / Henri pristrent, sil coronerent, / tote la lterre li livrerent; / ne voldrent pas Robert atendre, / qui a Jerusalem ert prendre, / n'il ne saveient qu'il fereit / ne se ja mais repaireireit; / e al realme rei estoet / ker sainz rei pas estre ne poet. / Henri s'en fist assez preier / ainz qu'il le volsist otreier, / son frere, ço dist, atendreit, / qui de Jerusalem vendreit; / mais li baron tant li preierent / e plusors tant le conseillierent, / que il fist ço qu il li distrent / e otreia ço que il quistrent." Wace, *RR*, vv. 10117–34.

Henry invades Normandy.[81] In the last instance, Wace describes how a "highly esteemed and learned" but anonymous knight, who held lands from both Robert and Henry, attempted to make peace between the brothers.[82] The knight, a rhetorical figure introduced to advance arguments that Wace is disinclined to make directly, travels to Henry's court and tells Henry that he should leave Normandy to Robert and not attempt to take any part of it from him. "Your father granted it to [Robert] when he died," the knight says. "He gave him his entire inheritance according to justice and seniority of birth. Therefore the crown you wear and the land you rule would have come to him, if reason had been maintained." The knight reminds Henry that "now things have turned out so that you received the kingdom and you ought to have advanced [Robert's] cause and left Normandy in peace, through seniority of birth and justice and through what is honorable and natural." He ends his argument by telling Henry that "you are fully aware that [Robert] is the elder and that you would be reproached because of this." Although Wace never directly accuses Henry of usurping the English throne, he hardly needs to do so. The inclusion of material like the knight's speech allows Wace to simultaneously insinuate criticism and distance himself from it, all while leading the reader to the inescapable conclusion that Henry's actions in accepting the throne were against justice, honor, reason, and nature, and that Henry was fully aware that he was transgressing the established order and infringing on Robert's rights when he took the throne.

---

81. "Robert vint de Jerusalem / frant joie en firent a Roem, / Normendie a tote saisie / e tote l'out en sa baillie, / n'i a trové nul aversaire, / par tot pout ço que il volt faire; / mais merveilles li ennuia / e merveilles se coreça / de Henri, son frere poisné, / qui reis esteit este son gré; / par ainzneage, ço diseit, / reis d'Engleterre estre deveit." Wace, *RR*, vv. 10319–30.

82. "Quant li reis out tot escolté / e cil se tout qui out parlé, / un chevelier en piez leva, / qui por le duc al rei parla; / de Normendie esteit venuz, / mult ert preisiez e coneüz; / cil tint del duc et tint del rei / e a chascun esteit par fei. / 'Sire,' Dist il, 'd'oltre mer vien, / hoem sui le duc e de lui tien, / e de vos tien jo e de lui / e hoem sui jo a amedui. / Ço que me covient me estoet dire, / ne me devez porter nul ire, / ker tote Engleterre avez / a vos trestot sol la tenez; / aveir deit li dus ensement / quantque a Normendie apent. / Vos tot deça, il tot dela, / chascun issi assez avra; / bien deit a chascun ço sofiere, / por nïent querreit altre empiere. / De Normendie que il tient / – mais nel fereiz pas de nïent – / vos l'en volez tolir partie, / mais li dus n'en soffera mie. / Costentin claimë e Danfront, / qui de son eritage sunt; / vostre pere lui otreia / quant il morut e il fina, / par dreiture e par ainznaage / il dona tot son eritage; / e par iço li aveinist, / se fust qui raisin li tenist, / la corone que vos portez / e la terre que vos tenez. / Mais ore est issi avenu / que vos avez le regne eü, / sil deüssiez bien avancier / e Normendie en pais laissier, / por ainznaag e por dreiture / e por enor e por nature; / bien saviez que il est ainznez / e que vos en sereiz blasmez.'" Wace, *RR*, vv. 10757–800.

Wace also offers an unflattering comparison of Henry I and Robert Curthose's personalities. He portrays Robert as honorable and decent, if occasionally duped by his more cunning and ruthless brother. In the midst of Robert's 1101 trip to England to challenge Henry for taking the crown in his absence, Wace tells us that Robert avoided attacking the strategically important stronghold at Winchester because he learned that Henry's queen was in childbed there, and he thought it too base to attack a lady in such circumstances.[83] Wace recounts that Henry repaid his brother's noble gesture in this instance by promptly devising an ambush in Alton Wood that Robert only narrowly escaped.[84] In another instance, Wace recounts that during William Rufus's reign a dispute had broken out between the brothers and Henry had retreated to Mont-Saint-Michel, where he was besieged by both Robert and William. Although Henry had plenty of food, he and his supporters were suffering from thirst. Henry sent word to Robert of their need and, in a display of filial love and courtliness, Robert sent Henry a barrel full of the best wine he could find and granted a truce for the whole day so that the besieged could collect water. William was furious with Robert for providing Henry with drink when he ought to have been starving him, but Robert replied that it would have been base to deny his brother food and drink when he asked for them.[85]

Unlike Robert, Henry appears to be motivated almost exclusively by hatred, pride, and greed. Henry harbors an excessive hatred for his brother, displays little clemency, and frequently resorts to deception in his pursuit of power.[86] In a particularly telling episode, Wace describes Henry's dispossession of William of Warenne and offers two interpretations of the event, neither of which exculpates Henry. In the first, Wace says that Henry conceived a hatred for William over an old slight. During William Rufus's reign, William of Warenne had nicknamed Henry "Stag's Foot" and jokingly said

---

83. "Barons semonst e chevaliers, / pria veisins e soldeiers, / od grant gent e od grant navie / e od noble chevalrie / passa mer e vint a Porsecestre, / d'iloc ala rendre Wincestre; / mais l'on li dist que la reïgne, / sa serorge, esteit en gesine, / e il dist que vilains sereit / qui dame en gesine assaldreit; / vers Londres fist sa gent torner / ker la quidout le rei trover." Wace, *RR*, vv. 10331–42.

84. "Al bois de Altone esteient ja, / quant li dus un home encontra / qui li dist que li reis veneit, / ultre le bois l'encontrereit; / ultre le bois li reis atent, / gart qu'il n'aut avant folement, / a l'eissir e al bois passer / le quide li reis desoter." Wace, *RR*, vv. 10343–50.

85. Wace, *RR*, vv. 9573–618.

86. Wace notes Robert's surprise and horror upon finally realizing that Henry hates him and wants to capture him. "Li dus fu mult espoëntez, / a merveille fu esfreez, / ses regnes tinit, si s'arestut; / lores a primes s'aparceut / que li reis Henri le haeit / a bien tost prendre le fereit." Wace, *RR*, vv. 10629–34.

that Henry was so skilled in hunting that he could determine how many antlers a stag possessed just by examining the animal's footprint. This was apparently so offensive to Henry that he chafed under the insult and never forgot it. Wace says that when Henry became king he remembered William's jokes, and that people reported that Henry hated William and dispossessed him for this reason alone.[87] Other people, Wace notes, said that Henry had dispossessed William out of a feigned hatred. These people accused Henry of sending William to Duke Robert to beg for his help in persuading the king to restore his land as part of a devious plan intended to force Robert to enter England a second time so that Henry could capture and imprison him.[88] In Wace's account, Henry can be seen as either overly proud and sensitive, prone to holding grudges, and ready to dispossess a baron out of spite, or as treacherous, greedy, and constantly scheming to imprison his brother and strip him of his inheritance.[89]

Wace initially treats both interpretations as plausible, but he clearly endorses the least attractive of them in the episode that follows.[90] After sug-

---

87. "Li reis Henri grant pose aveit / le conte Guillame haeit, / e se vos plaist, briemont diron / de la haenge l'achaison. / Quant Henri fu od le rei Ros, / qui tot tens fu mult glorios, / ainz qu'il eüst terre ne rente, / en chiens e en bois ert s'entent; / ses chiens aveit, en bois alout / e en chacier se delietout. / Quant il faiseit mote mener / mult l'oïsiez sovent corner, / e s'il voleit aler berser / brachez faiseit assez mener, / sovent, quant veneit a pleisir, / as trieges faiseit retenir; / de bois, de chiens, de venerie / conoisseit tote la maistrie; / solonc l'achaison qu'il aveit / cers e bisses e pors perneit. / Por les cers qu'il alout pernant / e por le bois qu'il cerchout tant, / li quens Guilleme le gabout, / Pié de Cers par gap l'apelout, / e sovent sore li meteit / et souvent par gap lui disoit / qu'as pas des cers aparceveit / de quanz ramors li cers esteit; / sovent Henri s'en coreçout, / mais por le rei que mult dotout / au conte mesler ne s'osout, / car li rois mout le conte amount; / Henri soffrout e escoltout / tel chose qui mult pesout. / Al terme que Henri fu reis / li remenbra des vielz gabeis / donc li quens le soleit gaber, / Henri ne pout mie oblïer; / por ceste achaison solement / – ço fu retrait entre la gent – / fu Willame del rei haïs / e de sa terre dessaisiz." Wace, *RR*, vv. 10513–54.

88. "Plusors dient, que que jo die, / que par engien e par veisdie, / par fause e par feinte haïne / fu faite ceste dessaisine, / e que li quens fu enveiez / por ço que il fu vezïez / en Normendie al duc parler, / ker mult saveit mal enarter. / Al duc se plainst des rei Henri, / qui por s'amor l'aveit haï; / sa terre en crient aveir perdue / se par lui ne li est rendue. / Par complaintes et par clamors / que li dus oï de plusors, / passa il mer sodeement / a Sohantone salvement, / sei dozieme de chevaliers, / estre servanz e escuiers; / le rei, ço dit, alout requerre / qu'a ses barons rendist lor terre. / Li reis, qui esteit a Wincestre / oï del duc l'afaire e l'estre, / tost oï dire qu'il quereit; / a sa gent dist qu'il le prendereit, / en sa prison le getereit, / ja mais ne li eschapereit." Wace, *RR*, vv. 10555–80.

89. Robert, it is true, was apparently violating the terms of the 1101 peace agreement by entering England uninvited to petition for redress of the barons' grievances, but Wace does not mention this. Wace also fails to mention that the earldom of Surrey was restored to William of Warenne as a result of Robert's actions, and that William went on to serve Henry loyally for another thirty-three years. Perhaps it was for this reason that people suspected William of Warenne's motives in appealing to Robert, and suspected Henry of having concocted a scheme to defraud his brother.

90. Wace, *RR*, vv. 10575–726.

gesting that Henry dispossessed William of Warenne out of cunning and deviousness, knowing that he was skilled in plotting to do harm, Wace reports that Henry sent William to the duke to seek redress. Wace observes that Henry knew this would compel his brother to come to him to plead on behalf of William and Robert's other partisans, whom the king had also dispossessed. Robert thus returned to England to seek redress of his barons' grievances. Upon hearing that Robert had entered England, Wace reports that Henry wanted to capture and imprison him. Robert of Meulan, however, protested that Henry should have mercy for God's sake and not cause his own brother such shame; instead, he proposed a plan to deprive Curthose of the annual payment of three thousand marks that Henry had promised him as compensation for the loss of England. Robert of Meulan rode out to meet Curthose and told him that the king was furious with him and intended to imprison him, but that he could escape this fate if he went to the queen and threw himself on her mercy. Curthose followed this advice and was granted safe conduct by the queen after relinquishing his claim to the annual payment. Henry may have been dissuaded from imprisoning Robert on this occasion, but Wace asserts that his deception enabled him to avoid having to compensate his brother for the loss of the English throne. In spite of having offered another plausible explanation for Henry's actions, the episode demonstrates that Wace thought he knew quite well why Henry had dispossessed William of Warenne—it was solely to draw his brother over to England in order to imprison him and deprive him of his inheritance.

Wace displays obvious sympathies for Robert throughout the *Roman de Rou*, defending both his rights as the firstborn and his character, and portraying him as motivated by justice and right. According to Wace, Robert's trips to England during Henry's reign were motivated by his entirely justified indignation over his brother's actions in taking the throne and by his desire to protect the magnates Henry had dispossessed for supporting him. During an interview with Henry after the king and Robert of Meulan had tricked him out of his compensation for England, Robert reassures Henry that he has not come with a force to deprive him of anything, although he reminds Henry that he wears a crown that should have been his. Instead, Robert says that he has released him from the money he was to pay him because they are brothers and because he loves and trusts him. Robert asks that they treat each other as brothers should, and requests that the king give him some of his fine things when he wishes. Robert is clearly trying to adjust the terms of their relationship into something more amicable here. The payment he was to have had resembled tribute and marked him as a hostile force rather than the king's brother. By suggesting that Henry give him some of his things when he wishes, as is right, Robert is clearly asking to be treated like a brother rather than an enemy (albeit while recognizing that he has already lost any hope of receiving the payment).[91] Wace also notes that Henry did not respond with generosity on this occasion, or with any gesture at all; the king merely thanked Robert for speaking in true courtly fashion and said he would do whatever was his duty.[92]

Perhaps the most important difference Wace draws between the two brothers is their respective willingness to either start or avert a civil war. Wace tells us that Robert was furious with Henry after he returned from Jerusalem for having taken the throne in his absence, and that he raised an army to assert his rights in England.[93] When the two armies finally faced each other, men on both sides appealed to Henry and Robert to prevent relatives and friends from slaughtering each other. Wace says that the barons made a special plea to Robert, not only as the injured party but as someone who had been to Jerusalem and should therefore act as an example to all.[94]

---

91. "'Ne sui,' dist il, 'pas ça venuz / comme par force, n'embatuz / por voz rentes amenuisier / ne por voz terres chalengier, / ne por aveir que me paiez / que par cosume me deiez; / mei ne devez costume rendre / ne jo ne la dei do vos prendre. / D'un pere e d'une mere fumes, / un pere e une mere eümes, / fraternité garder vos dei, / ausi a vos com vos a mei; / altresi gentil, ço savez, / comme jo sui, estre devez, / n'a entre nos nul avantage, / ço m'est avis, fors d'ainznaage, / e ço fu endreit vos tornez / des que vos fustes coronez; / la dignité de la corone / mult grant avantage vos done. / Por ço que jo vos aim e crei / les deniers quites vos otrei / que vos rendre me devïez, / tant com cest regne tendrïez; / quite vos claim, quite seiez, / por nïent plus me querrïez. / A la reïne ai tot doné / e vos en ai quite clamé. / A lié l'otei por vostre amor / e vos claim quite por m'enor; / quant vos plaira e vos voldreiz / de voz bels aveirs me dorriez, / de beaux avers me paierés / et je prendroy, car ce est drois.'" Wace, *RR*, vv. 10671–704.

92. "'Vostre merci,' ço dist li reis, / 'ore avez vos dit que corteis.' / Quant li dus fu asseürez / e il quida estre acordez, / le rei fist requerre e requist / por ses barons, e li reis dist: / aut s'en li dus quant li plaira, / il fera bien ço qu'il devra. / Li reis ne l'en volt faire plus / ne plus faire n'en pout li dus." Wace, *RR*, vv. 10705–14.

93. Wace, *RR*, vv. 10319–472.

94. "Al duc dient que pais feïst, / a al rei chose ne quesist / que li reis faire ne deüst / ne que faite ne peüst, / ker pois qu'il esteit coronez / ne deveit estre desposez; / mielz voldreit estre a mort feruz / que del regne fust abatuz. / Ne deit mie son frere abatre / ne si grant gent faire combatre; / de totes parz ad filz e peres / e d'ambes parz nevoz e freres. / 'Sire,' font il, 'merci, por Dé! / Qui al Sepulcre avez esté / vos nos devez toz assenser / e enseignier e doctriner. / Bataille fait mult a doter; / ne poet tel chose assembler / com li reis e com vos avez, / c'ommes n'i ait ocis assez; / tels amis perdre porrïez / que ja mais joie n'avrïez. / Ensorquetot al comencier / tel quide veintre e se fait fier, / qui a la fin s'en part vilment / e mult le fait hontosement; / faites pais, si vos accordez, / seiez amis com vos devez.'" Wace, *RR*, vv. 10413–40. It is important to note that Wace's sympathy for Robert Curthose does not extend to suggesting that he has the right to take the throne from Henry; instead, Wace appears to accept the argument that a king should not be deposed once he has been crowned.

Wace observes that Robert listened to reason and relented. He agreed to hold his anger and accepted an annual payment of three thousand marks in place of the crown that should have been his. When Henry determined to launch a similar invasion into Normandy, on the other hand, Wace recounts that no amount of reasoning or pleading could persuade him to desist.[95]

Wace's horror at the prospect of civil war is apparent in his comments surrounding these two episodes. In each case he dwells on the tragedy of relatives being forced to fight against each other and the barons' revulsion at the prospect, saying "a brother should not do this to his brother or make so many men fight each other; on both sides there were sons and fathers and on both sides nephews and brothers."[96] Although Wace never explicitly denounces Henry, he vigorously implies that forcing men into a civil war can only bring shame and dishonor on the perpetrator. In Wace's view, Robert took the nobler course and acted as an example to others, while Henry remained obstinate and needlessly forced relatives into battle.[97]

Wace's treatment of the grievances in each case also offers an implicit criticism of Henry. Whereas Robert invaded England to assert his rights as the firstborn and protest his brother's usurpation of the English throne while he was absent on crusade, Henry invaded Normandy over the Cotentin and Domfront, which Wace insists Henry had been forced to concede to Robert as part of the peace agreement that followed Robert's invasion of England in 1101.[98] According to Wace, Robert invaded England over le-

---

95. "Li messagier issi parleient, / de pais faire s'entremeteient; / mult volsissent, se il peüssent, / que li dui frere pais eüssent, / mais li reis ne li volt graer, / trieues ne volt al duc doner; / assez sovent a reprové / que li dus l'aveit mult gabé, / ja mais a lui pais ne fera, / quant il porra son droit avra. / Li messagier se departirent, / en Normendie revertirent, / ne porent rien vers le rei rendre; / or penst li dus de sei deffendre!" Wace, *RR*, vv. 10801–14.

96. "Ne deit mie son frere abatre / ne si grant gent faire combatre; / de totes parz ad filz e peres / e d'ambes parz nevoz e freres." Wace, *RR*, vv. 10421–24.

97. Henry's apologists, on the other hand, emphasize that Henry invaded Normandy only after Robert had violated the terms of their 1101 peace treaty, and Orderic insists that Bishop Serlo of Seés and others exhorted Henry to take Normandy from his brother. Orderic, *HE*, xi, VI:55–69.

98. "Li reis a faite cele fin / e out Danfront e Costentin; / Danfront aveit longues tenu / e Costentin en garde eü; / cez dous ne volt li reis laissier / e al duc l'estut otreier. / Issi fu entrels graanté / e issi fu asseüré / que li reis l'argent paiereit / e li dus a ço se tendreit." Wace, *RR*, vv. 10463–72. However, Wace says elsewhere that Robert was harassing both the Cotentin and Domfront after he returned from his second trip to England. Wace explains that Robert did this because of what was being said by those who had lost their fiefs in England (vv. 10727–38), but this makes little sense unless Henry was still pressing his claims to the Cotentin and Domfront. In any event, Robert replied to Henry's complaints that the Cotentin and Domfront were part of his fief and that he would do with them as he pleased (vv. 10745–56). Neither Orderic Vitalis nor Robert de Torigny mentions that Henry ever alienated his rights to Domfront or the Cotentin. Orderic attributes Henry's invasion of Normandy to Robert's violation of their peace agreement, while Robert de Torigny

gitimate injuries to his dignity and rights, while Henry invaded Normandy over land to which he no longer had any legitimate claim. As Wace has the "highly esteemed and learned" knight who is acting as Robert's messenger point out, Henry should have been satisfied with the kingdom he had gained at Robert's expense.[99] Henry should have advanced Robert's cause and left Normandy in peace. Instead, Henry sought to deprive his brother of lands that were rightfully his.

Perhaps most damning to Henry is the manner in which Wace portrays his refusal to make peace with Robert. Wace's characterization of Henry's actions throughout much of the *Roman de Rou* can only be described as malicious, grasping, and petty, and his refusal to be reconciled with Robert in this instance also exhibits these features. Henry complains that Robert has mocked him and for this reason he will never make peace with him.[100] Wace's explanation of Henry's actions in this case resembles one of the explanations he gives for Henry's dispossession of William of Warenne. In both cases Henry nurses a grievance that appears trivial in comparison with the reprehensible manner in which he retaliates—either dispossessing a baron out of spite or making war on his own brother without cause. His actions, as always, contrast unfavorably with those of Robert, who defends his vassals and attempts to restore their unjustly confiscated possessions, and who forgives his brother for stealing an entire kingdom from him.

The Battle of Tinchebray

Wace compounded these offenses to his patron's sensibilities by terminating his account of Henry I's reign at a particularly contentious moment—the battle of Tinchebray. Having struggled with his brother since taking the throne in 1100, Henry apparently determined to rid himself of Robert once and for all. He invaded the Norman duchy on spurious grounds in 1105, and defeated Robert at Tinchebray in 1106. After the decisive battle, Henry finally got what Wace suggests he had wanted all along: he captured Robert, imprisoned him for the remainder of his life, and took Normandy from him.

merely states that Robert sought every opportunity to provoke his brother until Henry could no longer tolerate it. Orderic, *HE*, xi, VI:57; and *GND*, viii, II:221.

99. Wace, *RR*, vv. 10765–800.

100. "Assez sovent a reprové / que li dus l'aveit mult gabé, / ja mais a lui pais ne fera, / quant il porra son dreit avra." Wace, *RR*, vv. 10807–10.

Wace attributes Henry's success in wresting Normandy away from his elder brother to his effective use of bribery and mercenaries, neither of which carried very positive connotations.[101] Henry came to Normandy, Wace recounts, armed with carts overflowing with treasure that he used to lure men into treason. In fact, Wace seems to take a special pleasure in naming some of the traitors and in describing the fate of one in particular. Robert fitzHamon had betrayed Robert Curthose and was pursued by the men of Caen and Bayeux for his crime.[102] He took refuge in the bell tower of the church in nearby Secqueville, but his pursuers set fire to it and forced him out. When he finally surrendered, his captors beat and threatened him, calling out for a rope for the traitor who had abandoned his rightful lord. Wace later notes that Robert fitzHamon served Henry well and that the king loved him greatly, but remarks that Robert had ruined his reputation when he abandoned the duke.[103]

Wace condemns not only the traitors who deserted Robert out of greed but implicitly condemns Henry himself. During the siege of Caen, Wace recounts that Henry and Robert fitzHamon devised a plan to take the city without a fight.[104] Certain wealthy men of Caen had fallen into Robert

---

101. "Li reis se fia es deniers / qu'il out a mines, as sestiers, / en Normendie trespassa, / mult out deniers, grant gent mena; / cil de Costentin le reçurent, / de sa venue mult lié furent; / od grant tonels, od grant charei / fist les deniers porter od sei. / As chastelains e as barons / qui orent tors e forz maisons, / as boens guerriers e as marchis, / a tant doné e tant pramis / que le duc Robert ont laissié / et por le rei l'ont guerreié; / neïs cil qui del duc teneient / e qui fiance li deveient / ont por le rei le duc querpi, / lor dreit seignor ont deguerpi. / Eis vos terre mult esfreé / e gent forment espoënté; / grant fu la guerre, si s'esmaient, / as cimitieres tot atraient, / ne laissoent rien es maisons / por roboors e por larrons. / Li reis a assez esterlins, / Mansels manda e Angevins / e Bretons qui od lui se tindrent, / qui volontiers al gaaig vindrent; / n'il n'en i saveit tant venir / comme li reis del retenir, / ne ja a livreison faillist / qui pois son terme ja tenist." Wace, *RR*, vv. 10851–82. "Le plus de la chevalrie / e le mielz de baronie / out li reis par ses dons od sei, / le duc laissoent por le rei." Wace, *RR*, vv. 11159–62.

102. "Robert que l'en dit filz Haimon / – tenuz esteit por haut baron – / qui l'enor tint de Torignié / e granz fieus out entor Croillié, / al duc son seignor fu meslez / e fu al rei Henri tornez. / A Sechevile en Beiessin / fu entrepris a un matin; / Beessin alout saisissant / e tot le païs porpernant. / Les maisnies le duc l'oïrent, / en Sechevile s'embatirent, / cil de Caan i acorurent, / de Baieues mult tost i furent. / Robert s'embati el mostier / sus en la tor desqu'al clochier, / mais il n'i pout gaires atendre / volsist ou non, l'estut descendre, / ker le feu i fu aportez / donc le mostier fu alumez; / mais por le feu s'est descendu / e as Baieues s'est rendu / Robert fu pris e bien gardez / e a Baieues fu menez; / a peine le pout l'en tenir / por manacier ne por ferir / les pautoniers quil menoent, / e mult sovent lu escrioent; / 'La hart, la hart al traïtor / qui a guerpi son dreit seignor!'" Wace, *RR*, vv. 11073–102.

103. "Li reis a mult Robert chieri / e Robert l'a mult bel servi; / por lui aveit le duc guerpi, / si en aveit mult malvais cri." Wace, *RR*, vv. 11239–42.

104. "Tant fu la parole menee, / mais mult fu entrels celee, / que ele fu issi finee, / del rei e des prisons graee / que li reis les prisons rendreit / e toz quites les clamereit / e riches homes les fereit,

fitzHamon's hands as his prisoners. Finding themselves in an untenable position, the men agreed to turn the city over to Henry in exchange for gifts and their freedom.[105] Wace notes that their scheme had to remain secret because the poorer inhabitants of Caen would never have consented to it. To prevent anyone from discovering their intentions, Henry and Robert fitzHamon had the men of Caen hand over hostages and fixed ransoms for them so that it would appear that they were buying their freedom rather than conspiring with Henry. Wace reports that the ransoms were fixed through "ruse and cunning" and "Caen was delivered through the enemies' machinations." He then decries the traitors who sold their loyalty, calling covetousness the root of all other sins and noting that the garden in which their secret meeting took place never again bore fruit.[106]

Wace clearly condemns the traitors and implies that their agreement with Henry was inspired by the devil himself, resulting in the barrenness of the very ground on which it transpired. The moral gloss Wace provides for this episode seems pedestrian enough; however, Wace is writing about his patron's grandfather (the source of Henry II's hereditary claims to both Normandy and England) and he appears to indict Henry for avarice along with his conspirators. Again, Wace never condemns Henry explicitly for his greed, but it is impossible to miss the parallel that he draws between Henry and the wealthy inhabitants of Caen, both equally willing to transgress the normal rules of conduct in order to gain land and money. Furthermore, Wace

---

/ aveirs e terres lor dorreit; / e les prisons Caan rendreient / e le rei dedenz recevreient. / Por ceste parols celer, / que l'en nes poisse destorber, / donerent li prison ostages, / filz e nevoz de lor lignages, / de lor raençons aquiter, / ker il lor aveit fait jurer; / par coverture e par veisdie / e par engien d'autre partie / furent les raençons nomees / e hostagies e fermees. / por deveer la gent menue, / que la chose ne fust seüe, / semblant firent de porchacier / e de lor raençons paier, / ker se la povre gent seüst / que l'ovre aler issi deüst, / ja li reis Caan nen eüst, / que grant barate n'i eüst; / mais par Tierri e par Raol / e par Nichole e par Aiol / e par lor riche parenté, / donc il aveient grant plenté, / e par lor proçains veisins, / qui vers Argences furent pris, / fu cele parole enartee / e a la povre gent celee." Wace, *RR*, vv. 11245–80.

105. Wace names these men as Thierry, Ralph, Nicholas, and Aiulf. Thierry has been identified as the son of Ralph fitzOgier, but the others are unknown. Cf. Orderic, *HE*, xi, VI:79, n. 5.

106. "Plusors a ceste ovre partirent / e ceste chose consentirent / donc jo ne vos sai les nons dire, / ne jo n'en voil mençonge escrire. / Male chose a en coveitise, / mainte male chose en est prise, / ele est racine de pechié, / tuit mals sunt par lié comencié. / Par pramesses que li reis fist, / qui a plusors terres pramist, / e por lor amis delivrer / qu'il ne poeient rachter, / e por ço que sovent seeient / que li baron al duc failleient, / sunt Caameis al duc failli / e torné sunt al rei Henri. / A cels tens aveit un gardin / a Caan, pres de Saint Martin, / entre Saint Martin e le mur / qui est joste la porte Artur; / iloc fu faite l'assemblee / e la parole graantee / de faillir al duc Robert. / Oïr poez miracle apert! / Ker onques pois cel parlement / – ço pois dire veraiement – / li gardin ne fructefia, / pome ne altre fruit ne porta." Wace, *RR*, vv. 11281–308.

calls our attention to another parallel. Henry, like the covetousness Wace denounces, is the source of all the other sins around him. It is Henry who instigates a civil war, it is Henry who trespasses in his brother's duchy without cause, and it is Henry who rewards anyone who betrays Robert. Taken as a whole, Wace's treatment of Henry I amounts to a campaign of innuendo that neither his audience nor his patron could have missed.

Just as Wace implicitly denounces Henry for his avarice, he also appears to condemn him for using such devious and dishonorable means to defeat his own brother and then shaming him with imprisonment. Wace suggests at the end of the *Roman de Rou* that Henry's treatment of his brother disgraced the king. At the beginning of his brief account of the battle of Tinchebray, Wace reminds us once again that Henry and Robert were born of the same parents, but that Henry had more money and men from England, and thus he did as he pleased.[107] Wace also reminds his reader that Henry held England in peace. These asides can only have been intended to provoke another comparison of Robert's and Henry's actions—Henry's ability to harass Robert came from the vast wealth of the kingdom that he had usurped from his brother, while the peace that England enjoyed derived from Robert's decision to cease pressing his own claims to the throne.

As the final verses of the *Roman de Rou* inch toward Robert's inevitable defeat and capture, Wace says that Henry continued taking Norman towns by force and bribing men with his wealth. He notes acerbically that more men abandoned Robert, lured away by Henry's promises. Finally, Robert and William of Mortain gathered what men they could, determined to lift the siege that Henry had set on the duke's stronghold at Tinchebray. Just as Wace depicts Robert fitzHamon as an archtraitor and the embodiment of an unworthy vassal for abandoning his lord in return for money and land, he presents William of Mortain as an exemplary vassal. He notes that he was loyal to his lord even in adversity, offered him good counsel to the end, rode with him into their final battle, and shared his imprisonment and misfor-

---

107. "Grant fu la guerre e grant fu l'ire / − mais tot ne pois conter ne dire − / del rei Henri e de son frere, / d'un pere nez e d'une mere; / li reis fu mult de grant poeir, / plus aveit gent e plus aveir / d'Engleterre qu'en pais teneit, / por ço faiseit que qu'il voleit. / Que vos ireie jo contant? / Tant ala li reis guerreiant, / chastels e viles porpernant / par force e par le soen donant, / qu'il a Tenechebrai assis / e environ le siege mis / so le conte de Moretoig, / qui n'esteit gaires d'iloc loig. / Li quens e li dus s'asemblerent, / trestoz lor boens veisins manderent; / le chastel voleient secorre / e le herneis dedenz rescorre, / mais al besoig li sunt failli / e par mal de lui departi, / par pramesses e par enors / que l'en aveit fait a plusors. / Li dus en son dreit se fiout / e en la gent qu'aveir quidout; / od tant de gent qu'od lui mena / cels del siege partir quida. / Tost fu la bataille assemblee, / mais n'out mie longue duree, / bien asaillirent cil qui vindrent / e cil de siege bien se tindrent; / n'i out gaires homes ocis." Wace, *RR*, vv. 11337–69.

tune. Uncharacteristically, Wace does not describe the battle of Tinchebray in detail. He says only that the besiegers fought well, the defenders held out well, and that scarcely any men were killed.

Robert and William were captured in the battle. Wace tells us that both were abandoned in their time of need by those who held fiefs from them.[108] He notes bitterly that the traitors received rewards from the king for their shameful actions, and that they were severely reproached for this by their peers. Wace observes that "the king had the duke and the count in his power, whoever might be honored or shamed."[109] He then moves to another assault on the men who betrayed Robert, asserting that there is no greater shame than for a man to betray his liege lord and reminding his audience that vassals are obliged to defend their lords with their lives and to guard their honor.[110] Deprived of its context, Wace's statement that the king had captured the duke and the count, whoever might be shamed, is hardly a searing indictment of Henry's actions; however, it appears wedged between two passionate denunciations of the men who abandoned Robert. The venomous barbs that Wace aims at the traitors were almost certainly intended to target Henry as well.

Wace goes on to declare treason the most heinous of crimes, and to assert that no one could do worse than to betray his liege lord. Urban Holmes interpreted this passage as a direct condemnation of Henry, but offered no rationale for his assertion.[111] Holmes may have been referring to the fact that Henry had apparently performed homage to Robert at some point in time.[112] It is more likely, however, that he was alluding to the belief that

---

108. "Tost fu li dus mis jus e pris, / li quens de Moretoig od lui, / en l'estor furent pris andui; / pris fu li dus, pris fu li quens, / nus ne fu rescos par les soens. / Plusors qui de lor fieus teneient / e qui od els estre deveient / lor seignor al besoig guerpirent, / e por la hone que il firent / del rei reçurent tels loiers / donc il orent mals reproviers." Wace, *RR*, vv. 11370–80.

109. "Li reis out le duc e le conte, / qui que feïst enor ou honte." Wace, *RR*, vv. 11381–82.

110. "Grant honte fait, ne poet graignor, / qui traïst son lige seignor; / nus hoem a seignor terrïen / ne deit faillir por nule rien, / menbre e vie li deit salver / e terrïen enor garder. / Mal fist qui son seignor guerpi; / li dus fu pris, li quens od lui." Wace, *RR*, vv. 11383–90.

111. Urban T. Holmes Jr., "Norman Literature and Wace," in *Medieval Secular Literature: Four Essays*, ed. W. Matthews (Berkeley, 1967), 66 and n. 56.

112. None of the chroniclers record the reason for this homage, but Orderic reports that Robert released Henry from it as part of the 1101 peace agreement. He says that Henry gave up the Cotentin but retained Domfront, and that Robert released him from the homage he had previously done him. Orderic Vitalis, *HE*, x, VI:318. Historians have thus assumed that Henry must have done homage to Robert in 1088 in return for the Cotentin. See Charles Wendell David, *Robert Curthose* (Cambridge, MA, 1920), 134–36; C. Warren Hollister, "The Anglo-Norman Civil War: 1101," *EHR* 88 (1973): 315–34, at 328–29; C. Warren Hollister, *Henry I* (New Haven, 2001), 142; and Tabuteau, *Transfers of Property in Eleventh-Century Norman Law*, 86 and nn. 348 and 349.

Robert, as the eldest brother, was Henry's natural lord. Even as reliable a partisan as Orderic articulates the case for Robert's natural lordship over Henry in the speech he attributes to Robert of Bellême (which will be discussed in more detail below).[113] This contention was apparently so prevalent, and so potent, that even Orderic felt obliged to address it. Wace also raises Robert's lordship over Henry in his speech for the "highly esteemed and learned" knight, who charges that Henry has already defied reason, justice, and nature in taking the English throne and is poised to do so again by invading his brother's duchy.[114] Although he never directly accuses Henry of rebellion against his lord and older brother, Robert, Wace certainly appears to be summoning this familiar allegation each time he condemns the treason against Robert and identifies Henry as its cause. Indeed, Wace may have assumed that Robert's natural lordship over Henry was such an obvious fact, and that Henry's rebellion against his brother was so evident, that it required no more blatant expression. If this is the case, then Wace's criticism of Henry I, and his protest against Henry II, is even more remarkable. His denunciations of treason take on a new dimension as they apply not only to the vassals who abandoned Robert but to Henry I himself, who upset the entire social order by illicitly rebelling against his older brother, stripping him of his inheritance, imprisoning him, and ruling Normandy in his place.

To return to Wace's otherwise cryptic comment that "the king had the duke and the count in his power, whoever might be honored or shamed," an apparently unrelated episode sheds significant light on this remark. As noted above, Wace asserts that Henry had wanted to imprison his brother in 1103, and had dispossessed William of Warenne in order to draw Robert to England. Robert of Meulan had pleaded with Henry on this occasion, telling him that he should not capture his brother and shame him with imprisonment.[115] Henry thus clearly shamed his brother Robert and his cousin William of Mortain by imprisoning them for the reminder of their lives. Wace's enigmatic comment that Henry "held the duke and the count, *whoever* might be shamed or honored" makes little sense, however, unless it is also meant to imply that Henry's actions brought shame upon the king himself. It is true that Wace never directly accuses Henry of acting ignobly or incurring disgrace, but he hardly needs to do so. Wace ineluctably draws

---

113. Orderic, *HE*, vi, III:94.

114. Wace, *RR*, vv. 10785–800.

115. Wace, *RR*, vv. 10575–94.

his reader toward this conclusion. Through layers of insinuation and innuendo, Wace argues that Henry's invasion of Normandy was unjust, that he was inspired by greed, that he caused men to commit the most base felonies, that he rewarded treason, and that he was guilty, at the very least, of dispossessing and imprisoning his own relatives without cause. And Wace's rhetorical strategy of attacking Henry I's legitimacy through thinly veiled insinuations was one that a contemporary audience could hardly have failed to grasp.

Just as Wace's idiosyncratic account of Henry's reign begins with his dubious accession to the English throne in violation of his brother's rights, it ends with Henry forcibly depriving Robert of Normandy without cause, and imprisoning his brother and cousin for the remainder of their lives. It is a powerful narrative move that underscores the controversial origins of Henry I's rule in both England and Normandy and, by extension, questions Henry II's own claims to legitimacy. Wace portrays Robert's loss of Normandy as the result of a societal breakdown at the most basic level, the feudal bond, which in turn was caused by Henry's greed and cunning. In the *Roman de Rou*, Robert's inability to protect Normandy is the direct result of the treason instigated by Henry, just as Robert's inability to reward his men is the result of Henry's opportunism in stealing the English throne and, with it, the country's immense wealth. It can hardly be overemphasized that the breakdown of Norman society's ordering mechanisms in the *Roman de Rou* is due to Henry's transgressions. It is Henry who steals the English throne from his older brother, Henry who launches an unjustified invasion into Normandy, and Henry who interferes in Robert's relationship with his vassals. Although Wace allows that Robert had flaws, that he was negligent in his spending and that he promised much but gave little, those flaws are also the direct result of his characteristic virtue, largesse.[116] Indeed, Robert's ability to reward his own vassals is really beside the point, as they were theoretically obliged to defend him regardless of his capacity to reward them.

---

116. "Li dus n'aveit gaires deniers, / ker il despendeit volentiers, / tot erent ses rentes faillies / e despendues ses aïes; / n'i poeient pas foisoner / a bien despendre e a doner. / Ses chastels faiseit redrecier, / les murs refaire e resforcier, / faire bretesches e quernels / e trenchies devant chastels. / A Chaem fist une trenchie / que encor poet estre enseignie, / qui va par la rue Meisine, / qui a la porte Milet fine; / une partie d'Ogne i vait / ou li floz montë e retrait. / Quant soldeiers li dus teneit / bien les paiout, quant il poeit, / e quant il nes poeit paier / e il nes osout corecier, / ker od li rei sepres tornoent / e od li rei le guerreioent." Wace, *RR*, vv. 10883–904. "Quant li dus doner ne poeit, / ou ne poeit or ne voleit, / par pramesses se deliverout, / mult prameteit e poi donout." Wace, *RR*, vv. 10931–34.

Wace ultimately casts Henry's invasion of Normandy as a battle between two types of rulers: Robert, who exhibits the values that Wace cherishes, and Henry, who deceives his brother, bribes Robert's men, and triumphs through ruse and cunning. Wace appears to have viewed the civil war between Robert and Henry as far more than a dispute over rights or lands. Although it was certainly a struggle to reunite the Anglo-Norman realm in allegiance to a single ruler, it was also a battle that determined which type of ruler and set of values would prevail. Much to Wace's apparent chagrin, Henry's ruthlessly efficient opportunism carried the day.

Wace may certainly have offended Henry II in any number of other ways, but his depictions of the Norman Conquest, William the Conqueror, and Henry I were particularly devastating because they directly attacked the edifice of Norman legitimacy. Since the Conquest, Norman legitimacy in England had rested on a meticulously constructed orthodoxy comprised of three fundamental tenets: that William the Conqueror was Edward the Confessor's only true and legitimate heir, that Harold was Duke William's own perjured vassal, and that the Conquest was a trial by battle in which God had weighed the merits of each side and determined the victor. Wace's portrayal of the Conquest not only failed to promote this orthodoxy, it completely eviscerated it.

Henry I's legitimacy rested on an equally artificial construct, and his reunification of the Anglo-Norman realm presented issues just as thorny as those raised by the Conquest. Henry had arguably usurped England from Robert Curthose and had indisputably taken Normandy from him by force. His apologists were clearly at pains to justify both actions, even as they lauded his accomplishments. They did so primarily by arguing that Henry was destined to possess all of his father's lands (often employing the argument that, of the Conqueror's sons, he was the only one to have been born in the purple) and that his triumphs indicated that he enjoyed God's favor. Should these providential arguments fail to satisfy Henry's detractors (and there were many), his apologists girded them with more mundane considerations. They focused on William Rufus's and Robert Curthose's shortcomings as rulers, the disorders in England and Normandy during their reigns, and presented both England and Normandy as desperately in need of a savior, which they had found in Henry.

Wace, however, entirely neglects the benefits of Henry's rule. Instead, he resurrects the disputes over the legitimacy of Henry's accession in England and his invasion of Normandy. Just as important, he counters the arguments of Henry's apologists with a defense of Robert Curthose's rights as the eldest of the Conqueror's sons. Although Wace generally resorts to insinuation in casting aspersions on the legitimacy of Henry's English reign, when he does state the case against Henry most clearly (as he does in the "highly esteemed and learned" knight's speech, where Henry's actions in accepting the throne are characterized as against justice, honor, reason, and nature), its effects are devastating. Finally, by ending the *Roman de Rou* with Tinchebray, Wace forces his reader to reconsider Henry's motivations in taking the duchy, the legitimacy of his actions, and the very legitimacy of his rule in Normandy. As he was writing for a monarch whose own legitimacy hinged upon that of Henry I, Wace's representation of Norman history must have dealt his patron a particularly unwelcome and disorienting blow.

Wace

One of the most important questions raised by this study is why Wace disparaged some of his patron's ancestors in such an unmistakable manner. Orderic Vitalis may have criticized William the Conqueror, and even Robert de Torigny lodged a complaint against Henry I for his appropriation of castles, but Wace was in an unusual position—he was employed by the king. Medieval histories are rife with denunciations of the mighty, but the men who produced works critical of a lineage were generally not engaged by one of its members to write a history of his family. Orderic was ostensibly writing the history of his monastic community of Saint-Évroul when he decided to criticize William the Conqueror, and Robert de Torigny was updating the *Gesta Normannorum ducum* on his own initiative. Other authors who were critical of Henry's ancestors, such as Henry of Huntingdon and Eadmer of Canterbury, were likewise writing without royal patronage and were thus free to criticize as they saw fit.

It is possible that Wace simply assumed that he was still as free to criticize the subjects of his history as he had been when he was writing the *Roman de Brut*, but this explanation is not entirely satisfactory. Wace's criticism of Henry I is too pointed, and his indirect attack on Henry II too transparent to be accidental. It seems more likely that Wace thought that a certain amount of criticism of Henry's ancestors was permissible when he began writing in 1160 (this applies to his critique of the Conquest and William the Conqueror), but that Wace escalated his criticism of Henry I due to Henry II's actions between 1160 and 1174, and that he purposely ended his history with Tinchebray after learning that he had been terminated. Wace had no single motive for his critical portrayal of Henry's ancestors; his history was shaped by his assumptions regarding the purpose of history writing and the duties of the historian, his own geographical location and experience, and by events that were occurring as he wrote.

We can gain some insight into Wace's refusal to produce a justificatory history by examining his understanding of his authorial role as it is revealed in his history, and what can be described as the "psychic baggage"—that tangle of prejudices and sympathies produced by one's circumstances and affiliations—that Wace brought with him to this project. Any attempt to discern the motives of Wace or Benoît (whose history and motives will be examined later) must, of course, be prefaced by the caveat that the scarcity of evidence severely limits what we can know about them. Any reconstruction of their biographies, therefore, can only be partial and the inferences drawn from them tentative.

Wace declares in the *Roman de Rou* that he is writing primarily to preserve the past, and he appears to have internalized the common didactic rationale for writing history, derived from classical authors and repeated so often throughout the Middle Ages that its significance has been diluted through constant repetition—that history provides us with examples of the deeds of the wicked and the good alike that should be used to enjoin virtuous behavior on the living. In the opening lines of part III of the *Roman de Rou*, Wace tells us he is writing "to remember the deeds, words, and ways of our ancestors, the wicked deeds of wicked men and the brave deeds of brave men."[117] Wace's exposition of the didactic purpose of history indicates that he understood history writing as an act of power, that he wielded his pen to rebuke the mighty, as well as to rescue the past from oblivion and inspire virtue among the living. In short, he sought to influence action in the present and shape the future by appealing to the past. His thinly disguised criticisms of both William the Conqueror and Henry I should thus be understood on one level as attempts to influence his patron. By pointing out the failings and mistakes of some of his predecessors, Wace hoped to encourage Henry II to avoid their errors. Since Henry II repeatedly insisted that he was merely restoring the government of his grandfather, Wace's critique of Henry I in particular must be understood as a negative appraisal of Henry II's attempts to expand royal power. By reminding his audience that Henry I's reign was predicated on his dubious ascent to the English throne and violent appropriation of Normandy, as well as his ruthlessness, cunning,

---

117. "Pur remembrer des ancesurs / les fiez e les diz e les murs, / les felunies des feluns / e les barnages des baruns." Wace, *RR*, vv. 1–4.

and greed, Wace implicitly argued that most aspects of Henry I's government were not worthy of restoration.

Wace also self-consciously presents himself as endeavoring to produce an accurate representation of the past.[118] The *Roman de Rou* is full of asides in which Wace variously declares that he will tell his reader the truth, or states that he does not know the truth of a certain matter and so prefers to give us the conflicting accounts he has found, as he does in the case of Harold Godwinson's trip to Normandy. Although Wace's statements testifying to the "truthfulness" of his narrative must be taken with a measure of skepticism—after all, he was hardly alone among medieval authors in claiming to establish a "true" account of events—Wace's singularity lies in his tendency to underscore these statements by actually following them with conflicting or subversive accounts. Wace forces his reader to consider variant tellings and interpretations, and he reveals the normally invisible process at the heart of most history writing in which the author disposes of less orthodox, or less flattering, variants in order to construct a coherent and satisfying narrative.

If Wace's primary desire was to present a "true" account of Norman history, then this goal required that he include potentially incendiary material, such as the Anglo-Saxon version of Harold's trip to Normandy, just as it compelled him to follow Orderic Vitalis's unflatteringly critical account of William the Conqueror's death, and to deviate from his sources in fashioning his own account of Henry I's reign. Although Wace apparently intended to "correct" previous histories of the Normans, which almost invariably erred on the side of praising the ducal line (with the notable exception of William Rufus) and legitimizing their actions at all costs, there are other ways to interpret Wace's apparent preoccupation with veracity.

A close inspection of several instances in which Wace appears to be wrestling with reconstructing an accurate account of events reveals that he is, in fact, playing a clever rhetorical game.[119] In his account of Harold's trip to Normandy, for instance, Wace presents the Anglo-Saxon version of events as normative. He says that "[Harold] took leave of King Edward; Edward openly refused him permission, forbade him and entreated him not to cross over to Normandy or speak to Duke William; he could easily be tricked there, for the duke was very astute. If he wished to have his hostages back, he should send other messengers." Wace then tells us that he has "found this

---

118. Matthew Bennett and Elisabeth van Houts offer the fullest discussions of Wace's apparent desire to establish a "true" account of events. Bennett, "Poetry as History?" 21–39; and van Houts, "Wace as Historian," 104–32.

119. See Le Saux, *Companion to Wace,* 171–72, 208–10, and 220–21.

account in writing, but another book has informed me that the king, to ensure that the kingdom passed to Duke William, his cousin, after his death, asked Harold to go to him. I do not know which explanation is correct, but we can find both in writing."[120] While Wace is trying to convince his reader of the truth of his account, he is also asserting that his sources—the authoritative Latin texts that medieval authors so often called upon as witnesses to the veracity of their own texts—can lie. Exposing such conflicts vividly reminded Wace's audience that he was reconstructing events from a host of rival Latin sources, some of which had to be inaccurate or contain outright lies since they could not be reconciled, and revealed that debate permanently obscured certain events, preventing any truly accurate and satisfying reconstruction of them.

Not only does he reveal that his sources can lie, Wace promotes one source over another in the structure of his account. By presenting Eadmer of Canterbury's Anglo-Saxon account as normative, Wace subtly indicates that he favors it above the other source he has found.[121] The other source is almost certainly one of the foundational texts of Anglo-Norman legitimacy and one of Wace's own sources, William of Poitiers's *Gesta Guillelmi*, but Wace mentions it in an almost offhand fashion.[122] This is remarkable because the most likely audience for Wace's history was the Anglo-Norman clergy and aristocracy. They would have been aware that Wace was crafting an account of Harold's trip to Normandy that subtly favored the Anglo-Saxon version of events, and Wace himself must have known that his audience would detect his revision and comprehend its import.[123]

On one level, then, Wace's apparent inability to determine which account is true is completely disingenuous. He has already suggested that the Anglo-Saxon account should be preferred simply by offering it as the standard against which he opposes the alternative interpretation he has found in another book. His assertion that he does not know which account is true,

---

120. "Al rei Ewart a pris congié, / e Ewart bien li deveia / e defendi e conjura / qu'en Normendie ne passast / n'al duc Guilliame ne parlast; / tost i porreit estre engigniez / ker li dus ert mult vezïez; / s'il voleit aveir ses hostages / si enveiast altres messages. / Issi l'ai jo trové escrit; / e uns altres livres me dit / que li rei le rova aler, / por le realme asseürer / al duc Guilliame, son cosin, / que il eüst emprés sa fin; / ne sai mie certe achaison, / mais l'un e l'autre escrit trovon." Wace, *RR*, vv. 5588–604.

121. Eadmer of Canterbury, *Historia novorum*, 5–6.

122. Poitiers, *GG*, 68–70.

123. Jean Blacker has suggested that Wace's refusal to construct a satisfying and coherent narrative by concealing contradictory material may have alienated his patron and led to his dismissal. Blacker, "'La geste est grande,'" 387–96, and Blacker-Knight, "Wace's Craft and His Audience," 355–63.

but that we can find both in writing, is thus a knowing wink at his audience and a dodge. It indicates that he is aware of the standard Norman line, but that he privileges the Anglo-Saxon version anyway. At the same time, Wace uses this strategy of demurring to avoid declaring unequivocally that he is rejecting the Norman version of events as inaccurate. Wace's habit of exposing such conflicts in the historical record clearly had political undertones. In this case, it questioned the traditional Norman claim that Edward the Confessor had sent Harold Godwinson to Normandy to confirm William as his heir, and revealed that William's claim to England was not beyond dispute.

A great deal of scholarly attention has also been focused on Wace's tendency toward evenhandedness in his history. Jean Blacker, Penny Eley, and Philip Bennett have characterized Wace's treatment of potentially divisive material such as the motivation for Harold's trip to Normandy and the battle of Hastings as impartial, especially when compared to accounts of the same events given by other eleventh- and twelfth-century authors.[124] Although Blacker in particular is careful to note that Wace never articulates the desirability of impartiality in his work, the idea that Wace attempts to be impartial in his reconstruction of the Conquest has much to recommend it. It is most evident in his very refusal to toe the Norman historiographical line. We should, however, resist the temptation to take this as evidence that Wace is apolitical. Although Wace often displays a laudable equity in his assessment of matters pertaining to the Conquest, this neutrality seems calibrated to promote reconciliation between the Anglo-Saxons and their Norman conquerors. Since Wace was writing for an audience that was increasingly composed of people of mixed Norman and Anglo-Saxon ancestry (as was Henry II), a certain degree of impartiality in his representation of the Conquest might have been welcome and even expected.

Wace's impartiality, however, does not extend to his representation of Henry I. Wace implies at every turn that Henry I was driven by greed and a hunger for power to routinely commit unscrupulous, and possibly illicit, acts, and he reveals a distinct preference for Robert Curthose. Wace's portrayal of Henry I may actually be more accurate than the previous, and overwhelmingly eulogistic, representations of the monarch had been, but it does not follow that it is therefore unbiased. Although one can still argue that Wace was advancing a variant account of history (one that conformed

---

124. Blacker, *Faces of Time*, 42; and Penny Eley and Philip E. Bennett, "The Battle of Hastings according to Gaimar, Wace and Benoît: Rhetoric and Politics," *Nottingham Medieval Studies* 43 (1999): 47–78.

more closely to his memory of Henry I), and was seeking to correct the one-sided narratives produced by Henry I's apologists, there is little here to indicate that he was truly impartial. His representation of Henry I appears calculated to remind his audience that the monarch was not the "Lion of Justice" apotheosized by writers such as John of Salisbury, Orderic Vitalis, and Robert de Torigny, and to refute the notion that Henry I's reign was a golden age deserving of restoration.[125]

To be sure, Wace's depiction of William the Conqueror's death functions in a similar manner, correcting the overly glowing assessments of that monarch and his accomplishments offered by William's apologists and restoring a good measure of human failing. We must, therefore, be extremely cautious in identifying impartiality as one of Wace's overarching principles. If anything, the apparent absence of bias is attributable to Wace's willingness to challenge and revise previous versions of Norman history (especially regarding those events recent enough to be within, and contradicted by, human memory). It does not mean that Wace lacked ulterior motivations or that he was nonpartisan. In all of these instances, Wace is consciously choosing to present an unflattering account of his patron's ancestors, and his "truth-telling" often has an agenda.

Whereas Wace provides his reader with ambiguous, contradictory, and even objectionable material, the Latin histories on which he relied share a common trait that is almost entirely absent from the *Roman de Rou*. They are obsessed with constructing the legitimacy of the Norman dynasty, and with very good reason. The Norman dynasty traced its descent from a pagan Viking, called either Rollo or Rou, who had invaded and appropriated Normandy. Its crowning glory had been the conquest of England. Histories of the Normans, since the first one written by Dudo of Saint-Quentin at the turn of the eleventh century, asserted the legitimacy and autonomy of the dynasty and set about transforming its dubious appropriation of Normandy into an act of providence. This was most clearly expressed in Dudo's account of Rollo's prophetic "dream of the birds," in which Rollo ascends a mountain where he is cleansed by a spring and then looks out to see that the earth below him is covered by a multitude of different birds, each having one red wing. According to the Christian cleric whom Dudo credits with interpreting Rollo's dream, the mountain is Francia, the cleansing spring

---

125. John of Salisbury refers to Henry I as the "Lion of Justice" and describes his imposition of order in book VI, chapter 18 of the *Policraticus*. John of Salisbury, *Policraticus*, ed. Cary Nederman (Cambridge, 1990), 118–22. Cf. Robert de Torigny's account of Henry I's reign in the *GND*, viii, II:196–280, and Orderic, *HE*, xi, VI:8–184.

denotes baptism, and the birds represent the people from various lands who will settle in Normandy and be united in their fealty to Rollo.[126] Dudo's history also provided the still young dynasty with a clear representation of ducal power passing from one generation to the next in an unbroken succession—something that tended to bolster its claims to legitimate rule in Normandy, and very likely something that Henry II wished to see in the history that he commissioned.

After 1066, the goal of Norman history writing shifted to promoting the legality of the Conquest and the legitimacy of Norman rule in England, most notably by casting the Conquest as a providential act and constructing William the Conqueror as Edward the Confessor's legitimate heir. The *Gesta Guillelmi*, *Gesta Normannorum ducum*, and the *Historia Ecclesiastica* all stress the legitimacy of the Conquest by focusing on William the Conqueror's designation as Edward the Confessor's heir, Harold's alleged perjury, and William's circumspection in pressing his claim after Harold's usurpation. They also uniformly emphasize that William appealed for and received papal approval to challenge Harold; they contend that the outcome of the battle of Hastings provided clear proof of God's favor for William's cause; and they note William's moderation in victory.[127] The historians of Orderic's generation may have had a slightly lighter burden to shoulder in justifying Henry I's accession in England and his takeover of Normandy, but they too labored for the cause of Norman legitimacy. In commissioning the *Roman de Rou*, Henry II almost certainly intended to extend the apology for Norman kingship to himself by commemorating his legitimacy as Henry I's rightful heir. He probably also hoped that the genealogical format of the history would help to ensure the unimpeded succession of his descendants by reiterating the almost unbroken succession of his ancestors.

Wace was not untouched by this pervasive concern over issues of legitimacy, but he differed from his predecessors in choosing to undermine the legitimacy of the Conquest and Henry I's reign, rather than laboring to promote it. Indeed, his tendency to contradict his sources results in a particularly damaging account of Henry I's early reign. Although still relying on Orderic's *Historia Ecclesiastica* and his redaction of the *Gesta Normannorum ducum*, as he did for most of his narrative, Wace also based his account of the Conquest and Henry I's reign on his own experience and memories,

---

126. Dudo, *History of the Normans*, 29–30.

127. Poitiers, *GG*, 68–72 and 100–142; *GND*, vi, II:76 and vii, II:158–70; and Orderic, *HE*, iii, II:134–44 and 168–84.

on his own research, and on the testimony he gathered from the people around him.[128] As a result, Wace's representation of Henry I in particular, and his interpretation of Norman history more generally, was likely shaped to a great extent by his own unique location in Normandy and his personal attachment to Norman history. Like Orderic, whose support for Henry I was so clearly conditioned by the geographical location of his monastery in a turbulent border region and the fact that the monks of Saint-Évroul were often at the mercy of the notoriously cruel Robert of Bellême, Wace's support for Robert Curthose appears to have been shaped by the region in which he lived, wrote, and researched.

Almost everything we know of Wace's life is derived from information divulged in the *Roman de Rou*. As a result, his biography consists primarily of those facts that he thought worthy of note. Wace tells us that he was born on the island of Jersey.[129] Although he does not note the year of his birth, it seems to have occurred around 1110.[130] On his mother's side he claims to have been descended from Turstin, chamberlain to Duke Robert the Magnificent of Normandy (1000–35). It may have been a family connection that gave him special knowledge of the affairs of the ducal household under both Duke Robert and Robert's son, William the Conqueror.[131] While describing his father's memories of watching William the Conqueror's preparations for the invasion of England, Wace refers to a time when he had been a *vaslet* (a boy not yet knighted).[132] This suggests that he was

---

128. See van Houts, "Wace as Historian."

129. "Jo di e dirai que jo sui / Wace de l'isle de Gersui, / al fieu de Normendie apent. / En l'isle de Gersui fui nez, / a Chaem fui petiz portez, / illoques fui a letres mis, / pois fui longues en France apris; / quant jo de France repairai / a Chaem longues conversai, / de romanz faire m'entremis, / mult en escris e mult en fis. / Par Deu aïe e par le rei / – altre fors Deu servir ne dei – / m'en fu donee, Deus li rende, / a Baieues une provende. / Del rei Henri segont vos di, / nevo Henri, pere Henri." Wace, *RR*, vv. 5301–18.

130. Based on his claims to have seen Henry I and the fact that he was still writing in the 1170s, scholars have concluded that Wace was most likely born in the first decade of the twelfth century. See van Houts, "Adaptation," 116; and *Le Roman de Rou de Wace*, III:15–18.

131. "Tosteins, ki ert ses chamberlencs, / de sa chambre maistre gardeins / – de par se mere fu sis aives – / pur ceo k'il fu curteis e saives, / li livra li ducs chiers corsainz / e reliques qu'il aveit ainz / en Jherusalem purchacies; / par Tostein les ad enveiees / a Ceresié, une abeïe / qu'il aveit faite en Normandie, / entre Costentin e Baieues, / de Saint Lo i cuntent treis lieues. / Grant fu li duels e grant dut estre, / mais issi plout al rei celestre, / del duc Robert, qui si fina, / grant fu li duels e mult dura; / wit anz aveit Robert vescue / puis ke il out le fieu tenu." Wace, *RR*, vv. 3223–40.

132. Wace remarks that he remembers his father's words well, although he was a *vaslet* at the time that he heard them. "Mais jo oï dire a mon pere / – bien m'en sovient, mais vaslet ere – ." Wace, *RR*, vv. 6423–24. See van Houts, "Ship List of William the Conqueror," 159–83, at 163, n. 22; van Houts, "Wace as Historian," 105, n. 12; and Bennett, "Wace and Warfare," 37–57, at 37.

originally destined for a military career before being taken to Caen as a young boy to receive a clerical education. After receiving elementary instruction in Caen, probably at Saint-Étienne, Wace tells us that he went to Paris to continue his studies. He says that he returned from the Île-de-France (probably before Henry I's death in 1135) and for a long time resided in Caen where he worked as a *clerc lisant*. Wace also tells us that he received a prebend as a canon of Bayeux from Henry II (in the 1160s), presumably as payment for the *Roman de Rou*. He seems to have remained in the region, most likely living and writing in Caen and Bayeux until his death in the late 1170s or early 1180s.[133]

From what little is known of Wace's life, he appears to have had very deep ties to Normandy and to have been born into a family of at least moderate means, perhaps even of some nobility. He could point to an ancestor who had served in Duke Robert's household and implies that he had initially been destined for a military career as a small child. He certainly says nothing to indicate that either his education or his ability to travel to Paris to study were extraordinary. Everything he reveals about himself fosters the impression that he came from a reasonably well-off Norman family with ancestral ties to the ducal household. Whether Wace was, in fact, descended from Duke Robert's chamberlain or was a member of the lesser nobility in Normandy, however, is largely irrelevant. The important point is that Wace constructs such an identity for himself, and it is from within this persona that he delivers his criticisms of William the Conqueror and Henry I.

By his own account, Wace spent the vast majority of his life in Caen and the Bessin, on the eastern border of the Cotentin—precisely the region that had been a main focus of contention between Henry I and Robert Curthose. Robert had either granted or mortgaged the Cotentin to Henry in

---

133. Wace may have continued to reside in Caen even after receiving his prebend, although he must have at least visited Bayeux on a fairly regular basis. He appears in three documents from Bayeux during this period: in an 1169 agreement between Bishop Henry II of Bayeux (1165–1204) and Abbot Gilbert of Troarn as *Wacius canonicus*; in a charter from 1174 that lists *Wascius* as one of the witnesses to an agreement between Richard of Le Hommet and the Bayeux chapter in the presence of Bishop Henry II; and in an undated document that refers to *Magister Wascius*. The documents were first discussed in E. du Meril, "La vie et les ouvrages de Wace," *Jahrbuch für Romanische und Englische Literatur* I (1859): 1–8. The first document is published in *Antiquus cartularius ecclesiae Baiocensis (Livre Noir)*, ed. V. Bourrienne, 2 vols. (Rouen-Paris, 1902), I:161–64 (no. cxxxv), and in R. N. Sauvage, *L'Abbaye de Saint-Martin de Troarn au diocese de Bayeux des origins au seizième siècle* (Caen, 1911), 81 (no. 2). The second document is published in *Antiquus cartularius*, I:54–56 (no. xlv). The third document is unpublished but is discussed by du Meril, "La vie," 6–7. See van Houts, "Wace as Historian," 105–6 and nn. 15–17.

1088, and had almost immediately attempted to take it back.[134] The lands of the Cotentin, Avranchin, and Bessin were the focus of disputes between the brothers for the next thirteen years.[135] Even after Henry's accession to the English throne in 1100 the Cotentin in particular remained a source of strife. Wace tells us that it was the ongoing dispute over the Cotentin that caused Henry to invade Normandy in 1105, resulting in Robert's capture at Tinchebray in 1106.[136] According to Wace, it was Henry's refusal to give up his claims in Normandy even after usurping the English throne that led to the civil war.[137] Wace's sources, however, blame Robert Curthose for provoking the war. Orderic specifically attributes Henry's invasion of Normandy to the fact that Robert broke the terms of his most recent treaty with Henry by reconciling with Robert of Bellême, whom Henry had recently exiled from England, while Robert de Torigny insists that Robert caused the war by squandering his inheritance and seeking every opportunity to provoke his brother's fury.[138] In his account of the civil war, Wace knowingly contradicts his sources and suggests that Henry was merely attempting to annex Normandy and subject it to his rule out of an apparently insatiable thirst for power.

The Norman civil war had been almost completely restricted to Wace's own territory, the Bessin, which had suffered the brunt of Henry's invasion. Henry looted and burned Bayeux in 1105, destroying the town and its cathedral. As C. Warren Hollister observed, "The burning of Bayeux was a horror not soon forgotten."[139] It was a trauma etched into the collective

---

134. There is some debate over whether this was a gift or a mortgage. Hollister agrees with Orderic and William of Malmesbury in asserting that Robert granted the Cotentin to Henry in return for three thousand pounds, but Robert de Torigny records that some people asserted that the Cotentin was only given to Henry in pledge for the money. Wace asserts unequivocally that Robert mortgaged the Cotentin to Henry. In any case, Robert attempted, unsuccessfully, to take the county back from Henry as soon as he had spent the money. Hollister, *Henry I*, 51; Orderic Vitalis, *HE*, viii, IV:120; William of Malmesbury, *GRA*, II:468; and *GND*, viii, II:205. It is also important to note that Henry did homage to Robert in return for the Cotentin. Although Robert is described as relinquishing this homage as part of the 1101 peace agreement with Henry, it remained the basis for charges that Henry had rebelled against his lord when he invaded Normandy in 1105. See David, *Robert Curthose*, 124; Le Patourel, *Norman Empire*, 343–44; Frank Barlow, *William Rufus* (New Haven, 2000), 70; Hollister, *Henry I*, 51; and Green, *Henry I*, 28.

135. C. Warren Hollister details the intricacies of the disputes in chapters 2, 3, and 4 of his biography of Henry I. See also Green, *Henry I*, chap. 1.

136. Wace, *RR*, vv. 10727–56.

137. Wace insinuates that Henry I stole the English throne from his brother, and that Henry knew this to be true. Wace, *RR*, vv. 10757–800.

138. Orderic, *HE*, xi, VI:47; and Torigny, *GND*, viii, II:221.

139. Hollister, *Henry I*, 188.

memory of the Bessinois, just as the names and deeds of the traitors had been indelibly impressed upon their minds. Henry then devastated the countryside between Bayeux and Caen, driving off the inhabitants to ensure that Robert and his men could not return to the region. The king next besieged Caen, which was strategically important as one of Normandy's economic and administrative centers. The townsmen of Caen, however, chose to surrender without a fight. This was precisely the area where Wace says he had spent most of his life, where he had received his early education during Henry I's reign, and where he lived out his later years. It was also presumably where Wace wrote and researched.

Even as reliable a partisan for Henry I as Orderic confirms that Wace was far from alone in his revulsion at the burning of Bayeux and the betrayal of Robert Curthose at Caen. Orderic reports that the townsmen of Caen, terrified by the burning of Bayeux and aware that Henry was hurrying toward them, sent to Henry to petition for peace before they suffered a similar fate.[140] He reports that the men of Caen made peace entirely on Henry's terms, expelled Robert's castellan, and turned the castle over to Henry. In return, Orderic says that Henry immediately handed over to the chief townsmen of Caen a manor (Orderic calls it Dallington, but Chibnall corrects this to Deddington) that has been called "Traitor's Manor" ever since.[141] It is worth noting again that many of Wace's more subversive claims are supported by his sources, and that the forceful defenses of the Conquest and Henry I's reign offered by men such as Orderic Vitalis and Robert de Torigny actually betray the anxieties surrounding these events. Had they been entirely unobjectionable, there would hardly have been a need to endorse them so vigorously and so often.

Wace also reminds us that he personally experienced Henry I's reign, asserting that he has known three Henrys (Henry I, Henry II, and the Young King Henry) and seen them all in Normandy.[142] In fact, this declaration seems designed to authenticate his inflammatory account of Henry I. It appears in the explicit of the *Roman de Rou*, in the midst of Wace's lament over the loss of his commission, and just after his account of the battle of Tinchebray. Although he was probably too young to remember the events of the civil war himself (he was probably born around 1110), Wace was

---

140. Orderic, *HE*, xi, VI:79.

141. Ibid., n. 6.

142. "Treis reis Henris ai coneüz, / en Normendie toz veüz; / d'Engletere e de Normendie / orent tuit trei la seignorie. / Li segont Henri que jo di / fu niés al premerain Henri, / né de Mahelt, l'empereriz, / e li tierz fu al segont filz." Wace, *RR*, vv. 11431–38.

likely to have grown up hearing local stories of Henry I's invasion and the horrors of the civil war, and he would have seen the scars they had left in the landscape around him. Henry had devastated Bayeux and burned its cathedral in 1105, the same cathedral in which Wace later served as a canon. Although it is unclear precisely when Bayeux cathedral was rebuilt (another fire in 1159 seems to have occasioned the total restoration of the building), similar catastrophic damage to other cathedrals such as Lisieux took thirty years to repair.[143] Bayeux's cathedral must have stood in a state of ruin or semiruin for decades, serving as a stark reminder of the brutality of Henry's invasion. The people Wace interviewed around Caen and Bayeux as he wrote his history some fifty years after the war may also have imparted their memories of it to him, memories that were conditioned by the fact that it was their land that Henry had invaded and ravaged, and it was their duke, recently returned from the Holy Land as a crusading hero, who had been deprived of his rights in England and then wrongfully dispossessed of his inheritance by his younger brother's treachery.

As Elisabeth van Houts has shown in her reassessment of Wace's account of the Conquest, Wace used both written and oral sources to supplement the Latin chronicles that form the basis of the *Roman de Rou*.[144] Wace appears to have scoured the archives of various Norman churches and monasteries and used their charters and other documents in crafting his account of the events leading up to and following the Conquest. He relied particularly on documents preserved in the cathedral archives at Bayeux and the ducal monasteries at Caen, but he also had access to documents held at the chief ducal monastery of Fécamp (where he was present at the translation of the bodies of Dukes Richard I and II in 1162).

Van Houts argues that, in addition to consulting a wide variety of documentary sources, Wace also interviewed his colleagues at Bayeux: men such as Richard de Bohun who was dean of the cathedral from 1137 to 1151 (before becoming bishop of Coutances), Philip of Harcourt who was bishop of Bayeux from 1142 to 1163, and Roger of Le Hommet who was archdeacon of Bayeux until 1161, when he became archbishop of Dol. These men would have shared family stories about their grandfathers' exploits in William the Conqueror's army.[145] Finally, she demonstrates that Wace also must

---

143. David Bates and Anne Curry, *England and Normandy in the Middle Ages* (London, 1994), 119; and Jacques Thirion, "La cathédrale de Bayeux," *Congrès archéologique* 132 (1978).

144. van Houts, "Wace as Historian," 103–32.

145. Ibid., 114.

have interviewed a great many of his contemporaries in Caen and Bayeux, especially the cathedral's extensive network of benefactors and servants. As van Houts correctly points out, many of these men and women were the grandchildren of the men who had accompanied William the Conqueror to England, and whom Wace lists as the Conqueror's companions. What van Houts does not mention, due to the fact that her focus is on examining Wace's depiction of the Conquest, is that many of the fathers of these same men and women had participated in the civil war between Henry I and Robert Curthose. One generation of their ancestors had taken part in the Conquest, and another had witnessed the Norman civil war. It seems certain that Wace would have asked them about their knowledge of more recent history, including Henry's invasion of Normandy, as he was collecting their family stories for the *Roman de Rou*. Indeed, Wace appears to have favored such oral testimony whenever it conflicted with the accounts found in his Latin sources.

The memories of the Bessinois, and the inhabitants of Bayeux and Caen in particular, were the recollections of the losing side in one of Anglo-Norman history's more important wars. Henry I had reunified the Anglo-Norman realm for the first time in almost twenty years, but he had done so by defeating and disinheriting his older brother, and dispossessing most of the Norman nobles who supported Robert. If we accept Wace's claim that he lived and wrote in this region during and after the time of Henry I, then we must assume that his account reflects this regional memory, its sympathy for its own duke and people, and its distaste for the invader. Many of the common people of Normandy had reacted with immediate horror to Henry's invasion of the duchy and the treason against Robert, as even Orderic's account of the burning of Bayeux and the surrender of Caen attests. And it is equally true that many of the Norman nobles, including those who had initially supported the king in return for money and gifts, quickly came to regret Henry's victory and resent his harsh rule. Within a few years of the supposedly decisive battle of Tinchebray, the Norman barons had already begun rebelling against Henry and forging alliances with anyone willing to confront the king.[146]

Since it is beyond doubt that Wace was intimately familiar with the defense of Henry I offered by his apologists, he cannot have rejected it lightly. Wace appears to have discarded their representations of Henry I because they were flatly contradicted by his own experience, memories, and research. By

---

146. See Green, *Henry I*, chaps. 5 and 6.

depicting Henry as a ruthless aggressor who invaded Normandy without adequate justification and dispossessed his own brother, Wace apparently felt that he was simply stating what many people, especially those living in Bayeux and Caen a generation after the civil war, already believed to be true. It is worth reiterating here that Wace was far from alone in his assessment of Henry I's character; the charges that he levels against the king are echoed in many of the English sources. *The Anglo-Saxon Chronicle*, Florence of Worcester, Eadmer of Canterbury, and Henry of Huntingdon, for example, variously criticize Henry's tyranny, his endless exactions, his method of bribing men to abandon Robert, and his dispossession of his brother and nephew. What sets Wace apart from these other historians is the fact that he voices such criticisms of Henry I within a vernacular history that was commissioned by Henry II and intended to shape the opinion of the French-speaking Anglo-Norman aristocracy and clergy. The stakes of circulating such criticisms in the vernacular were considerably higher than they would have been in a Latin history, as vernacular histories were, by definition, intended to be directly accessible to a much wider audience than their Latin cousins. Wace had thus committed the sin of choosing to express fairly common, but still quite subversive, views in an unusually public forum.

Perhaps the most important aspect of Wace's treatment of Henry I is that he appears to intentionally admonish Henry II through his criticism of Henry I. Like his grandfather, who arguably stole both kingdom and duchy from his eldest brother, Henry II appeared to be overstepping his authority, and he was certainly upsetting the established order by vigorously checking the power of his barons and interfering in the relations between his clergy and Rome. Of course, from Henry II's point of view, he was doing nothing of the sort. Henry II appears to have genuinely felt that he was restoring order rather than unsettling it, and that what can be described as his innovations were, in his eyes, merely forceful assertions of established traditions and privileges. In many senses, of course, Henry was absolutely right, but it was his misfortune to have misread some of the augurs. Whereas Henry's attempts to centralize royal government and professionalize its administration would ultimately succeed, his efforts to keep the Anglo-Norman clergy under royal control would fail as the clergy slowly distanced itself from the king and aligned itself with Rome. In any case, Wace appears to have been bent upon attempting to restrain Henry II's ambitions by reminding him that his legitimacy and authority in both England and Normandy were derived from very dubious sources (the Conquest and Henry I).

Wace's criticism of William the Conqueror, likewise, appears designed to chasten Henry II. By reminding his patron that England was conquered by a man with very tenuous claims to the kingdom, and that he was able to do so only with the assent and full cooperation of his barons and clergy, Wace apparently hoped to remind Henry II that he owed his very right to the English throne to the ancestors of the men whose power he was now curtailing.[147] Wace's portrayal of William's death and funeral also provide a warning to Henry II. In effect, Wace reminds Henry II that William abused his power, that he took land by force from one of his vassals, only to have it mar his legacy and almost prevent his burial. The obvious parallels between the offense William committed in seizing his vassal's land and Henry II's own actions in confiscating the properties and razing the castles of his barons would not have been lost on an aristocratic audience. The dispute over William's burial was a direct result of his failure to honor his seigneurial obligation to protect his vassals and promote their interests. Wace reminds us (and his patron) that, while William was powerful and feared during his life, his transgressions were exposed and punished after his death. It is also noteworthy that this episode, which Wace dwells on at great length, also happened to have occurred in Caen. This fact probably explains Wace's otherwise bizarre adaptation of Orderic's account of William's funeral. It seems very likely that Wace edited Orderic's account to reflect and conform to local memories of the event.

Implicit in Wace's criticism of Henry I, and in his indirect criticism of Henry II, is a distinct strain of nostalgia for a passing age.[148] Wace seems to

---

147. Wace's account of the Conquest stresses the indispensability of William's barons, his reliance on their counsel, and the necessity of persuading them to assist him. Wace, *RR*, vv. 5954–6180. See van Houts, "Ship List of William the Conqueror," 159–83.

148. Several of Wace's statements in the *Roman de Rou* describe the ideal functioning of the feudal bond, criticize those who fail to uphold their obligations, or wrestle with the complexities that competing loyalties create. "Mout ert prodons honnis qui sert mauvez seignor, / d'omme mauvez servir n'avra l'en ja honour." Wace, *RR*, II, vv. 1460–61. "Mais si home li ont preié / e por bien li ont conseillé / qu'a son seignor dreit en bataille, / que que il face aillors, ne faille. / Guillaume est sis naturels sire / e il sis hoem, nel poet desdire, / posa que il fist homage, / veiant son pere e son barnage; / n'a dreit el fieu ne en l'enor / qui s'en combat vers son seignor." Wace, *RR*, 3887–96. "Grant honte fait, ne poet graignor, / qui traïst son lige seignor." Wace, *RR*, vv. 11383–84. "Par Normendie fist banir / e comander e establir / que chevalier qui sis hoem fust, / qui terre e fieu de lui eüst, / en Engleterre ne passast / ne od le rei ne demorast, / ne hoem le rei ne devenist / ne serement ne li feïst, / en Normandie remainsist / e do son fieu le duc servist; / e cil qui d'Engleterre esteient / e en Engleterre maneient / en Engleterre remainsissent / e de lor fieus le rei servissent. / Ker nul, ço dit, a son espeir / - e quit bien que il diseit veir - / dous seignors bien ne servireit / ne egalment nes amereit, / que a l'un mielz ne se tenist / e que a l'un mielz ne volsist." Wace, *RR*, vv. 10819–38.

lament the passing of the old social order in which a more autonomous aristocracy shared in the duties of governing and acted as a counterbalance to the king, an order that was being threatened by Henry II's efforts to centralize power. Many of Wace's comments reveal that he viewed the relationship between the king and his barons as one of reciprocal obligation in which the aristocracy enjoyed a great deal of autonomy and was a necessary partner in governing (as was decidedly the case during Stephen's reign). The new standards being forged by Henry II and his counselors checked the power and autonomy of the barons, narrowed their role in governing by professionalizing the administration of justice, and insisted that the king's interests always outweighed those of his barons. Many of Henry's actions effectively sought to marginalize aristocratic authority, and the same can be said of Henry's actions with regard to the clergy as the king attempted to exert control over their affairs (most notably through the Constitutions of Clarendon).

Wace's history exposes the dangers of unchecked royal authority, and at least one historian has speculated that this was a result of Henry II's dispute with Thomas Becket.[149] It is quite likely that Wace took Becket's side against Henry in the dispute over clerical autonomy, but we need not look only to the Becket dispute to explain Wace's motivations. It cannot be overemphasized that Wace's motives for admonishing his patron were potentially numerous as Henry II regularly alienated his clergy, his barons, and his family with his attempts to monopolize power and regulate their affairs. Although he was undoubtedly a cleric, internal evidence from the *Roman de Rou* suggests that Wace also considered himself a member of the aristocracy.[150] And Wace displays notable sympathy for Henry II's sons and barons in his *Chronique Ascendante*. Indeed, he shifts the blame for their part in the great rebellion of 1173/74 onto the duplicitous French, whom he accuses of perpetually attempting to sabotage the Normans.[151] It is therefore likely that Wace's disaffection with Henry was a more general response to the seismic changes in the world around him, and that his criticisms of royal power were symptomatic of defiance in the face of these changes. Wace probably

---

149. Jean-Guy Gouttebroze has argued that Henry's attempts to control the relations between the clergy and papacy, and his campaigns to sanctify his ancestors Richard I, Richard II, and Edward the Confessor polarized the Anglo-Norman clergy, and that circumstantial evidence suggests that Wace aligned himself with the supporters of Becket and the papacy against the king. Gouttebroze, "Pourquoi congédier un historiographe," 289–311.

150. Wace, *RR*, vv. 3221–29.

151. Wace, *RR*, I, vv. 45–96.

viewed Henry as overbearing in his dealings with his barons and clergy, and with his own sons, and meant to chastise the king by reminding him that his grandfather's harsh rule was not universally viewed as a model of good governance. Whether Wace intended to rebuke Henry II for his treatment of his clergy, his barons, or his sons, he must have been aware that any attack on Henry I's legacy undermined the legitimacy and government of his grandson.

The order that Wace champions in the *Roman de Rou*, and that he seems to hope to restore, was already in crisis and passing as he wrote. Not only was Henry II reshaping government in every corner of his lands and exceeding his grandfather in his efforts to centralize power, Normandy itself had become a mere appendage to Henry's greatly expanded empire and the king's attention was often focused elsewhere. It should, therefore, not be entirely surprising that Wace chose to sound a note of rebellion in his history. The fact that Henry was actively redefining the relations between the king and his barons and clergy, and refusing to cede a measure of power to his sons, likely prompted Wace (like many other historians working during Henry II's reign) to textually embed the old ideals in his history, celebrate their virtues, and protest their passing. His portrayal of Robert Curthose in particular celebrates a conception of chivalry and lordship that was losing ground to the ruthlessly calculating realism that he attributed to Henry I and apparently saw traces of in Henry II.

With the old order passing before his eyes, we may reasonably ask what results Wace thought such reminders might produce. Did he think they had any chance of turning the tide, or was he merely indulging in some hopeless exercise? At the risk of appearing to equivocate, and without the benefit of much guidance from Wace, it was probably a bit of both. As a historian, and one with a particularly inquisitive mind at that, Wace could not have failed to notice that nothing stays the same. In fact, Wace often pauses to remind his readers of the transience of life and power, and the capriciousness of fortune. In the opening of part III, Wace recounts the triumphs of Alexander the Great and Julius Caesar, only to observe that "neither of these two men, who conquered so much, had so many lands and captured so many kings, had when he died any more of his own domain than his own length. What good has all of this done them . . . ? All that remains of them is their names."[152] Wace must have also realized that

---

152. "Cil dui vassal, ki tant cunquistrent, / tant eurent terres, tanz reis pristrent, / enprés la mort, de lur onur / ne out chescun ne meis sa lungar. / Quel bien lur feit, quel bien lur est / de lur pris et de lur cunquest? / Ne mais tant cum l'um veit disant, / si cum l'um le ad truvé lisant, / que Alisandre e

the very history he was writing amply demonstrated the principle that power is fleeting. He could see, for instance, that Henry I had grabbed the reins of power through sheer will and had centralized that power to an unprecedented degree, only to have it revert into the hands of the barons under Stephen. Wace may well have thought that this was a good indication that Henry II's efforts to achieve an even greater centralization of royal authority were ultimately doomed to failure, and that he could help restore the old balance by pointing this out to his patron.

Although Wace's history was clearly intended to be didactic and serve as a mirror for the prince, the efficacy of such any such work has always depended on the disposition of the prince in question and his willingness to accept instruction. Wace would probably have noticed that the mighty seldom heed the lessons of history, especially when those lessons run counter to their own desires. Henry II appears to have been no exception to this rule. From this point of view, no amount of admonition or instruction on Wace's part (or anyone else's part for that matter) was likely to produce the desired result. In some sense, Wace appears to have dutifully done what historians writing for the benefit of princes had always done. He pointed out fortune's faithlessness, the transient and blighted nature of temporal power, and hoped to have some influence on the king's behavior, while probably expecting little to actually come of his efforts. This is not meant to suggest that Wace knowingly squandered his energies on a futile enterprise. Correcting a historical record you believe to be flawed is not pointless, nor is attempting to redirect the course of events in the face of improbable odds.

Clearly, Wace did not succeed in persuading Henry II to temper his actions, and we can surmise that, in all likelihood, Wace lost his commission precisely for giving Henry II such unwelcome reminders about his ancestry, and the origins and limits of his power. As it happens, Wace appears to have taken a measure of revenge on Henry II in the version of the *Roman de Rou* that has filtered down to posterity. Wace ended his history on a controversial note with the battle of Tinchebray.

It is highly unlikely that in the fifteen years Wace spent working on the *Rou* that he failed to bring his narrative at least to the death of Henry I— roughly the point at which Benoît de Sainte-Maure's *Chronique* ends. It seems more likely that Wace had managed to complete a version of the *Rou*

Cesar furent, / tant i ad de eus que lur nuns durent." Wace, *RR*, vv. 119–28. In fact, Wace's choice to focus on Alexander and Caesar may be intended as an implicit criticism of secular rulers, as both were known for their tyranny, ultimate failure, and early deaths.

that terminated with the death of Henry I by the time he was replaced by Benoît around 1174. Elisabeth van Houts has argued that Wace terminated the *Roman de Rou* with Tinchebray because that is essentially where his major sources, the B and E redactions of the *Gesta Normannorum ducum*, ended.[153] Although her argument appears quite reasonable, on closer inspection it suffers from two flaws. First, by this reasoning the *Rou* would essentially end at 1070/71 (the terminus of the B redaction) or possibly at 1109/13 (the terminus of the E redaction), but certainly not at 1106. Second, we know that Wace also relied on Orderic's *Historia Ecclesiastica*, which continues slightly beyond Henry I's death in 1135. Van Houts was absolutely correct to indicate that three different versions of the *Gesta Normannorum ducum* with different terminus points provided the basic framework for both Wace's and Benoît's histories (Benoît was using the F redaction to which Robert de Torigny had appended material up to 1135/37), but Wace displays a clear ability to venture beyond the confines of the B and E redactions of the *Gesta Normannorum ducum*. In fact, as van Houts has also pointed out, Wace does so precisely by constructing his own account of Henry I's reign with the help of Orderic's *Historia Ecclesiastica*, William of Malmesbury's *Gesta regum Anglorum*, and the *Brevis Relatio*.[154]

The need to rely on sources other than the *Gesta Normannorum ducum* may have slowed Wace's progress, as van Houts has also suggested, but it hardly explains Wace's decision to end the *Rou* with Tinchebray.[155] It appears to have taken Wace roughly five years to complete the *Roman de Brut*, a work of only slightly less length than the *Roman de Rou* (the *Brut* consists of 14,866 lines, while there are a total of 16,930 lines in the *Rou*, including the *Chronique Ascendante* and the false start to part II).[156] Even allowing that compiling materials from diverse sources was an impediment to Wace's progress, it seems that fifteen years would still have been ample time for him to bring his history up to 1135—or at least up to some point other than Tinchebray.

The most compelling reason to believe that the *Roman de Rou* originally had some other terminus has more to do with the connotations of Tinchebray than it does with any of these ancillary arguments. The battle of

---

153. "The B and E redactions of the *GND* used by Wace essentially end at 1070/1, although they do include a few excursions up to the period 1109/13; the F redaction used by Benoît ends with King Henry I's death followed by a few chapters on the period 1135/7." van Houts, "Adaptation," 116.

154. Ibid., 118.

155. Ibid.

156. Wace appears to have written the entire *Roman de Brut* between 1150 and 1155. *Wace's Roman de Brut*, xii.

Tinchebray was not a natural terminus derived from the B or E redactions of the *Gesta Normannorum ducum*, and it most certainly was not a neutral event. On the contrary, it was one of the most contentious events in Norman history and a serious rupture in the ducal succession. It was the point at which Henry I defeated his eldest brother, Robert Curthose, and wrested from him control of Normandy, Robert's inheritance. After Tinchebray, Henry imprisoned Robert for the remainder of his life and ruled Normandy in his place. Robert died a prisoner in 1134, a year before Henry's own death in 1135. By ending the *Roman de Rou* with Tinchebray, Wace impugned the public memory of Henry I and offered an affront to Henry II. He effectively stated that the line of legitimate Norman dukes had ended with Robert and that Henry's usurpation marked the beginning of a reign of impostors. He also suggested, none too subtly, that Henry II's legitimacy rested on a particularly suspect foundation as a result of his grandfather's usurpation of Normandy (and arguably England).

It is especially telling that Wace defends Robert Curthose in the *Roman de Rou*, that he argues for Robert's rights and refuses to denounce him. Indeed, Wace seems to feel that Robert Curthose's rights as the firstborn son, and especially his hereditary right to Normandy, outweigh whatever arguments Henry's apologists could muster in favor of deposing him. Orderic, for instance, went to great lengths to construct a legal and ideological justification for Henry's actions. He offers the most comprehensive argument in favor of Henry's right to interfere in his brother's duchy in the speech he composes for Bishop Serlo of Séez, the former abbot of Saint-Évroul. The argument, based on principles apparently derived from the Peace of God, consists of three parts: that Robert Curthose is an ineffectual ruler who does not or cannot defend the Norman church and people; that a ruler is required to provide a minimum level of protection to the church and to the defenseless; and that Henry has an obligation to protect Normandy (his father's patrimony) if his brother cannot do so, regardless of the fact that he is not its duke.[157] It bears repeating here that Orderic and Robert de Torigny clearly felt the weight of the arguments against Henry's actions in invading Normandy and capturing Robert at Tinchebray, that they understood that Henry had done something terrible and exceptional, and that they realized that extraordinary arguments were necessary to justify his actions.

Like the burning of Bayeux, Tinchebray had left a harrowing impression on Norman memory. Even those who supported Henry in the sincere

---

157. Orderic, *HE*, xi, VI:60–68.

hope that he would restore order in Normandy recognized that they had to develop extraordinary arguments to justify his actions. Orderic's conflicted feelings about Henry's appropriation of Normandy are apparent throughout his account of the civil war. In his speech for Bishop Serlo, for instance, Orderic reports that Serlo exhorted Henry to take Normandy from Robert. The bishop tells Henry that God demands that he " 'be angry' to some purpose and, as David, prophet and king, teaches, 'sin not,' by taking up arms not for lust of earthly power but for the defense of *your* country."[158] Even while making the case for Henry's invasion, Orderic's speech for Bishop Serlo makes it clear that the prospect of such a war was profoundly disturbing to contemporaries. Orderic presumably would not have thought it necessary to insist that a Norman bishop assured Henry that he would be blameless in the eyes of God if Henry's intervention in Normandy were not deeply problematic. Nor would he have gone to such great lengths to demonstrate that it was Henry's Christian duty to depose his brother.

After the war, Orderic again defends Henry's deposition of Robert as a necessary evil. He recalls that Robert of Bellême went to Count Helias of Maine seeking to enlist his aid against the king, charging that Henry's "rebellion" had turned the world upside down. Robert asserts that "a younger brother has rebelled against an elder, a servant has conquered his master in war and thrown him into chains. Moreover, he has robbed him of his ancestral inheritance and, as a perjured vassal, has taken his lord's rights into his own hand."[159] Helias replies, "If indeed [Henry] has fought against his elder brother and lord, as you assert, he was driven to it by the most urgent necessity, in response to the invitation and prayers of churchmen who were wretchedly oppressed by reprobates." Orderic then asserts that Helias made a revealing admission: "Indeed, as the popular saying goes, 'wrong must be done to put an end to a worse wrong. . . . It is by the just judgment of God that victory has been bestowed by heaven on a friend of peace and justice, and the opposing party utterly destroyed.' "[160] Despite his efforts to advance

---

158. " 'Pro tanta natalis soli erumna probe rex utiliter irascere, et sicut Dauid propheta et rex commonet noli peccare, arma sumens pro defensione patriae non pro terrenae potestatis augendae cupidatate.' " Orderic, *HE*, xi, VI:62–64.

159. " 'Ecce iunior frater in maiorem surrexit, seruus in bello dominum suum superauit, et uinclis iniecit. Auitam quoque illi heredidatem abstulit, sicque periurus domini sui iura sibimet subiecit.' " Orderic, *HE*, xi, VI:94.

160. " 'Si contra fratrem suum ut asseris maiorem et dominum pugnauit ad hoc ipsum maxima necessitas compulit, et supplicato religiosorum qui miserabiliter a biothanatis conculabantur inuitauit. Porro sicut uulgus in cotidiana locutione perhibet malum debet fieri ut peius cesset. . . . Iusto iudicio Dei actum est quod amatori pacis et iusticiae uictoria celitus collata est, atque contraria pars

an argument supporting Henry's right to intervene in Normandy, even Orderic must finally concede that Henry's actions may have been wrong, or illicit, according to the laws of men. He resorts to asserting that Henry had to do wrong to end a worse wrong, and that his victory over Robert has proven that God favored him. Tellingly, Orderic also encourages us to discount the most forceful argument against Henry's actions by putting it directly into the mouth of Robert of Bellême, a man whom Orderic consistently portrays as a cruel, self-serving monster, and whom Orderic blames for most of Normandy's troubles during Robert's tenure.

It can be argued, of course, that Wace's protests were useless. Henry II was still king of England and duke of Normandy whatever Wace might say and in spite of anything his ancestors might have done. Even so, circulating such pointed criticisms was inflammatory and dangerous, especially in a vernacular history specifically designed to influence Henry II's nobles. It had the potential to encourage rebellion by reminding the Anglo-Norman aristocracy and clergy that Henry II's legitimacy rested on very unsteady ground, and it threatened to derail Henry II's plans for the succession of his children for precisely the same reason. The nobles and clergy still played a central role in accepting and crowning the king's heir, and this point would hardly have been lost on Henry II as his own bid for the throne might have been doomed to failure had the barons and clergy not come to view him as the legitimate heir over Stephen's son Eustace. To focus only on the fact that Wace's protest ultimately accomplished none of these things is to miss the point that it had very real and very destructive capacities that no contemporary could have failed to notice.

Finally, it is very likely that Wace's criticism of Henry II and his ancestors escalated in direct response to Henry's actions. Although Wace may have felt that a certain amount of criticism of the royal character and lineage was permissible (or even required) before he lost his commission, he most likely ramped up his criticism of Henry I in response to Henry II's many efforts to curtail the power of his barons and regulate the affairs of his clergy between 1160 and 1174. It also seems incredible that Wace would have presented a version of the *Roman de Rou* ending with Tinchebray to Henry II unless he intended to insult and provoke him. It is more likely that Wace either truncated an earlier version of the *Rou* to end with Tinchebray as a parting blow after he was replaced by Benoît de Sainte-Maure, or that he

---

penitus obruta est.'" Orderic, *HE*, xi, VI:96. See also David, *Robert Curthose*, 124; Le Patourel, *Norman Empire*, 343–44; Barlow, *William Rufus*, 70; and Hollister, *Henry I*, 51.

purposely closed with Tinchebray after learning that he had been fired. Wace was an old man by 1174, in his midsixties or midseventies; he had already received a prebend at Bayeux, presumably as payment for his work, and he had apparently seen the king's largesse decline over the previous decade.[161] When the humiliating news came that he had been replaced, Wace was approaching the end of his life, he had apparently already received compensation for his work, and he had little to fear in the way of retaliation from the king; he might have felt entirely justified and relatively safe in committing this last act of defiance, when it could do his professional life the least harm.

---

161. Wace's plea for financial support in the *Chronique Ascendate* indicates that this was the case.

CHAPTER 4

The *Chronique des ducs de Normandie*

Sometime around 1174, Henry II transferred the commission for a history of his Norman ancestors from Wace to Benoît de Sainte-Maure.[1] Obviously dissatisfied with the history that Wace had taken almost fifteen years to produce, yet equally unwilling to abandon the project, Henry appears to have searched for a more amenable author. In turning to Benoît, Henry chose an author with notable similarities to his

---

1. Wace is our only source of information regarding the transfer of the commission, although Benoît repeatedly names Henry II as his patron in the *Chronique*. The date of the transfer of the commission is unclear, but Wace speaks of it as having already happened when he closes part III of the *Roman de Rou*, presumably just after 1174. There has also been a debate surrounding the identity of the "Maistre Beneeit" Wace names as his successor. Léopold Constans, an early editor of the *Roman de Troie*, argued against identifying the author of the *Chronique* as Benoît de Sainte-Maure. *Le Roman de Troie, par Benoît de Sainte-Maure, pub. d'apres tous les manuscrits connus par Léopold Constans*, 6 vols. (Paris, 1904–12), VI:165. Current scholarly opinion, however, holds that the *Chronique des ducs de Normandie* and the *Roman de Troie* were both produced by Benoît de Sainte-Maure. See Benoît de Sainte-Maure, *Chronique des ducs de Normandie, publiee d'aprés le manuscrit de Tours*, I:150; Becker, "Die Normannenchroniken: Wace und seine Bearbeiter," 481–519, at 485; Paul Zumthor, *Histoire littéraire de la France médiévale* (Paris, 1954), 192, n. 371; Robert Bossuat, *Le Moyen Âge* (Paris, 1931), 140; Wace, *Roman de Rou*, trans. Burgess, xiv; Penny Ely, "History and Romance in the *Chronique des ducs de Normandie*," *Medium Aevum* 68 (1999): 81–95, at 81; H. B. Teunis, "Benoît de Sainte-Maure and William the Conqueror's *Amor*," *ANS* 12 (1990): 199–209, at 199; and Peter Damian-Grint, "*En nul leu nel truis escrit*: Research and Invention in Benoît de Sainte-Maure's *Chronique des ducs de Normandie*," *ANS* 21 (1999): 11–30, at 11.

predecessor. Benoît was close to the Anglo-Norman court and the popularity of his previous work, the *Roman de Troie*, had endowed him with a certain degree of fame.[2] Like Wace, Benoît had experience in adapting Latin histories for a vernacular audience and had dedicated his previous work to Queen Eleanor.[3] Benoît's *Roman de Troie*, a vernacular adaptation of Dares Phrygius's *De excidio Troiae historia* with material from Dictys Cretensis's *Ephemeris belli Troiani*, is a romanticized account of the strife between the ancient Greeks and Trojans, and modern historians have accordingly avoided it.[4] Indeed, Peter Damian-Grint goes so far as to wonder why Henry would have turned to a purveyor of romances for a dynastic history. This question, however, presumes that twelfth-century audiences recognized the same generic distinctions employed by modern scholars and that their expectations of the quality and veracity of a text were dependent on these distinctions. Although the *Roman de Troie* is very different in tone and content from the *Roman de Brut*, Damian-Grint's observation that "Benoît was not a historian at all but a writer of romance" posits a rigid generic distinction between history and romance when the late twelfth-century reality appears to have been more fluid (all of the *romans antiques* purport to translate authentic historical narratives).[5] It is worth remembering that neither *De excidio*

---

2. There are thirty manuscripts and twenty-eight fragments of the *Roman de Troie* still extant. For a full list of the extant manuscripts, see Constans, *Le Roman de Troie*.

3. *Roman de Troie*, vv. 13457–94. The dedication of the *Roman de Troie* to Eleanor would not necessarily have helped Benoît in securing Henry's patronage around 1174, as Eleanor had been arrested and imprisoned in 1173 for her role in assisting her sons in their rebellion against Henry, but it does not appear to have hurt him either. Indeed, Benoît may have received the commission not because of his dedication of the *Roman de Troie* to Eleanor but because he was an Angevin. Both Jean Blacker and Carin Fahlin have suggested that Benoît was from Sainte-Maure in the Touraine, where the earliest extant manuscript of the *Chronique* was produced. See Blacker, *Faces of Time*, 186, and Carin Fahlin, *Etude sur le manuscrit de Tours de la Chronique des ducs de Normandie par Benoît* (Uppsala, 1937), 172. Elisabeth van Houts, on the other hand, says that Benoît was "from the village of Sainte-Maur in Poitou," but she provides no evidence or rationale for her assertion. van Houts, "Adaptation of the *Gesta Normannorum*," 115–24, at 119. In either case, Benoît would have been born and probably raised in Angevin territory, and was thus likely to have been more closely attached to Henry II than to Eleanor.

4. See Stefan Merkle, "Telling the True Story of the Trojan War: The Eyewitness Account of Dictys of Crete," in *The Search for the Ancient Novel*, ed. James Tatum (Baltimore, 1994), 183–96.

5. Damian-Grint, "*En nul leu nel truis escrit*," 11. Damian-Grint goes on to demonstrate that Benoît is casting himself in the guise of historian in the *Chronique des ducs de Normandie*, and I would add that a brief review of the prologue of the *Roman de Troie* (vv. 1–140) reveals that Benoît constructs that work as a history as well. In fact, he employs many of the rhetorical strategies medieval authors normally marshaled to persuade their audiences of the veracity of their work. We are constantly reminded in the *Roman de Troie* that Benoît is "faithfully translating" Latin texts, texts that establish the authority and authenticity of his account. Benoît's description of Dares's account, which is derived from a Greek original allegedly produced by a Trojan eyewitnesses to the events described,

Troiae historia nor *Ephemeris belli Troiani* were regarded as pseudohistories in the twelfth century, and that they were preferred to the Homeric version precisely because they claimed to be eyewitness accounts.[6] It would therefore be more generous, and more accurate, to say that the *Roman de Troie* and the other *romans antiques* inhabit a shadowy region between history and literature in that they purport to represent history while catering to specific literary tastes. In spite of the highly romanticized and fictionalized qualities of the *Roman de Troie*, it seems arbitrary to insist that the majority of its twelfth-century audience did not regard it as history in much the same vein as Geoffrey of Monmouth's *Historia regum Britanniae* or Wace's *Roman de Brut*.[7] Benoît's ability to produce a wildly popular adaptation of such material was probably the very quality that recommended him to Henry as a replacement for Wace. Benoît came to this project then in much the same way and with many of the same credentials as Wace.

In spite of the similarities between Wace and Benoît, a great deal had changed since Henry II first commissioned a history of his Norman ancestors in 1160. In 1160 Henry was still a very young king laboring to restore royal authority in England, and attempting to impose his authority in Aquitaine. His marriage to Eleanor of Aquitaine in 1152 had been a major political coup, and was producing future heirs who were still too young to threaten their father (their oldest surviving child, Henry, was five years old in 1160 and their last child, John, was not born until 1167). In 1160 Henry appeared to be going from strength to strength. In spite of the considerable

---

stresses the authenticity of *De excidio Troiae historia*, and, as Damian-Grint points out, is contrasted with Homeric "lies." Finally, Benoît refers several times to the "estoire" that he is laboring to translate (*en romanz metre*). Damian-Grint has evaluated the same evidence, but reaches the conclusion that Benoît is using "estoire" to refer to Dares's account as an "original true narrative" and is certainly not referring to his own work. Damian-Grint, "*Estoire* as Word and Genre," 189–99, at 196. This statement, however, raises an obvious question. Why would Benoît stress the *auctoritas*, authenticity, and reliability of his source with such insistence? What purpose did it serve other than advancing a claim of veracity for his own text?

6. Cf. Merkle, "Telling the True Story of the Trojan War," 183–96; and Damian-Grint, "*Estoire* as Word and Genre," 189–99.

7. Although it is true that Geoffrey of Monmouth had his twelfth-century critics, William of Malmesbury, William of Newburgh, Gerald of Wales, Henry of Huntingdon, and even Wace among them, the undisputed popularity of the *Historia regum Britanniae*, which survives in at least 215 manuscripts, is a testament to the fact that Geoffrey's revisionist history was preferred to the histories of his detractors. For discussions of Geoffrey's revisioning of Anglo-Saxon history, his status as an authority, and the reception of the *Historia regum Britanniae*, see Leckie, *Passage of Dominion*; Julia Crick, *The 'Historia regum Britanniae' of Geoffrey of Monmouth*, 4; Michael Curley, *Geoffrey of Monmouth* (New York, 1994); and Valerie I. J. Flint, "The *Historia regum Britanniae* of Geoffrey of Monmouth: Parody and Its Purpose, a Suggestion," *Speculum* 54/3 (1979): 447–68.

tasks facing him, he was consolidating his power and looking toward the future of his dynasty. By 1174 Henry's world had changed dramatically. Although he was firmly ensconced as king of England, duke of Normandy and Aquitaine, and count of Anjou, Henry existed in a political landscape characterized by centrifugal tendencies, constantly struggling to keep his far-flung dominions intact. Friends, events, and Henry's own family now turned against him as often as not. After a prolonged and bitter fight with the king, his former friend and mentor, Archbishop Thomas Becket had won a martyr's crown in 1170. Henry was forced to perform penance twice for his role in the archbishop's murder—first at Avranches in 1172 and again at Canterbury Cathedral in 1174.[8] Queen Eleanor had been arrested and imprisoned in 1173 for encouraging her sons to rebel against their father and would spend the rest of Henry's life under guard.[9] Finally, three of Henry's sons had grown old and discontented enough to defy him. In 1173 all of Henry's sons but John, and many of his disaffected barons, had rebelled

---

8. Becket's murder in Canterbury Cathedral by four knights of Henry's household on December 29, 1170, produced widespread indignation and ignited a firestorm from which all of Henry's rivals—most notably Louis VII and King Stephen's brother, Count Theobald of Blois—hoped to gain some political advantage. See Roger of Howden, *Gesta Regis Henrici Secundi*, I:14–16; and Roger of Howden, *Chronica Rogeri de Houedene*, II:18–22. Becket was immediately celebrated as a martyr and canonized in March 1173; his reputation for having defied Henry only added to his fame. *Materials for the History of Thomas Becket*, ed. J. C. Robertson, 7 vols. (London, 1875–85), Epistolae, VII:545–46. It was only the measured response of Pope Alexander III that saved Henry from becoming a casualty of the backlash Becket's murder had unleashed. Rather than excommunicating Henry or laying England under interdict, Alexander excommunicated the murderers on March 25, 1171, and pronounced that the king was prohibited from entering a church until he had been reconciled to the church. *Materials for the History of Thomas Becket*, Epistolae, VII:478. Henry was reconciled to the church in a public ceremony at Avranches Cathedral on Sunday, May 21, 1172, after admitting that his anger had prompted his servants to kill Becket. Among the terms of the reconciliation were provisions that required Henry to renounce any innovations prejudicial to the church that had been introduced during his reign and to swear that he would not impede appeals to Rome. These provisions effectively annulled the Constitutions of Clarendon, which had been the source of Henry's troubles with Becket in the first place. *Materials for the History of Thomas Becket*, Epistolae, VII:517–18. Henry performed public penance at Canterbury Cathedral on July 13, 1174. William of Newburgh, "Historia rerum Anglicarum," I:183–85; Roger of Howden, *Gesta*, I:67 and *Chronica*, II:63–64; and Jordan Fantosme, "*Chronique de la guerre entre les Anglois et les Ecossois en 1173 et 1174*," in *Chronicles of the Reigns of Stephen, Henry II and Richard I*, ed. R. Howlett, 4 vols. (London, 1884–90), III:202–377, at 350–52.

9. Eleanor was arrested in 1173 attempting to reach the French court in order to join her sons in their rebellion against Henry. Gervase of Canterbury, *Historical Works*, I:242. She was imprisoned at Winchester and Salisbury after July 7, 1174. Eyton, *Court, Household and Itinerary of King Henry II*, 177 and 180. After 1184 she was sometimes allowed to appear or travel with Henry and was guarded less closely, but she remained Henry's prisoner until his death in 1189, when she was released by her son Richard. Roger of Howden, *Gesta*, I:74, 301, 304, 305, 313, 319, 334, 337, and 345; Ralph of Diceto, *Radulphi de Diceto Decani Lundoniensis Opera Historica*, II:67; and Matthew of Paris, *Matthaei Parisiensis Chronica Majora*, ed. Henry Richards Luard, 7 vols. (London, 1872–84), II:116.

against him. Although Henry had definitively put down the rebellion and restored order in 1174, reconciling with his sons and barons on terms favorable to them, the events of the early 1170s had bruised and battered him. Far from being cowed, Henry appears to have redoubled his efforts to assert his authority and assure the future of his dynasty.

Benoît entered the fray at a crucial stage when the king's authority had just been challenged on almost all fronts.[10] Henry may have emerged from these trials victorious (with the exceptions of having to admit his guilt in Becket's murder and rescind the Constitutions of Clarendon), but this did not mean he could assume his authority would never again be assailed. Indeed, his later years were punctuated by further rebellions by his sons and challenges from the French king, Philip Augustus. Whereas Wace had been hired to write a legitimizing, dynastic history in the wake of the crisis caused by the 1135 succession dispute and the civil war (at a time when Henry was trying to ensure the survival of his newly restored dynasty), Benoît was hired to rewrite that history in the wake of a massive assault on Henry's authority. Presumably Benoît was enlisted to correct the deficiencies of Wace's history and provide a more serviceable portrayal of Henry's ancestors. Although Benoît's rewriting of Norman history may not have delivered everything that Henry could have desired, his *Chronique des ducs de Normandie* was certainly more flattering to Henry's ancestors than Wace's *Roman de Rou* had been.[11]

In fact, Benoît appears to have discarded Wace's work completely and begun the project anew. Going back to essentially the same Latin sources Wace had used, Benoît extended the history to almost three times the length of Wace's work without significantly expanding its subject matter.[12] Benoît's most significant departure from Wace was his use of Robert de Torigny's

---

10. As noted above, the date of the transfer of the commission from Wace to Benoît is unclear, but I am inclined to believe that Henry made the decision after 1174. The internal evidence from Wace's *Chronique Ascendante* supports this view as it refers to events that occurred in 1174, and Wace would hardly have pleaded for largesse from his benefactor in the *Chronique Ascendante* if he already knew that he had been fired.

11. The Tours and London manuscripts are the only extant copies of the *Chronique*. The Tours manuscript is written in Benoît de Sainte-Maure's own dialect and was executed in the late twelfth century; the London manuscript was produced in the early thirteenth century. Cf. Benoît de Sainte-Maure, *Chronique des ducs de Normandie, publiee d'aprés le manuscrit de*, and Benoît de Sainte-Maure, *Chronique des ducs de Normandie, par Benoit, trouvére anglo-normand du XIIe siècle*.

12. The *Chronique des ducs de Normandie* consists of almost forty-five thousand lines while the *Roman de Rou* contains a mere sixteen thousand lines. While the *Roman de Rou* ends in 1106, it includes references to events as late as the death of William Audelin in 1120. The bulk of the *Chronique des ducs de Normandie* likewise terminates in 1106; only its final one thousand lines recount

F redaction of William of Jumièges's *Gesta Normannorum ducum*, rather than Orderic Vitalis' E redaction or the anonymous B redaction, upon which Wace had relied.[13] While Benoît used the *Gesta Normannorum ducum* to provide the frame for his narrative, he also included material derived from Dudo of Saint-Quentin's *De moribus et actis primorum normanniae ducum*, Orderic Vitalis's *Historia Ecclesiastica*, and William of Poitiers's *Gesta Guillelmi Ducis Normannorum et Regis Anglorum*.[14] Benoît may have also made use of Wace's *Roman de Rou*, although the occasional correspondences between the two works can also be attributed to coincidence.[15]

Although Benoît and Wace drew on essentially the same Latin sources for their works, Benoît's history departs dramatically from that of his predecessor in several important ways. The first is Benoît's providential contextualization of the history of the Norman dukes set out in the proemium of the *Chronique*. Benoît also differs substantially from Wace in his representation of the Norman Conquest, the death of William the Conqueror, and the reign of Henry I. Unsurprisingly, Benoît's portrayals of both Robert Curthose and Henry I invert the comparison of their relative merits made by Wace. Benoît's Robert is inept and prone to following the counsel of evil men, while Henry I is depicted as a necessary and worthy replacement for his incompetent older brother. Benoît also includes material not found in the *Rou* that reinforces Henry II's legitimacy, such as Henry I's designation of Matilda as his heir, a defense of Matilda's marriage to Geoffrey of Anjou, an account of the birth of Henry II, and apostrophes to Henry II.

---

the later events of Henry I's reign and his death in 1135. The *Chronique* closes with the death of Henry I and Stephen's usurpation.

13. William of Jumièges, *Guillaume de Jumièges, Gesta Normannorum ducum*, ed. Marx; and *The Gesta Normannorum ducum of William of Jumièges, Orderic Vitalis and Robert of Torigni*, ed. and trans. van Houts. Wace relied primarily on Orderic's E redaction of the *Gesta Normannorum ducum* and also used four anecdotes from the anonymous B redaction, whereas Benoît used Robert de Torigny's F redaction. See van Houts, "Adaptation," 116; and van Houts, "Wace as Historian," 106, n. 20.

14. *De moribus et actis primorum Normanniae ducum auctore Dudone sancti Quintini decano*, ed. Lair; *Dudo of St Quentin: History of the Normans*, trans. Eric Christiansen; Orderic Vitalis, *The Ecclesiastical History of Orderic Vitalis*; and *The Gesta Guillelmi of William of Poitiers*.

15. Peter Damian-Grint and Hugo Andresen point out that the assumption that Benoît had access to the *Roman de Rou* is based on little solid evidence and is merely possible rather than probable. Damian-Grint, "*En nul leu nel truis escrit*," 13; Hugo Andresen, "Über die von Benoît in seiner normannischen Chronik benutzen Quellen, insbesondere über sein Verhältnis zu Dudo, Wilhelm von Jumièges und Wace," *Romanische Forschungen* 1 (1883): 327–412, and 2 (1886): 477–538; and Hugo Andresen, "Zu Benoît's *Chronique des ducs de Normandie*," *Zeitschrift für romanische Philologie* 11 (1888): 231–40 and 345–70.

Finally, and most important, Benoît almost never strays from the Norman historiographical orthodoxy constructed by William of Poitiers and William of Jumièges, and on the rare occasions when he does deviate from it, he generally strengthens Norman claims to legitimacy rather than undermining them. Benoît appears to have understood that his primary function was to produce a defense of Norman kingship, and he goes to great lengths to aggrandize Henry's ancestors, magnify their deeds, and praise their virtues.

Providence and the Norman Dukes

Peter Damian-Grint has pointed out that the cosmographical and geographical exposition Benoît provides in the proemium of the *Chronique des ducs de Normandie* demonstrates a remarkable degree of sophistication and learning that presented his credentials as a scholar to his audience.[16] Damian-Grint concludes that "by beginning his work with an *ennaratio* of Biblical material, [Benoît] is laying claim to the highest possible *auctoritas*. . . . He is indicating that his history is to be read as the story of divine providence."[17] He goes on to note that Benoît articulates the importance of both the providential and exemplary justifications for writing history elsewhere in his text, and that the *Chronique* presents the history of the Norman dukes in both guises.[18] Damian-Grint focuses mainly on Benoît's exquisite craftsmanship in the proemium, but the fact that Benoît self-consciously constructs a providential framework for his history deserves further consideration.

Although Benoît's proemium may seem an unexpected discursus, he was, of course, working within a well-established tradition, at least one that was well established among Latin authors. As Damian-Grint has indicated, many Latin histories and one of Benoît's own Latin sources for the *Chronique* begin in a similar manner.[19] Orderic Vitalis's *Historia Ecclesiastica*

---

16. Benoît de Sainte-Maure, *CDN,* vv. 1–352. It is worth reiterating that this exposition of learning would have been superfluous if Benoît had not intended for his *Chronique* to be read as history. Damian-Grint, "Learning and Authority," 25.

17. Damian-Grint, "Learning and Authority," 42.

18. Ibid. and n. 79.

19. Ibid., 25 and n. 4. Benoît's proemium is unique in that is an original composition rather than a redaction of a Latin source, and it appears to be the first cosmographical text in the vernacular. Ibid., 25 and n. 1. I would add that Dudo of Saint-Quentin also includes a brief geographical exposition at the beginning of book I of *De moribus*.

begins with the Genesis account of the Creation and a geographical proemium that, sadly, has been considered so tangential to the rest of his narrative that it is often not reproduced in its entirety. The *Historia*'s modern
editor and translator, Marjorie Chibnall, includes only those portions of the
proemium considered to be Orderic's original work, and she reproduces
those passages without an English translation.[20] Although these proemia can
admittedly tend toward the soporific, they do serve a vital textual function
in declaring that the narrative that follows is an extension of biblical history.
The effect of both Benoît's and Orderic's proemia is thus to amplify the importance of their subjects. In Benoît's case, that subject is exclusively Henry
II's Norman ancestors and their rise to power. The providential framework
of the *Chronique* announces that God has orchestrated the ascent of the Norman dynasty, and insists that their continued prosperity, especially that of
Henry II, is attributable to divine favor. It also implicitly asserts that all Norman victories, whether over the English or other foes, have been the mani-
festations of God's judgment, which prove the virtue of their rulers and
reveal God's special affection for them.

The impact of Benoît's textual strategy can be demonstrated most clearly
by considering a text that does not present itself as providential history,
Wace's *Roman de Rou*. Wace's justification for historical writing is to rescue
the past from oblivion, and his history is exemplary and didactic, but nowhere does Wace stress the providential aspect of history. In the *Rou*, Norman history is presented as the deeds of men recorded so that posterity will
remember and perhaps learn from them, while the *Chronique* presents Norman history as evidence of God's continued regulation of human affairs and
proof of His affection for the Norman dukes.

The notion that God favors the Norman ducal line is implicit in Benoît's
approach, and Benoît gives this idea concrete expression in the body of his
history. As Penny Eley has noted, Benoît's presentation of the Norman
dukes reads like secular hagiography.[21] In portraying William the Conquer-
or's mother and father, for instance, Eley demonstrates that Benoît uses an
Old Testament type, that of Isaac and Rebekah, to shape his rendering of
Duke Robert's first glimpse of and reaction to Arlette.[22] The duke spies the

---

20. Orderic, *HE*, I. Portions of books I and II deemed to be redactions of biblical or other Latin
texts are not reproduced. Neither book I nor II is translated in Chibnall's edition.

21. Benoît de Sainte-Maure, *CDN*, vv. 33445–752. Eley, "History and Romance," 82. Eley is primarily concerned in her article with discovering the extent to which Benoît romanticizes Norman
history through examining his representation of female characters.

22. Eley, "History and Romance," 82.

lovely but bourgeois Arlette washing clothes in a stream. Stricken with longing for her, Robert sends his chamberlain to negotiate for her. Arlette's father may be the duke's social inferior, but he is mindful of his family's reputation and accordingly dubious of the proposed affair. He has to be convinced of the propriety of this liaison by Arlette's hermit uncle and Arlette herself. Eley also argues that Benoît presents the duke's request for Arlette as a type of annunciation in which Arlette's apprehension, humility, and modesty are emphasized, thus drawing a parallel between Arlette and Mary. According to Eley, Arlette's instantaneous conception of the future William the Conqueror during her first encounter with Robert "makes this as close to a miraculous birth as one could get without actually being blasphemous."[23]

There is another important aspect of this episode that Eley does not mention: Arlette's dream of a tree growing from her belly that covers all of Normandy and England.[24] The prophetic dream announces the conception of William who will unite Normandy and England, but it also echoes certain biblical dreams and prophecies. The most obvious parallel is with the Annunciation and Gabriel's reassurances to Mary that she has conceived through the Holy Spirit and her child will be called the "son of the Highest and the Lord God shall give unto him the throne of his father David and he shall reign over the house of Jacob for ever, and of his kingdom there will be no end."[25] Benoît's typological rendering of these events elevates a morally dubious situation and is calculated to preserve Arlette's reputation and remove the sting of arguments circulated by William's detractors (that William's illegitimacy and his mother's base blood disqualified him as ducal material), but it also fits perfectly into the providential framework of the history. Like all of Benoît's Norman dukes, William is predestined for greatness.

The Norman Conquest

Just as Benoît attributes the rise of the Normans to divine favor, he presents the conquest of England as the product of God's plan. It is, however, also partly due to careful human planning. Unlike Wace, who muddied the

---

23. Ibid.

24. Benoît, *CDN*, vv. 33711–52.

25. Luke 1:26–38.

waters of the Conquest by including Anglo-Saxon material that encouraged his readers to reach the conclusion that William the Conqueror was not Edward the Confessor's legitimate heir, Benoît presents only the Norman version of events.[26] He declares in unequivocal language that the childless Edward designated and confirmed William as his heir.[27] Benoît says that Edward confirmed his designation of William through the archbishop of Canterbury. Although Benoît does not name the archbishop or specify a date other than "years before," he is surely referring to Archbishop Robert of Canterbury's visit to Normandy in the spring of 1051, during which he was reported to have confirmed William as Edward's heir.[28] Benoît goes on to say that Edward wished to ensure the succession and thus sent Harold, the most powerful of his earls, to confirm a second time that his entire realm and everything pertaining to the English crown would pass to William. Following the Norman orthodoxy, Benoît also explains that one of Harold's tasks on this trip was to swear fealty to William.

Harold then sets off for Normandy on a specific mission at Edward's request, but is blown off course by a storm.[29] He is taken hostage by Count

---

26. Wace says that Harold wished to see William about the return of his brother and cousin, but that Edward strictly forbade it, warning Harold that William was cunning and likely to trick him if he attempted to secure their release. Wace then says that another book tells him that Edward sent Harold to confirm William as his heir, but he does not know which account is true. Wace, *RR*, vv. 5588–604 (all references to the *Roman de Rou* are to part III unless otherwise noted).

27. "La me convient a revertir, / E qui des or voudra oïr, / Saveir mun cum li dus Guilleaume / Conquist la terre e le reiaume / Sor Heriaut, qui s'ert coronné, / J'en retrairai la verité. / Evvart, li juz e li verais, / Qui Engleterre tint em pais / Cumme hauz reis, veirs crestiens, / Plains de douçor e de toz biens, / Ç'avint qu'enfant ne eir nen oct, / Si cum a Nostre Seignor ploct. / Deu duc Guilleaume le Normant / - Cumme eu siecle n'en ama tant - / Voct son eir faire, a c'entendeit, / Que nulee riens plus ne voleit. / L'arcevesque de Contorbire, / Li plus hauz hom de som enpire, / Oct en Normandie tramis / Les anz avant, si cum j'os dis, / Por afermer ce qu'il li donne / Tot le reiaume e la coronne. / Eissi esteit ja li aferes. / Por estre plus certains e meres / E qu'eu n'i sorsist encombrer / Revost l'ovre plus esforcier. / Heraut, qui quens ert deu païs / Trestoz li plus poesteïs / Que nul des autres deu reiaume, / Celui tremist au duc Guilleaume / Que deu renne enterine-ment / - Tot qui a la coronne apent - / Li feïst feeuté juree, / Eissi com ele ert devisee. / Vect qu'il l'en face serement / E qu'il l'en donge tenenment / Sor saintuaires conneüs. / Tot eissi est Heraut meüz." Benoît, *CDN*, vv. 38727–64.

28. Both William of Poitiers and William of Jumièges mention Archbishop Robert's visit to Normandy and report that he confirmed William as Edward's heir. Robert's trip most likely took place between mid-Lent and June 27, 1051, when Robert traveled to Rome. Poitiers, *GG*, 14; and Jumièges, *GND*, vii, II:157 and n. 6. See Barlow, *Edward the Confessor*, 107–9 and 220–21; and Eric John, "Edward the Confessor and the Norman Succession," *EHR* 94 (1979): 241–67. It should also be noted that Edward's initial designation of William, if it indeed occurred in 1051, came in the midst of his troubles with Earl Godwin.

29. "Sanz tarzer e sanz demorer / En vint as nex dreit a la mer. / Od ceus qu'oct en sa compeignie / Cuida sigler vers Normandie, / Mais trop lor fu la mers sauvage, / Quer grans tempers e forz

Guy who imprisons him in the hope of extracting a ransom. As in the *Roman de Rou*, Harold sends to William for help in his adversity and is rescued. William then entertains Harold, taking him to jousts and to fight against the Bretons.[30] Unlike Wace, who tells us that William hoped to gain something by keeping Harold himself, Benoît says nothing of the sort. After William and Harold returned from fighting the Bretons, Benoît says that William assembled a council at Bonneville where Harold swore an oath "of his own devising."[31]

The contrast between Wace's version of Harold's oath and Benoît's re-telling could not be more striking. In Benoît's version there is no coercion and no duplicity on William's part, the oath is not staged over a mass of hidden relics, nor is it dictated to Harold. Harold composes his own oath and, in return, William promises Harold his daughter Adeliza in marriage and half of England, with the provision that Harold will have these things after William has gained the crown.[32] William then sends Harold off in a

---

orage / Ne les i laissa arriver; / Ainces les convint devaler / Dreit em Pontif. La pristrent port / Eissi ateint e eissi mort / Meiuz vosistrent estre en Sezile. / Llas prist li quens Gui d'Abevile, / Quis tint e mist en sa prison, / Qu'aveir voudra lor raançon; / Tant com il se voundront amer, / Tant les convendra rachater. / Retenu fu Herauz e pris, / Mais au duc Guilleaume a tramis Por Faire li saveir ce plait / Ne ou il est ne cum li vait. / Si tost com il en soct le veir, / Ne mist plus l'ovre en non-chaleir, / Ainz tramist a Gui tot maneis, / Si li manda que sor son peis / Tendreit Heraut plus un sol jor; / Mais ce li requert par amor / Qu'il le li quit e soille e rende / Si que deu suen rien n'i despende, / Riens n'i perde, n'omme des suens. / Mais Gui n'en fist nul de ses buens, / Ainz en ert moct estorçonnos, / Quer de l'aveir ert coveitos. / Por ce manda li dus ses jenz / Sempres a millers e a cenz. / Vers Ou chevaucha, irascuz / Dum Heraut ne li ert renduz. / Sempres eüst mereiau mestrait / E a Gui teu damage fait / Qui ne fust pas de l'an entier / A restorer sain ne lejer. / Mais conseil crut, si fist que sage. / Ainz qu'en fust fait autre damage, / Li amena a ou tot quite. / S'il oct sa requests despite, / Toteveies en fist son buen, / C'um dener n'en retint deu suen. / Eissi fu Heiraut delivré." Benoît, *CDN*, vv. 38765–811.

30. "Tot dreit a Roem la cité / L'en amena li dus od sei. / Li fist teu joie e tel honnor / Cum il li poct faire graignor. / S'il oct eü point de meses, / De ses buens oct most e de s'ese. / O oz que li dus oct jostees / Moct granz e moct desmesurees / Por aler essillier Bretons, / Vers lui torçonnes e felons, / Qui nou deignoent sopleier, / Le mena od sei osteier. / La fist de lui si grant cherté / C'um tant n'ot de sa volunté, / Ne fu nul leu mais tant joïz." Benoît, *CDN*, vv. 38812–27.

31. "Quant cil afaires fu feniz, / Si josta li dus son concile, / Ce sui lisant, a Buenne Vile. / La fu li seremenz jurez / Qu'Heraut meesme a devisez, / Que tant cum Evvart vivreit mais / Le renne li tendreit em pais / Selonc sa force, au suen poeir, / Sanz fauser e sanz deceveir. / E après qu'il sereit feniz, / Ci que deu renne fust saisiz / Li tendreit vers toz hommes nez / Deci qu'il fust coronnez, / E des ice jor en avant / L'en sera mais par tot aidant. / Douvre, la Tor e le chastel, / Si fort com il est e si bel, / Baillera sempres si garniz / E de vitaille repleniz / A ceus des suens cui lui plaira / Qu'il a garder i rememtra; / E s'aillors vect chasteaus fermer / Desus le riviage de mer, / Despense e vivre e estoveir / Trovera tot deu suen aveir. / Eissi sor tot le saintuaire / Qu'en li voct aporter ne traire / Jura de sa main a tenir / Sanz rein fauser e sanz ganchir." Benoît, *CDN*, vv. 38828–56.

32. "E li dus, por lui mieus aveir, / Sanz fauser e sanz deceveir / E sanz muer vers lui corage, / Aeliz, la proz e la sage, / Sa fille, li otreie e donne, / Quant saisiz ert de la coronne, / E deu renne l'une

manner suitable for a future son-in-law, laden with gifts of fine horses, arms, gold, and silver. Following the *Gesta Normannorum ducum*, Benoît adds that Harold left his brother Wulfnoth with William as surety.[33]

Benoît's description of Harold's oath generally follows that of his sources, but a careful reading of the episode reveals two important differences. Benoît, like Wace before him, fails to assert that Harold swore fealty to William (in spite of the fact that this was the express purpose of his trip to Normandy), and the language of his oath is intentionally vague. Harold promises only that Edward will hold the kingdom in peace as long as he lives and that he will aid *whomever* is crowned and has possession of the kingdom after Edward's death, without ever mentioning William by name. He also promises to provision Dover and other castles, but cleverly declines to state for whose benefit. Furthermore, Benoît muses on whether Harold already knew of the crime he was going to commit when he left his brother in William's custody. The implication is that Harold's oath was purposely evasive, that he already knew he would usurp England upon Edward's death and was trying to swear an unenforceable oath. In contrast to the account of Harold's oath in the *Rou*, Benoît's account exonerates William completely and credits Harold with duplicity and cunning.

In spite of Harold's shrewd attempt to swear essentially nothing, Benoît insists that he is guilty of perjury when he usurps the English crown.[34]

---

meitié. / Moct l'en vect cil baisier le pié. / Itex furent lor covenanz. / Aveirs riches e beiaus e granz, / Chevaus, armes, or e agent / E maint autre cher garnement / Li donna tant ce fu merveille. / Eissi l'atorne e rapareille, / Sil conveie dreit a la mer, / Si l'en ra fait outre passer. / Au rei, qui li ert sire e druz, / Manda merciez e chers saluz." Benoît, *CDN*, vv. 38857–74.

33. "He made Harold stay with him for some time and took him on an expedition against the Bretons. Then after Harold had sworn fealty to him about the kingdom with many oaths he promised him that he would give him his daughter Adeliza with half the kingdom of England. Later he sent him back to the king with many gifts but kept as hostage his handsome brother Wulfnoth." [Quem aliquandiu secum demorari fecit et in expeditione contra Britones adduxit. Diende dux post quam Heraldus fidelitatem sibi de regno pluribus sacramentis firmauit, Adelizam filiam suam cum medietate Anglici regni se daturum eidem spopondit. Postremo ipsum cum multis muneribus regi remisit et pulchrum adolscentem Vulnothum fratrem eius obsidem retinuit.] *GND*, vii, II:160–61. William of Poitiers notes that Edward had sent Hakon and Wulfnoth to William as surety for William's succession and that William released Hakon out of respect for Harold. Poitiers, *GG*, 68 and 76. "Heraut oct un frere danzel, / Qu'o n'estoveit querre plus bel. / Vuilnoth oct non, corteis e sage, / Cel laissa au duc en ostage. / Ce ne sai ne ne vei mie / S'il pensoct ja la felonnie, / Quant il le laissa en tenance, / Quer unc ne li tint convenance / Ne fei ne serement ne lei. / por tel l'em mescharra, ce crei." Benoît, *CDN*, vv. 38875–84.

34. "Afeibleia li reis Evvarz / Si qu'ainz que trepassast li marz / fu morz, trepassez e feniz / E hautment enseveliz. / Gloriose fin oct e sainte / E qui fu moct ploree e plainte. / Heraut, de coveitise espris, / Sanz autre conseil quin fust pris / Saisi le renne demaneis. / Parjur e faus se fist li reis / Eissi sanz icele untion / E sanz cele sacratium / Qu'en deit faire a rei saintement / Le jor de son

Unlike Wace, who dwells on the scene of Edward's deathbed and reveals that the dying king left England to Harold in the face of coercion, Benoît avoids the mistake of his predecessor and makes short work of Edward's death. Edward dies a glorious and saintly, if extremely brief, death, and the covetous Harold immediately steals the crown on his own initiative. Benoît does not even allude to the possibility that Edward may have named Harold as his heir as he lay dying, nor does he suggest that he may have been pressured to do so. In fact, Benoît's description of Harold's actions emphasizes their solitary nature and his singular guilt. Deviating slightly from his sources, Benoît reports that Harold acted alone, without counsel, and that he made himself king without anointing, without sacrament.[35] Indeed, he declares that Harold committed a great wrong for which he was destroyed. The case Benoît builds against Harold is so definitive that its rigor surpasses even that of William the Conqueror's foremost apologist, William of Poitiers, who allowed that Harold had conspirators, was supported by his countrymen, and was consecrated, although improperly, by the excommunicate archbishop Stigand.[36]

William the Conqueror

While Wace essentially ends his account of William's life with the battle of Hastings and moves quickly to William's death, Benoît devotes almost three thousand lines to William's life after the Conquest. Not only is Benoît expansive where Wace is taciturn, but he includes material that bolsters Norman claims to legitimacy. Benoît reports William's clemency toward the conquered English in the wake of Hastings, the splendor of his coronation,

---

coronnement. / Eissi, sanz hule autre devise, / Parjur, faus, pleins de coveitise, / Se fist coronner a grant tort; / Por c'en fu puis destruis a mort. / Ne tint envers le duc fiance / Ne ostage ne convenance; / De son frere ne li sosvint. / Eissi oct le reiaume e tint." Benoît, *CDN*, vv. 38885–906.

35. This is almost certainly a reference to Harold's consecration at the hands of Archbishop Stigand who had been excommunicated by Pope Leo IX. The sentence was renewed by Popes Nicholas II and Alexander II, and Stigand was ultimately deposed in 1070. Poitiers, *GG*, 100 and n. 2. An alternative Anglo-Saxon tradition holds that Harold was consecrated by Archbishop Ealdred of York, whose priestly status and good relations with the papacy were not in question. See John of Worcester, *Chronicle*, II:600; and *Chronicon pontificum ecclesiae Eboracensis*, in *Historians of the Church of York*, ed. J. Raine, 3 vols. (London, 1879–94), II:348.

36. William of Poitiers reports that Harold acted with the connivance of a few wicked men and that he seized the crown with the acclamation of the bishops and magnates. Poitiers, *GG*, 100. The *GND* is more terse, reporting only that Edward died and Harold stole the crown, thus perjuring the fealty he had sworn to William. *GND*, vii, II:160.

his construction of Battle Abbey in memory of his victory over Harold, and the coronation of William's queen, Matilda, in 1068.[37] He focuses mainly on William's pacification of England and so details various rebellions against the king, including the revolt of the count of Boulogne, the risings in the north of England, the rebellions of Harold's sons and of the Earls Edwin and Morcar, as well as the invasions by King Swein of Denmark and the Saxons.[38] In each case, William emerges from the confrontation victorious, erects fortifications, and consolidates his power. Benoît presents the disorders caused by the rebels as a counterpoint to William's imposition of order and good government. He consistently presents the perpetrators as felons and the challenges to William's authority as having little motivation other than greed. Benoît does not even entertain the possibility that the English might have legitimate grievances against William or the Normans.[39] Ultimately, Benoît's recitation of the long list of rebellions only serves to magnify William's prowess in suppressing one uprising after another and establishing peace. In Benoît's account, William's continuous triumphs over his enemies actually demonstrate his worthiness to hold England.

After extolling William's success in restoring peace to England, Benoît moves to a discussion of William's troubles in Normandy.[40] Having repelled attacks from all sides in England, William returns to Normandy to find his duchy beset by the French.[41] William learns that his eldest son, Robert Cur-

---

37. Benoît, *CDN,* vv. 38973–9904. Benoît depicts William's coronation at Westminster as peaceful and orderly, neglecting its more chaotic aspects. He does not mention the fire set by the Normans, the terrified flight of most of the congregation, nor William's rushed consecration. Orderic comments that the disturbance during William's coronation instilled a distrust of the Normans in the English, and from that day forward the English sought revenge. Benoît, *CDN,* vv. 40061–124. Cf. Orderic, *HE,* iii, II:184; and Benoît, *CDN,* vv. 40125–39. Benoît's inclusion of Matilda's coronation is also significant as one of the arguments often advanced for Henry I's legitimacy as king of England is the fact that he was the only one of the Conqueror's sons to have been "born in the purple." Benoît, *CDN,* vv. 40713–54.

38. Benoît, *CDN,* vv. 40449–558, 40601–74, and 40675–712. Benoît does not mention William's betrayal of his peace agreement with Earl Morcar, Morcar's imprisonment, or Edwin's death at the hands of the Normans. Benoît de Sainte-Maure, *CDN,* vv. 40775–1025. Cf. Orderic, *HE,* IV:256–58. The invasion of King Swein and the Saxons are found in Benoît, *CDN,* vv. 41189–252.

39. Orderic Vitalis, on the other hand, makes quite clear that at least some of the insurrections were caused by Norman duplicity or brutality. Orderic reports, for instance, that the Earls Edwin and Morcar revolted due to William's refusal to honor his promise to allow Edwin to marry one of his daughters. Orderic, *HE,* iv, II:214. He also describes the uprising in York as the result of Norman injustice and tyranny. Orderic, *HE,* iv, II:216. Unlike Benoît, who praises William's tactics, Orderic explicitly condemns William for his brutal suppression of the rebellions in the north of England. Orderic, *HE,* iv, II:230–32.

40. Benoît, *CDN,* vv. 41415–54.

41. Benoît, *CDN,* vv. 41455–535.

those, has gone over to the king of France and prepares to march on Paris in a fit of indignation. William, of course, will fail to reach Paris. He advances only as far as Mantes, burning the town before being overcome by his final illness. Where Wace purposely obscured the fact that Robert was in open rebellion against his father at the time of his death, Benoît makes Robert's revolt and William's disappointment in his eldest son central themes in his depiction of William's death. Before setting out for Paris, William declares that Robert did not do well to depart from him, that he cannot suffer his son's disloyalty nor consent to his folly for fear he will only continue to do worse.[42]

When William falls ill and is taken to Rouen, Benoît reports that he called his sons Henry and William Rufus to him. He specifically notes that Robert was not called because he had gone over to the king of France and was fighting against his father.[43] Benoît employs a subtle strategy here in listing William's sons: he inverts their birth order, thereby giving Henry precedence over his brothers. It will not be the last time Benoît indicates a preference for Henry. Henry appears first, followed by William Rufus, while Robert is referred to as the third of the Conqueror's sons. The move is revealing. As we know, Henry will surpass his brothers, and Benoît appears to be preparing his reader for this; however, the move also implies that Robert has proven himself unworthy of his father's confidence and has been accordingly demoted.

Another theme running throughout Benoît's account of William's death is his piety, particularly his protection of churches and clerics. After calling his two faithful sons to him, Benoît says that William made amends to the town of Mantes, sending rich gifts to restore the churches he had destroyed.[44] William then confessed himself and prayed for God's mercy before offering some final advice to Henry and William Rufus. Selectively following Orderic's deathbed speech for William, Benoît has William recount his defense of the church and its rights, noting that he had not en-

---

42. "'N'a pas fait bien Roberz, mis fiz, / Dum il de mei s'est departiz / Por aler s'en dedevers eus, / C'um pere a fiz ne fu mains feus. / Si son deslei ne vuil soffrir / Ne sa fole ovre consentir, / Ne me deüst pas por ce nuire, / Qu'il en sera toz jorz le pire.'" Benoît, *CDN*, vv. 41491–98.

43. "Ses fiz apela ambedous, / Henris e Guilleaume li Ros. / Robert, li terz, n'i esteit mie, / Cil qui ert dus de Normendie, / Quer por moct poi de mauvoillance / S'en ert alez au rei de France. / Contre com pere aveit tencié / E plusors feiz mal espleitié." Benoît, *CDN*, vv. 41565–72. Orderic also reports that Robert was absent from William's deathbed. Orderic, *HE*, vii, IV:80.

44. "As iglises rapareillier, / Faire, covrir e radreicier, / Qui a Maante erent fondues, / Arses a few e abatues, / Donna e tramist riches dons / E fist granz satisfacions." Benoît, *CDN*, vv. 41581–86. Orderic is the only other source to make this assertion as far as I am aware. Orderic, *HE*, vii, IV:80.

gaged in simony, but had installed saintly men in clerical offices, that he had enriched the nine abbeys and the convent of nuns founded by his ancestors in Normandy, and that eighteen further abbeys and six more convents had been founded with his aid.[45] William confirms their foundations and revenues and enjoins his sons to follow him in these things.[46] He also advises his sons to live and reign in peace, to keep the company and counsel of good men in order to live a noble life, to love God, and to guard the poor and helpless. William then repents of his sins again, this time focusing on having caused the deaths of so many men in seizing England.[47] William states that

45. "'Most vos ai, fait il, toz amez / E chers tenuz e si gardez / E desfenduz que torz ne laiz / N'os a esté ne diz ne faiz. / Unc ne baissai en nule guise / Nul leu l'onnor de saint' iglise, / Ainz l'ai creüe e enoree / E si sa dreiture gardee / C'umues n'en fui simoniaus; / Ainz des sainz hommes, des leiaus, / L'ai enluminee en mainz leus, / Tant odtreié terres e fieus / Qu'a nof abeïes de moines / Estre les autres des canoines / E une sole de nonains / Que mes anceisors premerains / Aveient avant mei fondees. / Ne descreües ne mermees / Ne furent unc par mei nul jor, / Ainz puis que j'oi terre e honnor, / Sai que de lai mer, que de ça, / Qui bien a dreit les nonmera, / Unt esté faites e basties / Au meins dis e oit abeïes / De moins e sis de nonains, / E si sui bien de ce certains / C'um n'i destoli ne veiai / Ne a homme neu chalonjai / Riens que nus i vousist gerpir, / Donner n'acreistre ne osfrir. / De totes sui faitre e fonderes / E conseillanz e ajuerres. / Si sunt creües e montees / Qu'en totes ai croces donnees. / En icestes saintes herberges / N'ert pas li airs laiz ne tenerjes. / Dex des suens rais les enlumine: / Le puet l'on trover medecine / De confession, de salu, / La est si deiable vencu / Que sis enging ne sis assaut / Rien n'i monte ne rien n'i vaut. / La iert des or mais Dex serviz. / Seiaus e chartres e escriz / Ai fait de toz lor fondemenz, / De rentes e de chesemenz, / De ceus que j'ai fait endreit mei / E des autres chascuns par sei. / Tot ai e par tot confermé / Od principal auctorité. / Eissieu vuil a mes eirs gerpir / Qui aprés mei sunt a venir, / Qu'isieu tiengent d'or en avant, / E de par Deu le lor conmant.'" Benoît, *CDN*, vv. 41595–648.

46. "'Beiau fil, a vos vuil moct preier / E doucement le vos requier / Qu'en cestes choses m'ensigeiz: / Eissieu teneiz, eissieu gardiez / Cum je ai fait, quer hautement / E devant Deu e son la jent / Vivreiz e rennereiz en pais. / S'o buens hommes e od verais / Avez conseil e compaignie, / Noble e honneste iert vostre vie. / Par ceus ai esté honnorez / E fait totes mes volontez; / Par eus ai je terre tenue / E mainte grant victoire eüe. / Cil m'unt des traïtors vengié, / Qui m'eüssent mort e chacié / Mil feiz, s'il le peüssent faire. / De toz conseiz vos doins le maire: / Que Deu amez premierement, / E aprés vostre bone gent. / Justice amez sor tote rien, / N'aiez orguil ne felonie: / Cil aime Deu qui s'umelie. / Tiranz porvers e desleiez, / Ceus destruiez e abaissez; / La povre gent ne la petite / Gardez ne seit par vos despite. / A ceus des maisons besoignoses, / As religions soffraitoses / Enveiez voz dons e voz biens, / Qu'eissi serreiz veirs crestiens / Tos tens vos voille sovenir / Des mestier Damnedeu oïr; / Kar richece nule a aveir / Ne force au siecle ne poeir / Senz Deu amer n'est fors sol paine, / Vil chose e trespassable e vaine. / Honoré serreiz e garri, / S'eissi le faites cum j'os di; / E Deus sil vos don't maintenir / Cume je coveit e desir!'" Benoît, *CDN*, vv. 41649–92.

47. "'Par les granz torz que l'om m'a faiz, / Qui oi ne sereient retraiz, / Ai maint home ocis de mes mains, / Dunt mis corages n'est pas sains, / Mais doleros e reprentables; / Or m'en seit Deus veirs pardonables! / E por se qu'o ocisons / E od pesmes confusions / Oi le reaume e fui saisiz, / Ne sui si os ne si hardiz / Qu'en face don n'otreiement / A riens fors a Deu solement. / E il, qui toz les granz biens done, / Dunt le reiaume e la corone / Guillaume, mun fiz, qu'isieu voil, / C'unc jor ne me mostra orguil / Ne ne fist ovre contre mei. / E Deus li donge, e jo l'otrei, / Qu'eu regne seit reis coronez / E vive en cest siecle honroez!'" Benoît, *CDN*, vv. 41693–712.

his conscience is not clear on this account, and he declares himself wretched and contrite for the terrible destruction he wrought in conquering England. For this reason he says he cannot commit the kingdom to anyone but God, but he goes on to declare that he wants William Rufus to have the kingdom because he has never been arrogant or worked against him. Benoît then has William say that, if God grants it, he confirms the kingdom to Rufus, whom he hopes will reign as a crowned king and live honored in this world.

Upon hearing that his brother William is to have England, Henry comes to the king with tears in his eyes, asking what his father will leave him.[48] William replies that Henry is to have five thousand silver pounds from his treasure, but he warns him not to fight with his brothers, as they will be powerful men who can ruin him and drive him from the land. Unsatisfied, Henry asks what good the money will be if he has nothing else. William responds that Henry should put his faith in God and suffer his brothers to precede him because it is only right that William should have England and Robert Normandy. William then comforts Henry, telling him that he is certain that one day he will have everything his older brothers possess and surpass them in nobility, power, and wealth. Fearing unrest in England, William then prepares a sealed letter detailing his wishes and orders Rufus to leave for England to take possession of the honor God will give him.[49]

---

48. "Entre icez granz partissemenz, / Cez dons e cez devisemenz, / Dunt trestuit cil se merveilloent / Qui environ le rei s'estoent, / De sa memoire e de s'entente, / La ou chascuns d'eus se gaimente / Vient devant lui sis fiz Henris, / De lermes tot moillié le vis. / De sei n'oï mencion faire / Fors des secund frere e del maire, / Ne riens laissier ne riens doner / Ne riens en siecle deviser; / Plorant il a dit: 'Queu conrei / Pernez vos, beiau sire, de mei? / Cheles! Ne sui je vostre fiz? / Sui je es autres si partiz / Que riens ne prenge ne riens n'aie? / Certes, mult redot lor manaie. / Bien vei que trop petit m'amez, / S'os en autre sen n'en pensez.' / Dunc li dist li reis doucement: / – 'De mes bons esterlins d'argent, / Beau fiz, avreiz cinc mile livres, / Si gar, ne content ne n'estrives / Ensemble od eus jor a ton tort, / Kar il seront haut home e fort, / Si te porreient mesbaillir ' E la terre faire guerpir.' / Dunc dist Henris: 'De cest tresor, / Mais li denier en fussent d'or, / Cum le dei je aveir ne prendre, / Si je n'en ai ou jeu despende?' / – 'Beiau fiz, fait li reis, seiez sage / E si aies entier corage; / Qu'il ne seit dobles ne changjanz; / Si seies vers Deu entendanz, / E si soefre paisiblement / Que cist aient seignorement / Dedesus tei, car c'est dreiture / E bien e raison e mesure. / Engleterre a a sa partie / Guillaume, e Robert Normendie; / Tu avras tot, j'en sui certains, / Eissi que tes freres germains / Trespasseras toz de noblece, / De poesté e de richece. / Ne criem, ne dote, ne t'esmaies: / N'ai terre eü que tu nen aies; / Grant chose sera mult de tei, / Mais Deu e conseil aime e crei.'" Benoît, *CDN*, vv. 41713–63.

49. "Por ce que li reis out dotance / Qu'en Engleterre eüst turbance, / Tribous e noise e destorbier, / Kar le regne en sout costumier, / Si fist sa chartre seielee / Si cum la chose ert devisee; / Si la bailla od oilz pluros / A Guillaume, son fiz, le Ros, / Kar set que jamais nel verra. / Par cent feiees le baisa; / Comande que tost past la mer / Senz targer e senz demorer; / Prenge l'onor que Deus li done / E le reaume e la corone. / Au departir fu granz li dous: / Tirent sei barbes e chevous / E

Benoît is careful not to couch the transmission of the kingdom as passing from William to his son, but as passing from William back to God who will then grant it to William Rufus, in yet another demonstration of God's special affection for the Normans. Rufus does as commanded, but not before sharing a dramatic scene of grief with his father in which the two men rend their beards and hair while emitting sorrowful cries at the prospect of being permanently separated by the Conqueror's impending death.

Benoît's depiction of William's bequests to his sons differs from Wace's in several important ways. Most important, Benoît does not have William declare that he stole a kingdom to which he had no right, nor does he include any material that might lead his reader to suspect that the Conquest was illicit, unjustified, or even morally ambiguous. Benoît's portrayal of William's troubled conscience most closely resembles Orderic's account in that both assert that William dared not confirm England to anyone but God because of the sins he committed in acquiring it. Benoît does depart from Orderic, but in doing so he mutes Orderic's criticism of William rather than amplifying it as Wace had done. Benoît simply eliminates whole sections of Orderic's scathing attack on William's shortcomings, and nowhere does he echo Orderic's assessment of the innate ferocity of the Norman temperament. Whereas Wace ineluctably follows Orderic's critique of William's harsh rule to its logical conclusion, asserting that the conquest of England was illicit, Benoît refashions Orderic's William into a pious king who humbly repents of his misdeeds and does not want to compound them by arrogantly assuming he has the right to transmit England to his son. Benoît's William does, of course, express his preference for William Rufus and sends him to England to take possession of the kingdom, clearly with little doubt that God will grant it.

Benoît also differs from Wace in his representation of William's bequest to Henry. Unlike Wace, who insists that William left Henry with five thousand pounds and nothing else, Benoît is careful to include Orderic's reassurance that Henry will one day surpass his brothers and be lord of all his father's lands. Benoît also adds elements not found in Orderic, such as William's warning to Henry not to quarrel with his brothers, but these additions

---

crient hauz cris doleros; / E sospiranz e angoissos / Pasme se cil par maintes feiz, / Si angoissos e si destreiz / Que par poi li quers ne li part. / Monte, car des or li est tart / Qu'il ait del regne la saisine; / Sovent li moille la peitrine. / N'esteit mais a la mer venuz / Ne n'ert encor pas descenduz / Que l'om le fist certains e fiz / Que sis peres esteit feniz. / Dunc n'i out rien plus de sojor: / La mer passerent de cler jor, / E 'sil mena dol la semaine, / Sa joie refu tost prochaine. / Tote dolor mist en obli, / Quant del regne se vit saisi. / Coronez fu, n'i out contraire / Que ce vos i face a retraire." Benoît, *CDN*, vv. 41764–98.

serve to enhance Benoît's carefully constructed image of William as a benevolent ruler who is anxious to preserve peace and imparts sound advice to his sons. This particular comment also foreshadows the mistreatment Henry will later suffer at the hands of Rufus and Robert, whom Benoît will claim conspired to drive Henry from their lands without provocation.

Finally, Benoît barely addresses Robert Curthose, who is absent from William's deathbed. Robert's inheritance of the duchy of Normandy is referred to obliquely and only in the context of William's reassurance to Henry that he will one day surpass his brothers. William says that Rufus will have lordship of England and Robert of Normandy as is right and good, reasonable and wise, and leaves the matter at that. Benoît omits any explicit reference to Robert's rights as the firstborn or to the fact that Robert had already received the homage of the Norman barons. He does, however, make it clear that Robert's rebellion against his father was a black mark against him, and one that cost him England. He does so by emphasizing that William Rufus was rewarded with the kingdom specifically for his fidelity and by depicting the extreme emotional distress that accompanies Rufus's departure from his ailing father. In both instances Benoît sets up an obvious comparison between William Rufus, who is portrayed as a dutiful, loving, and worthy son, and Robert Curthose, who appears as a rebellious, selfish, and undeserving son.

After making restitution to Mantes, settling the matter of his sons' inheritance, and releasing his prisoners, William is prepared to give up the ghost.[50] Benoît reports that William died calling upon Mary just after prime had sounded on the morning of September 10.[51] Unlike Wace, Benoît dwells on

---

50. Benoît, *CDN*, vv. 41803–72.

51. Wace records the date as September 8, while Orderic gives the generally accepted date of September 9. "Dreit au disain jor de setembre, / Ce nos dit l'estoire e remembre, / Matin, quant prime fu oïe / A ma dame sainte Marie / E bien l'oct seü e enquis, / Dum torna cele part son vis. / Le cel esgarda comtremunt / Que la chere li muille e funt. / Ses mains jointes, od voiz pidose, / Prie la sainte gloriose, / La mere au fil deu Sauveor, / Que por sa sainte grant douçor / Od lui si l'acort e apair / Qu'en lui deiable part nen ait, / S'arme conduie es ceus amunt / La ou li suen cher ami sunt. / Eissi s'en est deu cors alee, / Quant cele parole oct finee, / Si paisiblement e si bel / Ne l'aperçut vil ne danzel. / Por le travailler deu parler / De ses granz choses deviser / Cuiderent se fust endormiz: / Por tel n'i sort ne braiz ne criz, / Neu post connoistre ne saveir / Nus d'entor lui jusque au seir, / E si dient la nuit entiere. / Trestot eissi, en teu maniere / En fist Deus son commandement. / Toz li poples, tote la jent / Furent esbahi e dotos, / Ploranz, pensis e poeros. / Unques ne sorent que fust mais / Ne grant dolor ne granz esmais. / Sempres maneis a esperon / S'en vunt e partent li baron, / Garnir ne vunt que que s'aviegne, / Quer n'i a cel qui trop ne crienge. / Cil de sa privee maisnee / n'i unt nule chose laissee. / Tot en unt si porté e rés / Que nule riens n'i a remés. / Tuit li plusor l'ont sol gerpi, / Alé s'en sunt e departi." Benoît, *CDN*, vv. 41873–916.

the details of William's demeanor—his clasped hands, his piteous voice, and the fervor of his devotion to the Virgin—adding that William passed away so peacefully and so well that those gathered around him thought he had only fallen asleep. Such details mark William's death as particularly pious, as does his meticulous attention to settling his affairs before his death. Benoît then recounts the chaos immediately following William's death. After the barons had hurried off to look after their possessions, William's retainers plundered his household, taking whatever they could and leaving him alone on the floor.

Unlike Wace, who had very little to say about William's abandoned corpse, Benoît follows Orderic in seizing the opportunity to meditate at length on the fleeting vanity of the world and the transience of earthly loyalty.[52] Everything dies, everything passes away, reverting to ashes and dust, observes Benoît. The joy of this world is nothing except the bubbles in a fountain, lasting only for a moment before ceasing to exist. William, who was powerful, noble, rich, and conquering, who was served by a hundred thousand knights, has no one to carry his body or bury him save the archbishop and clergy.

Although both Wace and Benoît depict the abandonment of William's corpse, Benoît's retelling of the episode resonates in a completely different way. Wace focuses relentlessly on William's theft of England in recounting his death, and this charge casts its shadow over his entire account of William's death and funeral. Although Wace tells us that William confessed himself, divided up his goods, and released his prisoners, he does so perfunctorily and then moves quickly to describe how William had captured and imprisoned his brother, Odo of Bayeux.[53] Benoît, on the other hand, carefully erects an

---

52. "Eiisi poez veer tot cler, / Si bien vos volez porpenser, / Saveir quex est la feiz mondainne, / Com ele est trepassable e vaine / E cum l'on a tost oblié / Ice que l'on a plus amé. / Tost fu la novele seüe / E par mainz rennes espandue / Que li reis Guilleaume ert feniz / E, si con retrait li escriz, / En Calabre e en Rome dreit / – Ne sai mie par quel endreit – / Sorrent certainement plusor / E l'ore e le terme e le jor / Qu'il ert feniz e trepassez, / Si cum l'on sot d'eus puis assez. / Ahi! Terrienne noblece / E tote mundainne richece, / Gloire, seignorementz d'empire, / Tant par teriez a despire / Que tot vostre soshaucement / Repaire e revert a neient! / Quer cil qui au siecle est plus beaus, / Plus freis, plus sages, plus noveaus, / Revert en cendre e en poudrier / Ainz le terme d'un an entier. / De tote la terre qu'il tint / Ne qui au siecle li avint / Ne li remaint fors poi assez: / Ce est itant, con vos savez, / Ou l'on l'enfeve sol envers / Queu menjucent laisarde e vers. / Nule riens n'est joie mondaine / Quel le boillon en la fontaine: / Tost fenist, tost trepasse / E tote nature se lasse; / Tot aneiente e tot tresvait. / Or oiez quex fu ci le plait: / Cist qui tant oct esté puissanz, / Nobles, riches, e conqueranz, / E cui serveient chevalers / Sovent a cenz e a millers, / Ci n'en poct pas dis aramir / A lui porter ne enfoïr; / Mais l'arcevesque e le clergié / E li convent vindrent irié / Od most haut procession / Faire la conmendation." Benoît, *CDN*, vv. 41917–65.

53. Wace, *RR*, vv. 9171–222.

edifice of piety and contrition around William's preparations for death. When William's corpse is abandoned in the *Rou* it is hardly a surprise. Wace's William was the ironfisted ruler of a violent people, feared rather than loved, and we almost anticipate that Wace's unruly Normans will exhibit such behavior once they are deprived of William's restraining influence. Benoît, however, does not prepare us for such a display. Benoît's William appears so benevolent and pious as he approaches death, and his Normans so comparatively docile, that the abandonment of William's corpse in the *Chronique* comes as a shock, and one that truly provides fodder for a meditation on the vanity of the world. Benoît's retelling also assures us just how well placed was William's faith in God. After all, it is only the clergy that tends to him in death as he is cast aside and forgotten by those who owed him loyalty in this world.

Benoît's account of William's funeral also differs significantly from Wace's description. Benoît tells us that William was taken to Caen to the abbey he had erected there. According to Benoît, a knight named Herluin took pity on William. Herluin had the body prepared and sent to Caen by boat, paying the expenses with his own money and traveling with the corpse himself, as there was no one else to do so.[54] Benoît records that a fire broke out at the instigation of the devil when the body arrived in Caen, burning over half the town and forcing everyone but the monks to abandon the king's body a second time.[55] When the fire was finally under control, the funeral proceeded with the clergy and nobility of Normandy, as well as William's son Henry, in attendance.[56] They buried William in great honor, Benoît

---

54. "A Caam iert le cors porté, / Eissi com il l'oct conmandé: / Jesir voleit en l'abeïe / Que il aveit faite e bastie. / Tuit, e parent e bienvoillant / E si plus dommaine serjant, / Erent alé, cui ça qui la, / Que nus le cors ne regarda, / Si que, ce me dit li latins, / Que uns chevalers, Herluïns, / Nez deu païs d'iloc entor, / Pleins de pitié e de dolor / Quant vit qu'eissi ert degerpiz / Od ses amis e od ses fiz / Envaï l'ovre hautement / Eissi que de som propre arjent / Fist aveir quanque fu mestier / A lui porter e a charjer / E a toz autres estoveirs. / Ainz que fust abaissiez li seirs, / L'orent en la nef mis en Seine. / Od moct escherie compaigne / S'en devalerent vers la mer, / Quer le tens esteit bel e cler. / La arriverent od le cors. / Dum s'en eissi li convenz fors / E li abés toz revestuz. / Ja si granz deos n'ert mais veüz / Com por lui fu faiz e menez, / Quant ne la vile fu entrez." Benoît, *CDN*, vv. 41965–94. This episode is also found in Orderic. Orderic, *HE*, vii, IV:102–4.

55. "Oiez que set deiable faire / Qui a trestoz biens est contraire: / Quant la jenz fu au cors alee, / Qui mainte lerme i oct ploree, / Si esprist la vile a adeir / Si qu'au cors ne poct remaneir / Homme ne fenne fors li moine. / Grant deol i sorst e gran essoine. / Porté l'en unt en l'abeïe, / E la vile plus que demie / Fu arsse trestote eissi ainz / Que li feus peüst estre estainz." Benoît, *CDN*, vv. 41995–2006.

56. "Tant fu li cors a enfoïr / Que l'on oct toz laissiez venir / Les evesques e les abez / E les hauz hommes renonmez / De par trestote de Normendie, / Ce retrait l'estoire e la vie. / De deol pales, descoloriz, / I fu e vint Henris, sis fiz. / Sol doze abez e sis evesques / E li setains li arcevesques /

recounts, but not before paying off a disgruntled Ascelin who charged that the ground on which the abbey sat belonged to his patrimony.[57] Unlike Wace, who never mentions the charitable Herluin but elaborates on Ascelin's challenge to William's burial at some length, Benoît hastily records Ascelin's importune disturbance and quickly moves on to the tears shed for William.[58] Benoît closes the funeral scene with an assertion that he has translated the history and the words as he found them written, including neither falsities nor lies.

Benoît's version of William's funeral shares several traits with Wace's account, but a comparison of the two reveals a significant divergence in tone and emphasis. Wace's account omits the figure of Herluin altogether, recording neither his pity for William nor his payment of the funeral expenses. Instead, Wace emphasizes the freak occurrences during the funeral (the fire and the challenge to the burial) that function as portents and shape his negative interpretation of William's funeral. Benoît, on the other hand, casts William's burial in a positive light by devoting a great deal of space to Herluin and his charity, explicitly describing the fire in Caen as the devil's work, and giving short shrift to Ascelin. Unlike Wace, Benoît does not mention the bishops' inquiry into Ascelin's charges, the amount of money he was given, or the assurances of restitution he received from the barons. Benoît also tells us that Herluin was a knight, but he deprives Ascelin of any status by remarking only that he was from the surrounding area. Benoît subtly encourages his reader to sympathize with both William's pitiful corpse and Herluin's generosity, while leading us to regard Ascelin as a troublemaker, probably of low status, whom the assembled nobles paid only in order to keep the peace during a solemn occasion.

Benoît's addition of an authorial disclaimer at the end of the episode suggests that he thought at least some of the material he had included might

---

Furent a son enterrement, / Qui moct par fu fait hautement / E bel e a moct grant honnor." Benoît, *CDN*, vv. 42007–19.

57. "La terre achata l'on le jor / Ou il fu enterrez e mis, / Quer uns Ascelins deu païs / Aveit la place chalongee / E requise mainte feiee: / Son patremoine ert, ce diseit, / La ou l'abeïe seieit. / N'en aveit eü nul retor / Avant deci qu'a iceu jor. / Mais lors l'en fu sis graanz faiz / Que puis en oct tote sa paiz. / Faite fu l'ovre e achevee, / Ou mainte lerme oct ainz ploree / Qu'il venissent au departir. / Tant puis bien dire, sanz mentir, / Translatee ai l'estoire e dite / D'eissi cum l'ai trovee escrite; / N'ai mis fauseté ne mençonge. / Danledeu pre qu'il vuille e donge, / Si sofert l ai gref labor, / Qu'au plaisir seit de mun seignor: / Ve vuil e quer sor tote rien, / Quer ov tant m'estereit ou bien." Benoît, *CDN*, vv. 42020–43.

58. Wace devotes sixty-one lines to Ascelin's challenge. Wace, *RR*, vv. 9279–340.

be offensive to Henry II.[59] Granted, Orderic appends a similar authentica-
tion to the end of his description of the funeral and Benoît may be imitat-
ing his source in this instance.[60] Both Benoît and Orderic had good reason
to endorse the authenticity of their accounts, as they were likely to cause
some of their readers indignation. In Orderic's case, he was not writing history for a royal patron but for the monastic community of Saint-Évroul;
still, he feared that some of his readers might think he had invented lies.
To counter this perception Orderic insists that he has "carefully investigated
and truthfully described what God's ordinance revealed in the duke's last
days. I neither compose a fictitious tragedy for the sake of gain, nor entertain cackling parasites with a wordy comedy, but truly record events of different kinds for studious readers."[61]

In spite of the fact that he had already tempered much of Orderic's stri-
dent criticism of William and the Normans, it obviously occurred to Benoît
that he might benefit from a similar endorsement of the veracity of his account; however, his differs from Orderic's in being addressed specifically to
his patron and in calling upon the authority of his sources. It is also notably
less surly in its tone. Benoît declares simply that has translated the history as
he found it written and introduced no lies before adding a plea in which he
hopes God will grant that the result of his labor pleases his patron. The aside
is directed to Henry II and asserts that any objectionable material found in
Benoît's representation of William's death and funeral should be blamed
squarely on Orderic rather than attributed to his own invention. It is particularly noteworthy that Benoît would make such a claim at this point in
his narrative. He had a variety of sources to draw on in reconstructing William's death, although none as comprehensive and detailed as Orderic's.
Benoît chose, just as Wace had, to use a source distinguished for its dim view
of William, its negative assessment of his English reign, and its problematic
depiction of his funeral. Although Benoît judiciously purged Orderic's account of its more abrasive elements, such as the noxious explosion of William's corpse during the funeral proceedings, he appears to have recognized

---

59. "Tant puis bien dire, sanz mentir, / Translatee ai l'estoire e dite / D'eissi cum l'ai trovee escrite;
/ N'ai mis fauseté ne mençonge. / Danledeu pre qu'il vuille e donge, / Si sofert i ai gref labor, /
Qu'au plaisir seit de mun seignor: / Ce vuil e quer sor tote rien, / Quer ov tant m'estereit ou bien."
Benoît, *CDN*, vv. 42034–42.

60. Orderic, *HE*, vii, IV:106–8.

61. "Subtiliter inuestigaui, et ueraciter enucleaui quae in lapsu ducis pie ostendit dispositio Dei.
Non fictilem tragediam uenundo, non loquaci comedia cachinnantibus parasitis faueo, sed studiosis
lectoribus uarios euentus ueraciter intimo." Orderic, *HE*, vii, IV:106.

the dangers inherent in using it at all, and to have hoped that his disclaimer would shield him from criticism.

Henry I

For his depiction of Henry I, Benoît turned to a notably partisan source, Robert de Torigny's F redaction of the *Gesta Normannorum ducum*.[62] Like Orderic before him, Robert de Torigny was an unabashed apologist for William the Conqueror's youngest son and saw in that monarch the resurrection of all of his father's noble qualities. Robert de Torigny was personally acquainted with both Henry I and his daughter Matilda who were patrons of, and frequent visitors to, the abbey of Le Bec where Robert penned his contributions to the *Gesta Normannorum ducum*.[63] Robert also added a book treating the deeds of Henry I that Matilda herself probably encouraged him to compose.[64] It is this book that Benoît relies on to construct his account of Henry I.

Benoît's portrayal of Henry I is accordingly distinguished by an extremely sympathetic rendering of Henry's character and rule, while his depictions of Robert Curthose and William Rufus most often emphasize their flaws. Although Benoît displays a good deal of restraint in tempering Robert de Torigny's more sycophantic fawning over Henry I and toning down his denigration of Robert Curthose, the resulting portraits of their characters and deeds are plainly at odds with those painted by Wace. Benoît completely inverts the assessment of Robert and Henry made by his predecessor: Henry emerges as a noble and deserving prince who patiently suffers the irrational cruelty of his brothers until God elevates him above them, while Robert is generally inept and foolish, although capable occasionally of rousing himself to mischief at the instigation of evil counselors.

After William's death, Benoît offers a brief sketch of the personalities of each of the Conqueror's sons. He begins with Henry, whom he describes as

---

62. Benoît's account relies on book VIII, which was composed entirely by Robert de Torigny and appended to the *GND*.

63. Elisabeth van Houts notes that Henry visited Le Bec frequently in the last two years of his life, and that both Henry and Matilda were generous patrons of the abbey. *GND*, I:lxxxiv. Robert de Torigny was a monk at Le Bec from 1128 to 1149, and was then prior of Le Bec from about 1149 to 1154. Robert was elected abbot of Mont-Saint-Michel in 1154 and remained there until his death in 1186. *GND*, I:lxxvii–viii.

64. *GND*, I:lxxxiv.

the most valiant, just, wise, noble, and discreet, praised by the entire world.[65] In fact, he declares that there was no better prince in his time, none more honored, or who loved to serve God more. Benoît's Henry is a lover of peace and justice, a giver of rich gifts, good wages, and joy to his men. No king was more renowned, none had more honor or more glory than Henry. Henry's brothers, on the other hand, are less distinguished for their virtues than for their failings. Indeed, Rufus and Robert only appear in order to magnify Henry's virtues by demonstrating the extent to which he surpassed them. Rufus was favored by his father, says Benoît, but became horrible and cruel after receiving the crown. Although generous with his money, Rufus is proud and hostile toward the church.[66] Robert is knightly, noble, and valiant, the flower of chivalry; but Benoît declares that he values neither good advice nor justice, and is unable to hold the land as his ancestors had.[67] Benoît concludes that Henry surpassed his brothers in intelligence, valor, and worth, and thus came to hold all the land they had possessed, "just as God willed."[68] The implication is that God removed Rufus, the king, and Robert, the

65. "Or est bien dreiz que je vos die / Que icist reis Henris premers / Fu vaillanz moct e dreitures / E sages e proz e discrez / E par tot le secle alosez. / Prince en son tens nul terrien / Ne fist plus honnor ne plus bien / Ne plus n'ama Deu a servir / Ne pais ne justice a tenir / Ne plus ne donna riches dons / N'a jenz plus larges livreisons, / Ne plus garies ne plus lees / Ne furent a rei ses maisnees. / Toz biens eslut, tote plentez, / Que reis n'i fu plus renonmez / Ne plus nen oct ennor ne gloire. / Por ce ert fait de lui memoire / Par tot le munt jusqu'a la fin. / Que de ses freres ne me tace, / Quer bien est dreiz que chascuns sace, / Quant li reis Ros fu coronnez, / Cum grant fu aprés sis aez. / Ses mors, sa fin, e sa manere, / Qui orrible fu trop e fere, / Ç'avum a dire e a retraire, / E de Robert, l'ainzné, le maire, / Cil qui fu fus de Normendie, / Sire e flors de chevalrie. / Si de cez deus brément retrai, / Si connois bien e vei e sai / Que ce ne fait fors embelir, / Enluminer e resplendir / L'ovre e les faiz deu noble rei; / Quer si chascuns est proz de sei, / Vaillanz au siecle e de grant pris, / Eu rei Henri, si com je truis, / Fu la valors set feiz doublee." Benoît, *CDN*, vv. 42072–109.

66. "De c'est moct bien chose provee / Que li reis Guilleaumes li Ros / Ne fu de rien tant desiros / Cumme d'aveir donner e prendre. / Nus hom n'ama tant a despendre / Ne n'en fu nus plus enprenanz, / Mains esmaiables, mains dotans, / Mais a ovres rert ententis / Dunc de tote jenz ert repris, / Que ne fust mestiers ne beoiz / A nuls reis sacrez ne ennoinz. / Trop fu assez d'estrange guise / Feus e eschis cers sainte iglise, / Vers clers e vers religions / E vers totes saintes maisons / Eissi que plusors feiz e maintes / En fu a Deu fait plusors plaintes." Benoît, *CDN*, vv. 42110–26.

67. "Robert, qui fu dus de Normanz, / Fu chevalers, proz e vaillanz. / Moct soct d'armes, most fu preisiez / E moct par en fu essauciez, / Mais haut conseil n'oct unques cher, / Buen ne feel ne dreiturer. / Ne soct pas si terre tenir / Ne si ne l'em poct avenir / Par sa coupe – ce fu dolors - / Com a ses autres anceisors." Benoît, *CDN*, vv. 42127–36.

68. "Por ce vos di li reis Henris / De sen, de valor e de pris / Les sormunta; si li avint / Que le tot oct e prist e tint, / E s'il as rennes departir, / Lors quant sis peres dut morir, / Fu si forsclos que rien n'enn oct, / Puis oct il tot, si con Dé ploct. / Puis fu le plus haut e le maire, / Eissi com je vos sai retraire / Sanz dire i chose que je puisse / Que je en l'estoire ne truisse." Benoît, *CDN*, vv. 42137–48.

eldest, in favor of Henry, the most worthy. Echoing the biblical tale of Jacob and Esau, Benoît portrays Rufus and Robert as valuing their birthrights too little and neglecting their duties, causing God to promote Henry, the youngest, above them.

Benoît's account of the events immediately following the death of William the Conqueror includes another reference to Robert's absence from his father's deathbed. This time, Benoît notes that Robert's companions in Abbeville are responsible for raiding the marches of Normandy, demonstrating that Robert's pride and his rebellion against his father are directly causing the depredation of his country.[69] Benoît goes on to describe Robert's quick reaction to the news of his father's death, his entry into Rouen, and his unhindered assumption of the ducal honor and lands. After discovering that Rufus has left to claim England, Robert is admonished by his men to challenge Rufus because he is the oldest son and the kingdom and the crown should rightfully be his.[70] Robert responds in disbelief to the news and, once he learns that Rufus has already been consecrated and anointed, a quarrel breaks out between the two brothers.

At this time, Benoît says that Henry was living in Robert's court and that Robert had either granted or mortgaged the Cotentin to Henry. This period of fraternal cooperation was to be short-lived. Benoît assures us that Robert was soon led by the counsel of evil men to seize Henry at Rouen and take away what he had granted to him.[71] Thus far Benoît's Robert has

---

69. "Uncore esteit son pere vif / Qu'a Abevile ert en Pontif. / La teneit grant chevalerie / Des plus preisiez de Normendie, / Qui a lui s'en erent alé / Tot folement e de lor gré / Por le novel seignorement / Que chascuns d'eus de lui atent, / E por acomplir lor corages, / Si cum est costume e usuages, / Que cil qui de mau faire unt tens, / Voler, coraige ne porpens / Funt desiros, parjur e faus. / Par cez ert tnat creüz li maus / Que les marches de Normendie / Qui erent d'icele partie, / Estieint a deol essillees / E robees plusors feiees; / Mais quant il fu cerntains e fiz / Que sis peres esteit feniz, / Vint a Roem sanz demorance. / Eissi sanz autre destorbance / E sanz content se fist seignor / De la cité e de l'onnor. / De rechef prist ses feeutez." Benoît, *CDN*, vv. 42175–99.

70. "Aprés fu moct amonestez / Qu'en Engleterre trepassast / E que a rei s'i coronnast / E chaçast son frere en essil, / Quer il, qui esteit l'aizné fil, / Deveit aveir – quer dreiz l'en donne - / E le reiaume e la coronne. / E il jura, ce truis escrit, / A ceus qui ce li orent dit / Que, s'il esteit en Alemaigne, / En Alixandre ou en Espaigne, / Si l'atendreient li Engleis / Tot mau gré lor e sor lor peis, / Ainz qu'a autre se sosmeïssent / Ne que cuide ne n'espeire mie / Que il ait fait tel estoutie / Ne sol li venist en penser / Qu'a rei se feïst coronner / Por sa teste ne por ses oiz, / C'um n'aveit esté faiz orguiz / Comparez fust si laidement; / Maid l'ovre aloct tot autrement. / Tot le veir en soct demaneis / Qu'enoiz ert e sacrez e reis: / Dunc fu entr'eus tex la haor / Qu'entre freres nen oct graignor." Benoît, *CDN*, vv. 42200–226.

71. "Od le duc Robert ert Henris, / De lui servir volonteris. / Sanz fauseté e sanz boisdie / Od lui aloct par Normendie. / Si cum me retraist li latins, / Cinc mile livres d'esterlins / Li aveit sis peres laissiez. / Ne sai donnez ou engajez / Li fu, ce sai bien, Costentin. / Mais sis freres a la parfin, / Qui saisi l'en oct buennement, / Li retoli vilainement. / Envers lui trova achaisons / Par mau conceil

acted shamefully, rebelling against his father, devastating his own country, listening to bad advice, and imprisoning his brother Henry without cause, but Benoît goes on to chide Robert further. He says that Robert "got what he deserved" (*si gaaigne qui si desert*). If he had loved, served, and obeyed his father, he would have had the entire kingdom and the crown, but he sealed his own fate by rebelling.[72] In fact, Benoît asserts that Robert's incompetence lost him the kingdom a second time. He could have deprived Rufus of the kingdom if he had acted wisely earlier. When Robert's supporters invaded England and captured several fortresses, Benoît says that Robert tarried in Normandy, partying with his men and sleeping in late.[73] Preoccupied with revelry, Robert failed to cross to England with reinforcements, causing his adherents to abandon their strongholds and forcing them to return to Normandy in shame. When peace was established between Robert and Rufus it was thus to Robert's detriment.[74] Benoît records that William

---

d'ommes felons. / Sanz ce que de rien s'en gardast / Ne que de lui point de dotast, / Le fist li dus a Roem prendre / Tant que le tot li oct fait rendre, / Si cum ainz li aveit laissié / Ne sai donné ou engaigié. / Sanz errer vers lui malement / Li toli si vilainement; / Unc puis ne fu, si com je truis, / Nul jor qu'eu ne l'en fust de puis / E que moct mains n'en fust Henris / Sis bienvoillanz e sis amis." Benoît, *CDN*, vv. 42227–52. Robert de Torigny and Benoît fail to mention that Robert imprisoned both Henry and the notorious Robert of Bellême because he suspected them of conspiring with William Rufus to deprive him of Normandy. Cf. William of Malmesbury, *GRA*, II:468; and Orderic, *HE*, vii, IV:148.

72. "Eissi oct la terre a estros / E le reiaume li reis Ros, / Si tot peisa au duc Robert; / Si gaaigne qui si desert. / S'il eüst som pere servi, / Amé, creeit e odbeï, / Le renne eüst entirerement / E quanqu'a la coronne apent, / Mais par sa coupe en est forsclos; / Deu tot en est botez defors. / Concorde firent entr'eus dous, / E se li dus fust engignos / E si sagement en ovrast / Com a ice li besoignast, / Le renne peüst tost aveir / E tot en fust fait son voleir." Benoît, *CDN*, vv. 42253–68.

73. "Enpris en fu riche besoigne, / Qu'Eustaces, li quens de Boloigne, / Ne tint au rei ne paiz ne treues / Ne li evesque de Baïues / N'o tot li quens de Moretuig / N'autres barons dum je n'ai suig / D'ici a ceste feiz nonmer. / Od tant quant qu'il porent mander / Passerent la mer sor Engleis / Si qu'ainz les quinze jorz deu meis / Orent Rovecestre en dommaine / Sanz grant traveil e sanz grant paine, / E les chasteaus d'icel empire / Qui sunt environ Contorbire. / Le duc mandoent tote jor / Que il venist saisir l'onnor, / E il entendeit a chacier / E a son jent cors aaisier / E a dormir granz matinees, / Soventes feiz assez vilaines, / Quer ses granz afaires domaines / Aloent assez bassement. / Se cil tindrent longement, / Ne lor poct unc aveir mestier, / Des qu'aler ne lor voct aidier / Ne passer le mer od ses jenz; / Si ne munta riens lor contenz, / Quer li reis Ros soventes feiz / Les teneit si a mort destreiz / Qu'endamagiez trop e laidiz / Li unt puis les chasteaus gerpiz / E voidié la terre ensement. / Sans faille moct hontosement / S'en revindrent en Normendie." Benoît, *CDN*, vv. 42269–303.

74. "Puis, ce truis escrit en la vie, / Fu a Caam lor concordance, / Que fist entr'eus li reis de France, / Qui au duc ert venuz aidier, / Quer od maint riche chevalier / Ert li reis passez od navie / Saisir e prendre Normendie. / A ou aveit sa jent jostee, / Quant la paiz d'eus fu porparlee, / Deu tot aveir encoragiez; / Mais eissi furent amaisiez / Que toz li meudres en fu reis, / E li dus en oct le sordeis, / Quer li reis ne se vect demetre; / Tant ne s'en soct nus entremetre / Deu chastel dunt il fust certain / Ne qu'il eüst pris en sa main / Que rendu li fust ne baillié / De ceus qu'i aveient laissié. / Le

Rufus gained parts of Normandy, including Fècamp and Eu, at Robert's expense, while Robert earned a reputation for ineptitude bordering on stupidity for having suffered such a disgraceful defeat.

Benoît next recounts a pact between Robert and Rufus to exclude Henry from their lands.[75] Acting in particularly unbrotherly fashion, they determine to drive Henry out, against the dying wishes of their father. Neither Robert de Torigny nor Benoît gives any reason for this sudden lack of filial affection toward Henry, but Orderic provides us with the relevant information. Orderic says that Henry was agitating for possession of some of his father's lands and had brought pleas against both of his brothers.[76] When his persistent supplications were not met with a satisfactory response, Henry determined to stage a rebellion and fortified Mont-Saint-Michel with the aid of some Norman and Breton followers. Benoît, however, suppresses any mention of Henry's rebellion. When he describes the siege of Mont-Saint-Michel it appears that Robert and Rufus are acting purely out of spite, harassing Henry without reason.

Benoît says that Henry was saved by a dispute that broke out between Robert and Rufus, during which he was able to escape and flee to Domfront. Orderic, on the other hand, notes that Henry recognized the ill-conceived nature of his rebellion and determined to save himself by asking his brothers for safe passage, which they granted.[77] Wace, who also recounts the siege of

---

duc, por lui deu tot aidier / A conquerre e a gerreier, / Fescamp teneit, Ou la contez / E autres buens chasteaus assez / Que li quens Guilleaumes, sis druz, / Li aveit bailliez e renduz. / Ausi li ert ferme e estable / Li quens Estievre d'Aubemarle / - Fiz fu Odon le Campeneis / E niés Guilleaume, li buens reis - / Ausi raveient plusors fait, / Qui ne remestrent pas fors plait; / Ne les voct pas quiter li reis. / Mau gré son frere e sor som peis / Les retint dedevers sei toz / Comme vasaus e comne proz." Benoît, *CDN*, vv. 42304–38.

75. "En ceste paiz dum j'os retrai / Poiez oïr estrange plai, / Fiere ovre e laide e crueeté: / Qu'icist frere unt entreus parlé / E afichié, dit e pramis / Que ne remaindreit pas Henris / En tot le renne qu'il teneient. / Ja entr'eus plus ne le laireient, / Qui que fust ennui ne contraire. / Lor poeir mistrent a ce faire. / Por veir deüssent il entr'eus / Non pas estre ver lui si feus: / Terre a son eus, chasteaus e bors / E autres tenemenz plusors / Dum il peüst vivre a honnor / Comme lor cher frere menor ... / Mais malement li unt mostré / Que de c'eüssent volunté, / Qu'eu Munt Saint Michel l'ont assis, / Ou il s'en ert foïz e mis. / La le cuiderent afermer / Tant que son cors vousist livrer. / Si feïst il par aventure, / Mais entr'eus sorst une rancure / Qui le siege fist departir / Tant que cil s'em poct bien eissir / Saus e quites, lui e sa jent. / Puis ne demora pas grantment / Qu'il oct Danfront par grant saveir, / Que uns vassaus li fist aveir / Qui en gardoct la fortelece; / Quer en danjer e en destrece / Les teneit Robert de Belesme; / - Unques nus huem ne reçut cresme / Plus pesme hul ne plus haïz / Ne plus de Danledeu partiz, / N'ou mains eüst amor ne fei / Ne plus amast faire deslei - / Nou poeit cil plus endurer / Qui le chastel deveit garder. / Henri i recoilli e mist, / Qui liez e toz joios s'en fist, / Qui sieu garda e le païs, / Qui tot esteit a dolor mis, / C'unc n'i deslia bof d'aree." Benoît, *CDN*, vv. 42339–83.

76. Orderic, *HE*, vii, IV:250.

77. Ibid.

Mont-Saint-Michel, offers a version of events that emphasizes Robert's courtesy and filial affection. He credits Robert with providing a truce for the besieged to gather food and with sending wine from his own supplies to relieve the thirst of his rebellious brother. He adds that, although Rufus was ready to depart in indignation when he learned that Robert had given aid to Henry, Robert made him remain in the area and effected a reconciliation between Rufus and Henry.[78] The episode as recounted by Robert de Torigny and Benoît, however, transforms Robert and Rufus into scheming, inhumane monsters determined to exclude Henry at any cost, just as it disguises Henry's rebellion against his brothers by converting it into the unreasonable persecution of an innocent man. Although Henry had reason to be upset with his brothers for refusing to maintain him in a manner befitting the son of a king, he was not as blameless as Benoît would have us believe, nor were Robert and Rufus so fiendish.

After narrating the siege of Mont-Saint-Michel, Benoît tells us that Rufus granted Henry lordship of the Cotentin, excepting Bayeux and Caen, and that Robert mortgaged the whole of Normandy to Rufus in 1096 in order to fight in the Holy Land.[79] Robert was thus away on the First Crusade and Henry was in England with Rufus when the king was mortally wounded while hunting in the New Forest on August 2, 1100.[80] Four days later, Henry was crowned at Westminster by Bishop Maurice of London.[81] Far from implying that Henry stole the English throne during Robert's absence, as Wace had done, Benoît tells us that Henry buried his brother and proceeded to London where he summoned the great men of the realm.[82] Benoît assures us that the assembled magnates then elevated Henry as their king, placing the crown upon his head without further delay. Benoît goes on to say that the country rejoiced that God had given them a king who would be a gentle and just father to the people, who would hold the realm

---

78. Wace, *RR*, vv. 9573–618.

79. Benoît, *CDN,* vv. 42399–411, 42543–55, 42477–542, and 42743–56.

80. Benoît, *CDN*, vv. 43027–108.

81. Henry was crowned on Sunday, August 5, 1100.

82. "Aprés – n'i out delaiement – / Le doleros enterrement / Qu'out fait faire li quens Henris / De son fere qui ert ocis, / Vint a Londres senz plus targer. / Dunc fist mander a Wemostier / Toz les granz homes de l'honor / Puis la mort son frere al quart jor; / E buen e mal e riche e sage / Comunaument od bon corage / L'unt receü a grant honor / E fait sor eus rei e seignor; / El chef out la corone assise, / Le jor n'i out autre devise." Benoît, *CDN*, vv. 43127–40.

in peace, love the church, and maintain justice.[83] Benoît describes Henry as full of the best virtues, severe toward evil men, but richly rewarding those who loved and served him. Most important, Benoît says that God gave proof of his affection for Henry by giving plenty and abundance to the people and lands that the king held for as long as he lived, and that Henry reigned kindly, with great faith and respect for God.

After the conquest of Antioch and Jerusalem, Benoît says that Robert was begged to stay in the Holy Land, but chose to return home out of folly.[84] Robert came back laden with riches, intending to repay Rufus for the loan he had taken. When he reached Normandy, however, there was no one to challenge him or demand repayment. Benoît notes that Robert thus resumed lordship of Normandy without repaying the mortgage he had taken, although he had the means to do so. Presumably this is meant to imply that Robert should have repaid Henry, who had succeeded William Rufus as king. Benoît then recounts Robert's reaction to the news of Henry's coronation, saying that Robert was furious and threatened to menace Henry with all his might.[85] Robert raised a navy and immediately set off for England. In response Henry assembled his own men, putting his faith in God and thinking it better to die in battle than relinquish the kingdom. The expected battle, however, never materialized. Benoît says that God effected concord, peace, and love between the brothers. A peace agreement was reached at Alton Wood where it was decided that Henry would remain king and hold the entire realm, but would pay Robert four thousand sterlings annually as compensation. Robert soon remitted this payment to Henry's queen, however, and so never received a single penny.[86] Wace

---

83. "Joie unt el regne, teu n'i out, / Kar chascun quida bien e sout / Que Deus tel rei lor ait tramis / Qui au grant pople e au païs / Sera peres douz e verais, / Qui le regne tendra en pais / E bones genz e sainte iglise / E qui mult maintendra justise. / Eissi fu il, ne fu veüz / Reis pleins de plus bones vertuz. / Nus ne maintint, que nos sachons, / Plus jor saintes religions, / Ne traïson ne felonie / Ne haï nul plus a sa vie. / As maus fu trop amers e feus, / Mais riches dons dona a ceus / Qui l'amerent e quieu servirent / E qui ses comandemenz firent. / De riches maisnees tenir / Ne se vout unques resortir; / Nul n'ama plus bons chevalers; / Leiaus reis fu e dreitures, / E Deus par saint demonstrance / Dona plenté e abondance / As genz, as terres, as païs / Qu'il tint dementres qu'il fu vis. / Boneüreement regna, / Mult le crut Deus e essauça." Benoît, *CDN*, vv. 43141–68.

84. Benoît, *CDN*, vv. 43387–408.

85. Benoît, *CDN*, vv. 43409–48.

86. "A Maheut, la bone reïne, / Ce truis en l'estoire latine / Ottreia cel premier aveir, / C'unc denier ne vout receveir: / Por bien le fist e por honor / A la dame de grant valor; / Mais cil n'eire pas sagement / Qui tant done qu'il s'en repent / E tant vout le suen departir / Que l'autrui li estoet tolir. / Mal espleite, de sei n'a cure: / Por ce vaut mult sen e mesure." Benoît, *CDN*, vv. 43449–60.

explicitly blames Henry and Robert of Meulan for purposely concocting a scheme to defraud Robert of this compensation, but Benoît completely obscures their deception, just as he omits any mention of Henry's plan to ambush Robert at Alton Wood. Benoît reports only that Robert generously gave his compensation to the queen, and concludes that, while this gesture was good and honorable, it was not very wise and Robert later repented of it.

Predictably, the peace between Robert and Henry concluded at Alton Wood did not last. Benoît says that after remaining in England for some time, Robert returned to Normandy with good intentions, but quickly lapsed into his old vices.[87] He did not listen to good counsel or attend to the business of ruling the duchy, but believed liars and evil men who wanted to stir up trouble between him and the king. Because of the wicked advice he received, Benoît reports that Robert often did things that confounded Henry.[88] When Robert began alienating most of the land and honors held by his predecessors to men Benoît describes as "simple and unwise," animosity returned.[89] Benoît says that Robert "gave away everything his ancestors had conquered and held with great effort, except the city of Rouen." This was the final straw for Henry. Benoît reports that he could no longer en-

---

87. "Aprés l'acordance e l'amor / Qu'orent entr'eus li dui seignur / Fu li dux Robert mult cheriz / En Engleterre e mult joïz. / Un lonc termine i esta puis / A grant aise, si cum je truis. / A ce n'esteit il mie eschis, / Riens n'i fu unc plus ententis. / Aprés, od maisnee escharie, / S'en retorna en Normendie. / Si donc vousist a ce entendre / Que bons princes deit soudre e rendre / - D'estre verais e dreiturers, / Senz laiz vices, bons justisiers, / Plein de conseil, plein de valor / Crienge e serve son creator / La gent gart qui il est baillee, / Que vers Deu ne vers eus n'enchee - / Eissi e od sei si aveir / Eüst li dux a son voleir / En fine paiz tote sa vie / La ducheé de Normendie; / Mais de tot ce ne li chalut. / N'ovra mie si cum il dut, / De bon conseil ne de verai / Ne tint unques conte ne plai, / Ainz se devint trop costumiers / De creire garçons losengiers / E mauvaise genz e vilanie, / Qui meteient travail e paine / De lui e son frere mesler. / Bien le porent a ce mener, / Kar de lor fol conseil hontos, / Vil e mauvais e haïnos, / Ne se saveit pas bien deffendre." Benoît, *CDN*, vv. 43461–95.

88. Benoît is following Robert de Torigny's description of the events. *GND*, viii, II:220–21.

89. "Sovent li faiseient emprendre / Choses multes laides a faire, / Qui au rei deveient desplaire, / E si faiseient eus sovent. / Ne dura mie longement / Lor bienvoillance e lur amors, / Ainz i retorna granz haors. / S'irié esteit vers lui le rei, / Mult i aveit choses por quei, / Kar li dux Robert ses honors, / Qui erent de ses anceisors, / Ses burs, ses viles, ses chasteaus, / La ou il les aveit plus beaus, / Ses bois, ses rentes, ses paages, / Cum simples hom e cum non sages / Donout e faiseit chasemenz, / E ç'assez a mauveises genz. / Ce que conquistrent a grant paine / E que tindrent a lor domaine / Si anceisor, parti de sei, / C'unc n'en prist cure ne conrei; / N'aveit plus i tenist a suen / Fors sol la cité de Roem. / Cele eüst il cent feiz donee, / S'el li fust chose graantee, / Mais li borgeis a mult grant paine / - C'unc n'en furent gent meins vilanie - / Neu li voudrent unc consentir. / Neu pout li reis Henris sofrir / Ne endurer teu deiable / Que d'autre home n'iert mais oïe, / Ne consentir si fait damage / As eirs d'eus ne de lor lignage." Benoît, *CDN*, vv. 43496–528. Cf. *GND*, viii, II:220–21.

dure his brother's behavior, nor sit idly while his brother squandered their patrimony.

Unsurprisingly, Benoît's description of the civil war in Normandy credits Robert and his evil counselors with causing the outbreak of hostilities by constantly provoking Henry and frittering away ancestral rights and lands. Equally unremarkably, Benoît does not dwell on the civil war or on the profound revulsion it provoked among contemporaries. He notes, with uncharacteristic but understandable brevity, that Henry's consternation over Robert's actions finally drove him to cross into Normandy; that he destroyed Bayeux with fire and took Caen in short order.[90]

Henry then proceeded to Tinchebray where Count William of Mortain had joined Robert, his cousin and his natural lord, in his folly.[91] Thinking they could best Henry, Benoît says that Robert and William "did an evil thing" that resulted in their downfall—they turned their forces on Henry and attacked him in a powerful charge. Henry withstood the assault. After defeating Robert and William of Mortain at Tinchebray, Benoît simply reports that Henry took them into his custody. He then goes on to note the almost bloodless nature of the battle, remarking that God skillfully ensured that Henry had not lost a single man, and that only fifty of Robert's men had died.[92] Thus was Normandy pacified. Benoît remarks that the duchy had been brought to shame and destroyed by Robert; under him it possessed neither law nor justice, but bred malice. Now there was peace, Normandy

---

90. "Mer passa od mult fieres genz, / N'en sai les milliers ne les cenz. / Baïes vint saisir e prendre, / Mais ne li voudrent mie rendre; / Mais tant i sist que il l'out prise, / Arse e detruite e a dol mise. / Caam – ne targa gaires puis - / Reprist aprés, si cum je truis." Benoît, *CDN*, vv. 43529–36.

91. "D'iloc ala, kar bien le sai, / Au siege de Tenerchebrai. / Au conte esteit de Moretoing, / Qui de lui amer n'aveit soing, / Ainz maintenit en la folor / Le duc, son naturel seignor, / Ja par lui ne li fust veee, / Contredite ne destorbee / Chose vis ne mauveis usage / Ne qui li tornast a damage. / Nen ert point li reis sis amis; / Por ç'out il son chastel assis, / Mais neu porent pas d'assaut prendre: / Bien le li quidout l'om defeendre. / Ne sai quanz jorz i aveit sis. / Li dux Robert entre tanz dis / E li quens orent genz mandees, / Oz fieres e desmesurees, / Barons, veisins e chastelains / E lor plus chers amis certains: / Del rei Henri se vengeront, / Ce dient, plus neu sofferont, / Ne, se lor force a ce s'adone, / Ne li remaindra la corone." Benoît, *CDN*, vv. 43537–60.

92. "La grant bataille fu finee, / N'i out puis autre demoree. / N'i out unc puis saette traite / Des qu'il conurent lor chaette, / Ne dedevers eus pris retor; / Pris i furent tuit li meillor. / Ceste mortele ovre haïe, / Qui si pesme esteit envaïe, / Fina Deus tot apertement, / Kar ce lis bien certainement / C'unc li reis le jor n'i perdié / Ne chevalier n'ome preisié, / Ne de l'autre part, tot acante, / Nen out ocis que sol cinquante. / Eisi par cest'ovre fenie / Fu rapaisee Normendie, / Qui par poi n'ert a honte alee, / Destruite e si a dol menee / Que n'i aveit dreit ne justice, / Qu'en terre n'aveit tant malice. / Icin fu pais, cin fu delivre / Tant cum li reis out puis a vivre. / Ici recovra sa douçur, / Sa joie, sa plenté, s'onor. / Par ceste bataille finee / Fu puis toz jorz boneüree / Tant cum li bons reis vesqui puis. / Des l'Incarnation, ce truis, / Aveit mil e cent e sis anz / Que ç'avint, ce sui je lisanz, / Si fu li tens de la bataille / En oitovre tot dreit, senz faille." Benoît, *CDN*, vv. 43611–42.

was delivered, and, under Henry, "she recovered her sweetness, her joy, her plenty, her honor."

The differences between Benoît's account of the civil war and that given by Wace are conspicuous and revealing. Wace cast Henry as a greedy opportunist who sowed treason among Robert's men, he lingered over the details of the burning of Bayeux and the betrayal at Caen, and he savored exposing the men who betrayed Robert, recording their evil deeds and commemorating their infamy. Benoît, however, describes Henry as motivated only by the need to preserve the duchy from his brother's incompetence. Benoît completely elides the horror of the burning of Bayeux, and never mentions the subterfuge and treason that enabled Henry to take Caen. Far from decrying the traitors who abandoned Robert as Wace had, Benoît adroitly transforms the terms of the debate. Rather than examining the treason among Robert's vassals and its causes (Benoît never mentions anyone betraying Robert), he notes only that William of Mortain had joined Robert, "his natural lord," in his "folly." The comment leads his reader to conclude that William of Mortain's exceptional loyalty to Robert, although derived from his obligation to defend his natural lord, was nonetheless ill conceived. Moreover, Benoît's explanation that God limited the casualties at Tinchebray indicates that the outcome of the battle was the product of the divine will, just as it seeks to shield Henry from criticism for having started the civil war.[93]

It should be noted that Wace had been no lone voice in the wilderness in expressing his disgust and horror at the civil war. Even Henry's apologists had viewed it as a lamentable, if necessary, evil and had struggled to construct a justification for Henry's invasion of Normandy that limited his responsibility. Orderic had clearly abhorred the necessity of using force against Robert, even though he fervently desired that Normandy be liberated from its duke and subjected to Henry's rule.[94] As Orderic succinctly observed in

---

93. Robert de Torigny makes this point more forcefully. "But God's judgment came upon them and both men along with many others were taken prisoner by King Henry's men and led before the king. In this manner did God concede a bloodless victory to a king who feared him, as once he did to his servant the Emperor Theodosius. In this battle none of the king's men perished and on the enemy's side scarcely sixty fell." ["Sed iudicio Dei super eos ueniente, capti sunt ambo et multi alii cum eis ab hominibus Henrici regis altque ante eum adducti. Concessit hoc modo Deus regi se timenti uictoriam incruentam, sicut quondam Theodosio imperatoris seruo suo fecerat. In enim conflictu ex suis nullus, ex aduersa parte uix .lx. corruerunt."] GND, viii, II:222–23.

94. Orderic's conflicted feelings about the civil war are apparent in his account of the events. Orderic, HE, xi, VI:60–69, 86–87, 96–97. Civil war was clearly hateful and to be avoided; it was only justifiable in the most dire circumstances, and even then exceptional arguments were necessary to defend it.

wrestling with the complexities of the Norman civil war and the moral ambiguity of Henry's actions, sometimes "a wrong must be done to put an end to a worse wrong."[95] In light of the almost indefensible nature of Henry's actions, the apologies offered by Orderic, Robert de Torigny, and Benoît had to rely on defaming Robert. Indeed, all of them were composed of three main elements: enumerating Robert's failings and provocations, stressing Henry's long patience with his brother, and emphasizing God's unequivocal judgment in the outcome of Tinchebray. Their assertions that Tinchebray resulted in so little bloodshed, and all of it on Robert's side, served to mitigate the horrors of the civil war, while further strengthening their claims that Henry's invasion was justified and that God favored his actions.

Benoît's assurance that Normandy once again flourished under Henry's rule is likewise designed to counter criticism of Henry for his extremely disquieting treatment of his brother and his illicit seizure of the duchy. Indeed, Benoît is at such pains to justify Henry's actions that he offers a summation of Robert's fate that again seeks to absolve Henry of blame: "Thus by [Robert's] excessive simplicity, by his immoderation, by his sloth, he lost land, lost honor, and lost all his merit; it was a loss and a great sorrow."[96] Benoît displays a glimmer of sympathy for the fallen duke here, and it may be quite genuine, but he does so while maintaining the position that Robert had to be deposed in order to preserve Normandy. It is not the only time that Benoît tempers his recriminations with praise, however backhanded, for Robert's virtues. It is a precarious balancing act that Benoît deftly executes on more than one occasion, and one that seems designed to firmly affix blame on Robert while maintaining the appearance of impartiality. Earlier in the *Chronique*, Benoît praised Robert as "the flower of chivalry," even as he repeated the standard charges against him—that he listened too much to evil counsel and was negligent in governing. Now, Benoît expresses regret, apparently unironically, that Robert's incompetence caused him to lose everything and tarnished his reputation.

Benoît is not alone in his representation of Robert as a once valiant and noble man brought to ruin by his flaws. "He was a very brave soldier," says Robert de Torigny, "who performed many noble deeds. . . . But as a ruler of the duchy he proved to be less effective."[97] This reluctance to paint

---

95. Orderic, *HE*, xi, VI:96–97.

96. "Eissi par sa tres grant simplece, / par son sorfait, par sa perece, / Perdi terre, perdi honor / E perdi tote sa valor: / Cu fu damage e granz dolors." Benoît, *CDN*, vv. 43679–83.

97. "Fuit hic Robertus miles fortissimus et multa nobiliter gessit, maxime quando a Christianis Anthiochia et Ierusalem super Sarracenos capte sunt. Ad regimen tamen ducatus minus utilis, prop-

Robert as completely devoid of redeeming qualities is partly due to the fact
that even Henry's partisans were keenly aware that Robert had done admi-
rable things, that he had returned from the Holy Land to a hero's welcome,
and that he was still the rightful duke of Normandy. Apparently in recognition of this last fact, Henry rarely used the title *dux Normannorum* while his
brother lived—an indication that, although Henry was the de facto ruler of
Normandy for eighteen years while Robert was his prisoner, there were still
limits to Henry's power and lingering doubts as to the legitimacy of his rule
in Normandy.[98]

Henry's supporters were acutely aware that his dubious actions had made
him vulnerable to criticism and that the vassals who had abandoned Robert
were likewise on very shaky moral ground. Finally, they recognized the
remarkable tenacity of human memory (a rather inconvenient fact in this
case). Although it is doubtful that contemporaries universally accepted the
argument that the once valiant, but now hopelessly inadequate, Robert had
to be deposed in order to save Normandy, even fewer people were likely to
accept an account that contradicted their own memories by focusing relentlessly on Robert's shortcomings without acknowledging his virtues. In spite
of its obvious weaknesses, it appears that this was the best defense that
Henry's apologists could muster, and that Benoît dutifully followed them in
promoting it.

Benoît concludes his account of Henry I's reign with a short list of the
king's accomplishments: restoring strongholds and towns in Normandy,
imposing peace throughout his realm and in lands far from him, subduing
the Welsh, and generously endowing monasteries and churches.[99] In spite of
its brevity, the list of Henry's deeds emphasizes the positive aspects of his
leadership, especially his ability to prevent internal wars between his magnates. Benoît also praises Henry's relations with the papacy, noting that
"Pope Innocent [II] came to Rouen for Henry's sake" where he granted
indulgences and received the king's support. With sparse, but very effective
strokes, Benoît paints Henry as a wise, benevolent, and supremely compe-

---

ter simplicitatem suam et propter consilia leuia, quibus nimium aurem acommodabat." *GND*, viii,
II:222.

98. E. B. Fryde and D. H. Greenway, *Handbook of British Chronology* (Cambridge, 1996), 30. Although Henry rarely styled himself *dux Normannorum*, even in charters pertaining to Normandy,
"Henricus dei gratia dux Normannorum" appeared on one side of his Great Seal after 1106. The
other side of the seal simply read "Henricus rex Anglorum," suggesting that Henry felt compelled
to emphasize God's intervention in his acquisition of Normandy.

99. Benoît, *CDN*, vv. 44215–46 and 44259–328.

tent ruler whose reign was favored by God and characterized by peace and prosperity, as well as good relations between the monarch and the church—a veritable golden age.

Following Robert de Torigny, Benoît declares that there was only "one deed for which Henry was reproved."[100] When Henry seized the castles of his enemies he enclosed and fortified them as though they were his own, keeping them for himself and his heirs. This is, in fact, the only aspect of Benoît's history to which Henry II might have objected. Henry II's restoration of his grandfather's government included returning the ownership of properties to those who had held them on the day of Henry I's death. Henry II also set about reclaiming Crown properties and vigorously enforcing royal control of castles. This single criticism of Henry I thus had the potential to remind Benoît's audience that the barons had objected to these confiscations during Henry I's reign. The magnates had viewed such actions as illicit and reproved Henry I for them, and their descendants might quite reasonably reprove Henry II for doing precisely the same thing. This criticism thus had the potential to undermine Henry II's claims to be legitimately recovering royal lands and prerogatives lost under Stephen. It is uncertain, however, whether Benoît would have understood the import of this criticism. He may have intended it as a thinly veiled condemnation of Henry II, but everything else about Benoît's history indicates that he was solicitous toward his patron and earnest in his attempts to construct Henry I's reign as a golden age worthy of restoration. Since he so closely follows Robert de Torigny in this case, we may assume that Benoît did not see the potential harm in including this detail.

The Empress Matilda and Henry II

Shortly after describing Henry I's accession to the English throne, Benoît recounts Henry's marriage to Edith-Matilda, the daughter of King Malcolm and Queen Margaret of Scotland.[101] Although Benoît praises Edith-Matilda's piety and character, he does not explicitly mention the importance of her royal Anglo-Saxon bloodline or her descent from Edmund Ironside. Although these facts go unstated, it is highly unlikely that Benoît's audience would have failed to note them as they were embedded

---

100. Benoît, *CDN*, vv. 44247–58.
101. Benoît, *CDN*, vv. 43169–94.

in the Anglo-Norman memory.[102] Benoît's real focus, however, is the two children Edith-Matilda bore Henry, especially their daughter Matilda.[103] Even Benoît's brief account of the premature death of Henry's only legitimate son, William Audelin, is interrupted with a reference to its implications for Matilda's future.[104] In the middle of depicting Henry's grief at William's death, Benoît notes that his only remaining heir was the empress Matilda before turning to a long digression on the chimerical nature of fortune and the wisdom of meeting both prosperity and adversity with moderation.[105] With a single well-placed stroke of bad luck, fortune had dashed Henry's meticulous plans to ensure the future of his dynasty and thrown the English succession into chaos. William Audelin, had he lived, would have been Henry's greatest legacy. Uniting the blood of the Anglo-Saxon and Norman royal houses in his person, he would have been Henry's undisputed heir, and, it was hoped, he would have healed the wounds opened by the Conquest. Instead, his premature death in 1120 ushered in fifteen excruciating years of uncertainty over the future of the Anglo-Norman dynasty.

Benoît returns to Matilda after recounting Tinchebray and detailing the extinction of Robert Curthose's line (his only legitimate son, William Clito, died in 1128 after threatening Henry's rule in Normandy and England for twenty years with his very existence; Robert himself died, still a prisoner, in 1134). In 1125 Matilda's first husband, the German emperor Henry V, died. Benoît says that Henry recalled his daughter to England, wishing to make her "heir to the entire kingdom, having no other children from his spouse. This he wanted all to swear to and none to renounce after his death."[106] Henry assembled his bishops and barons, making them "swear and grant [to her] everything that pertained to the crown. Then, just as he had devised, they all swore fealty [to Matilda] over sacred reliquaries."[107]

---

102. The marriage of Henry I and Edith-Matilda was widely recognized by contemporaries as uniting the Norman and Anglo-Saxon royal bloodlines.

103. Benoît, *CDN*, vv. 43195–272.

104. Benoît, *CDN*, vv. 43273–386.

105. Benoît, *CDN*, vv. 43331–33.

106. Benoît, *CDN*, vv. 43973–400.

107. "Fist ses evesques toz mander / E ses hauz homes assembler. / Veiant eus, li ostreie e done / Tot quant qu'apent a la corone. / Puis, si cum il l'a devisé, / Li jurerernt tuit feeuté / Sor chers renomez saintuaires, / Cume que otrnast li afaires, / Son lor valors e lor poeirs / A metre i tot cors e aveirs, / Li portassent fei e amor / E le regne entier e l'onor / Li gardassent mais feeument. / Ce jurerernt vers tote gent, / Mais bien diron cum il les tindrent / Ne cum les choses puis avindrent." Benoît, *CDN*, vv. 43983–98.

This was, Benoît says, "all put down on parchment before the work was finished."[108] Benoît makes no reference to any dissension among the barons, or to the fact that Henry's designation of a female heir was quite extraordinary for its time. Benoît chooses to elide the debate entirely and instead sets about praising Henry's creation of a marital alliance with Anjou—an alliance that proved to have dreadful consequences for the Anglo-Norman succession.

For a long time the lords of Anjou had warred with their Norman neighbors, each side burning the other's fortresses and laying the countryside waste.[109] "Henry, the good king of England" wished to bring this interminable fighting to a peaceful conclusion and make friends of these formidable enemies. Benoît, it should be noted, carefully avoids blaming either side for the hostilities, apparently finding it senseless to incite hatred for people who were now in-laws. In fact, he showers Count Fulk of Anjou with praise, and extols his son Geoffrey still more, calling him "a great knight, strong and handsome, prudent, wise, and conquering; there was no prince more valiant."[110] To this man, lord of Anjou, Maine, and the Touraine, Henry "gave his daughter and his heir, the Empress, the prudent, the wise."[111]

In bald contradiction of the known facts, Benoît records that "many great men were involved" and that the marriage was celebrated far and wide.[112] In fact, neither the Anglo-Norman barons nor Matilda were overjoyed by the alliance. The marriage was performed almost in secret and, when news of it finally reached Henry's magnates, it provoked angry recriminations. More than a few of the magnates threatened to abjure their oaths to Matilda on the grounds that they had not been consulted about the marriage and had certainly not consented to it. It was widely presumed that, were Matilda allowed to inherit, her husband would rule England and Normandy *iure*

---

108. "Tot sera mis eu parchemin, / Ainceis que l'ovre vienge a fin." Benoît, *CDN*, vv. 43999–4000.

109. Benoît, *CDN*, vv. 44001–70.

110. "Grant chevaler e fort e bel, / E proz e sage e conqueranz. / Prince n'esteit nus plus vaillanz." Benoît, *CDN*, vv. 44022–24.

111. "Doner e sa fille e son eir, / L'empereriz, la proz, la sage." Benoît, *CDN*, vv. 44034–35.

112. "Ici out riche mariage. / Tanz hautes genz s'en enremistrent / E tant parlerent e tant fistrent / Qu'il la li dona a moillier / E qu'il la li fist noceier. / Ja de plus haute renomee / Nen ert mais dame mariee. / Beneit fu li jostemenz / D'eus deus e li assemblemenz; / Si fait pareil cum voz oez / Ne quit que jamis seit trovez; / Teu dame ne teu chevalier / N'ert mais mie a trover leger / Tant cum le siecle a a durer. / Ici n'en voil gaires parler, / Qu'avant en ai grant ovre a faire / E a conter e a retraire." Benoît, *CDN*, vv. 44036–52.

uxoris (in his wife's right), and many of the Anglo-Norman barons could not stomach the prospect of being ruled by an Angevin count. Benoît, however, pretends to be blissfully unaware of these facts and notes only that Matilda bore Geoffrey three sons: Henry, Geoffrey, and William.[113] "These were the rightful heirs to the realm of England, legitimate, valiant, and seemly. Thus had the praiseworthy Empress come to the aid of her line."[114]

Matilda may have come to the aid of her lineage by producing legitimate male heirs, but Matilda's children were also Geoffrey's children, and the Anglo-Norman barons appear to have had little but loathing for him. Indeed, the backlash against Henry's decision to marry his daughter to the fifteen-year-old son of a count was so great that even Robert de Torigny felt compelled to defend it (although, he did so rather halfheartedly). Benoît, true to form, follows his source in this instance. He reproduces Robert de Torigny's genealogy of the counts of Anjou (which Robert de Torigny had lifted from the *Abbreviatio gestorum regum Franciae*) in an obvious attempt to counter criticism of the marriage and elevate Henry II's paternal ancestry.[115] For readers who might find it distasteful that Matilda followed her marriage to an emperor with a marriage to a count, Benoît reassures them that the Capetian kings of France (also known as the Robertians for their founder, Robert the Strong) trace their descent from the lords of Anjou.

According to this genealogy, the kings of France were descended from the ninth-century counts of Angers (later lords of Anjou).[116] Benoît tells us that Odo (d. 898), son of Robert the Strong (d. 866), ruled France for thirteen years during the minority of Charles the Simple (son of Louis the Stammerer and the great-great-grandson of Charlemagne).[117] Benoît reports that Odo was succeeded by his brother Robert, who held the crown for only one year before being killed at Soissons.[118] Benoît next asserts that both Robert the Strong and his grandson, Hugh the Great, "were princes

---

113. "De son seignor out treis belz fiz / En poi de temps l'empereriz: / Henris e Joufrei e Guilleaumes." Benoît, *CDN*, vv. 44053–55.

114. "Des or nen ert mais li reiaumes / D'Engleterre senz eir tenable, / Dreiz e vaillanz e covenable. / Fait a l'empereriz preisee / Si fait secors a sa lignee." Benoît, *CDN*, vv. 44056–60.

115. *GND*, viii, II:242–43. Robert de Torigny is summarizing the *Abbreviatio gestorum regum Franciae*, cc. 24–50 (*MGH SS* 9:402–3). See McKitterick, *Frankish Kingdoms under the Carolingians*, 267–75, 306–28, and genealogical tables 3 and 6.

116. Benoît, *CDN*, vv. 44071–170.

117. Benoît, *CDN*, vv. 44091–125. Both Robert de Torigny and Benoît say that Odo ruled for thirteen years, however, he was actually crowned on November 13, 888, and died ten years later on January 1, 898. Cf. *GND*, viii, II:242–43, n. 3.

118. Benoît, *CDN*, vv. 44126–43.

and dukes over the French," in spite of the fact that neither of them were kings.[119] He then recounts the death of Charles the Simple at the hands of Count Herbert of Péronne (more commonly known as Herbert of Vermandois), and the birth of Hugh Capet to Hugh the Great and his wife, Hadwig.[120] Benoît states that Hugh Capet was later crowned, and that it is from his line that the "heirs of Anjou are descended."

Although Robert de Torigny and Benoît correctly trace the origins of the Capetians back to Robert the Strong, count of Angers, they both fail to mention the precise relationship between the current kings of France and counts of Anjou. This may be because they were perfectly aware that the two lines were not, in fact, descended from a common ancestor and that this genealogy proved only that Robert the Strong, the progenitor of the Robertian/Capetian line, and some of his heirs had been counts of Angers centuries ago. The genealogy ignores the fact that the lordship of Angers was actually held by Fulk the Red, son of Ingelgerius, in the first half of the tenth century. Fulk the Red was a vassal of the Robertians/Capetians (first of Odo and then of Robert) from the Loire valley, but neither he nor his descendants were related to them.[121]

In spite of the false impression fostered by Robert de Torigny and Benoît, the dynasty that ruled Anjou in the early twelfth century, including Geoffrey of Anjou, was actually descended from Ingelgerius, not from Robert the Strong. Indeed, to my knowledge no Angevin history claims any such relation to the Capetians, and the Angevins would surely have had an interest in preserving such a tradition if they thought it remotely credible. In spite of the fact that this genealogy of the early Capetians proves nothing of the sort, it is significant that both Robert de Torigny and Benoît felt compelled to defend Matilda's marriage to Geoffrey by perpetuating the fiction that the Capetian kings sprang from the same line as the current lords of Anjou. Benoît closes his recitation of the genealogy with the claim that Matilda's mar-

---

119. "Sis pere, si cum nos lisons, / E Hue, sis fiz, - n'i rout plus - / Fu sor Franceis princes e dus." Benoît, *CDN*, vv. 44144–46.

120. "Hues li Maines prist oissor / La fille Othon, l'empereor; / E d'eus fu Huun Chapez nez, / Qui aprés fu reis corronez, / Toz li premiers, ç'os ai retrait, / Dunt icist sunt né e estrait. / Sil qui regné unt puis en France / Pristrent e unt de lui naissance: / Eissi des eirs d'Angou decendent." Benoît, *CDN*, vv. 44151–62. Hugh Capet was elected king of the West Franks on July 3, 987. Both Robert de Torigny and Benoît incorrectly identify Hadwig as the daughter of Otto I; she was actually the daughter of King Henry I of the Saxons and the sister of Otto I. Cf. *GND*, viii, II:244, n. 1.

121. Fulk the Red was viscount of Anjou after 898 and count by 941. McKitterick, *Frankish Kingdoms*, 322.

riage to Geoffrey was thus a noble match, in no way beneath her. In fact, he claims that "never was a woman born who was more honored than she."[122]

Benoît's assertion that Matilda was honored by her marriage to Geoffrey may be unintentionally ironic, but it serves a very useful purpose. It is meant to stave off criticism of the match and its offspring, especially Henry II. Indeed, the *Chronique*'s concluding passages (particularly Benoît's description of Henry I's designation of Matilda as his heir, his description of the barons and bishops swearing oaths to uphold Matilda's rights, and the catalogue of her children with Geoffrey) are all specifically designed to stress Henry II's status as Henry I's rightful and legitimate heir. Having cleverly linked Henry I's designation of Matilda as his heir with her production of legitimate children, Benoît immediately proceeds to elevate Geoffrey's lineage. Benoît then abruptly moves back in time to recount the death of Matilda's mother, Edith-Matilda, an event that had occurred a decade earlier in 1118, and Henry I's second marriage to Adeliza of Louvaine.[123] Benoît tells us that Henry's second marriage produced no children, but that he fathered six sons and seven daughters by concubines. These children, however, are clearly identified as the king's natural issue and their presence only serves to remind us again that the empress Matilda and her sons Henry, Geoffrey, and William are Henry I's only legitimate heirs.

It should come as no surprise that Benoît is so scrupulous in setting out Henry II's lineage and insisting on his legitimacy. The primary function of both the *Roman de Rou* and the *Chronique des ducs de Normandie* was to recount Henry II's lineage and their deeds, and both employ a genealogical format that emphasizes the continuity of the ducal/royal line and the regular passage of power from one generation to the next. Benoît, however, employs another recurring textual strategy designed to reinforce Henry II's lineage that is absent from the *Rou*. At three points in his narrative, Benoît breaks from his history to insert apostrophes praising Henry II—although it can be argued that there are actually four of these apostrophes, the fourth being the description of Henry II's birth discussed above. In each case, the apostrophes occur after the death of a duke and serve to link Henry II to his predecessors. Notably, they appear after the deaths of especially important dukes: Richard I, Richard II, and William the Conqueror.

---

122. "Ne fu au siecle femme ne, / Qui de lui ne fust honoree." Benoît, *CDN*, vv. 44169–70.

123. The empress Matilda was widowed in 1125 and married to Geoffrey of Anjou in 1127, a decade after Edith-Matilda died and Henry I remarried in 1118.

Dukes Richard I and Richard II were considered particularly devout rulers, known for restoring and reforming Norman monasteries. Indeed, they were regarded as almost saintly in the twelfth century.[124] Their tomb in a small chapel at Sainte-Trinité in Fécamp had been drawing pilgrims for a century and a half when Henry II and his bishops moved their bodies to a place of honor behind Sainte-Trinité's main altar in 1162. It is no surprise then that Benoît would choose to link Henry II to these ancestors above all others. After a description of Richard I's pious death and a notable account of an examination of the duke's miraculously preserved, sweet-smelling (and thus saintly) body, Benoît directs his attention to his patron.[125] In another reminder of Henry II's lineage, Benoît hopes God may grant that his work pleases "the good King Henry, son of Matilda." Although he also complains of the difficulty of his task, the struggle he endures to translate this history from the Latin, and his lack of anyone to guide him, save God (indicating that this may also be a plea for leniency should his work fail to please Henry), the apostrophe's placement serves above all to remind us that Henry is descended from an exceptionally saintly ancestor, one that Benoît "has no doubt is in angelic company."[126]

The apostrophe that appears after the death of Richard II has a similar effect. Benoît's description of Richard II's death emphasizes his piety, his preparations for a good death, and the sorrow of Normandy at his passing, but, unlike his father, Richard II's body displays no signs of saintliness.[127] Nonetheless, Richard II shares some of his father's sanctity, if only through proximity, as Benoît notes that Richard II's body was interred with his father's at Fécamp. This apostrophe actually has a much stronger effect than the first in that here Benoît explicitly links Henry II to both Richards and

---

124. Cf. Gouttebroze, *Le Précieux Sang de Fécamp*; Gouttebroze, "Pourquoi congédier un historiographe," 289–311; Bédier, "Richard de Normandie," 113–24; and Cazauran, "Richard sans puer," 21–43.

125. Benoît, *CDN*, vv. 28628–702. "Mil anz, quatre meins, e plus non, / Aveit des l'Incarnation / Deci qu'il trespassa de vie. / De lui est l'estoire fenie, / Ou merveilles aveit a dire, / Au translater e a l'escrire. / Or donge Dex par sa douçor / Qu'au plaisir seit de mun seginor, / Deu buen rei Henri, fiz Maheut, / Que si benigne cum il seuct / Seit a l'oïr e a l'entendre! / N'est pas de mes poors la mendre / Que de mesdire e de mesfaire / Chose que ni li deie plaire, / Quer ge sai bien, si m'est avis, / C'um moct sage homme e moct apris / Faut a poi dire assez sovent / Si qu'il en pert par gugement. / E ge qui jor ne nuit ne fin, / Qui si truis encombros latin, / Se g'i mesfaz n'est pas merveille, / Quer riens fors Deu ne m'i conseille." Benoît, *CDN*, vv. 28705–26.

126. "L'arme est de lui, n'en doton mie / En l'angelial compaignie." Benoît, *CDN*, vv. 28701–2.

127. Benoît, *CDN*, vv. 32001–48.

mentions Henry's orchestration of the translation of the ducal bodies.[128] He says that Richard II was placed in the abbey at Fécamp and richly buried there, but then the bodies of both Richards were removed. "This was overseen by the good king, he who was son of Matilda, the good empress, [it was done] by the good king Henry the second, flower of princes of the entire world, whose deeds are worthy of memory." Benoît goes on to wish that God may grant Henry II a litany of blessings—courage and victory, long life and prosperity, honor, joy, and peace. Thus ends Benoît's chapter on Richard II. It is noteworthy that the opening of the next chapter on Richard III begins with a reiteration of lineage, which again asserts the continuity of the ducal line.[129]

Although it has been noted that neither Wace nor Benoît emphasize the motives behind the translation of the bodies of Richard I and Richard II or discuss its meaning, perhaps they had no need to do so. As Jean-Guy Gouttebroze has argued, the very act of translation in the presence of a bishop was viewed as a tacit recognition of sanctity in the twelfth century.[130] Although Benoît never acknowledges that he is describing what can be construed as the formal recognition of the sanctity of Henry's ancestors in this passage, a contemporary audience may well have recognized it as such, and the presence of saints (or even quasi saints) in a lineage constituted a powerful argument for the continued dominance of their descendants.

---

128. "Mil e vint e sis anz compliz, / Si cum reconte li escriz, / Aveit des l'Incarnation / Tot entierement e plus non / Jusqu'au derrer jor de sa vie / A Fescape just en l'abeïe, / La fu richement enterrez, / Mais puis unt esté relevez / Cist e li peres, li premiers, / Li buens Richarz, li justisiers, / Par le buen rei, cil que fu fiz / Maheut, la buenne empereriz, / Par le buen rei Henri segunt, / Flors des princes de tot le munt / Cui faiz sunt digne de memoire, / A cui Dex dunt force e victoire, / Longe vie, prosperité, / Sanz ainsse e sanz aversité. / Saintisme e buenne seit sa fins! / Ci racheve li parchemins. / As buens, as frans, as cuers verais / Dunt Dex honnor e joie e pais!" Benoît, *CDN*, vv. 32049–70.

129. "Des deus Richarz ai translaté / Ce qui j'en truis d'autorité. / Li uns fu pere e l'autre fiz. / Dreiz est qu'aprés les lor escriz / Reseit li tiers, s'iert il, mun vuel. / Li uns fu pere e l'aure aiol, / Niés deu premier, fiz deu segunt, / Si cum l'estoire nos espont." Benoît, *CDN*, vv. 32071–78.

130. Jean-Guy Gouttebroze has argued that the translation of relics by a bishop in itself sufficed as ecclesiastical recognition of the deceased's sanctity at this time. He also argues that Wace's reluctance to explicitly acknowledge the sanctity of Henry II's ancestors played some part in his loss of the commission. Gouttebroze, "Pourquoi congédier un historiographe," 304. Cf. Amore, "Culto e Canonizzazione dei Santi nell'antichitá Cristiana," and Amore, "La canonizazzione vescovile." Wace says only that the bodies were "placed" behind the main altar. His description, however, allows that the bodies were moved to a place of honor, and the act could still be interpreted by his audience as a translation and thus as recognition of their sanctity. "A grant honur fu cunreez / e a grant honur fu enterrez. / Le cors de lui e de sun pere, / si que jel vi e jeo i ere, / furent de terre relevez / e triés le maistre autel posez; / la furent portez e sunt, / li moigne en grant cherité les unt." Wace, *RR*, vv. 2239–46.

The final apostrophe to Henry II appears after the death of William the Conqueror. As noted earlier, Benoît's William dies a very pious and orderly death, attended by his sons William Rufus and Henry. Benoît describes Normandy's deep mourning over the Conqueror's death, and stresses the point that Henry I was present at his father's funeral—an assertion otherwise found only in Robert de Torigny.[131] He then interjects the authorial disclaimer addressed to Henry II discussed above, before moving to the apostrophe to Henry II proper.[132] In the apostrophe Benoît notes that with great effort and God's help he is bringing his translation of the history of the Norman dukes to "the last Henry." In spite of the strain imposed by his task, he says that he would like to bring his history up to the reign of the "good king Henry II" and relate his noble deeds. Benoît then shifts back immediately to describing the virtues of Henry II's grandfather, Henry I.[133]

Like the two preceding apostrophes, this one serves to link Henry II to his ancestors, and it notably links him most forcefully to Henry I, whom Benoît has just identified in preceding passages as the most favored and most deserving of William the Conqueror's sons. The apostrophe also breaks the genealogical flow of the *Chronique* in a telling manner: it skips both Duke Robert Curthose and King William Rufus, either of whom should logically follow their father in a dynastic history, and gives pride of place to Henry I, who at this point possesses neither of his father's territories or titles. Just as he had done earlier in reversing the birth order of the Conqueror's sons, Benoît subtly promotes Henry I ahead of both of his elder brothers and foreshadows his ascendancy. The substitution seeks to reshape our conception of the Norman ducal/royal line by suggesting that Henry I is the Conqueror's only "true" heir, and making it appear that the ensuing descriptions of Robert Curthose's and William Rufus's reigns are merely detours that must be taken before we can return to the main thread of the narrative—

---

131. Benoît, *CDN*, vv. 42007–33; and *GND*, vii, II:194–95.

132. Benoît, *CDN*, vv. 42034–42. "Quant par le don e par l'etrei / De l'autisme soverain Rei, / Qui les enfantez fait raisnables, / Escientos e entendables, / E qui au muz donne eloquence, / Oiemenz e intelligence, / Ai translaté des dus normanz, / D'eus l'estoire qui moct est granz / E ou moct ai trové a dire / E grant estuide e grant martire / Deci qu'au rei Henri l'ointains, / Qui d'eus fu uns soverains / Nen est dreiz qu'a lui me recreie, / Qu'a tenir ai la dreite veie / En ordre continuaument / Deci lai ou mist cuers s'atent, / Jusqu'au buen rei Henri segunt, / Que ç'otreit Dex e vuille e don't / Que je les suens hauz faiz retraie! / Ce peise mei que tant delaie, / Qu'ausi cum l'on plastrist e taint / La maisiere sor quei l'on paint, / Por faire ses traiz plus formez, / Plus soutis e plus colorez, / Rai je long tens plastri por paindre / Sanz desveer e sanz mei faindre. / Por c'l sui tant assiduios, / Volenterif e dessiros / Que de ça fust l'ovre acomplie." Benoît, *CDN,* vv. 42043–71.

133. Benoît, *CDN,* vv. 42072–89.

and the main line of the ducal/royal lineage. By placing Henry II in the middle of this bit of genealogical tinkering, Benoît further suggests that his accession in England and Normandy was both normal and inevitable—it proposes that Henry II is Henry I's true heir, just as Henry I was William the Conqueror's true heir. Finally, as Benoît shifts rapidly between Henry I and Henry II, he encourages his reader to associate Henry II with his grandfather, and especially with the list of Henry I's virtues that follows the apostrophe to Henry II.

Benoît's intent to include Henry II in his history also deserves our attention. The statement not only links Henry II to his predecessors by asserting his rightful place in this dynastic history, it suggests, as many other scholars have noted, that the *Chronique* is unfinished in its present state. Elisabeth van Houts has argued that Benoît ended his *Chronique* with the death of Henry I because that it where his primary source, Robert de Torigny's F redaction of the *Gesta Normannorum ducum*, terminates.[134] Although this explanation is perfectly plausible, it ignores the fact that there may have been another very good reason for terminating the *Chronique* with Henry I—Stephen's usurpation. The additional effort of having to compose his own history of the reigns of Stephen and Henry II, or of finding other source material to adapt, would have presented a hurdle for Benoît, but one that hardly seems insurmountable. Benoît's loquacity and his tendency to greatly expand on his sources, which drew out the length of his project considerably, may have slowed his progress to such an extent that it was impossible for him to continue his history to Henry II's reign. It seems likely, however, that the problems inherent in memorializing Stephen's reign presented Benoît with significant impediments in and of themselves.

Henry II viewed Stephen's reign as a suspension of lawful government, one that had broken the legitimate line of ducal/royal succession and had very nearly deprived him of his inheritance. Stephen's appearance in the middle of a dynastic history of the Normans commissioned by Henry II would, therefore, be extremely problematic. Any such history would have to follow Matilda's struggle to win her inheritance back from Stephen, and would thus be a vivid reminder of the recent civil war that might be unwelcome on several fronts. It would recall the bitter struggle between the Normans and Angevins for control of the Anglo-Norman realm, which would, in turn, dredge up Norman memories of Angevin brutality—a prospect that Henry II can only have wished to avoid.

---

134. van Houts, "Adaptation."

Even more troubling from Henry II's perspective, the commemoration of both Stephen's usurpation and his own accession would graphically demonstrate the power of the clergy and aristocracy to affect the succession. In the first case, many of the barons and clergy had abjured their oaths to Matilda and chosen to elevate Stephen to the throne, whereas in the latter, Henry's own accession was made possible by the decision of a majority of the barons and clergy to accept him as the rightful heir to the throne over Stephen's son Eustace. Both precedents promised to be more damaging than useful to Henry's project of enshrining hereditary right as the sole basis of kingship, and thereby removing the hazards posed by the tradition of clerical and baronial assent to kingship.

Even though Benoît does mention Stephen and his usurpation, the mention is very brief and of an entirely different nature than a commemoration of his reign would have been. Following Robert de Torigny, Benoît inserts a passage recounting the histories of William the Conqueror's daughters before ending the *Chronique* with a description of Henry I's death.[135] Both Benoît and Robert de Torigny recount that William's fourth daughter, Adele, was married to Count Stephen of Blois, and that their son Stephen became king after the death of Henry I. There are, however, a few revealing differences between the two accounts.

Robert de Torigny tells us that "[Stephen] was made king of the English after the death of his uncle King Henry."[136] He goes on to explain that this was because Henry's heir, Matilda, was in Anjou with her husband and children when her father died. She had left Normandy, he says, due to a recent quarrel with her father over his reluctance to be reconciled with William Talvas—he completely elides the fact that Matilda and Geoffrey's recent rebellion had caused the estrangement between father and daughter, and that William Talvas's support for Matilda during the rebellion was the root of the tension between Talvas and the king.[137] Robert de Torigny says that Henry had not acted out of contempt for Matilda, "his beloved daughter," in this dispute, but was only biding his time in reconciling with Talvas so that his barons would maintain their fear of him. Robert de Torigny alludes to the role of the barons and clergy in Stephen's usurpation by stating that Stephen "was made king of the English," but he avoids condemning anyone for this turn of events. He does not indict either Matilda or Stephen; indeed,

---

135. Benoît, *CDN*, vv. 44329–500 and 44501–44.

136. *GND*, viii, II:262–65.

137. *GND*, viii, II:264, n. 3.

his language excuses both of them. Although Robert de Torigny was a loyal supporter of Matilda's, he is just as careful in his avoidance of characterizing Stephen's accession to the throne as a usurpation as he is in veiling Matilda's rebellion against her father. Benoît, on the other hand, narrates the events a bit differently.

According to Benoît, when King Henry died Stephen went to the bishop of Winchester, who happened to be his brother Henry.[138] Bishop Henry was lord and master of the land, explains Benoît, and was very eager to help his brother. He comments that Stephen was made king by treason (*rei en fist par seduction*), with Bishop Henry's aid, and that Henry I's heir, the empress Matilda, was deprived of her inheritance by those who had promised to uphold her rights. Benoît says that they disregarded their oaths and made Stephen king through a disgraceful crime (*par trop laide mesprison*). Benoît then returns to Robert de Torigny's description of the falling out between Matilda and her father in which he characterizes the whole affair as a misunderstanding and emphasizes that the empress was not at fault.[139] Like Robert de Torigny, he neither mentions Matilda's rebellion nor the real reason for Henry's displeasure with William Talvas.

Whereas Robert de Torigny never characterizes Stephen's accession as a usurpation, Benoît clearly does. He accuses both Stephen and Bishop Henry of Winchester of treason and betrayal in the strongest terms, of abjuring their oaths and breaking their sworn fealty to Matilda. Although Robert de Torigny was perhaps forced to treat Stephen's accession gingerly due to the fact that Stephen was king of England and duke of Normandy at the time when Robert was writing, Benoît labored under no such restraint. Quite the opposite was true—Benoît was writing for Matilda's son, and his narration of Stephen's usurpation is accordingly much more forceful and direct. Benoît's indictment of Stephen is notable for its rancor, as well as for its revealing linkage between the two brothers. Although Robert de Torigny mentions that Stephen gained the crown with the help of his brother, Benoît goes much further in accusing the brothers of a criminal conspiracy.[140]

---

138. "Cist, quant li reis Henris fu morz / E alez fu sis granz efforz, / Si cum l'evesque de Wincestre, / Qui de la terre ert sire e mestre, / L'out apareille e enpris, / Out tost por son frere tramis. / Rei en fist par seduction / E par trop laide mesprison, / Kar eir en ert l'empereriz / E vers li erent tuit pleviz. / N'i regarderent covenance / Ne serrement nul ne fiance." Benoît, *CDN*, vv. 44449–60.

139. Benoît, *CDN*, vv. 44461–80.

140. Robert de Torigny returns briefly to the subject of Stephen's accession after a genealogical digression. When he returns to the topic, he notes that Stephen was aided in gaining the throne by his brother Henry, bishop of Winchester; however, he never characterizes Stephen as a usurper.

In Benoît's retelling, Bishop Henry is an indispensable accessory to Stephen's usurpation and is condemned along with Stephen. Benoît's charges of treason and betrayal implicitly extend to much of the Anglo-Norman nobility and clergy as well, many of whom indisputably broke their oaths and their fealty to Matilda when they accepted Stephen as king.

Benoît's treatment of Stephen's accession is extremely brief, but it perfectly illuminates the thorny issues raised by mentioning Stephen at all. Although Benoît treats Stephen's elevation to the throne as an unjust usurpation, and thus rejects the legitimacy of his reign, this only raises another set of problems. Benoît cannot indict Stephen without at least implying that many others were to blame. Unfortunately, those "others" happened to be the ancestors of Henry II's own magnates and clergy. This reminder of the complicity of their forebearers in Stephen's usurpation could be either insulting or empowering to Benoît's audience—the aristocracy could either conclude that their fathers and grandfathers had consented to this crime or that they had effected it. Neither of these options was particularly advantageous for Henry II. Of course, another lesson might be drawn from Stephen's example—that interfering with the succession by excluding the king's acknowledged heir could bring about another disastrous civil war. This would obviously have been a much more salutary conclusion from Henry II's point of view, but the fact remains that memorializing Stephen, even as a usurper, had the potential to backfire spectacularly. Henry II's magnates might be persuaded that they should defer to the king's wishes for the succession, or they might be alienated by the implicit shaming of their ancestors, just as they were being vividly reminded of their own power to transform the succession.

Benoît did not include Henry II's reign in the *Chronique*. His history ends with Henry I's death and the foreshadowing of Stephen's reign. Benoît does, however, manage to adroitly insert Henry II into his dynastic history of the Normans in several other ways. His constant emphasis on Matilda's status as Henry I's rightful heir inevitably recalls to mind Henry II's place within the royal/ducal lineage whether or not Henry II is explicitly mentioned—and he most often is. Furthermore, whenever Benoît does mention Henry II, he almost always links him clearly to Matilda by identifying him as the son of the empress. He quite often links Henry II to other members of his family as well, through the placement of apostrophes that

---

Instead, he subtly insists on Matilda's rights by always referring to her as Henry's heir. *GND*, viii, II:274–75.

deftly juxtapose, and thus associate, Henry II with his most important maternal ancestors: Richard I, Richard II, William the Conqueror, and Henry I. Although his history does not recount the deeds of Henry II, Benoît ensures that his patron is a constant presence in the *Chronique*, and unflaggingly labors to present him as the rightful heir to the Anglo-Norman realm.

Benoît de Sainte-Maure

The texts produced by Wace and Benoît, although admittedly similar in some respects, ultimately present two very different views of Norman history. Most profoundly, Wace's *Roman de Rou* challenged previous versions of Norman history, fundamentally altering what had been the dominant narrative (especially as it was presented in his main source, the *Gesta Normannorum ducum*) by revealing the messy complexity of the past and illuminating the defects of dukes and kings. Benoît, on the other hand, was clearly more interested in praising the glorious deeds of the Normans, smoothing out the rough edges of history, suppressing inconvenient facts, and softening or concealing the more unpleasant aspects of Henry II's ancestors. Presumably, Benoît was more inclined to please his patron than was Wace.

Similar conflicts are also apparent in Wace and Benoît's diverging contextualizations of their subject. The *Rou* is almost entirely didactic and revisionist in nature, while the *Chronique* refracts a triumphalist account of Norman history through the well-worn lens of providence. Benoît's history of the Normans is an account of the manifestation of God's plan that effectively legitimizes Norman actions, whereas Wace's history is a series of events impelled primarily by human actions that are motivated, in turn, by very human desires. Where Benoît magnifies the deeds and greatness of Henry II's Norman ancestors, Wace's account generally deprives the Norman dukes and kings of the benefit of divine favor and undermines the legitimacy of William the Conqueror and Henry I by exposing ambiguities and revealing base motivations. Although Wace's and Benoît's representations of Norman history diverge in important ways, their motivations are very similar in certain respects. Benoît's interpretation of Norman history, like Wace's, was likely shaped to a great extent by his physical location and his personal affiliations. Likewise, Benoît's history was colored by his understanding of his role as a historian and influenced by contemporary events. This, however, is where the similarities end. As will become apparent, Benoît came from another region, he held very different allegiances from Wace, he had a much more pragmatic understanding of his role as a historian, and he seems to have found most of the events of Henry's reign far more agreeable.

Benoît appears to have been more content with the new regime forming under Henry II in which power increasingly coalesced in the hands of the king and his administrators at the expense of the barons and clergy. Although Benoît was not as forceful an advocate for royal authority as some of his predecessors, most notably Robert de Torigny and Orderic Vitalis in their defenses of Henry I, Benoît nonetheless assumed the role of apologist for Henry II in both his extravagant apostrophes to his patron and in his adulation of Henry I. The minute differences between Benoît's representation of Henry I and the depictions of the monarch found in his sources are probably due to the fact that Benoît was a product of a different time and place. Benoît was not a Norman, nor had he lived through the chaos of Robert Curthose's rule (as had both Robert de Torigny and Orderic); he thus lacked their visceral need to defend Henry and legitimize his rule.

Unlike Wace, who helpfully constructs such a strong Norman identity for himself and who appears to have felt a personal connection to the Norman ducal line and an investment in its history, Benoît de Sainte-Maure is much more elusive. Almost nothing is known of his life. As a native of the Touraine, or possibly Poitou, we can reasonably assert that Benoît was an outsider when it came to Norman politics and history.[141] He certainly does not reveal any personal connection to the history he recounts or to the region in which it occurred, and he appears to have produced his work outside of Normandy, in Tours or the surrounding area.[142] In fact, Jean Blacker suggests that Benoît may have been a "monk at Marmoutier near Tours, where John of Marmoutier was writing his *Gesta Consulum Andegavorum* for Henry at roughly the same time as Benoît was composing his poem."[143] Whether at Marmoutier or elsewhere in the Touraine, Benoît lived and

---

141. Benoît does not tell us where he was born or raised. Jean Blacker and Carin Fahlin suggest that Benoît was from the area around Tours, where the oldest manuscript of the *Chronique des ducs de Normandie* was produced. Blacker, *Faces of Time*, 186, and Fahlin, *Etude*, 172. Elisabeth van Houts, on the other hand, says that Benoît was "from the village of Sainte-Maur in Poitou," but provides no rationale for her assertion. van Houts, "Adaptation," 119. In the absence of any evidence other than Benoît's cognomen, we can say only that he was probably an Angevin who came from Saint-More in the Touraine, or possibly from near Sainte-Maur. We can also say with some assurance that he was neither English nor Norman, nor did he pretend to be.

142. van Houts, "Adaptation," 119, and Fahlin, *Etude*, 133 and 171–72.

143. Blacker, *Faces of Time*, 186.

wrote in a location fairly removed from the turbulent scenes of Norman history.

Benoît's interest in the history he was commissioned to produce was thus almost certainly of a different order and magnitude than Wace's interest had been. Wace's affection for his native *pays* and his strong opinions regarding its history and its rulers clearly outweighed any obligation he felt toward his patron, but Benoît's loyalty was not similarly divided. Benoît came from Angevin-controlled territory and had been attached to Henry II's court since the early 1160s when he dedicated the *Roman de Troie* to Queen Eleanor. Although Benoît was an outsider when it came to Norman history, both the Touraine and Poitou were close enough to Normandy to have felt the reverberation of events there. The Angevins had been instrumental in assisting Geoffrey, Matilda, and Henry II in pressing their claims to England and Normandy after Henry I's ill-considered decision to marry Matilda to Geoffrey of Anjou had provoked many of the Anglo-Norman barons to renounce their oaths to Matilda and elevate her cousin Stephen in her place. In a very real sense, Geoffrey of Anjou had cost Matilda the throne as the Normans could not stomach the prospect of being ruled by an Angevin count. Although the fighting was restricted to Normandy, and the Normans decried the brutality they had suffered at Angevin hands, the succession dispute and ensuing war had left an impression on the Angevins as well.

As an Angevin, Benoît may have harbored old prejudices against the Normans, and he probably derived some satisfaction from the fact that Geoffrey of Anjou's son now sat on the English throne. In fact, Henry II's accession could be seen as an Angevin triumph. Benoît would therefore have had good reason to emphasize the legitimacy of Henry II's claim to the Anglo-Norman realm, and little sympathy for any arguments to the contrary. He also would have recognized that praising the deeds of Henry's Norman ancestors could serve only to augment the king's authority, and Benoît's willingness to commend Henry's Norman ancestors is evident throughout the *Chronique*. Benoît articulates a fervent desire to please Henry in his apostrophes to his patron, and he performs an astonishing feat of thaumaturgy, countering Norman disdain for Geoffrey of Anjou with a specious genealogy asserting that the counts of Anjou were descended from the same bloodline as the Capetian kings of France. Henry II's decision to transfer the project to an Angevin author thus paid off as Benoît's version of Norman history glorifies Henry II and his ancestors, whether Norman or Angevin, in a conventional and predictable manner.

Although Benoît reveals almost nothing of his biography, is less present as an authorial voice, and less inclined to contradict his sources than Wace, we catch glimpses of Benoît's personal opinions on the rare occasions when he chooses to follow one narrative thread from his sources rather than another, or when he omits information found in his sources. These indications are extremely oblique, but they reveal that Benoît was quite sympathetic to the arguments of Henry I's apologists that a ruler's duty to provide good governance ultimately outweighed his lack of birthright. Rather than expending a great deal of effort on constructing an ideological or legal basis for Henry's intervention in Normandy, as Orderic had done, Benoît follows Robert de Torigny in cleverly recasting the terms of the debate.[144] Both men simply assert that Robert Curthose provoked Henry by squandering his inheritance and neglecting his duties as a ruler. They portray Henry's invasion of Normandy as a completely appropriate response to this incitement, and then represent Henry's victory over Robert at Tinchebray as the manifestation of God's judgment.[145]

Benoît's account of Henry I's rise to power thus emphasizes that his appropriation of England and Normandy was favored by God and justified by the benefits of his rule, regardless of the manner in which he came to the English throne or acquired Normandy. It effectively counters Wace's argument for the primacy of Robert Curthose's birthright with an apology for Norman (and Angevin) kingship that gives precedence to the king's duty to maintain justice, peace, and order. By appealing to the proofs of God's favor for Henry I's actions, Benoît asserts that Robert was unworthy of his birthright and had to be replaced. Again, Benoît differs slightly from Orderic in this. In his attempts to justify Henry's actions, Orderic makes a strong case for royal power as a necessary restraint on aristocratic power. As noted above, it was Robert Curthose's reluctance, or his inability, to restrain Robert of

---

144. Benoît and Robert de Torigny both implicitly advance the argument that Robert had forfeited his birthright, but they tend to focus on the allegation that Robert frittered away his patrimony, rather than on the contention that he did not provide good governance. Nor do they offer anything approaching the comprehensive exposition of the argument made by Orderic (through the speech for Bishop Serlo of Séez described above) that Robert had to be deposed because he failed to protect the innocent and the defenseless. Orderic, *HE*, xi, VI:60–68.

145. "Sed iudicio Dei super eos ueniente, capti sunt ambo et multi alii cum eis ab hominibus Henrici regis atque ante eum adducti. Concessit hoc modo Deus regi se timenti uictoriam incruentam, sicut quondam Theodosio imperatoris seruo suo fecerat." [But God's judgment came upon them and both men along with many others were taken prisoner by King Henry's men. In this manner did God concede a bloodless victory to a king who feared him, as once he did to his servant the Emperor Theodosius.] *GND*, vii, II:222. "Fina Deus tot apertement, / Kar ce lis bien certainement / C'unc li reis le jor n'i perdié / Ne chevalier n'ome preisié, / Ne de l'autre part, tot acante, / Nen out ocis que sol cinquante." [This conclusion God very skillfully brought about, for as we can most certainly read, the king that day did not lose a knight or esteemed man, on the other side, all counted, they had only fifty men killed.] Benoît, *CDN*, vv. 43611–24.

Bellême that appears to have been the decisive factor in Orderic's support for Henry I. Although Orderic clearly struggled with the morality and justice of Henry I's invasion of Normandy and his violation of his brother's sovereignty, he concluded that Henry I's ability to impose peace and stability (particularly by restraining Robert of Bellême) ultimately outweighed Robert Curthose's rights. Neither Benoît nor Robert de Torigny appears to have been as torn by this conflict. They give short shrift to Robert's rights, but emphasize his incompetence, his tendency to act on bad advice, and the fact that he squandered his inheritance.

Benoît's endorsement of royal power does have limits, however, and is somewhat balanced by the manner in which he tempers Robert de Torigny's praise of Henry I and condemnation of Robert Curthose. Like Robert de Torigny, Benoît also offers a single, but telling, criticism of Henry I's reign—that Henry appropriated the castles of his nobles and treated them as his own. Benoît may simply be following Robert de Torigny in this instance, or it may be that this subject was so important to the aristocracy that both men were forced to acknowledge it. Certainly, Benoît's audience would have readily extended this criticism of Henry I to his grandson, as Henry II was guilty of precisely the same thing. In any case, these instances are so few that they do not significantly detract from Benoît's general readiness to assert the preeminence of royal power and rights.

In addition to his royalist sympathies, Benoît emphasizes filial devotion in his treatment of William the Conqueror's sons. Although Benoît is following his sources in contrasting Robert's rebelliousness with the affection displayed by William Rufus and Henry toward their father (and this certainly serves to justify Robert's loss of England), these reminders of the behavior that sons should exhibit toward their fathers seem designed to comment on contemporary events as well. It is difficult to read Benoît's portrayal of Robert Curthose without conjuring associations with Henry II's own sons, who were so frequently in rebellion against him during the period when Benoît was writing. Benoît's location, whether in the Touraine or Poitou, would have placed him in the thick of these disputes between the king and his sons. Anjou and Aquitaine had both been involved in the Great War of 1173/74, and the Young King Henry and Geoffrey were in rebellion against their father once again, this time attempting to take Aquitaine from Richard, when Young King Henry died in 1183.[146] Richard in particular continued to rebel against his father throughout the

---

146. Warren, *Henry II*, 591–93.

1180s, and both Richard and John were in open rebellion at the time of Henry's death in 1189. Where Wace's history appears to rebuke Henry II for his treatment of his barons, clergy, and sons, Benoît's history seems to admonish Henry's sons for their treatment of their father. Benoît's declaration that Robert "got what he deserved" when he lost England as a result of his numerous rebellions against his father seems to be a warning to Henry II's sons that their distinctly unfilial behavior could rightly cost them their inheritance as well.

Granted, it would have been just as difficult for Henry II to disinherit his sons as it had been for William to completely disinherit Robert (Robert had already received the homage of the Norman barons and William could not revoke that). In his efforts to ensure the succession of his children, Henry had not only crowned the Young King Henry twice but Richard had been formally recognized as duke of Aquitaine in 1172 and Geoffrey was invested with Brittany in 1181.[147] After the death of the Young King, Henry attempted to redistribute his lands by requiring Richard to give up Aquitaine in exchange for England, Normandy, and Anjou (Henry still seems to have been intent on having his oldest surviving son inherit this reconstituted patrimony, and disposing of Eleanor's duchy separately).[148] When Richard refused, Henry threatened to promote Geoffrey above Richard by endowing him with England, Normandy, and Anjou; after Geoffrey's death in 1186, Henry kept his surviving sons, Richard and John, in the dark about his plans for the succession in an attempt to enforce their obedience.[149] It seems quite likely that these rebellions and Henry II's efforts to bring his sons to heel were on Benoît's mind as he denounced Robert's disobedience and praised the devotion of Rufus and Henry. Perhaps he even envisioned a situation in which John, the youngest, might be promoted above his brothers in recognition of his faithfulness, just as Henry I had once been promoted above his brothers. There is a certain irony, of course, in the way events ultimately played out: John's fidelity to his father proved limited, and although he did eventually succeed to all of his father's dominions, he was unable to hold them.

Unlike Wace, who frequently articulates his concern for veracity, Benoît is notable for his relative silence on the matter.[150] This is not to say that

---

147. John Gillingham, *Richard I* (London, 2002), 40, and W. L. Warren, *King John* (Berkeley, 1973), 574.

148. Warren, *Henry II*, 596.

149. Ibid., 597–99.

150. See Blacker, *Faces of Time*, 51.

Benoît does not promote his history as an accurate representation of the past by appealing to the *auctoritas* of his Latin sources or presenting himself as a learned authority; it is simply meant to emphasize that Benoît rarely has occasion to directly assert that he is telling his audience the truth. This distinction between the two authors is partly a result of their differing treatment of their sources. Where Wace is regularly driven to assert his veracity due to the sheer volume of subversive and contradictory material he includes, Benoît tends to conform to his sources and give objectionable material a wide berth. Since his deviations from his sources are slight, and they are generally omissions rather than additions or contradictions, he is rarely compelled to attest to his own veracity. Likewise, Benoît evinces no concern for impartiality and, unlike Wace, he rarely appears to display it. His version of Norman history is unabashedly royalist.

As suggested above, an explanation for Benoît's apparent desire to please Henry II can be gleaned from what little is known of his biography. Benoît was raised in Angevin-controlled territory and was an alien in the Anglo-Norman realm. He was probably closely attached to Henry II's Angevin court, and, as an Angevin, he might have felt some compulsion to gloat over Henry's accession to the English throne. As the second author entrusted with this commission, he was also likely to have been more aware of Henry's expectations. There has been some controversy, however, over whether Benoît de Sainte-Maure had access to the *Roman de Rou* and was responding directly to his predecessor's text. Peter Damian-Grint has contended that the widely held assumption that Benoît had access to the *Roman de Rou* is based on little solid evidence and is merely possible rather than probable.[151] Although the textual correspondences between the histories are slight, and Damian-Grint is quite right to point out the lack of solid evidence directly connecting the texts, it seems likely that Benoît would have had at least some access to Wace's text, if for no other reason than to use it as a negative example. Wace had worked on the *Roman de Rou* for almost fifteen years before he was fired, and it seems improbable that Henry II and his counselors would have risked having Benoît deliver yet another subversive version of Norman history by not advising him of his predecessor's failings and providing him with the materials necessary to avoid repeating Wace's mistakes. As this historiographical project was important enough to warrant a second attempt after such a great effort had already been ex-

---

151. Damian-Grint, "*En nul leu nel truis escrit*," 13.

pended, Henry II or his counselors must have at least briefed Benoît on their expectations.

Benoît's portrayal of Henry I's reign is distinctly more flattering than Wace's, and this is largely due to his reliance on Robert de Torigny's F redaction of the *Gesta Normannorum ducum*. Robert de Torigny was one of the most vociferous of Henry I's champions. Initially a monk of Le Bec (1128–49), he served as prior of the monastery (1149–54), and finally as abbot of Mont Saint-Michel (1154–86).[152] His F redaction of the *Gesta Normannorum ducum* dates from c. 1139 and extends the history of the Norman dukes to 1137.[153] During his years at Le Bec, Robert had personal contact with both Henry I and the empress Matilda, who were patrons of the monastery and frequent visitors.[154] Indeed, Matilda herself may have suggested that Robert add book VIII (which deals exclusively with Henry I's reign and the disputed succession after his death) to the *Gesta Normannorum ducum*.[155] Robert also proved to be one of Matilda's staunchest supporters and his additions to the *Gesta Normannorum ducum* emphasize the legitimacy of her claim to the Anglo-Norman realm.[156] His account of Henry I is thus one that implicitly strengthens Henry II's authority by extolling the virtues and promoting the rights of his mother and grandfather.

It is no wonder then that Benoît should have switched to Robert de Torigny's account. In fact, it seems very likely that Henry II or his counselors furnished Benoît with Robert de Torigny's work to ensure that he delivered a laudatory account of Norman history. Although we have no direct evidence that they did so, presenting Benoît with an almost foolproof source surely would have served their interests. Whether Benoît chose Robert's account of his own accord or had it pressed upon him, the shift in source material provided him with an extremely positive account of Henry I's reign that stressed Matilda's right to succeed her father, and hence emphasized the legitimacy of her son Henry II. Robert explicitly described Matilda's sons, Henry, Geoffrey, and William, as the legitimate heirs to the English throne and emphasized that they united the royal Anglo-Saxon and Norman blood

---

152. *GND*, I:lxxvvii.

153. *GND*, I:lxxix.

154. Henry I was a friend of Abbot Boso of Bec, under whom Robert de Torigny served as prior. The king was a regular visitor, especially in 1134–35, as was Matilda. *GND*, I:lxxxiii–xxxiv.

155. Abbot Boso may have suggested the addition of book VIII, but van Houts argues that the initiative probably came from Matilda herself. Ibid.

156. *GND*, I:lxxxvii–xxxviii.

carried by their grandparents, Henry I and Edith-Matilda.[157] Benoît repeated exactly these points in the *Chronique*. In addition to providing a source unencumbered by nuance or doubt, the switch to Robert de Torigny's redaction allowed Benoît to discard the *Roman de Rou* entirely without having to construct his own account of Henry I's reign. A potential avenue to unwanted representations of the past was thus avoided.

Henry II also had another excellent reason to pay more attention to this second attempt at commemorating his lineage. The historiographical project itself appears to have changed as a result of shifting political circumstances. When Wace was first commissioned to produce a vernacular history of the Normans in 1160, Henry appears to have been interested primarily in memorializing his dynasty and enshrining the principle of hereditary right as the sole basis of kingship. After the rebellion of 1173/74, Henry may well have been more concerned with projecting his authority and suppressing dissent. Many of Henry's barons in England, Normandy, Aquitaine, Anjou, and Brittany had joined the Great War in 1173 out of frustration with Henry's ongoing efforts to curtail their power, limit their role in governing, prevent their private wars, seize their castles, and crush their territorial ambitions. Although the peace that concluded the war offered favorable terms to the barons, Henry did nothing to redress the grievances that had caused them to rebel in the first place. If anything, he intensified his efforts to assert royal rights and curb baronial power in the years following the rebellion. There is thus good reason to believe that Henry would have been more hostile than usual to any kind of criticism after 1174, and that the revolt and its aftermath played a significant role in Wace's firing. Wace might have been able to get away with a certain amount of discreet criticism of the royal lineage in the 1160s, but Henry would have been in no mood for Wace's defense of baronial power or his unpleasant reminders about the failings of his ancestors in the wake of such a large-scale rebellion. By the time Benoît received the commission he would certainly have been aware of the dangers of delivering a history that challenged Henry's authority by publicly maligning his ancestors in the vernacular as Wace had done.

Although Benoît expresses the desire to bring his history up to the time of Henry II's reign in one of his apostrophes to his patron, and this statement has been taken to indicate that the *Chronique* is thus incomplete in its current form, it seems highly unlikely that Henry II would have been re-

---

157. He also rebukes the nobles who denied the throne to Matilda, although not as harshly as one might expect. *GND*, viii, II:240–42.

ceptive to this idea.[158] Considering how far astray Wace had gone in his project, and the length of time that had already been consumed in attempting to produce just one serviceable history that concluded with the reign of his grandfather, it is doubtful that Henry II would have had the patience for such an extension. Whether or not Henry's patience was wearing thin, there would have been a far greater problem had Benoît attempted to bring his history up to Henry II's reign—he would have had to deal with Stephen and the civil war. It is difficult to imagine any circumstances in which the prospect of memorializing Stephen would have appealed in the least to Henry II. Indeed, it is likely that Benoît himself would have recognized the folly of such an enterprise. Even if he had wanted to include Henry II's reign, how could Benoît bridge the almost twenty-year gap between Henry I's death and Henry II's accession—that period of civil war that Henry II consistently asserted was a suspension of legitimate government. If these vernacular histories were meant to provide Henry II with a means of cementing his grip on power and promoting an orderly succession based on the principle of hereditary right, Stephen's usurpation and his reign were almost insurmountable problems. They were well within human memory; eliding them while bringing the history up to the present would have only drawn attention to their absence, and treating them would have been even more perilous.

Not only did Stephen's accession to the throne clearly and painfully illustrate the power of the barons and clergy to determine the succession, commemorating Stephen's reign in a vernacular history also had the potential to vividly remind them of just how much they had lost under Henry II. Stephen had viewed his magnates and clergy as his partners in governing and had ceded them a degree of autonomy and power that Henry II found intolerable. Much of Henry's early reign had been devoted to reining in what he considered to be the inordinate power the barons had acquired under Stephen. As a result, many of Henry II's barons probably remembered Stephen's reign as a time when their interests were more often served by the king. After all, Stephen had once been one of them and had gladly relied on their assistance, while Henry seemed intent on restricting their

---

158. Elisabeth van Houts has pointed out that Benoît chose to end his history at the point where his source terminated. She does not clearly indicate why Benoît stopped there, but seems to suggest that the time it would have taken Benoît to construct his own account working from various other sources prevented him from doing so. I suggest, on the other hand, that his reversal may have been largely due to the fact that Henry II would have objected to any memorialization of Stephen's reign. Cf. van Houts, "Adaptation."

power. In fact, Henry II's efforts to reverse the trends that had characterized Stephen's government had generated such profound discontent among the barons that it had resulted in their wide-scale rebellion during the Great War. According to at least one contemporary chronicler, the nobles had joined the cause of Henry's sons only because it offered them a convenient means of protesting Henry's policies and reasserting their power.[159]

It seems, therefore, that we should understand Benoît's declaration that he wished to include Henry II's reign in his history as an instance in which he sought to flatter his patron, and we should not be surprised that he later regained his senses. The sentiment behind Benoît's intention to extend his history to Henry II's reign might have been welcome, but the actual logistics of producing such an extension would have been daunting and its utility questionable at best. The fact that the *Chronique* does not address Stephen's or Henry II's reigns in detail may well derive from a conscious decision to project contemporary political concerns onto the more distant, and safer, past. Although almost all of the issues at stake in this debate over the guiding principles of Anglo-Norman political ideology had their origins in, or had been exacerbated by, the Anarchy and Henry II's efforts to reclaim royal power, the reigns of Stephen and Henry II were too recent, and their politics too raw and apparent, to address them directly.

---

159. Ralph of Diceto makes precisely this point. Ralph of Diceto, *Radulfi de Diceto Decani Lundoniensis Opera Historica*, I:371.

Conclusion

Since there were already perfectly good Latin histories of his Norman ancestors that would have served Henry II's purposes (Robert de Torigny's F redaction of the *Gesta Normannorum ducum* would have done an excellent job), and neither Wace nor Benoît significantly extended the material covered by their Latin sources, Henry II must have commissioned a vernacular history of his dynasty in the hope that it would reach the widest audience possible—a mixed audience that was not necessarily literate in Latin. It is possible, of course, to argue that Henry merely wanted a vernacular history of his ancestors that he could read. Although this may have played into his decision, I strongly doubt that it was his only motive for two reasons. The first reason is that private reading appears to have been uncommon in the twelfth century. Both Wace and Benoît indicate that they expect their histories to be read aloud before an audience, not read privately by the king, and the act of reading aloud is implicit in the titles of *clerc lisant* and *maistre lisant* that both authors claim for themselves. Second, in commissioning a dynastic history in Old French, Henry was actually appropriating a genre that had been pioneered by the Anglo-Norman nobles and clergy, who had already been commissioning and consuming vernacular verse histories recounting the deeds of the Britons, Anglo-Saxons, Trojans, and Romans since at least 1135. These histories were tailored to the tastes of Henry's own barons and clergy, those with

whom he competed for power in the Anglo-Norman realm, those who
wielded influence and might orchestrate a rebellion or affect the succession.
In short, Henry appropriated the preferred genre of the Anglo-Norman
aristocracy and clergy and used it in an attempt to insist on his own interpretation of Norman history and the legitimacy of the very policies that
had incensed his nobles and clergy.

The larger mission of Henry II's historiographical enterprise was to portray Henry I's government as a golden age of peace, prosperity, and order
that Henry II was restoring, to forcefully articulate royal arguments in what
amounted to an ongoing public debate over the proper balance of power
between the king and his nobles and clergy, and to enshrine hereditary right
(and arguably primogeniture) as the only consideration governing the royal
succession. How likely is it though that the contemporary Anglo-Norman
nobility or clergy would have been swayed by such a history? They had
their own memories and there was no shortage of competing narratives.
Wace himself demonstrates that this was the case in the way he narrates
events occurring in the Bessin (the area surrounding Bayeux and Caen).
Surely Henry II was not so naïve as to think that he could convince a contemporary audience that their memories were defective and that other narratives were lies?

Even though Henry must have hoped to influence the present by selectively representing the past, he must have also taken a longer view and
wished to control the memory of his dynasty in the eyes of posterity. Like
a countless number of monarchs and counselors before them, Henry II and
his advisers grasped that they could seek to influence the present and future
by controlling the representation of the past.[1] As Wace himself and other
historians have reminded us, human memory ultimately fades and variant
representations fall away. Although the desired effects might not be produced immediately and in every quarter, the king apparently hoped to produce a royalist interpretation of the past that would eventually take hold and
spread. Henry's choice to disseminate this history in the vernacular, and in
a genre favored by the Anglo-Norman nobles, is particularly important in
this regard. A Latin history conveying a royalist account of the past might
have been useful, but it would surely have reached a more limited audience.
By commissioning this history in the language of the Anglo-Norman aris-

---

1. See Geary, *Phantoms of Remembrance*; Yitsak Hen and Matthew Innes, eds., *The Uses of the Past in the Early Middle Ages* (Cambridge, 2000); McKitterick, *Carolingians and the Written Word*; McKitterick, *History and Memory*; McKitterick, "Constructing the Past," Coleman, *Ancient and Medieval Memories*; and Goffart, *Narrators of Barbarian History*.

tocracy and clergy, Henry attempted to ensure that it would circulate widely among the very classes whose opinion he most desired to influence.

As for influencing the present, we may surmise that the Anglo-Norman nobility, while stung by Henry's efforts to curb their power, also desired order and were not anxious to revisit the recent past of disputed succession and civil war under Stephen. Nearly twenty years of chaos, shifting allegiances, and fighting had resulted in an almost universal revulsion at the prospect of another succession dispute—hence the willingness of the barons and clergy to assist Henry II in reaching an agreement with Stephen regarding the succession in 1153. The civil war appears to have instilled circumspection in all but the most incorrigible (Hugh Bigod being the most obvious and belligerent exception to this rule). Henry's efforts to monopolize power could still inspire indignation and his authority could still be challenged, as the revolt of 1173/74 testifies, but even this rebellion did not seek to overthrow the established order, only to moderate what the barons considered to be excessive royal claims to power and interference in their affairs.

Henry must have also hoped that the genealogical format of these histories would assist him in inculcating hereditary right as the sole basis for succession. This was likely to have been only slightly problematic for his intended audience. Henry's insistence on hereditary right was primarily intended to strip the barons and clergy of their power to affect the royal succession, and it bears repeating here that every succession since that of William the Conqueror had been disputed. William's own accession as duke of Normandy had been contested due to his illegitimacy, and his claim to England had been disputed, as both he and Harold Godwinson claimed to be Edward the Confessor's heir. William's decision to leave England to his second son had led to rancorous division between those magnates who accepted William Rufus as king and those who championed the rights of Robert Curthose, the eldest. In accepting Henry I as king upon Rufus's death, the barons and clergy had chosen once again to exclude Robert Curthose.

The succession of Henry I's son might have been less problematic, had he survived his father. At the time of William Audelin's death in 1120, however, there was still rampant disagreement over whether he or his cousin William Clito was the legitimate heir to the throne. After William Audelin's death, much of the nobility and clergy assumed that William Clito would succeed Henry I, but the king would not hear of it. He spent the next eight years doing everything in his power to ensure that Clito would never succeed him. By 1134 all of the legitimate, direct male descendants of William the Conqueror other than Henry I were dead, creating a new problem—Henry's only remaining legitimate child was female. Although hereditary right, legitimate birth, and royal designation were clearly factors in determining succession, the barons and clergy had some latitude in choosing whom to elevate to the throne, and they used it. They had exploited this element of choice in rejecting Matilda, despite having taken numerous oaths to uphold her rights during her father's lifetime. And they had exercised this prerogative most recently in choosing to support Henry II's claim to the throne over that of Stephen's son Eustace. Stephen's surviving son, William, was not even considered for the throne after Eustace's death, in spite of the fact that he had the same hereditary claims as Eustace. Unfortunately for both Eustace and William, clerical and baronial favor had already shifted to Henry II.

The elective principle was still strong enough during Henry II's reign that the magnates and clergy could effectively destroy the king's plans for the succession upon his death. It was precisely this level of exploitable ambiguity in the Anglo-Norman succession that Henry II sought to eradicate by enshrining the supremacy of hereditary right. Applying some form of primogeniture to the royal succession also seems to have been among Henry's goals, as the dynastic settlement of 1169, the crownings of the Young King Henry, and the king's efforts to redistribute his lands after 1183 attest. Indeed, both the *Roman de Rou* and the *Chronique des ducs de Normandie* implicitly advanced the principle of primogeniture, in that they both illustrated the traditional passage of Normandy, the patrimony of the Norman dukes, to the duke's eldest son (the duchy had once passed to the duke's brother when Richard III died in 1027 and his brother Robert succeeded him).[2]

Whereas both Wace's and Benoît's histories inherently advocated the practice of primogeniture by illustrating that it had been the standard for transmission of the Norman duchy, they took different approaches to the issue as it applied to the Anglo-Norman realm. Wace explains the fact that the Anglo-Norman realm had been divided between William Rufus and Robert Curthose by arguing that William the Conqueror had no right to name his heir to England. Even so, Wace later evinces sympathy for those partisans who believed that Robert Curthose, as the eldest son, should have inherited all of his father's lands. Indeed, Robert might have inherited both

---

2. Richard had a son, Nicholas, who was probably very young in 1027 and was displaced by his uncle. Garnett, *Conquered England*, 142–52.

Normandy and England had he not been in open rebellion against his father at the time that he died. Benoît, on the other hand, shows no anxiety over the division of Normandy and England, as Robert still received the whole of his father's patrimony and William received the kingdom his father had won by conquest. The most important difference between Wace and Benoît is that Wace always insists on the primacy of primogeniture, while Benoît accepts the separate transmission of patrimony and conquest, and implicitly argues that failure to maintain one's patrimony and provide good government can nullify one's birthright (as he does when he advocates Henry I's deposition of Robert Curthose). Although this argument supported the legitimacy of Henry I's reign, it admittedly had the potential to backfire on Henry II and his heirs if pushed to its logical conclusion that any younger son could rightly deprive his older brother of the patrimony by force if he squandered his heritage or proved to be an utter failure as a ruler. Presumably, this was thought to be such an exceptional circumstance that it did not significantly threaten the general application of primogeniture to the succession.

Accepting the application of hereditary right and primogeniture to the royal succession had potential benefits for the nobility. After all, if these principles were the only considerations germane to the royal succession, it could only help the aristocracy in their attempts to assert that the same principles applied to them; it thus promised to limit royal interference in noble successions and aid the nobility in establishing their own hereditary dynasties.

Although most of Henry's reforms were salutary, we must not lose sight of the fact that he transformed the rules governing both royal and noble successions during his reign. Henry's decision to crown the Young King Henry during his own lifetime had been a complete innovation. The practice may have been customary in France, but it was not so in England. Moreover, Pope Celestine II had banned any innovations concerning the English crown in the early 1140s. When Pope Eugenius III and Archbishop Theobald of Canterbury invoked this ban to justify their refusal to crown Eustace, Henry of Huntingdon noted that "the pope in a letter had forbidden the archbishop to elevate the king's son as king. It was understood that this was because Stephen had seized the kingdom contrary to the oath [he had taken to support Matilda]."[3] The ban may have been designed to punish

---

3. Huntingdon, *HA*, x.32, 759. It is important to note that he presents Matilda's right to the throne as rooted in her designation as Henry I's heir and in the oaths the barons (including Stephen) had sworn to uphold her rights, not as being based on her having the better hereditary claim.

Stephen for perjuring himself and prevent him from transmitting the crown to his son, but the fact remains that no English king before Henry had ever crowned his heir during his own lifetime. Stephen had clearly tried to import this practice in order to ensure the succession of his own son, but his efforts had been thwarted. Henry knew from his mother's experience that designations and oaths were insufficient, and he was astute enough to recognize that crowning his heir would prevent the nobles and clergy from meddling in the succession. Still, Henry could not appeal to English tradition on this point. Fortunately, his Norman ancestors had a tradition of recognizing heirs *inter vivos* and associating them in government—a tradition that was clearly illustrated in these dynastic histories—that Henry could use to legitimate the practice of crowning his heir.[4]

Henry's introduction of *mort d'ancestor* had also been an innovation, even if it had only formally endorsed the already widespread practice of hereditary succession among the nobility. Henry had already begun applying the principle of hereditary right to noble successions through *mort d'ancestor* by 1166. Since there was technically no right of inheritance in the feudal tenure system, a vassal's fief theoretically reverted to his lord upon his death and the lord had no legal obligation to transmit the fief to the dead man's heir. Practice, of course, was another matter entirely. Heirs generally assumed their father's fiefs upon payment of a relief and performance of homage to the lord from whom the fief was held, and twelfth-century lords generally confirmed fiefs to their vassal and that vassal's heirs. Henry's innovation in introducing *mort d'ancestor* was thus to make the disseisin (dispossession) of the deceased's family illegal and to ensure that a presumptive heir could take possession of his father's fief, even when faced with a recalcitrant lord.[5]

By introducing these changes, Henry hoped to enunciate clear rules governing successions that would benefit not only his own dynasty but those of noble families as well. Accepting this new order thus had some distinct advantages for the nobility, insofar as it promised to aid them in perpetuating their own dynasties. It must be admitted that accepting the new regime also threatened to set a dangerous precedent by implicitly condoning Henry's expansion of royal power, but it cannot have been clear to anyone at the time that Henry's successors would be as successful in maintaining that power as

---

4. Cf. Garnett, *Conquered England*, chap. 3.

5. Assize of Northampton, clause 4; *Select Charters and Other Illustrations of English Constitutional History*, 179–80; Warren, *Henry II*, 342; and Bloch, *Feudal Society*, chap. 15.

Henry had been in claiming it. Rather than accepting this new order and all of its innovations as permanent, the nobility and clergy probably accepted those elements they found advantageous and resisted those they did not. They likely assumed that power would revert to them upon Henry's death, just as it had upon his grandfather's death, and waited to fight under more propitious circumstances.

One of the most fascinating aspects of this early foray into royally commissioned, vernacular historiography is that Wace's subversive history emerged from it at all. The very existence of the *Roman de Rou* should be taken as a measure of the resistance Henry II met in his drive to monopolize power, and a reminder of the dangers inherent in royal attempts to control the representation of the past.[6] The great irony of this project is thus that Henry II spent most of his reign pursuing a vernacular history that would strengthen his dynasty's grip on power, only to have Wace's subversive version of Norman history win in the end. The surviving manuscript evidence suggests that the *Roman de Rou* enjoyed a greater circulation than the *Chronique*. There are three extant manuscripts of the *Roman de Rou* dating from the thirteenth and fourteenth centuries, as opposed to two manuscripts of the *Chronique*. And, while both works were adapted into prose in the thirteenth century, the prose *Rou* appears to have been more widely copied than the prose *Chronique*; there are two extant copies of the prose *Rou* (and another eight manuscripts at the Bibliothèque nationale de France that are dependent on it), versus a single copy of the prose *Chronique*.[7]

On the basis of its content and what we can infer regarding the circumstances of its production, Benoît's *Chronique* appears to represent an "official" version of Norman history that opposes Wace's subversive history. This binary opposition of official and subversive provides a useful, if rudimentary, lens through which to view the debate over the nature of power, lordship, and authority in a period of crisis and transformation that is contained in the pages of these histories. To be sure, the debate was not confined solely to these vernacular histories; it raged in other texts produced

---

6. Cf. Jason Glenn's discussion of the divergent interpretations of history offered by Richer and Flodoard of Reims. Jason Glenn, *Politics and History in the Tenth Century: The Work and World of Richer of Reims* (Cambridge, 2004), esp. chaps. 10, 11, and 12.

7. See the bibliography for a list of the extant manuscripts of the *Roman de Rou* and *Chronique des ducs de Normandie*. There are two manuscripts containing a prose version the *Roman de Rou*, one at the Bibliothèque nationale de France (BN fr. 16939) and the other at the British Library (BL Royal Fr. 15.E.VI), along with another eight manuscripts at the Bibliothèque nationale de France that contain a prose history that depends upon the *Roman de Rou*, as opposed to one copy of the prose *Chronique* held at the J. Paul Getty Museum (Getty, Ms Ludwig XIII 4).

during Henry II's reign as well.[8] Although most often centered on the events of the past, its true concern was determining the guiding principles of political ideology in the present and future. Wace and Benoît represented conflicting sides in this debate, one amenable and one antithetical to the expansion of royal power. Whereas Benoît promoted Henry II's agenda by praising his ancestors and portraying their dominance as the direct result of God's will, Wace protested the destruction of the old social order and admonished his patron by presenting an inflammatory account of Anglo-Norman history.

Benoît's adulatory account of Henry I and his reign buttressed Henry II's efforts to consolidate power by providing a precedent for his actions, while Wace's negative depiction of Henry I and his greed and treachery undermined any such effort to use his reign as a positive example. Benoît's representation of Henry I's reign as a golden age of justice, peace, and close relations between monarch and papacy, which was predicated on Henry I's ability to impose his will and curb the power of his vassals, offered a compelling justificatory precedent for Henry II's expansion of royal power. Given the likelihood of greater royal oversight of the *Chronique*, Benoît's history is almost certainly an official attempt to mitigate the damage Wace had inflicted by rebutting his account of the past. We can surely say that Benoît's narrative advanced the royal cause, while Wace seems to have felt obliged to caution Henry II and remind him of the potentially deleterious consequences of his policies in much the same way that a vassal was expected to offer sound counsel to his lord. Indeed, Wace's greatest crime may have simply been underestimating the power of the new medium of vernacular verse historiography, and the danger that any subversive content disseminated through that medium posed to royal power. He may not have grasped that admonitions that were permissible in a Latin history with a necessarily restricted circulation were transformed into something far more hazardous when circulated in a language that was accessible to, and specifically intended to reach, so many.

---

8. Among the most notable are the following. Robert de Torigny, "*Chronica Roberti de Torigneio, Abbatis Monasterii Sancti Michaelis in Periculo Maris*," in *Chronicles of the Reigns of Stephen, Henry II and Richard I*, ed. R. Howlett, 4 vols. (London, 1884–90), IV:81–315; William of Newburgh, "*Historia rerum Anglicarum*," I:1–408 and II:409–53; Gerald of Wales, "*De instructione principum*," in *Giraldus Cambrensis, Opera*, ed. Brewer, Dimmock, and Warner; Gervase of Canterbury, *Historical Works*; Ralph Niger, *Radulphi Nigri Chronica*, ed. R. Anstruther (London, 1851, and New York, 1967); Ralph of Diceto, *Radulphi de Diceto Decani Lundoniensis Opera Historica*; John of Salisbury, *Policraticus*, Corpus Christianorum Series 118 (Turnhout, 1993); and Walter Map, *De Nugis Curialum*, ed. M. R. James (Oxford, 1914).

What should be abundantly clear is that neither author passively described the past, but actively constructed it and reshaped its meaning in accordance with his own preoccupations and biases. Their narrative choices expose deep and abiding concerns surrounding moments of rupture in the recent past, and they use these ruptures as forums for debating present realities and future possibilities by manipulating their representations and embedding arguments within them. Although it is perhaps easier to identify these fissures and plumb their attendant worries in the *Roman de Rou*, Benoît's attempts to elide these ruptures are just as revealing. By trying to disguise, or deny, those moments in which power was transferred, taken, or exercised in questionable circumstances, he draws our attention to these episodes and magnifies their importance. It should also be apparent that Benoît's efforts to conceal these ruptures would have been countered by human memory, as well as by rival narratives such as the *Roman de Rou*, at least in the short term, and that a contemporary audience could not have failed to apprehend his sleight of hand.

The Anglo-Norman nobility must be given credit for pioneering the new genre of vernacular verse historiography, but Henry II had been prescient in co-opting this genre and using it to disseminate a royally authorized history of his dynasty. Although Wace presented him with a subversive version of Norman history, and Benoît's history appears to have been met with an almost total lack of interest, the important point remains that Henry II adopted the preferred historiographical genre of the Anglo-Norman aristocracy and used it in an attempt to enhance the prestige of his own dynasty and ensure its survival—and he did so almost a full century before any similar effort to enshrine a royal ideology in a vernacular history was made elsewhere in Europe.[9] Despite its failures and frustrations, Henry's experiment in using the vernacular to promote a royal agenda heralded the beginning of a new age of vernacular history writing. Vernacular historiography would hereafter be co-opted again and again, and pressed into the service of competing aristocratic and royal agendas both in England and on the Continent.[10]

---

9. The Capetians adopted the practice of patronizing vernacular histories in the thirteenth century. The *Grandes Chroniques de France* was begun at Saint-Denis during the reign of Louis IX, and was followed by Joinville's *Life of Saint Louis* in the early fourteenth century. *Les grandes chroniques de France, selon que elles sont conservées en l'église de Saint-Denis en France, publiées par M. Paulin Paris* (Paris, 1836–38); and Jean de Joinville, "The Life of Saint Louis," in *Chronicles of the Crusades: Joinville & Villehardouin*, trans. M. R. B. Shaw (New York, 1985).

10. For aristocratically commissioned vernacular histories in early thirteenth-century Flanders, see Spiegel, *Romancing the Past*.

Bibliography

Critical Editions and Translations of the *Roman de Rou*

Wace. *The Roman de Rou*. Translated by Glyn S. Burgess with the text of Anthony J. Holden and notes by Glyn S. Burgess and Elizabeth M. C. van Houts. Isle of Jersey, 2002.

——. *Le Roman de Rou de Wace*. Edited by Anthony J. Holden. 3 vols. Paris, 1970–73.

——. *Maistre Wace's Roman de Rou et des ducs de Normandie*. Edited by Hugo Andresen. Heilbronn, 1877–79.

——. *Roman de Rou et ducs de Normandie*. Edited by François Pluquet. Rouen, 1827–29.

Manuscripts of the *Roman de Rou*

A   London, British Library, Royal 4.C.XI, ff. 249r–278r. Beginning of the thirteenth century. Contains part III only.

B   Paris, Bibliothèque nationale de France, fr. 375 (formerly fr. 6987), ff. 219r–240v. End of the thirteenth century. Contains part III only.

C   Paris, Bibliothèque nationale de France, nouv. acq. fr. 718, ff. 1a–149a. End of the fourteenth century. Contains part III only.

D   Paris, Bibliothèque nationale de France, Duchesne 79, ff. 1r–83r. A seventeenth-century copy, of which three further copies are also extant (see Holden, vol. 3, p. 24). Contains the *Chronique Ascendante*, part II, and part III. The Duchesne copy is the only extant source for the *Chronique Ascendante* and part II, but it appears to offer a faithful representation of an older model.

A2 London, British Library, Royal 13.A.XVIII, f. 115. Fragment. Fourteenth century. Contains the first forty-four lines of part III; probably copied directly from A.

Critical Editions of the *Chronique des ducs de Normandie*

Benoît de Sainte-Maure. *Chronique des ducs de Normandie, publiee d'aprés le manuscrit de Tours avec les variantes du manuscrit de Londres par Carin Fahlin*. 2 vols. Uppsala, 1951.

——. *Chronique des ducs de Normandie, par Benoit, trouvére anglo-normand du XIIe siècle: Publiee pour la premiére fois d'aprés un manuscrit du Musée britannique, par Francisque Michel*. Paris, 1836–44.

Manuscripts of the *Chronique des ducs de Normandie*

T   Tours, Bibliothèque municipale de Tours no. 903. End of the twelfth century. Written in the dialect of the author.

B   London, British Library, Harley 1717. First half of the thirteenth century.

Additional Primary Sources

Abbreviatio gestorum regum Franciae. MGH SS 9: 402–3.

Actes des comtes de Flandre, 1071–1128. Edited by Fernand Vercauteren. Paris, 1938.

Ailred of Rievaulx. *Life of Edward the Confessor.* In *Patrologia Latina: Patrologiae Cursus Completus,* edited by J. P. Migne, 195:737–90. 221 vols. Paris, 1844–55.

Ancient Charters, Royal and Private, prior to A.D. 1200. Edited by J. H. Round. London, 1888.

Anglo-Norman Political Songs. Edited by Isabel S. T. Aspin. Anglo-Norman Text Society 11. New York, 1971.

The Anglo-Saxon Chronicle: A Revised Translation. Translated by Dorothy Whitelock, with David C. Douglas and Susie I. Tucker. London, 1961.

Anonymous monk of Battle Abbey. "*The Brevis relatio de Guillelmo nobilissimo comite Normannorum,* Written by a Monk of Battle Abbey: Edited with an Historical Commentary by Elisabeth M. C. van Houts." In *Chronolgy, Conquest and Conflict in Medieval England: Camden Miscellany XXXIV,* 1–48. Camden Miscellany, 5th series, 10, 1997. Reprinted with an English translation in Elisabeth M. C. van Houts. *History and Family Traditions in England and the Continent, 1000–1200.* Aldershot, 1999.

Antiquus cartularius ecclesiae Baiocensis (Livre Noir). Edited by V. Bourrienne. 2 vols. Rouen-Paris, 1902.

Bede. *The Ecclesiastical History of the English People; The Greater Chronicle; Bede's Letter to Egbert.* Edited by Judith McClure and Roger Collins. Oxford, 1994.

Benoît de Sainte-Maure. *Le Roman de Troie, par Benoît de Sainte-Maure, pub. d'apres tous les manuscrits connus par Léopold Constans.* 6 vols. Paris, 1904–12.

British Library, Department of Manuscripts. *Index of Manuscripts in the British Library.* 8 vols. Cambridge, 1984–85.

The Carmen de Hastingae Proelio of Guy of Amiens. Edited and translated by Frank Barlow. Oxford, 1999.

The Chronicle of Battle Abbey. Edited and translated by Eleanor Searle. Oxford, 1980.

Chronicles of the Reigns of Stephen, Henry II and Richard I. Edited by R. Howlett. 4 vols. London, 1884–90.

Chronicon Angliae Petriburgense. (i) *Chronicon Angliae Petriburgense.* Edited by J. A. Giles. London, 1845; (ii) *The Peterborough Chronicle, 1070–1154.* Edited by Cecily Clark. Oxford, 1970.

Chronicon Monasterii de Abingdon. Edited by J. Stevenson. London, 1858.

Chronicon Monasterii de Bello. Edited by J. S. Brewer. London, 1846.

Chronicon pontificum ecclesiae Eboracensis. In *Historians of the Church of York,* edited by J. Raine. 3 vols. London, 1879–94.

Chroniques anglo-normandes. Recueil d'extraits et d'écrits relatifs à l'histoire de Normandie et d'Angleterre pendant les XIe et XIIe siècles; publié, pour la première fois, d'après les manuscrits de Londres, de Cambridge, de Douai, de Bruxelles et de Paris, par Francisque Michel. Imprimé sous les auspices et avec l'autorisation de M. Guizot, ministre de l'instruction publique. Rouen, 1836–40.

Chroniques des Comtes d'Anjou et des Seigneurs d'Amboise. Edited by Louis Halphen and René Poupardin. Paris, 1913.

"De obitu Willelmi." In *Guillaume de Jumièges, Gesta Normannorum ducum*, edited by Jean Marx, 145–49. Caen, 1914. English translation in R. Allen Brown. *The Norman Conquest of England*, 47–50. Woodbridge, 1995.

Domesday People: A Prosopography of Persons Occurring in English Documents, 1066–1166. Edited by K. S. B. Keats-Rohan. 2 vols. Woodbridge, 1999–2002.

Dudo of Saint-Quentin. (i) *De moribus et actis primorum Normanniae ducum auctore Dudone sancti Quintini decano.* Edited by Jules Lair. Caen, 1865; (ii) *Dudo of Saint-Quentin: History of the Normans.* Translated by Eric Christiansen. Woodbridge, 1998.

Eadmer of Canterbury. (i) *Eadmeri Historia novorum in Anglia.* Edited by Martin Rule. London, 1884; (ii) *Eadmer's History of Recent Events in England: Historia novorum in Anglia.* Translated by Geoffrey Bosanquet. London, 1964.

English Historical Documents, vol. 2 (1142–1189). Edited by David C. Douglas and G. W. Greenaway. London, 1953.

"Extrait de la Chronique ou histoire manuscrite de Normandie." *Recueil des historiens des Gaules et de la France.* 24 vols. Paris, 1738–1904. 11:320–43 and 13:220–56.

Florence of Worcester. *Florentii Wigorniensis Monachi, Chronicon ex Chronicis.* Edited by B. Thorpe. 2 vols. London, 1848–49.

Geffrei Gaimar. (i) *Estoire des Engleis: History of the English.* Edited and translated by Ian Short. Oxford, 2009; (ii) *Estoire des Engleis.* Edited by A. Bell. Oxford: Blackwell, 1960; (iii) *Estoire des Engleis.* Translated by T. D. Hardy and C. T. Martin. London, 1888–89.

Geoffrey of Monmouth. (i) *The Historia regum Britannie of Geoffrey of Monmouth. 1, Bern, Burgerbibliothek, MS. 568.* Edited by N. Wright. Cambridge, 1984; (ii) *The Historia regum Britannie of Geoffrey of Monmouth. 2, The First Variant Version: A Critical Edition.* Edited by N. Wright. Cambridge, 1988; (iii) J. C. Crick. *The Historia regum Britannie of Geoffrey of Monmouth. 3, A Summary Catalogue of the Manuscripts.* Cambridge, 1989; (iv) J. C. Crick. *The Historia regum Britannie of Geoffrey of Monmouth. 4, Dissemination and Reception in the Later Middle Ages.* Cambridge, 1991.

Gerald of Wales. *Giraldus Cambrensis Opera.* Edited by J. S. Brewer, J. F. Dimmock, and G. F. Warner. 8 vols. London, 1861–91.

Gervase of Canterbury. *The Historical Works of Gervase of Canterbury.* Edited by William Stubbs. 2 vols. London, 1879–80.

Gesta Abbatum Monasterii Sancti Albani: Chronica Monasterii S. Albani: Gesta Abbatum Monasterii Sancti Albani, a Thoma Walsingham. Edited by H. T. Riley. London, 1867.

Gesta Stephani: The Deeds of Stephen. Edited by K. R. Potter. London, 1955.

Les grandes chroniques de France, selon que elles sont conservées en l'église de Saint-Denis en France, publiées par M. Paulin Paris. Paris, 1836–38.

The Great Rolls of the Pipe of the Reign of Henry the Second, 5th to 34th years. 30 vols. London, 1884–1925.

Henry of Huntingdon. *Henry, Archdeacon of Huntingdon: Historia Anglorum, The History of the English People.* Edited and translated by Diana Greenway. Oxford, 1996.

Herbert of Bosham. *Materials for the History of Thomas Becket.* Edited by J. C. Robertson. 7 vols. London, 1875–85.

Hugh the Chantor. *History of the Church of York.* Edited by C. Johnson. London, 1961.

Jean de Joinville. "The Life of Saint Louis." In *Chronicles of the Crusades: Joinville & Villehardouin.* Translated by M. R. B. Shaw. New York, 1985.

John of Hexham. "*Historia regum.*" In *Symeonis Monachi Opera Omnia,* edited by T. Arnold. II:284–332. 2 vols. London, 1882–85.

John of Marmoutier. "*Gesta consulum Andegavorum et dominorum Ambaziensium.*" In *Chroniques d'Anjou,* edited by Paul Marchegay and André Salmon. Paris, 1856.

——. "*Historia abbreviata consulum Andegavorum.*" In *Chroniques d'Anjou,* edited by Paul Marchegay and André Salmon. Paris, 1856.

——. "*Historia Gaufredi ducis Normannorum et comitis Andegavorum.*" In *Chroniques des comtes d'Anjou et des seigneurs d'Amboise,* edited by Louis Halphen and C. Poupardin, 172–231. Paris, 1913.

John of Salisbury. *Historia Pontificalis: Ioannis Saresberiensis Historia Pontificalis: John of Salisbury's Memoirs of the Papal Court.* Edited by Marjorie Chibnall. London, 1956.

——. *The Letters of John of Salisbury, I, The Early Letters (1153–1161).* Edited by W. J. Miller and H. E. Butler, revised by C. N. L. Brooke. London, 1955.

——. (i) *Policraticus: Iohannis Saresberiensis Episcopi Carnotensis Policratici sive De Nugis Curialium et Vestigiis Philosophorum.* Edited by C. C. J. Webb. 2 vols. Oxford, 1909; (ii) *Policraticus.* Edited by Cary Nederman. Cambridge, 1990; (iii) *Policraticus.* Corpus Christianorum Series 118. Turnhout, 1993.

John of Worcester. *The Chronicle of John of Worcester.* Edited by R. R. Darlington and P. McGurk. Translated by Jennifer Bray and P. McGurk. 3 vols. Oxford, 1995.

Jordan Fantosme. (i) *Jordan Fantosme's Chronicle.* Edited and translated by R. C. Johnston. Oxford, 1981; (ii) "*Chronique de la guerre entre les Anglois et les Ecossois en 1173 et 1174.*" In *Chronicles of the Reigns of Stephen, Henry II and Richard I,* edited by R. Howlett, III: 202–377. 4 vols. London, 1884–90.

Layamon. *Brut.* Edited by G. L. Brook and R. F. Leslie. 2 vols. London, 1963 and 1978.

Les chroniques de Normandie. Edited by Francisque Michel. Rouen, 1839.

Liber niger Scaccarii. Edited by Thomas Hearne. 2 vols. London, 1774.

Materials for the History of Thomas Becket. Edited by J. C. Robertson. 7 vols. London, 1875–85.

Matthew of Paris. *Matthaei Parisiensis Chronica Majora.* Edited by Henry Richards Luard. 7 vols. London, 1872–84.

The Oldest Anglo-Norman Prose Brut Chronicle: An Edition and Translation. Edited by Julia Marvin. Woodbridge, 2006.

Orderic Vitalis. *The Ecclesiastical History of Orderic Vitalis.* Edited and translated by Marjorie Chibnall. 6 vols. Oxford, 1969–80.

Patrologia Latina: Patrologiae Cursus Completus. Edited by J. P. Migne. 221 vols. Paris, 1844–55.

Ralph Niger. *Radulphi Nigri Chronica.* Edited by R. Anstruther. London, 1851, and New York, 1967.

Ralph of Coggeshall. *Radulphi de Coggeshall Chronicon Anglicanum.* Edited by J. Stevenson. London, 1875.

Ralph of Diceto. *Radulphi de Diceto Decani Lundoniensis Opera Historica.* Edited by William Stubbs. 2 vols. London, 1876.

Reading Abbey Cartularies: British Library Manuscripts Egerton 3031, Harley 1708 and Cotton Vespasian E XXV. Edited by B. R. Kemp. 2 vols. London, 1986–87.

Recueil des Actes de Henri II, roi d'Angleterre et duc de Normandie, concernant les provinces françaises et les affaires de France. Edited by L. Delisle and E. Berger. 4 vols. Paris, 1906–27.

Recueil des historiens des Gaules et de la France. Publiée sous la direction de M. Léopold Delisle et édité par Martin Bourquet. Westmead, 1967.

Red Book of the Exchequer. Edited by Hubert Hall. 3 vols. London, 1896.

Regesta Regum Anglo-Normannorum, 1066–1154. III, *1135–1154.* Edited by H. A. Cronne and R. H. C. Davis. Oxford, 1968.

Richard of Hexham. "*Historia Ricardi, Prioris Ecclesiae Haugustaldensis, De Gesta Regis Stephani.*" In *Chronicles of the Reigns of Stephen, Henry II and Richard I,* edited by R. Howlett, III: 137–78. 4 vols. London, 1884–90.

Robert de Torigny. (i) "*Chronica Roberti de Torigneio, Abbatis Monasterii Sancti Michaelis in Periculo Maris.*" In *Chronicles of the Reigns of Stephen, Henry II and Richard I,* edited by R. Howlett, IV: 81–315. 4 vols. London, 1884–90; (ii) *Chronique de Robert de Torigni.* Edited by L. Delisle. 2 vols. Rouen, 1872.

Roger of Howden. *Chronica Rogeri de Houedene.* Edited by William Stubbs. 4 vols. London, 1868–71.

——. *Gesta Regis Henrici Secundi.* Edited by William Stubbs. 2 vols. London, 1867.

Select Charters and Other Illustrations of English Constitutional History from the Earliest Times to the Reign of Edward the First. Edited by William Stubbs. Oxford, 1900.

Suger, Abbot of Saint-Denis. *Vie de Louis le Gros par Suger, suivie de l'Histoire du Roi Louis VII.* Edited by A. Molinier. Paris, 1887.

Symeon of Durham. "*Historia Regum.*" In *Symeonis Monachi opera omnia,* edited by Thomas Arnold, II: 3–283. 2 vols. London, 1882–85.

Thomas Rhymer. *Foedera, Conventiones, Litterae, et Acta Publica.* Edited by A. Clarke and F. Holbrooke. 7 vols. London, 1816–69.

Vita Aedwardi Regis: The Life of King Edward Who Rests at Westminster, Attributed to a Monk of St. Bertin. Edited and translated by Frank Barlow. London, 1962.

Wace. (i) *Le Roman de Brut.* Edited by Le Roux Lincy. 2 vols. Rouen, 1836–38; (ii) *Le Roman de Brut.* Edited by Ivor Arnold. 2 vols. Paris, 1938, 1940; (iii) *Wace's Roman de Brut, A History of the British People: Text and Translation.* Edited and translated by Judith Weiss. Exeter, 1999.

Walter Map. *De Nugis Curialum*. Edited by M. R. James. Oxford, 1914.

William of Jumièges, Orderic Vitalis, and Robert of Torigny. *Gesta Normannorum ducum (GND)*. (i) *Guillaume de Jumièges, Gesta Normannorum ducum*. Edited by Jean Marx. Caen, 1914; (ii) *The Gesta Normannorum ducum of William of Jumièges, Orderic Vitalis and Robert of Torigni*. Edited and translated by Elisabeth M. C. van Houts. 2 vols. Oxford, 1992–95.

William of Malmesbury. (i) *De gestis regum Anglorum Willelmi Malmesbiriensis Monachi*. Edited by W. Stubbs. 2 vols. London, 1887–89; (ii) *William of Malmesbury, Gesta regum Anglorum: The History of the English Kings*. Edited and translated by R. A. B. Mynors, completed by R. M. Thomson and M. Winterbottom. 2 vols. Oxford, 1998–99.

——. *Historia Novella*. Edited by K. R. Potter. London, 1955.

William of Newburgh. "*Historia rerum Anglicarum*." In *Chronicles of the Reigns of Stephen, Henry II and Richard I*, edited by R. Howlett, I:1–408 and II:409–53. 4 vols. London, 1884–90.

William of Poitiers. *The Gesta Guillelmi of William of Poitiers*. Edited and translated by R. H. C. Davis and Majorie Chibnall. Oxford, 1998.

Secondary Studies

Aird, William M. "Frustrated Masculinity: The Relationship between William the Conqueror and His Eldest Son." In *Masculinity in Medieval Europe*, edited by Dawn M. Hadley, 39–55. Harlow, 1999.

——. "Northern England or Southern Scotland? The Anglo-Scottish Border in the Eleventh and Twelfth Centuries and the Problem of Perspective." In *Government, Religion and Society in Northern England, 1000–1700*, edited by John C. Appleby and Paul Dalton, 27–39. Stroud, 1997.

——. *Robert Curthose*. Woodbridge, 2008.

Albu, Emily. "Dudo of Saint-Quentin: The Heroic Past Imagined." *HSJ* 6 (1994): 111–18.

——. *The Normans in Their Histories: Propaganda, Myth and Subversion*. Woodbridge, 2001.

Althoff, Gerd. *Family, Friends, and Followers: Political and Social Bonds in Medieval Europe*. Cambridge, 2004.

Althoff, Gerd, Johannes Fried, and Patrick Geary, eds. *Medieval Concepts of the Past*. Cambridge, 2002.

Amore, Agostino. "Culto e Canonizzazione dei Santi nell'antichitá Cristiana." *Antonianum* 52 (1977): 38–80.

——. "La canonizazzione vescovile." *Antonianum* 52 (1977): 231–66.

Amt, Emilie. *The Accession of Henry II in England: Royal Government Restored, 1149–1159*. New York, 1993.

Anderson, Carolyn B. "Double Vision: Historiographers, Chroniclers, Romances, and the Invention of Royal Character, 1050–1377." PhD diss., Stanford University, 1992. *Dissertation Abstracts International* 59 (1993).

——. "Narrating Matilda, 'Lady of the English,' in the *Historia novella*, the *Gesta Stephani*, and Wace's *Roman de Rou*: The Desire for Land and Order." *Clio* 29 (1999): 47–67.

——. "Wace's *Roman de Rou* and Henry II's Court: Character and Power." *Romance Quarterly* 47 (2000): 67–82.

Andresen, Hugo. "Über die von Benoît in seiner normannischen Chronik benutzen Quellen, insbesondere über sein Verhältnis zu Dudo, Wilhelm von Jumièges und Wace." *Romanische Forschungen* 1 (1883): 327–412, and 2 (1886): 477–538

——. "Zu Benoît's *Chronique des ducs de Normandie.*" *Zeitschrift für romanische Philologie* 11 (1888): 231–40 and 345–70.

——. "Zu Wace's *Rou*, Bd. II 50 v. 511 und 529." *Zeitschrift für romanische Philologie* 12 (1888): 525–26.

Arnoux, Matthew. "Before the *Gesta Normannorum* and beyond Dudo: Some Evidence on Early Norman Historiography." *ANS* 22 (2000): 29–48.

Ashe, Laura. *Fiction and History in England, 1066–1200.* Cambridge, 2007.

Aurell, Martin. *La cour Plantagenêt (1154–1204): Actes du colloque tenu à Thouars du 30 avril au 2 mai 1999 sous la direction de Martin Aurell.* Poitiers, 2000.

——. *L'empire des Plantagenêt.* Paris, 2003.

Bachrach, Bernard. "Henry II and the Angevin Tradition of Family Hostility." *Albion* 16 (1984): 112–30.

Barlow, Frank. "The Constitutions of Clarendon." *Medieval History* 1/1 (1991): 39–52.

——. *Edward the Confessor.* Berkeley, 1970.

——. "English Kings and the Church (1066–1154)." *Medieval History* 3 (1993): 171–77.

——. *The Feudal Kingdom of England, 1042–1216.* London, 1988.

——. *Thomas Becket.* London, 1986.

——. *William Rufus.* New Haven, 2000.

Bartlett, Robert. *England under the Norman and Angevin Kings, 1075–1225.* New York, 2000.

Bates, David. *Normandy before 1066.* London, 1982.

Bates, David, and Anne Curry, eds. *England and Normandy in the Middle Ages.* London, 1994.

Bauduin, Pierre. "Chefs normands et élites franques, fin IXe–début Xe siècle." In *Les Fondations scandinaves en Occident et les débuts du duché de Normandie. Colloque de Cerisy-la-Salle (25–29 septembre 2002)*, edited by Pierre Bauduin, 181–194. Caen, 2005.

Baumgartner, Emmanuèle. "Écrire, disent-ils. À propos de Wace et de Benoît de Saint-Maure." In *Figures de l'écrivain au Moyen Age: Actes du Centre d'Études Médiévales de l'Université de Picardie (Amiens, 18–20 mars 1988)*, edited by D. Buschinger, 37–47. Göppingen, 1991. Reprinted in *De l'Histoire de Troie au livre du Graal: Le temps, le récit (XIIe–XIIIe siècles)*, 15–25. Orléans, 1994.

Bautier, R.-H. "L'historiographie en France aux Xe et XIe siécles." In *La storiografia altomedievale. Settimane di studio del centro italiano di studi sull'alto medioevo* 17/2: 793–850. Spoleto, 1970.

Becker, Philippe Auguste. *Der gepaarter Achtsilber in der französischen Dichtung.* Abhandlungen der philologisch-historischen Klasse der Sächsischen Akademie der Wissenschafte 43, 1. Leipzig, 1934.

——. "Die Normannenchroniken: Wace und seine Bearbeiter." *Zeitschrift für romanische Philologie* 63 (1943): 481–519.

Beckerman, John. "Succession in Normandy, 1087, and in England, 1066: The Role of Testamentary Custom." *Speculum* 47/2 (1972): 258–60.

Bédier, Joseph. "Richard de Normandie dans les chansons de geste." *Romanic Review* 1 (1910): 113–24.

Beeler, John. *Warfare in England, 1066–1189.* Ithaca, 1966.

Bennett, Matthew. "Poetry as History? The *Roman de Rou* of Wace as a Source for the Norman Conquest." *ANS* 5 (1983): 21–39.

——. "Stereotype Normans in Old French Vernacular Literature." *ANS* 9 (1987): 25–42.

——. "Wace and Warfare." *ANS* 11 (1989): 37–57. Reprinted in *Anglo-Norman Warfare: Studies in Late Anglo-Saxon and Anglo-Norman Military Organization and Warfare*, edited by M. Strickland, 230–50. Woodbridge, 1992.

Bennett, Philip E. "La Chronique de Jordan Fantosme: Épique et public lettré au XIIe siècle." *CCM* 40/1 (1997): 37–56.

——. "L'Épique dans l'historiographie anglo-normande: Gaimar, Wace, Jordan Fantosme." In *Aspects de l'épopée romane: Mentalité, idélogies, intertextualité*, edited by H. van Dijk and W. Noomen, 321–39. Groningen, 1995.

Benton, John F. " 'Nostre Franceis n'unt talent de fuïr;' The Song of Roland and the Enculturation of a Warrior Class." *Olifant* 6 (1979): 237–58.

Bernstein, Dorothy. "The Blinding of Harold and the Meaning of the Bayeux Tapestry." *ANS* 5 (1982): 40–64.

Berthelot, Anne. *Histoire de la littérature française du Moyen Âge.* Rennes, 2006.

Bezzola, Reto R. *Les Origines et la formation de la littérature courtoise en occident (550–1200).* 3 vols. Paris, 1958–63.

Bibliothèque national de France. *Catalogue général des manuscrits français.* 18 vols. Paris, 1868–1918.

Billoré, Maïté. "Y a t-il une 'oppression' des Plantagenêt sur l'aristocratie en Normandie à la veille de 1204?" In *Plantagenêts et Capétiens: Confrontations et héritages*, edited by Martin Aurell and Noël-Yves Tonnerre, 145–61. Histoires de famille: La parenté au Moyen Age 4. Turnhout, 2006.

Bisson, Thomas. *The Crisis of the Twelfth Century: Power, Lordship, and the Origins of European Government.* Princeton, 2009.

Blacker, Jean. " 'Dame Custance la gentil': Gaimar's Portrait of a Lady and Her Books." In *The Court and Cultural Diversity: Selected Papers from the Eighth Triennial Congress of the International Courtly Literature Society, The Queen's University of Belfast, 26 July–1 August 1995*, edited by Evelyn Mullally and John Thompson, 109–19. Woodbridge, 1997.

——. *The Faces of Time: Portrayal of the Past in Old French and Latin Historical Narrative of the Anglo-Norman Regnum.* Austin, 1994.

——. " 'La geste est grande, longue et grieve a translater': History for Henry II." *Romance Quarterly* 37 (1990): 387–96.

——. "Where Wace Feared to Tread: Latin Commentaries on Merlin's Prophecies in the Reign of Henry II." *Arthuriana* 6/1 (1996): 36–52.

Blacker-Knight, Jean. "Transformations of a Theme: The Depoliticization of the Arthurian World in the *Roman de Brut*." In *The Authurian Tradition: Essays in Convergence*, edited by Mary Flowers Braswell and John Bugge, 54–57. Tuscaloosa, AL, 1988.

———. "Wace's Craft and His Audience: Historical Truth, Bias, and Patronage in the *Roman de Rou*." *Kentucky Romance Quarterly* 31 (1984): 355–63.

Bloch, Marc. *Feudal Society*. Translated by L. A. Manyon. 2 vols. Chicago, 1965.

Blumenfeld-Kosinski, Renate. "The Earliest Developments of the French Novel: The *Roman de Thèbes* in Verse and Prose." In *The French Novel: Theory and Practice*, 1–10. French Literature Series 10. Columbia, SC, 1984.

———. "The Gods as Metaphor in the *Roman de Thèbes*." *Modern Philology* 83 (1985): 1–11.

———. "Introduction: The Middle Ages." In *The Politics of Translation in the Middle Ages and the Renaissance*, edited by Renate Blumenfeld-Kosinski, Luise von Flotow, and Daniel Russell, 17–27. Ottawa, 2001.

———. "Old French Narrative Genres: Towards a Definition of the *Roman Antique*." *Romance Philology* 34 (1980): 143–59.

Blumenfeld-Kosinski, Renate, Duncan Robertson, and Nancy Bradley Warren, eds. *The Vernacular Spirit: Essays on Medieval Religious Literature*. New York, 2002.

Boissonnade, P. "Les comtes d'Angoulême: Les ligues féodales contre Richard Coeur de Lion et les Poésies de Bertran de Born (1176–1194)." *Annales du Midi* 7 (1895): 275–95.

Bongert, Yvonne. *Recherches sur les cours Laïques de Xe au XIIIe siècles.* Paris, 1949.

Bossuat, Robert. *Le Moyen Âge.* Paris, 1931.

Boussard, J. *Le comté d'Anjou sous Henri Plantagenêt et ses fils (1151–1204).* Paris, 1938.

———. "L'enquête de 1172 sur les fiefs de chevalier en Normandie." In *Recueil de travaux offert à M. Clovis Brunel—par ses amis, collègues et élèves*, I:193–208. 2 vols. Paris, 1955.

———. *Le gouvernement d'Henri II Plantagenêt.* Paris: Librarie d'Argences, 1956.

Bradbury, Jim. "Fulk le Réchin and the Origin of the Plantagenets." In *Studies in Medieval History Presented to R. Allen Brown*, edited by Christopher Harper-Bill, Christopher J. Holdsworth, and Janet L. Nelson, 27–41. Woodbridge, 1989.

———. "Geoffrey V of Anjou, Count and Knight." In *The Ideals and Practice of Medieval Knighthood III. Papers from the Fourth Strawberry Hill Conference 1988*, edited by Christopher Harper-Bill and Ruth Harvey, 21–38. Woodbridge, 1990.

———. *Stephen and Matilda: The Civil War of 1139–1153.* Far Thrupp, 1996.

Braet, Herman. "Le Songe de l'arbre chez Wace, Benoît et Aimon de Varennes." *Romania* 91 (1970): 255–67.

Brand, Paul A. " 'Multis vigiliis excogitatam et inventam': Henry II and the Creation of the English Common Law." *HSJ* 2 (1990): 197–222.

Brial, Michel-Jean-Jacques. "Robert Wace, chanoine de Bayeaux, historien-poète." *Histoire Littéraire de la France* 13 (1869): 518–30.

Broadhurst, Karen M. "Henry II of England and Eleanor of Aquitaine: Patrons of Literature in French?" *Viator* 27 (1996): 53–84.

Brooke, Z. N., and C. N. L. Brooke. "Henry II, Duke of Normany and Aquitaine." *EHR* 61 (1946): 81–89.

Brooks, Nicholas, ed. *Latin and the Vernacular Languages in Early Medieval Britain*. Leicester, 1982.

Brosnahan, Leger M. N. "A Collation of Wace's *La Geste des Normanz*." *Manuscripta* 16 (1972): 83–97.

Brown, R. A. *English Medieval Castles*. London, 1954.

——. "Framlingham Castle and Bigod." *Proceedings of the Suffolk Institute of Natural History and Archaeology* 25 (1950): 127–48.

——. "Royal Castle Building in England, 1154–1216." *EHR* 70 (1955): 353–98.

Buda, Milada. *Medieval History and Discourse: Toward a Topography of Textuality*. New York, 1990.

Bull, Marcus, ed. *France in the Central Middle Ages (900–1200)*. Oxford, 2002.

Buttrey, Dolores. "Authority Refracted: Personal Principle and Translation in Wace's *Roman de Brut*." In *The Politics of Translation in the Middle Ages and the Renaissance*, edited by Renate Blumenfeld-Kosinski, Luise von Flotow, and Daniel Russell, 85–106. Ottawa, 2001.

Carruthers, Mary. *The Book of Memory: A Study of Memory in Medieval Culture*. Cambridge, 1990.

Carruthers, Mary J., and Elizabeth D. Kirk, eds. *Acts of Interpretation: The Text in Its Contexts, 700–1600: Essays on Medieval and Renaissance Literature in Honor of E. Talbot Donaldson*. Norman, OK, 1982.

Cazauran, Nicole. "Richard sans Peur: Un personage en quête d'auteur." *Travaux de Littérature* 4 (1991): 21–43.

Chance, Jane. *Medieval Mythography*. Gainesville, 1994.

Chauou, Amaury. *L'idéologie Plantagenêt: Royauté arthurienne et monarchie politique dans l'espace Plantagenêt, XIIe–XIIIe siècles*. Rennes, 2001.

Chibnall, Marjorie. *Anglo-Norman England, 1066–1166*. Oxford, 1993.

——. "The Empress Matilda and Her Sons." In *Medieval Mothering*, edited by John Carmi Parsons and Bonnie Wheeler, 279–94. New York, 1996.

——. *The Empress Matilda: Queen Consort, Queen Mother, and Lady of the English*. Oxford, 1991.

——. "L'avènement au pouvoir d'Henri II." *CCM* 37/1–2 (1994): 41–48.

——. *The Normans*. Oxford, 2000.

——. *The World of Orderic Vitalis: Norman Monks and Norman Knights*. Woodbridge, 1984.

Clanchy, Michael. *From Memory to Written Record: England 1066–1307*. Oxford, 1993.

——. "Remembering the Past and the Good Old Law." *History* 55 (1970): 165–75.

——. "The Written Word: From Domesday Book to Caxton." In *The Making of Britain: The Dark Ages*, edited by Lesley M. Smith, 163–77. London, 1984.

Coleman, Janet. *Ancient and Medieval Memories: Studies in the Reconstruction of the Past*. Cambridge, 1992.

Copeland, Rita. *Criticism and Dissent in the Middle Ages*. Cambridge, 1996.

———. *Rhetoric, Hermeneutics, and Translation in the Middle Ages: Academic Traditions and Vernacular Texts*. Cambridge, 1991.

Cooper, Alan. "'The Feet of Those That Bark Shall Be Cut Off': Timorous Historians and the Personality of Henry I." *ANS* 23 (2001): 47–67.

Crane, Susan. *Insular Romance: Politics, Faith, and Culture in Anglo-Norman and Middle English Literature*. Berkeley, 1986.

Crouch, David. *The Beaumont Twins: The Roots and Branches of Power in the Twelfth Century*. Cambridge, 1986.

———. *The Birth of Nobility: Constructing Aristocracy in England and France, 900–1300*. New York, 2005.

———. *The Image of Aristocracy in Britain, 1000–1300*. London, 1992.

———. *The Reign of King Stephen, 1135–1154*. London, 2000.

———. *William Marshall: Court, Career, and Chivalry in the Angevin Empire, 1147–1219*. London, 1990.

Curley, Michael. *Geoffrey of Monmouth*. New York, 1994.

Damian-Grint, Peter. "*En nul leu nel truis escrit*: Research and Invention in Benoît de Sainte-Maure's Chronique des ducs de Normandie." *ANS* 21 (1999): 11–30.

———. "*Estoire* as Word and Genre." *Medium Aevum* 66 (1997): 189–99.

———. "Learning and Authority in Benoît de Sainte-Maure's Cosmography." *Reading Medieval Studies* 24 (1998): 25–52.

———. *The New Historians of the Twelfth-Century Renaissance: Inventing Vernacular Authority*. Woodbridge, 1999.

———. "Robert Courteheuse et Henri Beauclerc, frères ennemis dans les estoires de Wace et de Benoît." Academia.edu. http://www.academia.edu/1883723 /Robert_Courteheuse_et_Henri_Beauclerc_freres_ennemis_dans_les_ estoires_de_Wace_et_de_Benoit (accessed March 14, 2013).

———. "Truth, Trust and Evidence in the Anglo-Norman *estoire*." *ANS* 18 (1996): 63–72.

Darlington, Reginald, R. *Anglo-Norman Historians*. London, 1947.

David, Charles Wendell. *Robert Curthose, Duke of Normandy*. Cambridge, MA., 1920.

Davis, R. H. C. *King Stephen, 1135–1154*. Berkeley, 1967.

———. *The Normans and Their Myth*. London, 1976.

Dean, Ruth. *Anglo-Norman Literature: A Guide to Texts and Manuscripts*. London, 1999.

de Boüard, M. "À Propos des sources du *Roman de Rou*." In *Recueil de travaux offert à M. Clovis Brunel–par ses amis, collègues et élèves*, I: 178–82. 2 vols. Paris, 1955.

de Bréquigny, Louis-Georges Oudart Feudrix. "Notice du *Roman de Rou et des ducs de Normandie*, manuscrit de la Bibliothèque Nationale 6987; autre coté 75672: manuscrit de la Bibliothèque de l'Arsenal, intitulé au dos, Roman De Rou." *Notices et Extraits des Manuscrits de la Bibliothèque Nationale* 5 (1795): 21–78.

Deliyannis, Deborah Mauskopf, ed. *Historiography in the Middle Ages*. Leiden, 2003.

Diggelmann, Lindsay. "Marriage as Tactical Response: Henry II and the Royal Wedding of 1160." *EHR* 119/483 (2004): 954–64.

Dor, Juliette. "Langues française et anglaise, et multilinguisme à l'époque d'Henri II Plantagenêt." *CCM* 37/1–2 (1994): 61–72.

Douglas, David C. "Companions of the Conqueror." *History* 27 (1943): 129–47.

——. *The Norman Achievement*. Berkeley, 1969.

——. "Rollo of Normandy." *EHR* 57 (1942): 417–36.

——. *William the Conqueror: The Norman Impact upon England*. Berkeley, 1964.

Duby, Georges. *The Chivalrous Society*. Berkeley, 1977.

——. "The Culture of the Knightly Class: Audience and Patronage." In *Renaissance and Renewal in the Twelfth-Century*, 248–262. Oxford, 1982.

——. *Dames du XIIe siècle: Héloïse, Aliénor, Iseut et quelques autres*. Paris, 1995.

——. "Dans la France du Nord-Ouest au XIIe siècle: Les 'jeunes' dans la société aristocratique." *Annales* 24 (1964): 835–46.

——. *The Knight, the Lady, and the Priest: The Making of Modern Marriage in Medieval France*. Translated by Barbara Bray. New York, 1983.

——. *William Marshal: The Flower of Chivalry*. New York, 1985.

Duggan, Anne. "*Ne in dubium*: The Official Record of Henry II's Reconciliation at Avranches, 21 May 1172." *EHR* 115/462 (2000): 643–58.

——. *Thomas Becket*. Oxford, 2004.

du Meril, E. "La vie et les ouvrages de Wace." *Jahrbuch für Romanische und Englische Literatur* I (1859): 1–8.

Dunbabin, Jean. *Captivity and Imprisonment in Medieval Europe, 1000–1300*. New York, 2002.

Ehlers, Joachim. "Die 'Historia Francorum Senonensis' und der Aufstieg des Hauses Capet." *Journal of Medieval History* 4/1 (1978): 1–24 and 107.

Eley, Penny. "History and Romance in the *Chronique des Ducs de Normandie*." *Medium Aevum* 68 (1999): 81–95.

Eley, Penny, and Bennett, Philip E. "The Battle of Hastings according to Gaimar, Wace and Benoît: Rhetoric and Politics." *Nottingham Medieval Studies* 43 (1999): 47–78.

Eyton, R. W. *Court, Household, and Itinerary of Henry II*. London, 1878.

Fahlin, Carin. *Etude sur le manuscrit de Tours de la Chronique des ducs de Normandie par Benoît*. Uppsala, 1937.

Farmer, Sharon. *Communities of Saint Martin: Legend and Ritual in Medieval Tours*. Ithaca, 1991.

Fawtier, Robert. *The Capetian Kings of France: Monarchy and Nation, 987–1328*. Translated by Lionel Butler and R. J. Adam. London, 1960.

Ferster, Judith. *Fictions of Advice: The Literature and Politics of Counsel in Late Medieval England*. Philadelphia, 1996.

Flint, Valerie I. J. "The *Historia regum Britanniae* of Geoffrey of Monmouth: Parody and Its Purpose, a Suggestion." *Speculum* 54/3 (1979): 447–68.

Frappier, J. "Vues sur les conceptions courtoises dans les littératures d'oc et d'oïl au XIIe siècle." *CCM* 2 (1959): 135–56.

Freeman, Edward A. *The History of the Norman Conquest of England, Its Causes and Its Results*. New York, 1873.

Fryde, E. B. and D. H. Greenway. *Handbook of British Chronology*. Cambridge, 1996.

Fuch, Barbara. *Romance*. New York, 2004.

Galbraith, Vivian H. "The Literacy of the English Medieval Kings." *Proceedings of the British Academy* 21 (1935): 201–37. Reprinted in *Kings and Chroniclers: Essays in English Medieval History*, edited by V. H. Galbraith, 78–111. London, 1982.

Garnett, George. *Conquered England: Kingship, Succession, and Tenure 1066–1166*. Oxford, 2007.

———. "'Franci et Angli': The Legal Distinction between Peoples after the Conquest." *ANS* 8 (1986): 109–37.

Geary, Patrick. *Phantoms of Remembrance: Memory and Oblivion at the End of the First Millennium*. Princeton, 1994.

Genestal, Robert. "La formation du droit d'aînesse dans la coutume de Normandie." In *Travaux de la Semaine d'histoire du droit normand tenue à Jersey du 24 au 27 mai 1923, avec le concours de la Société des gens de droit de Jersey, de la Société jersiaise et de la Société d'histoire du droit normand, sous la présidence de Sir W. Venables Vernon et de M. E. Pilon*, 221–40. Caen, 1928.

Gillingham, John. *The Angevin Empire*. London, 1984.

———. "The Context and Purposes of Geoffrey of Monmouth's *History of the Kings of Britain*." *ANS* 8 (1991): 99–118.

———. "The Cultivation of History, Legend, and Courtesy at the Court of Henry II." In *Writers of the Reign of Henry II*, edited by Ruth Kennedy and Simon Meecham-Jones, 25–52. New York, 2006.

———. *The English in the Twelfth Century: Imperialism, National Identity, and Political Values*. Woodbridge, 2000.

———. "Gaimar, the Prose *Brut*, and the Making of English History." In John Gillingham. *The English in the Twelfth Century: Imperialism, National Identity, and Political Values*, 113–22. Woodbridge, 2000.

———. *Richard I*. London, 2002.

Glenn, Jason. *Politics and History in the Tenth Century: The Work and World of Richer of Reims*. Cambridge, 2004.

Gneuss, Helmut. *Language and History in Early England*. Aldershot, 1996.

Goetz, Hans-Werner. *Geschichtsschreibung und Geschichtsbewusstein im hohen Mittelalter*. Berlin, 1999.

Goetz, Hans-Werner, ed. *Hochmittelalterliches Geschichtsbewusstsein im Spiegel nichthistoriographischer Quellen*. Berlin, 1998.

Goez, Werner. *Translatio Imperii*. Tübingen, 1958.

Goffart, Walter A. *The Narrators of Barbarian History (A.D. 550–800): Jordanes, Gregory of Tours, Bede, and Paul the Deacon*. Princeton, 1988.

Gouttebroze, Jean-Guy. "Entre les historiographes d'expression latine et les jongleurs: Le clerc lisant." In *Le Clerc au moyen âge*, 215–30. Aix-en-Provence, 1995.

———. "Exclusion et intégration des Normands Hasting et Rollon." In *Exclus et systèmes d'exclusion dans la littérature et la civilisation médiévales*, 299–311. Aix-en-Provence, 1975.

——. "Henry II Plantagenêt: Patron des historiographes anglo-normands de langue d'oïl." In *La Littérature angevine médiévale: actes du colloque du samedi 22 mars 1980*, 91–105. Angers, 1981.

——. "Le Diable dans le *Roman de Rou*." In *Le Diable au Moyen Âge: Doctrine, problèmes moraux, représentations*, 213–34. Aix-en-Provence, 1979.

——. *Le Précieux Sang de Fécamp*. Paris, 2004.

——. "Pourquoi congédier un historiographe, Henri II Plantagenêt et Wace (1155–1174)." *Romania* 112 (1991): 289–311.

Gransden, Antonia. *Historical Writing in England*. 2 vols. London, 1974–82.

——. *Legends, Traditions, and History in Medieval England*. London, 1992.

Green, Dennis. *The Beginnings of Medieval Romance: Fact and Fiction, 1150–1220*. Cambridge, 2002.

Green, Judith A. *The Aristocracy of Norman England*. Cambridge, 1997.

——. *The Government of England under Henry I*. Cambridge, 1986.

——. "Henry I and the Origins of the Court Culture of the Plantagenets." In *Plantagenêts et Capétiens: Confrontations et héritages*, edited by Martin Aurell and Noël-Yves Tonnerre, 485–95. Histoires de famille: La parenté au Moyen Age 4. Turnhout, 2006.

——. *Henry I: King of England and Duke of Normandy*. Cambridge, 2006.

——. "King Henry I and the Aristocracy of Normandy." In *La "France anglaise" au Moyen Age, colloque des historiens médiévistes français et britanniques. Actes du 111e Congrès national des sociétés savantes (Poitiers, 1986), Section d'histoire médiévale et de philologie*, I, 161–73. Paris, 1988.

——. "'A Lasting Memorial': The Charter of Liberties of Henry I." In *Charters and Charter Scholarship in Britain and Ireland*, edited by Marie Therese Flanagan and Judith A. Green, 53–69. Basingstoke, 2005.

——. "Le gouvernement d'Henri Ier Beauclerc en Normandie." In *La Normandie et l'Angleterre au Moyen Age. Acts du Colloque de Cerisy-la-Salle (4–7 octobre 2001)*, edited by Pierre Bouet and Véronique Gazeau, 61–73. Caen, 2003.

——. "Robert Curthose Reassessed." *ANS* 22 (2000): 95–116.

Greenway, Diana. "Authority, Convention and Observation in Henry of Huntingdon's *Historia Anglorum*." *ANS* 18 (1996): 105–21.

Grundmann, Herbert. *Geschichtsschreibung im Mittelalter*. Göttingen, 1965.

Guenée, Bernard. *Histoire et culture historique dans l'Occident médiéval*. Paris, 1980.

——. *Politique et histoire au Moyen Âge: Recueil d'articles sur l'histoire politique et l'historiographie médiévale (1956–1981)*. Paris, 1981.

Guillot, Olivier. "La conversion des Normands à partir de 911." In *Histoire religieuse de la Normandie*, edited by Brigitte Beaujard, 23–53. Chambray, 1981.

——. "La conversion des Normands peu après 911: Des reflets contemporains à l'historiographie ultérieure (Xe–XIe s.)." *CCM* 24 (1981): 101–16 and 181–219.

Hall, H. *Court Life under the Plantagenets*. London, 1890.

Hanning, Robert W. *The Vision of History in Early Britain: From Gildas to Geoffrey of Monmouth*. New York, 1966.

Hardy, Thomas Duffus. *Descriptive Catalogue of Materials relating to the History of Great Britain and Ireland, to the End of the Reign of Henry VII.* 3 vols. London, 1862–71; New York, 1966.

Harford, Thomas J. *A Comprehensive Study of Layamon's Brut.* Lewiston, NY, 2002.

Haskins, Charles H. "Henry II as a Patron of Learning." In *Essays in Medieval History presented to T. F. Tout,* edited by A. G. Little and F. M. Powicke, 71–77. Manchester, 1925.

———. "The Materials for the Reign of Robert I of Normandy." *EHR* 31 (1916): 257–68.

———. "Normandy under Geoffrey Plantagenet." *EHR* 27 (July 1912): 417–44.

———. *Norman Institutions.* Cambridge, 1918.

Hen, Yitzhak and Matthew Innes, eds. *The Uses of the Past in the Early Middle Ages.* Cambridge, 2000.

Heslin, Anne. "The Coronation of the Young King in 1170." In *Papers Read at the Second Winter and Summer Meetings of the Ecclesiastical History Society,* edited by G. J. Cumming, 165–78. Studies in Church History 2. London, 1965.

Hicks, Sandy. "The Impact of William Clito upon the Continental Policies of Henry I of England." *Viator* 10 (1979): 1–21.

Holden, Anthony J. "De Nouveau le vers 3 du *Roman de Rou*: Á propos de deux articles récents." *Romania* 89 (1968): 105–15.

———. "L'Authenticité des premières parties du *Roman de Rou*." *Romania* 75 (1954): 22–53.

———. "Nouvelles remarques sur le texte du *Roman de Rou*." *Revue de Linquistique Romane* 45 (1981): 118–27.

Hollister, C. Warren. "The Anglo-Norman Civil War: 1101." *EHR* 88 (1973): 315–34.

———. "Anglo-Norman Political Culture and the Twelfth-Century Renaissance." In *Anglo-Norman Political Culture and the Twelfth-Century Renaissance,* edited by C. Warren Hollister, 1–16. Woodbridge, 1997.

———. "The Anglo-Norman Succession Debate of 1126: Prelude to Stephen's Anarchy." *Journal of Medieval History* 1/1 (1975): 19–41.

———. "The Campaign of 1102 against Robert of Bellême." In *Studies in Medieval History Presented to R. Allen Brown,* edited by Christopher Harper-Bill, Christopher J. Holdsworth, and Janet L. Nelson, 193–202. Woodbridge, 1989.

———. *Henry I.* New Haven, 2001.

———. "Henry I and the Anglo-Norman Magnates." *ANS* 2 (1980): 93–107, 184–88.

———. "Henry I and the Invisible Transformation of Medieval England." In *Studies in Medieval History Presented to R. H. C. Davis,* edited by Henry Mayr-Harting and R. I. Moore, 119–31. London, 1985.

———. *The Impact of the Norman Conquest.* New York, 1969.

———. "The Magnates of Stephen's Reign: Reluctant Anarchists." *HSJ* 5 (1993): 77–87.

———. *The Military Organization of Norman England.* Oxford, 1965.

------. *Monarchy, Magnates and Institutions in the Anglo-Norman World*. London, 1986.

------. "Normandy, France and the Anglo-Norman Regnum." *Speculum* 51 (1976): 202–42.

------. *The Twelfth-Century Renaissance*. New York, 1969.

------. "War and Diplomacy in the Anglo-Norman World: the Reign of Henry I." *ANS* 6 (1984): 72–88.

------. "William Rufus, Henry I, and the Anglo-Norman Church." *Peritia: Journal of the Medieval Academy of Ireland* 6–7 for 1987–88 (1993): 119–40.

Hollister, C. Warren. ed. *Anglo-Norman Political Culture and the Twelfth-Century Renaissance: Proceedings of the Borchard Conference on Anglo-Norman History, 1995*. Woodbridge, 1997.

Holmes, Urban T. "Norman Literature and Wace." In *Medieval Secular Literature: Four Essays*, edited by W. Matthews, 46–67. Berkeley, 1967.

Holt, James. "1153: The Treaty of Winchester." In J. C. Holt, *Colonial England, 1066–1215*, 271–90. London, 1997.

------. "The *Casus Regis*: the Law and Politics of Succession in the Plantagenet Dominions, 1185–1247." In J. C. Holt. *Colonial England, 1066–1215*, 307–26. London, 1997.

------. "Feudal Society and the Family in Early Medieval England: I. The Revolution of 1066." *TRHS* 5/32 (1982): 193–212.

------. "Feudal Society and the Family in Early Medieval England: II. Notions of Patrimony." *TRHS* 5/33 (1983): 193–220.

Howlett, David. *The English Origins of Old French Literature*. Portland, 1996.

Hudson, John. *The Formation of the English Common: Law and Society in England from the Norman Conquest to Magna Carta*. London, 1996.

------. *Land, Law and Lordship in Anglo-Norman England*. Oxford, 1994.

Hyams, Paul R. "Henri II comme juriste eut-il une politique de réforme?" *CCM* 37/1–2 (1994): 85–89.

Innes, Matthew. "Introduction: Using the Past, Interpreting the Present, Influencing the Future." In *The Uses of the Past in the Early Middle Ages*, edited by Yitsak Hen and Matthew Innes, 1–8. Cambridge, 2000.

Jackson, W. T. H. *The Challenge of the Medieval Text: Studies in Genre and Interpretation*. Edited by Joan M. Ferrante and Robert W. Hanning. New York, 1985.

Jaeger, C. Stephen. *The Origins of Courtliness: Civilizing Trends and the Formation of Courtly Ideals, 939–1210*. Philadelphia, 1985.

Jirmounsky, M. M. "Essai d'analyse des procédés littéraires de Wace." *Revue des Langues Romanes* 63 (1925): 261–96.

John, Eric. "Edward the Confessor and the Norman Succession." *EHR* 94 (1979): 241–67.

Johns, Susan. *Noblewomen, Aristocracy, and Power in the Twelfth-Century Anglo-Norman Realm*. Manchester, 2003.

Jolliffe, J. E. A. *Angevin Kingship*. London, 1963.

------. "The *Camera Regis* under Henry II." *EHR* 68 (1953): 1–21 and 337–62.

Jordan, Victoria B. "The Role of Kingship in Tenth-Century Normandy: Hagiography of Dudo of Saint-Quentin." *HSJ* 3 (1991): 53–62.

Kealey, Edward J. *Roger of Salisbury, Viceroy of England*. Berkeley, 1972.

Keefe, Thomas. *Feudal Assessments and the Political Community under Henry II and His Sons.* Berkeley, 1983.

———. "Geoffrey Plantagenet's Will and the Angevin Succession." *Albion* 6 (1974): 266–74.

Keller, Hans-Erich. "The Song of Roland and Its Audience." *Olifant* 6 (1979): 259–74.

Kemp, Eric. *Canonization and Authority in the Western Church.* London, 1948.

Kennedy, Ruth, and Simon Meecham-Jones, eds. *Writers of the Reign of Henry II: Twelve Essays.* New York, 2006.

Kibler, William W., ed. *Eleanor of Aquitaine, Patron and Politician.* Symposia in the Arts and the Humanities 3. Austin, 1976.

Krappe, Alexander H. "Le Songe de la mère de Guillaume le Conquérant." *Zeitschrift für französische Sprache und Literatur* 61 (1937): 198–204.

Kuttner, Stephan. "La réserve papale du droit de canonisation." *Revue historique de droit français et étranger* 4/18 (1938): 172–228.

Langille, Édouard. " 'Mençunge ou folie?' Commentaire sur la mise en 'romanz' de Wace." *Dalhousie French Studies* 39–40 (1997): 19–32.

Lawton, David, Wendy Scase, and Rita Copeland, eds. *New Medieval Literatures.* 3 vols. Oxford, 2000.

Leckie, R. William. *The Passage of Dominion: Geoffrey of Monmouth and the Periodization of Insular History in the Twelfth Century.* Toronto, 1981.

Legge, M. Dominica. *Anglo-Norman in the Cloisters: The Influence of the Order upon Anglo-Norman Literature.* Edinburgh, 1950.

———. *Anglo-Norman Literature and Its Background.* Westport, 1978.

———. "Clerc Lisant." *Modern Language Review* 47 (1952): 554–56.

———. "La précocité de la littérature anglo-normande." *CCM* 8 (1965): 327–49.

———. "L'influence littéraire de la cour d'Henri Beauclerc." In *Melanges offerts à Rita Lejeune*, 679–87. Gembloux, 1969.

Le Maho, Jacques. "Les Normands de la Seine à la fin du IX siècle." In *Les Fondations scandinaves en Occident et les débuts du duché de Normandie. Colloque de Cerisy-la-Salle (25–29 septembre 2002)*, 161–79. Edited by Pierre Baudin. Caen, 2005.

Lemarignier, J-F. *Recherches sur l'Hommage en March et les Frontières Fèodales.* Lille, 1945.

Le Patourel, John. *Feudal Empires: Norman and Plantagenet.* London, 1984.

———. *Norman Barons.* 1066 Commemoration Series of the Hastings and Bexhill Branch of the Historical Association 4. London, 1966.

———. *Normandy and England, 1066–1144.* Reading, 1971.

———. *The Norman Empire.* Oxford, 1976.

———. "The Norman Succession, 996–1135." *EHR* 86 (1971): 225–50.

LePetit, Jean. "La Normandie sous les premiers ducs d'après le *Roman de Rou*." *Art de Basse-Normandie* 63 (1974): 3–35.

Le Saux, Françoise H. M. *A Companion to Wace.* Cambridge, 2005.

Lewis, Andrew W. *Royal Succession in Capetian France: Studies on Familial Order and the State.* Cambridge, 1981.

Leyser, Karl. "The Anglo-Norman Succession, 1120–1125." *ANS* 8 (1991): 225–41.

Lifshitz, Felice. "Dudo's Historical Narrative and the Norman Succession of 996." *Journal of Medieval History* 20 (1994): 101–20.

Lot, Ferdinand. *Fideles ou Vassaux? Essai sur la nature juridique du lien qui unissait les grands vassaux à la royauté depuis le milieu du IXe jusqu'à la fin du XIIe siècle.* Paris, 1904.

Loud, G. A. "The 'Gens Normannorum'–Myth or Reality?" *ANS* 4 (1982): 104–16.

Lyons, Faith. "Clerc lisant and maître lisant." *Modern Language Review* 56 (1961): 224–25.

Mason, Emma. "Henry I: Decoding an Enigma." *Medieval History* 1/3 (1991): 17–33.

Matheson, Lister M. *The Prose Brut: The Development of a Middle English Chronicle.* Tempe, 1998.

Mayer, Lauryn S. *Worlds Made Flesh: Reading Medieval Manuscript Culture.* New York, 2004.

McKitterick, Rosamond. *The Carolingians and the Written Word.* Cambridge, 1989.

———. "Constructing the Past in the Early Middle Ages." *TRHS* 6/7 (1997): 101–30.

———. *The Frankish Kingdoms under the Carolingians, 751–987.* London, 1983.

———. *History and Its Audiences: Inaugural Lecture Given by Rosamond McKitterick in the University of Cambridge, 15 May 2000.* Cambridge, 2000.

———. *History and Memory in the Carolingian World.* Cambridge, 2004.

———. *Perceptions of the Past in the Early Middle Ages.* Notre Dame, 2006.

McKitterick, Rosamond, and Binski, Paul. "History and Literature: Sacred and Secular." In *The Cambridge Illuminations: Ten Centuries of Book Production in the Medieval West*, edited by Paul Binski and Stella Panayotova, 235–40. London, 2005.

Merkle, Stefan. "Telling the True Story of the Trojan War: The Eyewitness Account of Dictys of Crete." In *The Search for the Ancient Novel*, edited by James Tatum, 183–96. Baltimore, 1994.

Mooers, Stephanie. "Backers and Stabbers: Problems of Loyalty in Robert Curthose's Entourage." *Journal of British Studies* 21/1 (1981): 1–17.

Mooers, Stephanie Lleueen. "Networks of Power in Anglo-Norman England." *Medieval Prosopography* 7/2 (1986): 25–54.

———. "A Reevaluation of Royal Justice under Henry I of England." *American Historical Review* 93/2 (1988): 340–58.

Moore, O. H. *The Young King Henry Plantagenet (1155–1183) in History, Literature, and Tradition.* Columbus, 1925.

Morse, Ruth. *Truth and Convention in the Middle Ages: Rhetoric, Representation, and Reality.* Cambridge, 1991.

Mortimer, Richard. *Angevin England, 1154–1208.* Oxford, 1994.

———. *Edward the Confessor: The Man and the Legend.* Woodbridge, 2009.

Musset, Lucien. "Ce que l'on peut savoir du traité de Saint-Clair-sur-Epte." *Annuaire des cinq départements de Normandie* 147 (1981): 49–82. Reprinted in Lucien Musset, *Nordica et Normannica: Recueil d'études sur la Scandinavie ancienne et médiévale, les expéditions des Vikings et la fondation de la Normandie*, 377–81. Paris, 1997.

———. "Considérations sur la genèse et le tracé des frontières de la Normandie." In *Media in Francia: Recueil de mélanges offerts à Karl Ferdinand Werner*, edited by Georges Duby, 309–18. Paris, 1989. Reprinted in Lucien Musset, *Nordica et Normannica: Recueil d'études sur la Scandinavie ancienne et médiévale, les expéditions des Vikings et la fondation de la Normandie*, 403–13. Paris, 1997.

Nelson, Janet. "The Rites of the Conqueror." *ANS* 4 (1982): 117–32.

Newman, Charlotte E. *The Anglo-Norman Nobility in the Reign of Henry I: The Second Generation*. Philadelphia, 1988.

———. "Henry I's Old and New Men: Social History and Prosopography." *Medieval Prosopography* 1/2 (1980): 35–43.

Norgate, Kate. *England under the Angevin Kings*. 2 vols. London, 1887.

Ong, Walter. "Orality, Literacy, and Medieval Textualization." *New Literary History* 16/1 (1984): 1–12.

Orme, Nicholas. "Lay Literacy in England, 1100–1300." In *England and Germany in the High Middle Ages: Essays In Honour of Karl J. Leyser*, edited by Alfred Haverkamp and Hanna Vollrath, 35–56. Oxford, 1996.

Otter, Monika. *Inventiones: Fiction and Referentiality in Twelfth-Century English Historical Writing*. Chapel Hill, 1996.

Paris, Gaston. "Wace, *Roman de Rou*, hgg. von Andresen." *Romania* 9 (1880): 592–614.

Partner, Nancy. *Serious Entertainments: The Writing of History in Twelfth-Century England*. Chicago, 1977.

Partner, Nancy, ed. *Writing Medieval History*. Oxford, 2005.

Peltzer, Jörg. "Henry II and the Norman Bishops." *EHR* 119/484 (2004): 1202–29.

Philipot, J. H. *Maistre Wace, a Pioneer in Two Literatures*. London, 1925.

Poole, A. L. "Henry Plantagenet's Early Visits to England." *EHR* 47 (1932): 447–52.

Poole, R. L. "The Dates of Henry II's Charters." *EHR* 22 (1908): 79–83.

———. "Henry II Duke of Normandy." *EHR* 42 (1927): 569–72.

Potts, Cassandra. "'Atque unum ex diversis gentibus populum effecit': Historical Tradition and the Norman Identity." *ANS* 28 (1996): 139–52.

Powicke, F. M. "The Angevin Administration of Normandy." *EHR* 21 (1906): 625–49; and 22 (1907): 15–42.

———. *The Loss of Normandy, 1189–1204: Studies in the History of the Angevin Empire*. Manchester, 1961.

Richardson, H. G. "The Letters and Charters of Eleanor of Aquitaine." *EHR* 74 (1959): 193–213.

Ritchie, R. L. G. *The Normans in Scotland*. Edinburgh, 1953.

Roblin, Michel. "Petromantalum, Saint-Clair et le Vexin." *Journal des savants* 1 (1976): 3–31.

Rollo, David. *Historical Fabrication, Ethnic Fable, and French Romance in Twelfth-Century England*. Lexington, 1998.

Round, J. H. *Feudal England: Historical Studies on the Eleventh and Twelfth Centuries*. London, 1964.

———. "A Glimpse of the Young King's Court." *Feudal England* (1964): 381–84.

——. "Mr. Freeman and the Battle of Hastings." *EHR* 9 (1894): 209–60. Reprinted in *Feudal England: Historical Studies on the Eleventh and Twelfth Centuries*, edited by J. H. Round, 258–321. London, 1964.

——. "Wace and His Authorities." *EHR* 8 (1893): 677–83.

Sanders, I. J. *English Baronies. A Study of Their Origin and Descent, 1086–1327.* Oxford, 1960.

Sassier, Yves. *Louis VII.* Paris, 1991.

Sauvage, R. N. *L'Abbaye de Saint-Martin de Troarn au diocese de Bayeux des origins au seizième siècle.* Caen, 1911.

Sayers, William. "The *jongleur* Taillefer at Hastings: Antecedents and Literary Fate." *Viator* 14 (1983): 79–88.

——. "Old French *s'esterchir:* Horse Rearing and Rearing Horses." *Romanische Forschungen* 106 (1994): 217–24.

Scammell, Jean. "The Formation of the English Social Structure: Freedom, Knights, and Gentry, 1066–1300." *Speculum* 68/3 (1993): 591–618.

Schimmelpfennig, Bernhard. "Heilige Päpste-päpstliche Kanonisationspolitik." In *Politik und Heiligenverehrung im Hochmittelalter,* edited by Jürgen Petersohn, 73–100. Vorträge und Forschungen, 42. Sigmaringen, 1994.

Schirmer, Walter F. and Brioch, Ulrich. *Studien zum literarischen Patronat im England des 12. Jahrhunderts.* Cologne, 1962.

Scholz, Bernard. "The Canonization of Edward the Confessor." *Speculum* 36/1 (1961): 38–60.

Searle, Eleanor. "Fact and Pattern in Heroic History: Dudo of Saint-Quentin." *Viator* 15 (1984): 119–37.

——. *Predatory Kinship and the Creation of Norman Power, 840–1066.* Berkeley, 1988.

——. "Women and the Legitimisation of Succession at the Norman Conquest." *ANS* 3 (1981): 159–70.

Sheehan, Michael. *The Will in Medieval England: From the Conversion of the Anglo-Saxons to the End of the Thirteenth Century.* Toronto, 1963.

Shopkow, Leah. "The Carolingian World of Dudo of Saint-Quentin," *Journal of Medieval History* 15 (1989): 19–37.

——. *History and Community: Norman Historical Writing in the Eleventh and Twelfth Centuries.* Washington, DC, 1997.

Short, Ian. "Gaimar et les débuts de l'historiographie en langue française." In *Chroniques nationales et chroniques universelles,* edited by Danielle Buschinger, 155–63. Göppingen, 1990.

——. "Gaimar's Epilogue and Geoffrey of Monmouth's *Liber vetustissimus.*" *Speculum* 69 (1994): 323–43.

——. "Patrons and Polyglots: French Literature in Twelfth-Century England." *ANS* 14 (1992): 229–49.

——. " 'Tam Angli Quam Franci': Self-Definition in Anglo-Norman England." *ANS* 18 (1996): 153–75.

Shwartz, Susan M. "The Founding and Self-Betrayal of Britain: An Augustinian Approach to Geoffrey of Monmouth's *Historia Regum Britanniae.*" *Medievalia et humanistica* 10 (1981): 33–53.

Smith, R. J. "Henry II's Heir: The Acta and Seal of Henry the Young King, 1170–83." *EHR* 116/466 (2001): 297–326.

Somerset, Fiona, and Nicholas Watson, eds. *The Vulgar Tongue: Medieval and Postmedieval Vernacularity*. University Park, PA, 2003.

Southern, R. W. "Aspects of the European Tradition of Historical Writing." *TRHS* 5/20 (1970): 174–96; 5/21 (1971): 159–79; 5/22 (1972): 159–80; and 5/23 (1973): 243–63.

——. *Medieval Humanism and Other Studies*. Oxford, 1970.

——. "The Place of Henry I in English History." *Proceedings of the British Academy* 48 (1962): 127–69.

Spiegel, Gabrielle. "Forging the Past: The Language of Historical Truth in the Middle Ages." *The History Teacher* 17 (1984): 267–83.

——. "Genealogy: Form and Function in Medieval Historical Narrative." *History and Theory* 22 (1983): 43–53.

——. "History, Historicism and the Social Logic of the Text in the Middle Ages." *Speculum* 65 (1990): 59–68.

——. *The Past as Text: The Theory and Practice of Medieval Historiography*. Baltimore, 1997.

——. "Political Utility in Medieval Historiography: A Sketch." *History and Theory* 14 (1975): 314–25.

——. *Romancing the Past: The Rise of Vernacular Prose Historiography in Thirteenth-Century France*. Berkeley, 1993.

Stafford, Pauline. "Cherchez la femme: Queens, Queen's Lands and Nunneries: Missing Links in the Foundation of Reading Abbey." *History* 85 (2000): 4–27.

——. *Queen Emma and Queen Edith: Queenship and Women's Power in Eleventh-Century England*. Oxford, 1997.

——. *Unification and Conquest: A Political and Social History of England in the Tenth and Eleventh Centuries*. London, 1989.

Stein, Robert M., and Sandra Pierson Prior. *Reading Medieval Culture: Essays in Honor of Robert W. Hanning*. Notre Dame, 2005.

Stenton, Doris. *English Justice between the Norman Conquest and the Great Charter, 1066–1215*. Philadelphia, 1964.

Stenton, Frank. "English Families and the Norman Conquest." *TRHS* 4/26 (1944): 1–12.

Stock, Brian. *The Implications of Literacy: Written Language and Models of Interpretation in the Eleventh and Twelfth Centuries*. Princeton, 1983.

——. "Literacy and Society in the Twelfth Century." In *The Spirit of the Court: Selected Proceedings of the Fourth Congress of the International Courtly Literature Society*, edited by Glynn S. Burgess and Robert A. Taylor, 1–4. Woodbridge, 1985.

——. "Medieval Literacy, Linguistic Theory, and Social Organization." *New Literary History* 16/1 (1984): 13–29.

Strevett, Neil. "The Anglo-Norman Civil War of 1101 Reconsidered." *ANS* 26 (2004): 159–75.

Strickland, Matthew. "Against the Lord's Anointed: Aspects of Warfare and Baronial Rebellion in England and Normandy, 1075–1265." In *Law and*

Government in Medieval England and Normandy: Essays in Honour of Sir James Holt, edited by George Garnett and John Hudson, 56–79. Cambridge, 1994.

Strohm, Paul. *England's Empty Throne: Usurpation and the Language of Legitimation, 1399–1422*. New Haven, 1998.

Stuip, René. "La Conquête de l'Angleterre dans la littérature française du XIIe siècle." *Rapports-Het Franse Boek* 58 (1988): 123–31.

Tabuteau, Emily. *Transfers of Property in Eleventh-Century Norman Law*. Chapel Hill, 1988.

Teunis, H. B. "Benoît de Sainte-Maure and William the Conqueror's *Amor*." *ANS* 12 (1990): 199–209.

Thirion, Jacques. "La cathédrale de Bayeux." *Congrès archéologique* 132 (1978).

Thomas, Hugh. *The English and the Normans: Ethnic Hostility, Assimilation and Identity, 1066–1220*. Oxford, 2003.

——. *Vassals, Heiresses, Crusaders, and Thugs: The Gentry of Angevin Yorkshire, 1154–1216*. Philadelphia, 1993.

Thompson, James. *The Literacy of the Laity in the Middle Ages*. Berkeley, 1939.

Thorndike, Lynn. "Elementary and Secondary Education in the Middle Ages." *Speculum* 15 (1940): 400–408.

Tolhurst, Fiona. "The Britons as Hebrews, Romans, and Normans: Geoffrey of Monmouth's British Epic and Reflections of Empress Matilda." *Arthuriana* 8/4 (1998): 69–87.

Tomchak, Laurie. "Wace's Work: Patronage, Repetition and Translation in the *Roman de Rou*." PhD diss., University of California, Irvine, 1983. *Dissertation Abstracts International* 44 (1984): 3380A.

Truax, Jean A. "Politics Makes Uneasy Bedfellows: Henry I of England and Theobald of Blois." In *On the Social Origins of Medieval Institutions: Essays in Honor of Joseph F. O'Callaghan*, edited by Donald J. Kagay and Theresa M. Vann, 273–304. The Medieval Mediterranean: Peoples, Economies and Cultures, 400–1453, 19. Leiden, 1998.

Türk, Egbert. *Nugae curialium: Le règne d'Henri II Plantagenêt 1154–1189 et l'éthique politique*. Genève, 1977.

Turner, Ralph V. "Changing Perceptions of the New Administrative Class in Anglo-Norman and Angevin England: The Curiales and Their Conservative Critics." *Journal of British Studies* 29/2 (Apr. 1990): 93–117.

——. *Men Raised from the Dust: Administrative Service and Upward Mobility in Angvin England*. Philadelphia, 1988.

——. "The Miles Literatus in Twelfth- and Thirteenth-Century England: How Rare a Phenomenon?" *American Historical Review* 83 (1978): 928–65. Reprinted in *Judges, Administrators and the Common Law in Angevin England*, edited by Ralph V. Turner, 119–36. London, 1994.

——. "The Problem of Survival for the Angevin 'Empire': Henry II's and His Sons' Vision versus Late Twelfth-Century Realities." *American Historical Review* 100/1 (Feb. 1995): 78–96.

Tyson, Diana B. "Patronage of French Vernacular History Writers in the Twelfth and Thirteenth Centuries." *Romania* 100 (1979): 180–222.

Valin, R. *Le duc de Normandie et sa cour (912–1203): Étude d'histoire juridique.* Paris, 1909.

van Caenegem, R. C. *The Birth of the English Common Law.* Cambridge, 1973.

van Houts, Elisabeth M. C. "The Adaptation of the *Gesta Normannorum ducum* by Wace and Benoît." In *Non nova, sed nove: Mélanges de civilisation médiévale dédiés à Willem Noomen,* edited by M. Gosman and J. van Os, 115–24. Groningen, 1984. Reprinted in Elisabeth M. C. van Houts, *History and Family Traditions in England and the Continent, 1000–1200,* 115–24. Aldershot, 1999.

——. "The *Gesta Normannorum ducum*: A History without an End." *ANS* 3 (1981): 106–18.

——. *History and Family Traditions in England and the Continent, 1000–1200.* Aldershot, 1999.

——. "Le roi et son historien: Henri II Plantagenêt et Robert de Torigni, abbé du Mont-Saint-Michel." *CCM* 37/1–2 (1994): 115–18.

——. *Memory and Gender in Medieval Europe, 900–1200.* Toronto, 1999.

——. "The Memory of 1066 in Written and Oral Traditions." *ANS* 19 (1997): 167–79.

——. "The Norman Conquest through European Eyes." *EHR* 110/438 (1995): 832–53.

——. "The Political Relations between Normandy and England before 1066 according to the *Gesta Normannorum ducum.*" In *Les Mutations socio-culturelles au tournant des XIe–XIIe siècles. Etudes anselmiennes (IVe section). Colloque organisé par le CNRS sous la présidence de Monsieur Jean Pouilloux, membre de l'Institut. Abbaye Notre Dame du Bec, Le Bec-Hellouin 11–16 juillet 1982,* 85–97 and 191–92. Paris, 1984.

——. "The Ship List of William the Conqueror." *ANS* 10 (1988): 159–83.

——. "The Trauma of 1066." *History Today* 46/10 (1996): 9–15.

——. "Wace as Historian." In *Family Trees and the Roots of Politics: The Prosopography of Britain and France from the Tenth to the Twelfth Century,* edited by Katherine S. B. Keats-Rohan, 104–32. Cambridge, 1997. Reprinted in Elisabeth M. C. van Houts, *History and Family Traditions in England and the Continent, 1000–1200,* 103–32. Aldershot, 1999.

Vauchez, André. *La sainteté en occident aux derniers siècles du moyen âge d'après les procès de canonisation et les documents hagiographiques.* Rome, 1981.

Vaughan, Sally. *The Abbey of Bec and the Anglo-Norman State, 1034–1136.* Woodbridge, 1981.

Viellard, Françoise. "Deux historiens normands du XIIe siècle, Guillance de Saint-Pair et Wace." *Revue de l'Avranchin et du Pays de Grabville* 78 (2001): 325–52.

Wallace-Hadrill, J. M. "The Franks and the English in the Ninth Century: Some Common Historical Interests." In J. M. Wallace-Hadrill. *Early Medieval History.* Oxford, 1975.

Warren, W. L. *The Governance of Norman and Angevin England, 1086–1272.* Stanford, 1987.

——. *Henry II.* Berkeley, 1973.

Watkin, Thomas Glyn. "The Political Philosophy of the Lord King." In *Communities and Courts in Britain, 1150–1900*, edited by Christopher Brooks and Michael Lobban, 1–12. London, 1997.

Webber, Nick. *The Evolution of Norman Identity, 911–1154*. Woodbridge, 2005.

Werner, Karl Ferdinand. "Die Legitimität der Kapetinger und die Entstehung des 'Reditus regni Francorum ad stirpem Karoli.'" *Die Welt als Geschichte* 12 (1952): 203–25.

——. "Dieu, les rois et l'histoire." In *La France de l'an mil*, edited by Dominique Iogna-Prat under the direction of Robert Delort, 264–81. Paris, 1990.

——. "Gott, Herrscher und Historiograph: Der Geschichtsschreiber als Interpret des Wirkens Gottes in der Welt und Ratgeber des Könige." In *Deus qui mutat tempora: Menschen und Institutionen im Wandel des Mittelalters. Festgabe für A. Becker*, edited by E.-H. Hehl, et al., 1–31. Sigmaringen, 1987.

——. "Les sources de la légitimité royale à l'avènement des Capétiens (Xe–XIe siècle)." In *Le sacre des rois: Actes du Colloque international d'histoire sur les sacres et couronnements royaux, Reims 1975*, 49–60. Paris, 1985.

——. "L'historia et les rois." In *Religion et culture autour de l'an mil*, edited by D. Iogna-Prat and J. Picard, 135–43. Paris, 1990.

White, Graeme J. *Restoration and Reform, 1153–1165: Recovery from Civil War in England*. Cambridge Studies in Medieval Life and Thought, Fourth Series 46. Cambridge, 2000.

White, Hayden. *The Content of the Form: Narrative Discourse and Historical Representation*. Baltimore, 1987.

Wormald, Patrick. *The Making of English Law: King Alfred to the Twelfth Century; Legislation and Its Limits*. Oxford, 1999.

Yver, Jean. "Les caractères origineaux du groupe de coutumes de l'Ouest de la France." *Revue historique de droit français et étranger* 4/24 (1952): 18–79.

Zatta, Jane. "Translating the *Historia*: The Ideological Transformation of the *Historia regum Britannie* in Twelfth-Century Vernacular Chronicles." *Arthuriana* 8/4 (1998): 148–61.

Zumthor, Paul. *Histoire littéraire de la France médiévale*. Paris, 1954.

INDEX